The Capitalist City

IDEAS is a new Blackwell series which makes available in paperback some of the most adventurous writing in the social and humane sciences in recent years, extending the frontiers of research, crossing disciplinary borders and setting new intellectual standards in international scholarship. Published and forthcoming titles include:

Jean Baechler, John A. Hall and Michael Mann,
Europe and the Rise of Capitalism

Colin Campbell, *The Romantic Ethic and the Spirit of Modern Consumerism*

William Connolly, *Political Theory and Modernity*

Philip Corrigan and Derek Sayer, *The Great Arch*

John A. Hall (ed.), *States in History*

Alan Macfarlane. *The Culture of Capitalism*

Derek Sayer, *The Violence of Abstraction*

Michael Peter Smith, *City, State and Market*

Neil Smith, *Uneven Development*

The Capitalist City

Global Restructuring and Community Politics

EDITED BY
Michael Peter Smith
& Joe R. Feagin

First published 1987
First published in paperback 1989
Reprinted 1991

Basil Blackwell Ltd
108 Cowley Road, Oxford, OX4 1JF, UK

Basil Blackwell, Inc.
3 Cambridge Center
Cambridge, Massachusetts 02142, USA

British Library Cataloguing in Publication Data

The Capitalist city: global restructuring
    and community politics.
    1. Cities and towns
    I. Smith, Michael Peter   II. Feagin, Joe R.
    307'.14   HT151
    ISBN 0–631–151182–6
    ISBN 0–631–15618–6 (Pbk)

Library of Congress Cataloging in Publication Data

The Capitalist city:
    Includes index.
    1. Urban economics.   2. Urbanization.
3. Capitalism.   4. Urban policy.   I. Smith, Michael P.
II. Feagin, Joe R.
HT321.C364   1987   330.9173'2   86–26841
ISBN 0–631–151182–6
ISBN 0–631–15618–6 (Pbk)

Typeset by Cambrian Typesetters, Frimley, Surrey
Printed in Great Britain by Athenaeum Press Ltd, Newcastle upon Tyne.

Contents

PART I

Introduction

1

Cities and the New International Division of Labor: An Overview

Joe R. Feagin and Michael Peter Smith

INTRODUCTION

The world of modern capitalism is both a worldwide net of corporations and a global network of cities. There are world command cities such as New York, London and Tokyo, which have extraordinary concentrations of top corporate decision-makers representing financial, industrial, commercial, law and media corporations. Even a cursory examination of such 'first-tier' cities shows the intimate relationship between the web-like organization of modern capitalism and the network of cities across the globe. The major organizational units in the capitalist web are the large international banks and transnational corporations; the latter today account for 70–80 per cent of world trade outside the centrally planned socialist countries (Clairmonte and Cavanagh, 1981: 5). The top 500–1000 multinational corporations not only sit at the summit of a pyramid of interrelated capitalistic firms of all sizes but they also create a truly transnational economy, one whose primary geographical nodes are the world's cities.

But most cities are not at the world command level; indeed, different cities occupy a variety of niches in the capitalist world economy. There are the specialized command cities which concentrate the headquarters operations of particular industries, such as the auto companies in Detroit, Michigan, and the rubber companies in Akron, Ohio. There are divisional command cities like Houston, Texas, with its absence of top oil firm headquarters and its high concentration of major divisions of top oil firms. There are cities specializing in a particular type of manufacturing production such as steel-making in Birmingham, Alabama and car manufacture in Birmingham, England. There are state command cities like Washington, D. C. and Brazilia. And there are numerous cities which are difficult to classify because of the diversity of their economic and state functions, such as the huge cities

We are indebted to James Simmie, Mark Gottdiener and Kelly Riddell for their useful comments on an earlier version of this chapter.

of Singapore, Mexico City and São Paulo in the Third World. None the less, all these cities are linked together by the organizational web of transnational corporations, their facilities, subsidiaries, suppliers and subcontractors. Major cities, as the places where the transnational corporate web is grounded physically, are the cotter pins holding the capitalist world economy together.

These interconnected networks of firms and cities have been described in terms of such concepts as a capitalist world economy or 'the new international division of labor'. The latter phrase has become particularly common since the publication of the seminal book of the same name by Fröbel, Heinrichs and Kreye. Published in 1980, this book defined the new international division of labor as the shifting world market for labor coupled with the shifting world market for production sites (cf. also Cohen, 1981). Plant closures in core industrial countries are part of these changing markets, as are new plant startups in Third World countries. Disinvestment and unemployment in one city in one nation can be linked to investment and employment in another nation. The shifting investments of transnational corporations can determine the future of labor, production sites, cities and nations.

Before we examine this changing global economy in detail, we should note that a shifting international division of labour is not, in fact, new. For at least two centuries capitalists have expanded operations across state boundaries to exploit raw materials, labor, production sites and overseas markets. Writing in the mid-nineteenth century, Marx (1967: 451) described the 'new and international division of labor' that this global expansion entailed:

By constantly making a part of the hands [workers] 'supernumerary' modern history, in all countries where it has taken root, gives a spur to emigration and to the colonisation of foreign lands, which are thereby converted into settlements for growing the raw materials of the mother country; just as Australia, for example, was converted into a colony for growing wool. A new and international division of labor, a division suited to the requirements of the chief centres of industry, springs up, and converts one part of the globe into a chief agricultural field of production, for supplying the other part which remains a chiefly industrial field.

This was a major step in the global division of labor under capitalism – peripheral agricultural dependency on core industrial centers – but over time nations outside the core became much more than suppliers of agricultural and raw materials for the 'chief centers of industry'. Gradually, their agricultural and raw materials production for export was paralleled by industrial production for export. The newly industrialized nations and their cities thus became increasingly important in the world economic order. In recent decades a new international division of labor has emerged, one that no longer involves medium-sized firms with distinctive national identities exchanging goods across national boundaries, but rather one that increasingly involves transnational firms investing heavily in many countries and trading goods and services with one another, or transnational firms' subsidiaries trading within the globally extended framework of one large corporation.

The scholarly contributions to this volume highlight several important propositions about urban development in this transforming global economy of modern capitalism:

1 The causes, character and significance of urban development can best be understood by analyzing cities in terms of their transnational linkages, especially their connections within the world capitalistic economy, its dominant multinational firms, and its processes of economic restructuring.

2 Moving through stages of economic growth and change, many major cities in the world economy tend to specialize in particular raw materials, production, distribution, marketing, and financial and other 'service' activities, while other cities house complex combinations of such activities.

3 The restructuring of global, national and local economies is intimately intertwined with state action and mediation; the role of the state can be generative or reactive.

4 Economic restructuring and state restructuring are intrinsically associated with household and community restructuring, and thus with geographical (spatial) transformation.

5 Household and community restructuring are not mere by-products of economic and state restructuring; the everyday activities of people living in households and communities – informalization, immigration, formation of networks, and political action – are constitutive elements in the process of urban transformation; they shape as well as reflect the global flows of labor and capital and the character of state policies.

THE GLOBAL ECONOMY OF CAPITALISM: STRUCTURING AND RESTRUCTURING

Foreign investment

A distinguishing feature of global restructuring has been the expansion of US investment abroad and the sharp increase in foreign investment in the US, both trends which Glickman's chapter in this book (see Chapter 3) examines in some detail. Glickman notes that US assets abroad in 1983 were $226 billion, a tripling of assets since 1970, while direct foreign investment in the US went up tenfold, from $13 billion to $134 billion, in the same period. Large multinational firms have been moving capital in both directions. These capital flows signal the scale of the global economic restructuring which has been taking place since at least the late 1960s. The capitalist world system periodically undergoes global restructuring, typically in response to shifts in international competition. There are a number of forces and processes here: the concentration of investment capital in a decreasing number of firms, peripheral industrialization and the 'global assembly-line', intensified transnational competition, changes in the mode of production, large-scale labor migration flows, and capital restructuring by core country multinationals to re-establish favorable conditions for profitability in an increasingly competitive global environment.

Corporate cities

Noting the global context of urban economies is becoming commonplace in the social science literature, but clarity about what this global context means is much less common. The central economic actors in the international division of labor are the top 500–1000 multinational corporations. These major organizations have created an integrated, worldwide network of production, exchange, finance and corporate services arranged in a complex hierarchical system of cities. The headquarters executives of these corporations are particularly effective at global scanning for the optimal labor costs and control factors, resource costs, markets and state subsidies. Clearly, these large companies have been able to integrate their operations on a global scale (Cohen, 1981: 302–4). As can be seen in Table 1.1, the headquarters facilities of the largest 500 multinational firms (excluding banks) are disproportionately located in the major cities of core countries.

TABLE 1.1 *Headquarters location of the world's largest transnational firms,*
1984

City	Metropolitan area population (000s)	Number of firms
1 New York	17,082	59
2 London	11,100	37
3 Tokyo	26,200	34
4 Paris	9,650	26
5 Chicago	7,865	18
6 Essen	5,050	18
7 Osaka	15,900	15
8 Los Angeles	10,519	14
9 Houston	3,109	11
10 Pittsburgh	2,171	10
11 Hamburg	2,250	10
12 Dallas	3,232	9
13 St Louis	2,228	8
14 Detroit	4,315	7
15 Toronto	2,998	7
16 Frankfurt	1,880	7
17 Minneapolis	2,041	7

TABLE 1.1 (Continued)

City	Metropolitan area population (000s)	Number of firms
18 San Francisco	4,920	6
19 Rome	3,115	6
20 Stockholm	1,402	6
21 Turin	1,191	5
22 Hartford, CT	1,020	5
23 Fairfield, CT	100	5
24 Seoul	6,889	4
25 Atlanta	2,190	4
26 Montreal	2,828	3 .
27 Stuttgart	1,835	3
28 Cologne	1,810	3
29 Cleveland	2,174	3
30 Milan	3,775	3
31 Basel	580	3
32 Eindhoven, Netherlands	374	3
33 Midland, MI	100	3
34 Genoa	830	2
35 Zurich	780	2
36 Akron, OH	606	2
37 Winston-Salem, NC	291	2
38 Peoria, IL	320	2
39 Ashland, KY	100	2
40 Wilmington, DE	100	2
41 Bethlehem, PA	100	2
42 Southfield, M1	100	2
43 Moline, IL	100	2
44 Philadelphia	5,254	2
45 Johannesburg	3,650	2
46 Madrid	4,515	2
47 Melbourne	2,722	2
48 Munich	1,955	2
49 San Diego	1,788	2
50 Cincinnati	1,481	2
51 Rotterdam	1,090	2

Sources: Rand McNally Commercial Atlas & Marketing Guide, Rand McNally & Co.: Chicago, 1986; *Statistical Abstract of the US*, US Department of Commerce Bureau of the Census, 1985; *Ward's Business Directory*, vol. 3, Information Access Co.: Belmont, CA, 1985.

Banks are excluded from the data sources. Size is in terms of sales. The population figures listed above are Ranally Metropolitan Areas (RMAs), which include outlying urbanized areas (e.g. suburban towns) around the city giving the area its name.

The New York metropolitan area is the headquarters capital of the core cities, capturing 59 of the top 500 transnational firms, including 18 of the top 100. London and Tokyo are at roughly the same level in the 1980s; both now house the headquarters of more than 30 of the top transnationals. Somewhat less important are Paris, Chicago, Essen, Osaka and Los Angeles with 14–26 each of the top 500 companies, followed by an industrial grouping including Houston, Pittsburgh and Hamburg. All cities with five or more of the top 500 companies are in the United States, Great Britain, France, Germany, Italy, Canada, Sweden and Japan. More countries are included when we examine cities with only 2–4 of the top 500 firms. These include Australia, Belgium, the Netherlands, and the first 'Third World' country, South Korea. (South Africa is an ambiguous case.) When cities with only one large transnational firm are examined, we find many more countries represented, including a scattering of firms in underdeveloped countries from Brazil to India.

Another instructive way of examining the relationship between transnational firms and cities is to list the 17 largest cities in the world using 1984 data (see table 1.2). This population ranking may have changed somewhat

TABLE 1.2 Firms in the world's 17 largest cities

City	Metropolitan area population (000s)	Firms
1 Tokyo	26,200	34
2 New York	17,082	59
3 Mexico City	14,600	1
4 Osaka	15,900	15
5 São Paulo	12,700	0
6 Seoul	11,200	4
7 London	11,100	37
8 Calcutta	11,100	0
9 Buenos Aires	10,700	1
10 Los Angeles	10,519	14
11 Bombay	9,950	1
12 Paris	9,650	26
13 Peking	9,340	0
14 Rio de Janeiro	9,200	1
15 Cairo	8,500	0
16 Shanghai	8,300	0
17 Chicago	7,865	18

Source: See table 1.1.

since the 1984 survey, but five of the world's largest cities here have *no* transnational headquarters. Two of these, not surprisingly, are in The People's Republic of China, but the other three are in Brazil, India and Egypt. And four other cities, in Argentina, Brazil, Mexico and India, have only one transnational firm. While most of the world's largest corporations are in large cities, it is clear that city size is not necessarily correlated with economic power. In short, a handful of cities house *all* the top firms. If we extend this list to the world's cities over one million (a total of 162) we find that 75 per cent have *no* multinational firms' headquarters.

Multinational corporations have expanded dramatically since the Second World War, both in their outreach into non-capitalist areas of the globe and in their own corporate structure. This industrial expansion typically involves investment in labor and fixed capital, ranging from factories, headquarters offices and warehouses, to ports and toxic waste disposal facilities. The decisions as to where to locate these fixed capital activities are shaped by a complex array of political and economic issues and relationships, not just those pertaining to a particular firm or set of firms, but also to the trends in the world economy. Moreover, this worldwide network of fixed capital and labor investments by transnationals has been matched by the creation of a web of international banking corporations and markets, a development that John Walton's paper (chapter 17) highlights. Coupled with the growth of the financial web, has been the expansion of other transnational-related services, such as law, accounting and advertising corporations (cf. Cohen, 1981: 288). And, perhaps most important of all, the large transnational firms are the foundation on which not only service-related firms, but also a huge array of small to middle-sized commercial and industrial corporations, are grounded. A little-researched dimension of the modern global economy is the major multiplier effect that the top multinationals have on the diffuse urban economies in which they operate. A great many, perhaps most smaller corporations, as well as the office and shopping center developments in which they are located, would not exist were it not for the multinationals operating in or headquartered there.

Capital centralization and export industrialization

A major driving force behind the expansion of this capitalist world economy is the centralization of capital, the process whereby smaller firms merge into or are taken over by a larger firm, or large firms come together. Mergers and takeovers proliferate in times of economic crisis, as healthier firms take over those in economic difficulty. This increase in capital under a unified command can facilitate a more rapid shift in large-scale productive activities from one region to another than would be possible under a smaller firm. It also allows larger-scale investments. With the development of large concentrations of capital under a unified command, it is easier for the larger firms to take advantage of worldwide labor conditions (N. Smith, 1984: 146). Together with competition and periodic crises in profitability, concentration generated the search for cheaper and more 'disciplined' labor pools. In addition, a sharp drop in the cost of sea and air transport and satellite communications has facilitated corporation decision-makers to utilize the huge disparities in wages across cities, regions and nations. Thus Third World nations and their cities have been able to compete with core countries in labor-intensive production, as well as with state subsidies for production. In response to this competition, three reactions have taken place in core countries: (1) the general exporting of older labor-intensive jobs; (2) the automating of core jobs to increase the productivity of the higher-wage workers there; and (3) as Sassen-Koob points out in this book (chapter 6), the creation of new low-wage jobs concentrated in a few large core cities as a result of increased subcontracting, customized production for affluent markets, and labor-intensive, mass production for low-income markets in those cities.

Direct foreign investment in labor-intensive production by transnational firms is not new. However, from the 1910s to the late 1960s much of that capital investment was for plants to produce for *local* markets overseas. Since the 1970s manufacturing in foreign countries for re-export to the US and other core countries has grown dramatically, catapulting cities in the periphery into much greater importance as industrial cities. This is a central dimension of the new international division of labor. In the last two decades the world capitalist system has switched substantially, and for the first time in its history, to overseas volume production of manufactured products in Third World cities for re-export to the home markets in core cities. One analysis of Asian countries found that the proportion of re-export sales increased from less than 10 per cent to more than 25 per cent between 1966 and 1977 for US-affiliated firms: the proportion was a remarkable 70 per cent for electrical machinery (Grunwald and Flamm, 1985: 3). By 1981 about 22 per cent of manufacturing imports into the US from developing countries were assembled abroad by US firms for re-export. The process of globalization of manufacturing, vertically integrated across national boundaries began with textiles and garment manufacturing, then spread to radios, TVs and automobiles. Most recently, hi-tech electronics products (e.g. semiconductors) have become part of this global factory (Grunwald and Flamm, 1985: 6–7).

'Export' industrialization has brought major changes to cities in both developed and developing nations, since their links to the world economy are increased and their dependence upon multinational firms and outside investors is increased. In the Third World, the net effect of this type of industrialization is usually negative in terms of inequality, dependency and the costs of urban growth (Grunwald and Flamm, 1985: 8). Capitalist expansion has emphasized the goal of accumulation, which creates a situation of affluent development in certain areas of the core cities at one 'pole' of the world economy and dependent development or under-development in peripheral cities at the other. Yet the pockets of affluence created in core cities, in turn, generate demands for customized production and personal services performed by low-wage workers, thereby contributing to uneven development within growing cities at the core. As Perry makes clear (chapter 5), the new pattern of capitalist expansion has also made peripheral previously prosperous core industrial cities like Buffalo, New York.

Yet the underdeveloped capitalist countries are not identical. One should make a clear distinction between the leading eight or nine 'underdeveloped' capitalist economies and the rest; indeed these leading countries account for an estimated three-quarters of manufactured exports, such as textiles, clothing and electronics, from all underdeveloped capitalist economies. The expansionist industrial bourgeoisies in countries such as South Korea, Hong Kong, Singapore, Taiwan, Malaysia, India, Indonesia, Brazil and Mexico not only facilitate core country transnational penetration of their own economies with free trade zones, tax write-offs, and weak regulation but also develop their own transnational corporations (e.g. South Korea's huge Hyundai conglomerate) which exploit the more undeveloped capitalistic economies.

In addition, private–public partnerships to promote economic development are common in the leading underdeveloped countries. As Clairmonte and Cavanagh (1981: 5) note, export manufacturing is dominated by subsidiaries of multinational firms, 'but the pattern is changing toward one of dependent partnership by domestic state and private capital'. Big firms in these countries are sometimes jointly owned private–state oligopolies. The critical urban aspect of this second-tier of peripheral capitalist economies can be seen in the fact that the principal cities in such leading underdeveloped countries play a much more important role in the world economy (and politics) than those cities in the dozens of lesser peripheral nations such as Peru, a country discussed in Wilson's article (chapter 9) in this volume.

Some contradictions

As is suggested by the increasing tendency towards uneven development within leading urban growth poles at the core, the globalization of production has inherent contradictions for the developed 'pole' nations. One contradiction can be seen in the abandonment of existing fixed capital in plants, warehouses, offices, and the like in declining cities of core industrial countries. The abandoned fixed capital investments of US industrial corporations in Detroit, Buffalo and Pittsburgh illustrate this – a point highlighted in Hill and Feagin's and Perry's chapters in this book (7 and 5). From the 1920s to the 1980s the movement of surplus capital into Third World countries, as well as into Europe after World War II, at first created prosperity for US export-oriented corporations. Yet this export capital has periodically created new corporate competitors, which come back later to threaten and reduce the profitability of US corporations, and thus generate a search for enhanced profitability. Meanwhile, US workers face plant closures that are linked to the flight of capital overseas. For example, the move of capital overseas in the seven-year period 1975–82 displaced 170,000 workers in the textile/garment industry alone, and another 75,000 jobs in the electrical industry (Grunwald and Flamm, 1985: 223).

Global expansion of core country multinationals is also linked to the global expansion of the US and its NATO allies' military establishments. While corporate capitalists like to speak of themselves as 'peacemongers' desiring to integrate even the Communist bloc into their world economy, it is also the case that the US and other NATO navies guarantee multinational access to harbors on all the oceans. In times of energy crisis, for example, the US Sixth Fleet protects the interests of US firms in Middle East oil. US military power is still seen as crucial to the political stability necessary to ensure corporate profitability in many developing countries. The constant threat of class- or religious-based revolutions (e.g. Iran), as well as of political terrorism directed against the core nations of the capitalist world economy, has led to the systematic expansion of the military of these core nations since 1945. Thus in 1985 the US alone had 241,000 sailors at sea and 480,000 soldiers stationed overseas, the latter not only in West Germany, but in 39 other countries and territories including Bermuda (1380), Panama (10,270), Italy (10,170), Greece (2900), Spain (12,000), Turkey (3800), Japan (71,760), South Korea (44,160), Egypt (1500), and the Philippines (17,410). There are in fact thousands of US military bases and installations in these 40 countries and territories. In addition, half the world's nations today have military dictatorships, most with extensive trade with US transnationals tied to the US military–industrial complex (Sivard, 1985: 13; Arkin and Fieldhouse, 1985: 147). These countries also have cities which are havens for corporations seeking a docile labor force, a friendly government and supportive state policies.

After World War II, the Pentagon divided the globe into regions for military planning, with a high-ranking military officer in command, an arrangement no other country has established (Anon., 1986: 2). This global military planning does not distinguish clearly between the needs of the nation-state and those of its transnationals. As an Air Force General expressed it in a National War College study, an 'indirect' national security strategy argues for the protection of Americans through the proliferation of American values around the globe, using as one dissemination mechanism 'multinational enterprise', whose 'growing arsenal of foreign-based business operations is working for us around the clock. Its osmotic action transmits and transfuses not only American methods of business operation, banking, and marketing techniques; but our legal systems and concepts, our political philosophies' (Barnet and Muller, 1974: 101). The multinational corporation is part of the broad American national security plan, which includes the most massive global military organization in world history.

Yet this global military expansion has its own built-in contradictions. The hundreds of billions of dollars spent to buttress this expansion have produced a very heavy drain on the tax resources available to the US and its NATO allies. This drain is now so great that it threatens the international banks which are an essential part of the debt structure created to finance the military expansion. In addition, the massive military expenditures are a major reason for the sharp curtailment of welfare state programs in core countries, an austerity which, in turn, has created conditions conducive to popular mobilization, particularly in Europe.

In the United States, where the modern mass consumption paradise has been enshrined, the key American values of individualized consumption and personal security in homogeneous local communities have none the less been threatened by the labor market restructuring and spatial reorganization of US cities that is occasioned by global economic restructuring. Thus, a final contradiction is that even in the most advanced capitalist country, the fundamental bases of mass consent – anticipated improved standards of middle-income mass consumption and the availability of 'good communities' and urban facilities for social reproduction – are being undermined by the $300 billion commitments to military hegemony. Some of the political implications of this contradiction are discussed below in the chapters by Nash, Perry, Fainstein, and Smith and Tardanico (chapters 13, 5, 15 and 4).

THE RESTRUCTURING OF CITIES

Fundamental economic restructuring at the global level means restructuring in those other critical contexts within which the world's households live, including the city and the community. We shall now focus upon the city. We visualize five basic types of urban restructuring that are part of the global revolution that analysts since Marx have called the 'new international division of labor':

a economic restructuring in cities;
b state restructuring in cities;
c household restructuring (including migration) in cities;
d community (and community politics) restructuring in cities;
e spatial restructuring in cities.

ECONOMIC RESTRUCTURING

Economic change in US cities

In order to make sense of the economic restructuring which underlies the many changes in households, communities, cities and states, we shall start with a breakdown of the changes which characterize major US cities such as Detroit, Houston, Los Angeles and New York. We shall then examine European and Third World cities. In looking at US cities one can distinguish at least five different aspects of the economic restructuring there. These are (1) plant closure, (2) plant start-ups, (3) corporate center development, (4) the expansion of service and other types of jobs related to the office developments, and (5) corporate expansion in outlying areas.

Plant closures have become commonplace in the US and European cities, as manufacturing decentralizes around the globe. In chapter 8 of this volume, Soja notes the loss of thousands of manufacturing jobs in Los Angeles in older unionized industries such as autos, rubber and steel. Similarly, New York City lost half a million jobs between the 1960s and 1980s. The chapter by Hill and Feagin (chapter 7) documents the fact that plant closures and disinvestment can occur in any city, whether it be an old industrial city like Detroit or a more recent industrial 'boomtown' like Houston. The reasons for economic restructuring in these cities have been variously ascribed, and they include renewed competition from Europe and Japan, profit cycles in mature industries, and the desire of industrial capital in core countries to renegotiate the terms of past concessions to organized labor. Indeed, many of the lost manufacturing jobs were well-paid, and were so because of decades of political struggle by core country trade unions.

Although plant closures receive considerable media attention, they are not the only sign of economic change. Another feature of economic restructuring can be seen in plant start-ups, even in those US cities which have suffered many plant closures. In the 1970s and 1980s an estimated 6000 manufacturing 'sweatshops' were opened in New York, Los Angeles and Chicago, employing a total of 85,000 workers, particularly immigrant women workers from Asia, Mexico and Central America (Anon., 1984: 7). One reason for the rise of these 'sweatshops' in garment and electronics manufacturing is the requirement of engineers and designers to have some manufacturing facilities nearby for prototype and related production requirements. Moreover, it is important to note that the movement of capital, interregionally or internationally, is linked to the migration of labor. The availability of a vast reservoir of illegal immigrant labor lacking the basic right of citizenship and willing to work for low wages is a major factor contributing to the rise of these new sweatshops and their spatial concentration in large US core cities (M. P. Smith, 1987). As documented by Sassen-Koob (chapter 6), other factors contributing to the growth of new labor-intensive, low-wage manufacturing facilities in core cities include: (a) subcontracting by formal sector firms to informal sector subcontractors to avoid state regulation of the labor process; (b) the growth of a low-income mass market of immigrants and displaced workers who can only consume cheaply produced goods; and (c) the increased demand for customized products by retailers catering to gentrified high-income service workers in restructured metropolitan cores.

The expansion of office-related corporate activities in core cities has increased white-collar employment, from top corporate executives to typists and filing clerks. This is a critical feature of the economic restructuring in many, but by no means all, American cities. The construction of millions of square feet of office space in central cities has been linked to the centralization of corporate decision-making and communications functions in corporate headquarters and in major subsidiary facilities, as well as in the very large number of firms (e.g. law firms) servicing corporate headquarters (Feagin, 1983: 64–5). From London to New York or Tokyo major transnational firms have created not only a huge nested complex of personal and business service firms, but also an array of small and medium-sized commercial and industrial corporations crucially dependent on the transnational enterprises. This organizational centralization of transnationals is associated with a number of organizational trends among large corporations, including the tens of thousands of mergers since 1960, reorganization in the face of increased foreign competition, and 'economies of scale' that come from a centralized communications center. The concentration and centralization of capital in fewer firms is often associated with a concentration of office headquarters and major subdivisions in selected cities. Most jobs in the corporate centers are distributed across three basic categories: better-paying managerial and professional jobs, lower-paying clerical and sales jobs, and low-paid service jobs. Rapid growth in headquarters cities, or in the central core of such cities, can also bring a range of social costs, such as inadequate water and sewerage supplies (Feagin, 1985).

The number of low-paid service jobs has increased so dramatically in many cities that it is sometimes viewed as a distinct type of economic restructuring. In part, this is because personal, commercial and clerical service work has grown in such places as a kind of multiplier effect of the conversion of these core cities to corporate headquarters operations and to tourist, professional service, restaurant and entertainment meccas (Sassen-Koob, 1983; and chapter 6). While some producer service jobs pay a good wage, the majority of jobs are low-waged. For example, 'more than 60 per cent of the service jobs in New York City pay salaries below the Bureau of Labor Statistics' living standard for a low income family of four, while 25 per cent of full-time service workers earn less than the poverty level' (McGahey, 1983: 23). The numerous office complexes in central cities require large numbers of low-paid workers to clean them, as well as a large cohort of restaurant workers, laundry workers, dog walkers, residential construction workers, and the like to serve the better-paid white-collar workers who work in the complexes or who reside in central city areas. Indeed, many low-paid 'service' and construction workers serve the higher-paid 'service' workers; a fact which suggests the basic flaw in the idea of a unified 'service society' found in much of the social science literature. Here again we see capital flows into the central city linked to labor migration from the underdeveloped countries.

A fifth major type of economic restructuring, especially in larger US cities, has involved corporate expansion in suburban areas (M. P. Smith, 1979: 238–40). In numerous US cities the downtown corporate center development has been paralleled by a decentralized pattern of development in outlying areas. Office and industrial parks sprawl outwards across the landscape to the hinterlands of cities from San Francisco, Los Angeles and Houston, to Atlanta and Boston. New industrial complexes, some with thousands of firms like northern California's 'Silicon Valley', have been constructed on the outskirts of large cities (Rogers and Larsen, 1984). In the case of Los Angeles (described in Soja, chapter 8) plant closures on a large scale have coexisted not only with corporate center development but also with extensive new plant openings in the electronics and aerospace industries, high-technology firms which are clustered in outer cities, mostly on the western edge of the Los Angeles basin. This coexistence of different types of economic restructuring is common in US and other core country cities. Yet it does not mean that the US economy and other core economies are becoming 'post-industrial' in composition. Deindustrialization is often followed by reindustrialization. As Soja emphasizes in regard to Los Angeles, the manufacturing sector there has indeed changed, from old industrial to high-tech production and garment sweatshops, but the fundamental rationalization and labor processes of capitalism have not been significantly altered.

Economic restructuring: the level of region

So far we have emphasized economic restructuring *within* cities, from the corporate center to the 'second round' of corporation-related suburbanization. Moving up a level to that of regional economics, we should note briefly the often-cited regional economic restructuring which has affected particular groups of cities and their hinterlands. A leading example in the United States is the economic surge of cities in the 'Sunbelt' (Southern tier) states from the 1960s to the 1980s and the decline of many cities in the industrial heartland of the Midwest. In the last decade we have also seen uneven city development in New England. Boston, for example, once an area in decline, in the late 1970s and early 1980s was booming in the fields of electronics and computers. In this economic restructuring it is usually sets of cities within the regions that are the primary sites of the economic trends. For example, in many ways the restructuring in Detroit (noted by Hill and Feagin, chapter 7) is similar to that in Youngstown, Cleveland and Pittsburgh, cities in the same region. The economic restructuring in Los Angeles discussed by Soja, moreover, is in a number of ways similar to the economic shifts in San Francisco and other West Coast cities. And economic restructuring in New York has some parallels in Boston and Philadelphia, although in the latter cases there are perhaps more differences than similarities.

A major caveat to a simplistic approach to regional restructuring is that all regions contain cities which diverge from what may be commonly called the dominant trend. Thus in the economically troubled industrial heartland there are cities which remain economically healthy, like Minneapolis, which has a diversified economy with a dozen major corporations' headquarters there (and in the twin city of St Paul) – companies ranging from food giants like General Mills to the high-tech firms 3M and Control Data. With a major university and leading medical center, this city has a well-educated labor force and a high quality of life. Minneapolis and, to a substantial event, Milwaukee demonstrate that some cities in the mid-western region prosper in a sea of industrial decline. The reverse phenomenon can be seen in the Sunbelt region during the 1960s to 1980s. While Dallas, Houston and Phoenix were booming, cities like New Orleans and Birmingham were stagnating or in decline. In a 1977 University of New Orleans survey the city of New Orleans was rated the poorest of the 50 larges US cities and was also notorious for its overcrowded housing and police–community conflict (Macdonald, 1984: 88–9). Despite extensive efforts by its local state officials throughout the 1970s and 1980s, New Orleans has been unable to diversify its tourist and oil-dependent economy (Smith and Keller, 1983). By the late 1970s Birmingham was a dying steel town, the only major metropolitan area in the Sunblet with two figure unemployment rates. A lack of economic diversity, a focus on steel-related industry, made Birmingham vulnerable to the same sort of disinvestment as that found in Youngstown and Pittsburgh in the industrial heartland (Macdonald, 1984: 84–5). *Within* US regions there is as much differentiation in urban economic health as there is *between* regions.

STATE RESTRUCTURING IN CITIES

Uneven development across cities, regions and nations is not a mechanical process of economic relations in isolation from other important factors. Cities change not only as a result of the requirements of global or local capital but also as a result of state policy at the local and national level. There are, in effect, two worldwide 'logics', an economic (capitalistic) logic and a state logic; these have for a century or more been inextricably interrelated. Changing urban development patterns are best understood as the long-term outcomes of actions taken by economic and political *actors* operating within a complex and changing matrix of global and national economic and political *forces*. It is historically-specific political-economic processes through which contemporary corporations must work rather than expressing general economic laws of capitalist development.

Indeed, even a cursory glance at the contemporary world scene reveals many examples of these processes, including free trade zones, varying tax concessions, public–private organizations like MITI in Japan, and legislation requiring that manufactured products have some local content. A distinctive political-economic history accounts for the uneven pattern of urban development in the United States. This is why the particular forms of uneven urban development in the United States – declining inner cities, sprawling suburban development, extreme race and class segmentation of residential communities, and pronounced population dispersal of affluent communities to the hinterlands – are not found in the same form in other advanced capitalist states. For example, government action over many decades has established a tax system in the US which allows rapid depreciation of fixed capital investments, such as plants and office building, for tax purposes. Rapid depreciation has facilitated unprecedented levels of plant closures and also of office block construction – two dimensions of economic restructuring just examined. These tax laws represent economic growth-oriented state action, as well reflecting the substantial lobbying of a coalition of powerful real estate corporations since the 1930s (Feagin, 1983).

Paralleling each type of urban economic restructuring previously discussed for cities are distinctive types of government action, mediation or involvement. In the case of plant closures it is usually the undiversified cities which depend on one economic sector that face the most difficulty. Locational specialization, which may be functional for producers operating on a global scale, leaves specialized localities highly vulnerable to economic crisis and marginalization, to the problem of large numbers of displaced workers, and to heightened pressure on national and local government officials to intervene to save the steel mill or car plant. Local and national governments have responded in a variety of ways to plant closures. In the US the market-centered ideologies of local growth coalitions have led them to lobby local governments to set up economic development commissions to attract new industries to replace those in decline. In chapter 13 June Nash examines the impact of the restructuring of General Electric plants on the city of Pittsfield, Massachusetts. Major plant closures there were met by a proliferation of development commissions and private consulting firms working with local government officials to promote Pittsfield as a place for new industry; the relatively high wage levels of unionized workers there were seen by the local growth coalition as anti-business elements in need of change.

Moreover, as Glickman explains (chapter 3) a variety of capital–labor coalitions have developed to lobby local and federal governments to deal with the impact of global restructuring on US cities. Thus the city government of Detroit, the Chrysler Corporation and the United Auto Workers union worked together for a federal loan guarantee for an auto firm in serious trouble because of foreign competition. In some cases the local or regional state has become involved in negotiations with firms threatening an imminent departure – negotiations involving state intervention in regard to tax concessions. For example, in 1985–86 many Michigan cities faced great pressure from General Motors to reduce local taxes on GM plants, otherwise they would be closed down.

Sometimes new state structures are created in the most unlikely places, such as generally *laissez-faire* South Carolina, which regularly advertises itself as the state which would never 'kill the goose that laid the golden egg'. The South Carolina government created an Agency for Displaced Workers to cope with the spate of plant closures in textiles, machine products and light manufacturing which have blighted the area in the last decade. Underlining the global roots of these developments, a skilled, displaced textile worker was recently recruited to go to Guatemala to train workers there to operate the textile machine he once operated in South Carolina, but which a local machinery salesman had sold to a factory owner in Guatemala. When confronted with the fact that his temporary job would only intensify displacement of other US textile workers, since the Guatemalan firm produced for export to the US market, the worker simply replied: 'I've got to look out for me and my wife' (Anon., 1985: 19). In this instance, the textile mill worker's household survival strategy was an impediment to the development of either community or class consciousness as a collective basis for resisting more plant closures at home.

As a result of the, admittedly scattered, grassroots worker resistance to plant closures in the US, the US Congress has introduced plant closure legislation, and some city and regional governments have actually passed limited plant closure laws. However, in the US government response to plant closures has for the most part been more market-driven and concessionary than in some European countries, a point documented in Nash and Body-Gendrot (chapters 13 and 11).

More generally, the federal state has come under increased pressure to protect US firms and workers against the adverse effects of renewed international competition. Aggressive foreign policy has attempted to reassert economic hegemony with the tools of the state. Glickman (chapter 3) discusses the protectionist pressures which have forced the federal state to legislate on behalf of US-based firms and unionized workers, such as the 'voluntary' quotas on imported Japanese cars.

The other dimensions of urban economic restructuring we discussed in the previous section have also involved other forms of state action. Direct state involvement in the opening of sweatshops in certain US cities has been limited. Some government agencies 'turn a blind eye' to violations of labor, health and safety laws. Federal involvement is indirect, but it does include the encouragement of some Third World (e.g. Vietnamese) immigration that provides low-wage garment and electronics workers. Broadly considered, the foreign policy of the US government has accelerated some types of immigrant from Mexico, Central America and parts of Asia.

Urban redevelopment and the state

Corporate expansion in US central cities has involved the most extensive state intervention and mediation. Beginning in the 1950s, federally-funded, large-scale urban redevelopment and urban renewal programs facilitated the development of office buildings, shopping centers, convention centers, hotels and tourist attractions. Billions of dollars were spent by local and federal governments to demolish older housing and other buildings in inner city areas. Private investment flowed into the construction of new buildings on the government-susidized, cleared land. Local governments also provided other substantial subsidies in the form of tax concessions, relaxation of regulations, and public capital investments in infrastructure (Fainstein, et al. 1983; Feagin, 1983).

By the 1970s conventional urban renewal, and the massive clearance programs, had been scrapped to be replaced by new forms of 'public–private partnership'. In the face of the accelerated movement of capital investment on the global scale in the past decade, a multitude of alliances have been forged at the state and local levels between public officials and various business interests to promote new business investment, particularly in inner cities. These political alliances have played a key role in exacerbating uneven urban development patterns. The primary tool used to extract resources to support the goals of this network of economic and political elites has been the tax concession. These partnerships are managed by quasi-public development organizations variously called Downtown Development Authorities (DDAs), Economic Development Corporations (EDCs), and Local Development Companies (LDCs). They usually implement their decisions without referenda or legislative approval of specific projects. They have a great deal of discretion over the use of public funds and the granting of tax concessions. When viewed in isolation, the achievements of these organizational networks have been impressive in revitalizing declining areas.

For example, in the case of Atlanta, a new kind of metropolitan-wide growth coalition has been formed in response to the economic crisis there. Using a network of international business contacts made as a result of his United Nations ambassadorship, Mayor Andrew Young initiated an aggressive campaign to attract international business. Atlanta and its six surrounding counties have launched a $3 million campaign to promote the metropolitan area as an attractive location for services, sales, distribution and high-technology industries. Atlanta's effort to forge metropolitan-wide political unity in the face of intensified competition for international capital investment illustrates a major political consequence for local government officials of the most common current definition of urban crisis – an awareness that both too rapid growth and too little growth in the economic base of local community life can expand the role of the state as a facilitator and regulator of economic growth processes and as a mediator of economic decline.

In the case of Houston's unprecedented economic decline in the mid-1980s, the local Chamber of Commerce created an Economic Development Council, composed of developers, bankers and newspaper editors (the 'growth coalition'), with an annual budget of $3 million to advertise and promote the city as a good place to do business. Pressure was put on city and county governments to provide half the funding for what has become a *private*–public partnership. Too little growth in this case was the trigger for the local growth coalition to create in 1984 a new organization, rare in the Sunbelt region of the US, designed to seek a greater diversity of capital investments for a city long tied to the exigencies of the petroleum and petrochemical industries (Feagin, 1987).

The expansion of low-wage service (and construction) jobs in large cities has involved the same indirect state involvement as in the case of sweatshops, particularly US foreign policy action which has encouraged or accelerated Third World migration to the US. These immigrants not only undertake low-wage factory jobs but also do a substantial part of the low-wage service work in cities. This immigration has had other political impacts as well. The rapid infusion of migrants tied to new localities through either informal kinship, friendship, neighborhood or village networks or through more formalized associational support networks (e.g. the social movement in California to grant 'sanctuary' to refugees from Central American) may create service and political management problems for local government officials. In Miami, Cuban and Haitian migration, and massive government support for the Cubans, contributed to the anger seen in black rioting there in the early 1980s (Macdonald, 1984: 59–72; Smith, 1987). And in many cities of the Southwest there have been loud complaints about illegal immigrants taking jobs local citizens could do. The pressure on the local state to restrict social services for these immigrants has been great, as has similar pressure on the federal government to impose legislated barriers to their immigration.

State involvement in corporate expansion in the localities outside central cities has also included tax concessions and other tax subsidies, as well as direct capital investments in water ways, roads, and other types of infrastructure facilities. Public–private partnerships similar to those in downtown areas have developed in many outlying localities of major US cities.

State reaction in European nations

State involvement is not unique to US cities. Three authors in this volume consider the reaction of European states to global economic restructuring and to the impact that restructuring has had on cities and on people's movements. For example, international competition has had a severe impact on the French auto and steel industries. In her chapter in this book (chapter 11), Sophie Body-Gendrot (cf. also Body-Gendrot 1982: 272–88) discusses the large-scale state intervention which this competition has caused. The extreme centralization of state power in a country like France means that local officials do not have to experience great popular pressure to take actions in the face of plant closures and high unemployment in their cities. Whatever the central state's political composition (Socialist or Gaullist), it has taken the blame for localized deindustrialization and plant closures. One of the ironies of recent French history is that urban workers have had to endure a high rate of unemployment and massive industrial restructuring under a Socialist government. State action in France oscillated between a leftist Keynesianism of state intervention on behalf of ailing industries and a more conservative policy, since 1983, focusing on industrial competitiveness and austerity. The failure of left-wing governments in France to deal with unemployment and deindustrialization has in turn precipitated strikes and new right-wing movements calling for the expulsion of immigrant workers.

Desmond King (chapter 10) details similar deindustrialization problems and market-oriented state responses in Great Britain. Thus London lost 40 per cent of its manufacturing jobs between 1959 and 1975, a loss which is a key cause of uneven development in London and urban decline in many other industrial cities. King attributes much of the decline in London and other older, densely concentrated cities to changes in the global economy favoring investment in cities in developing countries. In his view older European cities cannot adapt readily to the rapidly changing needs of new corporate investments. The Thatcher government in Britain has not ignored distressed areas, but rather has aligned itself with market-oriented public policies. In Great Britain, central state action has often taken the form of encouraging and facilitating private investment in decaying areas of cities, using such market-oriented solutions as urban enterprise zones. As an example, King notes the sale in 1981 of publicly owned land in the depressed Docklands area of London to private developers, a development strategy opposed by local residents.

In her article on West German cities in this volume Mayer (chapter 16) documents processes of economic restructuring – urban disinvestment, redevelopment, gentrification – similar to those in US cities. In West Germany the federal state's industrial policy has worked in recent years to restructure industrial production towards industries which are the most competitive on the world market. Morever, state intervention in central city redevelopment has come to West Germany later than in the US, although the reason has been the same – to enhance the profitability of corporations operating in inner city areas. Thus in 1971 West Germany's Urban Development Act increased state power to redevelop inner city areas. This intervention at the local level, as in the US, gave community-based protest groups a centralized target. There have been squatter movements pressing for housing reform, as well as an array of community movements protesting against redevelopment, airport expansion, and a general lack of access to state decision-making. Mayer notes that, because political access at the local level is much less available to community groups in West Germany, these groups have moved to participation in the new alternative political parties (e.g. the 'Greens') at the national level. Yet many of these citizen groups have been co-opted into existing administrative structures but have not significantly expanded local democracy in West German cities. Mayer even suggests that a hidden function of these urban movements has been to facilitate urban redevelopment programs under state control.

RESTRUCTURING OF URBAN HOUSEHOLDS IN CITIES

Each type of economic restructuring in core country cities can also be linked to a restructuring of urban households. Enzo Mingione (chapter 14) deals with the survival strategies of worker households in industrialized nations of the US and Western Europe in crisis periods, as well as in 'normal' times. The expansion of informal economies, of such things as maintenance work, has become very important in areas with large-scale disinvestment; it is clear that women are central to these informal economies. This expansion of informal economies is, in part, a response to cutbacks in welfare programs by governments around the globe.

Plant closures are often very disruptive to workers and their households, as well as to other households (e.g. small businesses) serving the local economy. In US cities, as elsewhere, plant closures can force household restructuring, from 'moonlighting', to family breakdown and divorce, to serial migration (that is, migration of successive family members) to other cities. At the very least, plant closures place a great burden on the basic building blocks of communities and cities – the household units.

Economic restructuring in the form of sweatshop expansion in US cities affects yet other urban households. Often crossing national borders, households in Third World countries 'loan' themselves, or selected members, for work in US sweatshops. The provision of low-wage work in New York, Los Angeles or Chicago can mean the relocation of Mexican, Asian or Caribbean households to American cities. Households may be temporarily or permanently restructured across national boundaries in line with shifting capital investments.

Corporate center restructuring has had an impact not only on the households directly tied to the office workplace, but also to households displaced by corporate center construction. In this case household restructuring involves the migration of better-paid managerial and professional works to inner city areas, often to luxury apartments or gentrified homes, whose construction involves the displacement of middle- and low-income households. Other corporate center employees become involved in the major segregation of households in the suburbs and work-places in the inner city.

As in the case of sweatshop expansion, the increase in service (and construction) jobs associated with corporate center expansion has had an impact on household restructuring, particularly for immigrant and ethnic minority households in inner city areas. As in the sweatshop case, the Third World immigrant households supply workers for the lower-paid service positions, thus breaking up and reconstituting families across national borders. Moreover, local minority (citizen) families working in this service sector may secure employment as a result of corporate center expansion, yet still be a victim of higher rents or displacement resulting from corporate growth and urban displacement.

Economic restructuring in the form of corporate expansion to outlying areas has an effect on worker households which varies by wage level. The affluent upper tier can locate in nuclear family units in outlying small communities or luxury suburban apartments, with the segregation and isolation for household members that these residential patterns entail. The lower tiers of workers may face a reverse commuter scenario, commuting from inner-city areas to corporate offices and plants in outlying suburbs, a daily journey which can produce a serious financial and psychological drain on moderate-income households.

RESTRUCTURING OF COMMUNITIES AND COMMUNITY POLITICS

Even though the processes producing community change are encapsulated in wider political and economic structures and are affected by international processes of investment, production and trade, the point of impact for people is not only the household but also the particular *place*, the community space, which is the locus of inter-household organization, the cares of everyday life, and community politics. These micro-social structures – neighborhoods and communities – are the bases of acculturation and thus of the creation of human and family identity. Hence local practices, springing from the actions of people in households, neighborhoods, community organizations, and local political jurisdictions, are the central elements in collective action that the chapters by Smith and Tardanico (chapter 4), Fainstein (chapter 15) and Mayer (chapter 16) chronicle.

The unfolding of capital restructuring creates profoundly destabilizing conditions of everyday life in the cities most immediately affected. Recent research has sought to connect the unfolding world economy to the arena of grassroots politics in both core and peripheral cities. Smith and Tardanico (chapter 4) explore the web of interconnections linking the micro-structures of household and neighborhood life in core and peripheral cities to the wider arenas of the global economy, the state and community politics. Starting from the premise that the processes of production and reproduction are inseparably connected to the dynamics of local community life, Smith and Tardanico draw upon the previously only loosely connected literatures on global restructuring, household survival strategies and collective action theory to draw out the actual means by which the consciousness, intentionality and everyday practices of common people force changes in the planning, implementation and consequences of state and business policies, thereby shaping and reshaping urban culture, economy and politics. Their chapter extends the discussion of households in the informal economy to encompass activities taking place within, between and outside households that contribute to the formation of the social networks that become the building blocks of collective responses to the economic crisis ranging from group migration to community protest action.

One of the key collective responses to urban restructuring has been the urban social movement. Such popular movements, as Fainstein's chapter illustrates, are often based in residential projects and neighborhoods and reflect demands for improved public services and expanded input into the political sphere. While urban social movements are often successful on specific local issues, they are not easily integrated into city-wide or regional movements. Fainstein's analysis, as well as recent work by Castells (1983), attempts to deal with the possibilities for a coalition of the hundreds of community groups resisting public service deterioration in the face of corporate disinvestment.

In her chapter on Pittsfield, Massachusetts, Nash (chapter 13) concludes with the important point that corporate dominance over workers has historically involved an implied commitment to a community and to people who work in production: a type of 'social contract'. But the rapid movement of jobs overseas and the creation of automated plants in the US, Nash argues, is destroying the legitimation for that corporate hegemony, as workers gradually perceive the destruction of the social contract between capital and labor. Thus, in the current crisis, the workplace as well as the community remain a potential local focus of collective action against the destruction of human structures. The forms of resistance or accommodation to local crises of disinvestment, unregulated growth or uneven development have varied from nation to nation and place to place (Smith and Judd, 1984). Where popular resistance has occurred, its form, development and effectiveness have depended upon the issue being targeted; the resources available; the political channels available for expressing discontent; the character of existing or emergent forms of community organization connecting affected individuals, households and social networks to the political process; and the prevailing structure and culture of local politics (M. P. Smith, 1987).

Economic restructuring such as plant closure has a major impact on communities, not only because households are situated in spatially defined communities, but also because communities are usually linked to major corporations in a symbiotic way. Communities grow up, historically speaking, with local investments in plant and other means of production and distribution. As the building blocks of towns and cities, communities are situated localities with homes, churches, schools, small businesses, and the like woven together into a social fabric that is both a daily network of everyday life and a household safety net. Thus plant closures not only break up families but also disrupt, often quickly, the social mesh of community life. In the US, for instance, in industrially declining communities such as Detroit, Michigan and Youngstown, Ohio, school taxes are not paid, and school governing bodies must close down schools or reorganize, even though there are still children of unemployed workers to be taught. Local services may deteriorate. Small businesses, even churches, may go bankrupt.

Sweatshop expansion in cities can create new urban communities, such as in the new Central American and Asian enclaves in Los Angeles, New York, Chicago and Houston, as well as in the immigrant enclaves of London. These are the new ghettos of US inner cities and are often differentiated themselves, as can be seen in the distinctive Salvadorean, Guatemalan, Honduran and Mexican areas of cities like Los Angeles and Houston. These communities are relatively new, and they range from relatively stable family-centered communities to areas with high turnover and transiency. Many such immigrant communities are further 'impoverished' in effect, when their residents send large amounts of money back to their poverty-striken families in their countries of origin. Demands on the local state for public assistance may eventually emanate from these new community areas, as the new residents come to identify themselves with their new territory. However, substantial barriers to the development of such community consciousness, such as lack of citizenship and persisting identification with places of origin, must first be overcome for such local demands to develop, not to mention the resistance of the indigenous residents.

Past corporate center redevelopment has destroyed some older communities in central areas, particularly minority (e.g. black, Puerto Rican) areas and those with large concentrations of retired and elderly, as in the South of Market area in San Francisco (Hartman, 1984). Urban renewal not only remade the physical profile of central cities from Boston to San Francisco, but also displaced and destroyed whole communities of 'disposable' human beings, often numbering in the thousands. Homes, friendship networks and living space for low and middle-income city-dwellers have been destroyed, sometimes precipitating significant community conflict ranging from lawsuits slowing urban renewal in the South of Market area in San Francisco to the large-scale ghetto disturbances in Newark, Detroit and Los Angeles.

The expansion of services in inner cities has had similar effects on communities as sweatshop expansion. Indeed, some cities in core countries have seen new immigrant communities, linked to service jobs, develop distinct from older immigrant communities. For example, research by Rodriguez (1986) in Houston's Latin American immigrants indicates that the development of different undocumented ('illegal') immigrant communities is related to different phases of economic development. Houston's older undocumented Hispanic communities provided labor for the area's earlier indusrialization phases in the 1925–65 period, while undocumented communities that are developing today provide labor for services. Today's new undocumented communities still provide workers for labor-intensive industrial enterprises, but these communities additionally provide workers for jobs associated with the developing business service sector. Examples of jobs directly connected to business are messengers and office cleaners, while the jobs indirectly connected range from restaurant workers to housemaids. Moreover, even without collective protest, new communities of Third World immigrants may indirectly put new political pressures on the local state for better services and housing. For example, the indigenous minorities who perform the service jobs have had some difficulty in finding decent housing in central city areas which have undergone urban renewal. The presence of new immigrant groups intensifies demand for the limited supply of cheap rented housing, thus driving up rents. Sub-letting in other minority communities has sometimes been the result, yet another underlying condition behind ghetto riots.

Corporate expansion in outlying city areas has fed the development or redevelopment of suburban communities, sometimes bringing the classic range of urban problems to suburbia. This can be seen in the Silicon Valley development south of San Francisco. This high-tech industry expansion has created serious environmental (e.g. toxic waste) and housing problems for local communities, as well as a crisis in local infrastructure and taxation. It has sometimes created new suburban and ex-urban enclaves of better-paid computer and electronics workers, as well as enclaves of low-paid Asian and Mexican workers (Rogers and Larsen, 1984: 184–229). Rising housing costs have sometimes forced lower-paid workers to abandon original communities of settlement in areas like Silicon Valley. In addition, in cities like Los Angeles and Houston suburban corporate development has brought a scattering of office tower blocks to the suburbs and major residential and shopping center developments twenty miles from the city center. Thus, economic restructuring in US cities can also entail a great deal of metropolitan sprawl.

RESTRUCTURING URBAN SPACE IN CITIES

As the foregoing discussion has suggested, the physical and geographical profile of urban development has been shaped in many ways by the interplay of global capitalism, the state, and the activities of urban residents. Perhaps because of its scale and scope the impact of global capitalism has been easiest to identify. Major economic investment and location decisions shape the built environment of cities, from the expansion of outlying residential areas to the number and location of ancillary industries, office towers and shopping precincts. Surplus capital from existing manufacturing industries may be channelled into real estate projects; and new manufacturing industries attract real estate capital into Sunbelt cities. As manufacturing industries change in response to the global reorganization of capitalism, the built environment of cities also experiences physical change. Private property and industrial investment are central dimensions of modern capitalism, and they set the broad parameters within which land and housing patterns emerge. Each type of economic restructuring involves investment or disinvestment in the physical facilities of production – plants, offices, warehouses, shops – and in the housing for workers in those means of production. Production and consumption (housing) construction require a complex of other constructions, from roads, water and sewerage systems to government offices.

Disinvestment in the form of plant closures has a negative multiplier effect on urban development. It means not only abandoned factories but also abandoned offices, warehouses, shops and housing. And it means a deterioration in state infrastructure facilities (e.g. water systems) which are paid for by the taxes on production. Most urban decay is the physical outcome of corporate decisions to move fixed capital expenditures to other areas of a city or to other cities around the nation or around the globe. A plant closing can mean urban decay in only one part of a city as in the uneven development pattern which can be seen in Cleveland, Buffalo or Detroit; or it can devastate an entire city, as in Youngstown, Ohio.

New plants in inner cities, particularly the sweatshops of Los Angeles, Chicago and New York, have made only a modest impact on the built environment. Most have been located in existing, even abandoned, buildings. But they do signal the cyclical process of disinvestment and investment which proceeds in a series of stages over a particular city's lifetime. Many a city area has been abandoned, thus reducing the price of land and building so providing the framework for later economic development. Some urban areas may be in permanent physical decline, while others experience periodic resuscitation.

Corporate centralization restructuring has brought office development to major central cities, literally elevating the skylines. Clusters of office towers are charateristic of San Francisco, Los Angeles, Chicago, Minneapolis, Detroit, New York and Houston, as well as a dozen other major cities. Billions in investment capital have flowed into this distinctive type of fixed capital. Harvey (1985), building on the insights of Lefebvre (1970), has argued that the secondary circuit of real estate investment is an important outlet for surplus capital which cannot find opportunities for above-average profit in production (e.g. manufacturing) investments. (See Gottdiener, 1985, for a detailed critique of Harvey's position.) Coupled with office construction has been the building of related facilities, often government-subsidized through urban renewal, such as hotels, convention centers, and quality department stores. Even though some older cities have successfully converted to corporate-professional cities, it should not be assumed that this developmental pattern is likely to become the typical pattern of urban transformation. Research has documented the robust growth of service employment in the past decade, along with continuing industrial decline. The data support the concusion that, despite notable exceptions like New York and Los Angeles, overall the central city share of the new dynamic has not been adequate to provide real economic regeneration in most older cities.

This expansion of office space is a major reason for the large numbers of inner city service employees, who must maintain, in the most direct sense, the massive physical plant. Many of these employees are housed in inner city slum areas, the large areas of deteriorating housing into which little private or public investment flows. They make their own investments in the older central city housing, generally slowing its deterioration and abandonment.

The spatial impact of corporate investment in outlying areas of large cities in the US has in a number of cases been dramatic. Silicon Valley, for example, has plants and offices for 2000 companies where there was once mostly open space. Residential communities have proliferated. In Houston decentralized development in the 17 business activity centers outside the downtown area has proliferated an assortment of office complexes and shopping facilities at the periphery. There is a bimodal distribution of development, in the center and in the outlying ring.

State policies, sometimes in support of capital accumulation, sometimes more autonomously, sometimes intentionally and sometimes by their unintended effects, have also played a key role in restructuring urban space. National and local taxation policies promote particular patterns of investment and household consumption; regulatory policies affect the flow of credit, mediate the labor process in the formal sector, and manage (or fail to manage) the flow of immigrants across national borders. State policies allocating responsibility for the social costs of capitalist production, such as pollution control and assisting displaced workers, vary across regions and nations, entering into the calculus of factors affecting investment decisions and capital flows between core and periphery.

Depending on the balance of social forces embodied in state policies, the economic development policies of the local and regional state vary from purely capital-serving tax concessions to more balanced 'linkage' development policies where local state officials are able to impose pro-neighborhood and other political conditions on the development process. Concessions of the latter sort have been extracted from developers by progressive governments in cities such as San Francisco, Boston, Los Angeles and Santa Monica, California, where neighborhood pressure has been an important factor in local politics (see Clarke, 1987).

The crucial variable producing popular responsive policies affecting urban development is the extent to which the networks of ordinary people in households, communities and workplaces can combine to produce forms of organization leading to the effective expression of demands for better neighborhood and working conditions, improved urban public services, and the self-management of their communities. From the Third World squatter settlements, discussed in the next section, to core country women's organizations demanding child-care facilities, to the progressive neighborhood movements in the United States, to urban social movements in Europe, it is clear that popular praxis matters. It is an essential element in community politics; and when it is present, the balance of power within the state, and hence the state role in urban restructuring, becomes more than a matter of capital accumulation.

CITIES IN THE THIRD WORLD: THE GLOBAL ASSEMBLY LINE

As we noted previously, global restructuring has had major consequences for cities in the core countries, including plant closures and job losses linked to such phenomena as re-export manufacturing in countries in the periphery. Much of the global assembly-line is now located in the city economies of the Third World, from Mexico City, to São Paulo, Singapore, Seoul and Manila. In Third World nations a dominant city often develops, one that is 6 to 15 times the size of the next largest city. Reviewing the literature on these 'primate' cities, Timberlake (chapter 2) notes that this urbanization phenomenon occurs for several reasons, including the fact that Third World export-oriented economies usually need only one shipping outlet, as well as the fact that the development of railroads has usually focused on transit to that one city. In addition, the destruction of local industry and trade by the increase of multinational investment tends to reduce the number of large cities. And the primate city, unlike cities in the US, is usually the only city with a significant finance capital market centered on facilitating exports and foreign investment.

In many Third World cities the new international division of labor has had two major effects: (1) an increase in export-processing industries, and (2) a significant increase in the use of the informal economic sector to support these formal sector industries. We have already discussed these export-processing industries. Their increase has led to a significant expansion of the manufacturing proletariat in Third World cities, a segregated workforce with men tending to work in basic industries (e.g. steel) and women working on consumer products (e.g. television sets). Today the occupational structure of industrializing cities in the Third World also includes a large tertiary or informal sector which some analysts have termed as 'marginal'. Reviewing the literature, Timberlake notes that this work (e.g. scavenging, domestic work, piecework at home) is not marginal but is inexorably linked to a system of modern capitalistic production. Moreover, the home workers also help reproduce industrial workers.

This combination of formal sector jobs and informal sector support activities has been a spur to economic development in many Third World cities, even though it is development dependent on the needs of multinational corporations. Even so, some cities in underdeveloped countries have been bypassed by this distorted type of transnational development. Cities like Lima, are losers in the new international division of labor, for Lima has captured little of the new re-export industrial production characteristic of the global assembly-line. As described by Patricia Ann Wilson (chapter 9), Lima has faced a distinctive type of economic restructuring. Once a center of assembly-line production for local markets, Lima has become a peripheral, backwater city, as production for export markets, even for Peru, has shifted to cities like Mexico City and São Paulo.

In her chapter (chapter 12) Helen Safa examines dependent urbanization in Latin America, the most urban of all developing regions. Latin American cities, initially colonial markets exporting raw materials, have recently been dominated by export-led growth linked to manufacturing. The increasing internationalization of manufacturing production has created a competitive search for cost-cutting. This competitive search has led to much sub-contracting to the informal sector, not only in garments, but also toys and electronics. Safa discusses in detail the importance of these informal economies in Latin American cities. The informal sector produces many goods and services for the formal sector. Enterprises in the formal sector often subcontract production to the informal sector, just as is the case in the sweatshops of Los Angeles, Chicago and New York. Noteworthy here is the role of the state. Latin American governments have facilitated the use of home, and other informal sector, production to reduce the labour costs of transnational corporations. A key role of the state in Latin American cities has been to facilitate production and, wherever possible, to repress worker organization and dissent. The state also mediates the contradictions of this pattern of development by attempting to respond to the demands of urban social movements by co-optative management of neighborhood services and state-sponsored citizen participation schemes.

We see here an impact as well on households and communities. Women workers are important not only in manufacturing but also in the informal economy. One type of work segregation in Latin American cities involves the use of younger, single women in export-oriented manufacturing plants, with older, married women with children working in their households and thus in the informal sector, a point Safa's chapter emphasizes. In Third World cities much of the labor in the informal sector, as well as in agriculture, is done by women and children. This is true of subsistence farming in the rural areas from which men have migrated to work in urban industries. In his article Timberlake cites studies documenting the fact that the penetration of foreign capital into Third World cities exacerbates the existing patriarchal family relationships there, often thus leading to a type of superexploitation of women workers as a group.

In Third World cities, as elsewhere, communities are the seedbeds of protest. Citizen protest has become characteristic of many of these cities in the last decade. One reason is the austerity forced on governments in underdeveloped capitalist countries by the principal organs of finance capital in the core capitalist countries. As John Walton notes (chapter 17), the current international debt crisis which affects most Third World countries is rooted in the attempt by the US to regain a favorale trade balance through its aid programs and in the huge loans made by the international banking system, centered in US banks, to these countries. The new international production system has been paralleled by this new world banking system to support industrial investments directly, and indirectly through loans to Third World governments committed to actions favoring export- and transnational-oriented production. (Socialist states such as Allende's Chile were boycotted.) When the debt crisis appeared, the IMF and private banks imposed new austerity programs on governments in developing countries. These programs, as Walton demonstrates for 22 countries, have led to major strikes and food riots, urban protest which has forced most governments to rescind cuts in welfare provision. This community-based collective action has in turn forced the IMF and the international banks to renegotiate their loan schedules with the countries in turmoil. In most countries the state is the target of urban protests, since it is the most 'visible' enemy of the poor. Much collective protest has targeted the state for providing poor public services, such as transport and water supply, and poor housing, and most protest has been based in working-class neighborhoods and squatter communities.

CONCLUSION

We have traced in this introductory chapter the impact that transnational corporate expansion, complementary state actions, and popular response by urban households have had on cities and communites around the globe. We have seen the many ways in which the world economy is indeed an integrated, worldwide, political-economic system laced together by transnational corporations and situated physically and geographically in those distinctive spatial places that we call cities. We have seen that, just as the activities of capital and the state constitute powerful constraints on the everyday activities of ordinary people, the key activities of households – immigration, informalization, and political mobilization – constitute household survival strategies which, in their turn, affect the accumulation strategies of global capital, the political management strategies of the state, and the character of urban life.

REFERENCES

Anon. (1984) 'Sweatshop renaissance', *Dollars and Sense*, no. 86 (April): 6–7.
—— (1985) 'Carolinian Finds a Textile Job, in Guatemala', *New York Times*, 14 April: 19.
—— (1986) 'Militarism in America', *The Defense Monitor*, 15: 1–6.
Arkin, William M. and Richard W. Fieldhouse (1985) *Nuclear Battlefields*, Cambridge: Ballinger.
Barnet, Richard L. and Ronald E. Muller (1974) *Global Reach*, New York: Simon and Schuster.
Body-Gendrot, Sophie (1982) 'Governmental responses to popular movements: France and the US'. In Norman I. Fainstein and Susan S. Fainstein (eds) *Urban Policy Under Capitalism*, Beverly Hills: Sage, pp. 277–91.
Castells, Manuel (1983) *The City and the Grassroots*, Berkeley: University of California Press.
Clairmonte, Frederick and John Cavanagh, (1981) *The World in Their Web*, London: 2ed Press.
Clarke, Susan (in press) 'More autonomous policy orientations: an analytical framework'. In Clarence N. Stone and Heywood T. Sanders (eds), *The Politics of Urban Development*, Lawrence: University Press of Kansas.
Cohen, R. B. (1981) 'The new international division of labor, multinational corporations and urban hierarchy'. In Michael Dear and Allen J. Scott (eds), *Urbanization and Urban Planning in Capitalist Society*, London: Methuen, pp. 287–315.
Fainstein, Susan S., Norman I. Fainstein, Richard Child, Dennis R. Judd and Michael Peter Smith, (1983) *Restructuring the City*, New York: Longman.
Feagin, Joe R. (1983) *The Urban Real Estate Game*, Englewood Cliffs, NJ: Prentice-Hall.
—— (1985) 'The social costs of Houston's growth', *International Journal of Urban and Regional Research*, 9: 164–85.
—— (1987) 'Local state response to economic decline'. In Dennis Judd and Michael Parkinson (eds), *Urban Development in Britain and the U.S.* [provisional title]. Manchester: University of Manchester Press.
Frobel, Folker, Jurgen Heinrichs and Otto Kreye (1980) *The New International Division of Labor*, Cambridge: Cambridge University Press.
Gottdiener, M. (1985) *The Social Production of Urban Space*, Austin: University of Texas Press.
Grunwald, Joseph and Kenneth Flamm (1985) *The Global Factory*, Washington, D.C.: The Brookings Institution.
Harvey, David (1985) *The Urbanization of Capital*, Baltimore: Johns Hopkins University Press.
Lefebvre, Henri (1970) *La Revolution urbaine*, Paris: Gallimard.
Macdonald, Michael C. D. (1984) *America's Cities*, New York: Simon and Schuster.
McGahey, R. (1983) 'High tech, low hopes', *New York Times*, 15 May; 23.
Marx, Karl, (1967) *Capital*, vol. 1. New York: International Publishers.
Rodriguez, Nestor (1986) 'Differential development of undocumented immigrant communities'. Unpublished manuscript, University of Houston.

Rogers, Everett M. and Judith K. Larsen, (1984) *Silicon Valley Fever*, New York: Basic Books.

Sassen-Koob, Saskia (1983) 'Recomposition and peripheralization at the core'. In Marlene Dixon and Susanne Jonas (eds), *From Immigrant Labor to Transnational Working Class*, San Francisco: Synthesis Publications.

Sivard, Ruth L. (1985) *World Military and Social Expenditures*, Washington, D.C.: World Priorities Organization.

Smith, Michael Peter (1979) *The City and Social Theory*, New York: St Martin's Press.

—— (1987) 'Global capital restructuring and local political crises in U.S. cities', in Jeffrey Henderson and Manuel Castells (eds), *Global Restructuring and Territorial Development*, London: Sage.

Smith, Michael Peter and Dennis R. Judd (1984) 'American cities: The production of ideology'. In Michael Peter Smith (ed.) *Cities in Transformation*, Beverly Hills: Sage, pp. 173–96.

Smith, Michael Peter and Marlene Keller (1983) 'Managed growth and the politics of uneven development in New Orleans'. In Susan S. Fainstein et al., *Restructuring the City*. New York: Longman, pp. 126–66.

Smith, Neil (1984) *Uneven Development*, Oxford: Basil Blackwell.

PART II

Theoretical Perspectives: The Global Economy, the State and the City

2

World-System Theory and the Study of Comparative Urbanization

Michael Timberlake

INTRODUCTION

Most aspects of large-scale social change have now been examined through the lens of what is called world-system theory. Not surprisingly this is true of urbanization processes. It is not surprising because the scale and pace of urbanization is dramatic and markedly uneven across regions of the world. According to recent estimates, over 40 per cent of the world's population now live in urban areas, and this is expected to increase dramatically (United Nations, 1984b).[1] There is tremendous global unevenness in this regard, with some 70 per cent of the European and US population living in places defined as urban, but less than one-third of Africa's population living in cities and towns and an even smaller percentage in China and South Asia. But there is variation within the Third World as well, ranging from Latin America, where nearly 70 per cent of the population is classified as urban, to about 30 per cent in Africa. However, concern with urbanization goes beyond its mere scale. In less developed countries (LDCs), there is much discussion of the problems created by the rapid tempo of urbanization and of the alleged imbalances in the way in which urbanization has proceeded. Major cities are said to be disproportionately large compared to other cities in a region, migration from rural to urban areas too rapid, and employment opportunities in the urban industrial sector too limited. Cities in some more developed countries are experiencing disturbing changes as well. For example, in the United States there is much discussion of the disastrous effects on cities of 'deindustrialization'.

In this chapter I shall review some of the literature on these urban imbalances, suggesting why they have become a source of concern and how they have been interpreted from global political-economy perspectives – in particular the world-system framework but also its predecessor, dependency theory. I shall also suggest what implications there might be for the study of urban change of three important general criticisms of world-system theory.

Before discussing urbanization, a review of the basic claims made by world-system theorists is in order.

THE WORLD-SYSTEM APPROACH

The increasing significance of neo-Marxian theories of development, beginning in the late 1960s within sociology in the United States, and the corresponding decreasing significance of developmentalist modernization theories were, in retrospect, inevitable. It was all too clear that the foreign policies of the US government with respect to foreign aid and military intervention were doing little to stem massive poverty, inegalitarianism and political repression in LDCs. To the contrary, voices from within the less developed countries were suggesting that involvement of the metropolitan countries all too often exacerbated these problems. In the universities in the United States, students faced with the possibility of killing and dying in Vietnam found little use for the modernization approach either. Instead they were receptive to the theories of development which related social change in less developed countries to relationships between these countries and other politically and economically powerful countries. But these Marxist and neo-Marxist theories of development needed legitimation before they could truly compete with the developmentalist approaches in the production of 'normal science' research. Legitimation came from two directions.

Immanuel Wallerstein's work has been enormously influential in recasting questions about fundamental social change. His early essays on the world system (1979) laid out the major assumptions of his theory, and his first two volumes (four are planned) of *The Modern World-System* (1974, 1980) used the theory to interpret social change historically. Wallerstein's work falls easily with an accepted tradition of macro-historical sociology and 'grand theory'. His work has served as an inspiration to numerous other more recent efforts at comparative historical research.

The second set of works that served to legitimate research critical of the developmentalist approach has been centered at Stanford University on the work of John Meyer, his colleagues and students. Their efforts, beginning in the early 1970s, were aimed at putting into practice the key concepts of Latin American *dependentistas* and Wallersteinian world-system theory for hypothesis-testing in quantitative, cross-national studies. This opened the way for publishing *ostensibly* neo-Marxist development research in major American sociology journals, most of which are strongly biased towards quantitative research. Together, these two new directions in comparative sociological inquiry made it possible for faculty and graduate students in university social science departments to pursue Marxian interpretations of development without putting an early end to their careers.

There are several excellent reviews of world-system theory available (e.g.

Chase-Dunn and Rubinson, 1977, 1979; Chirot and Hall, 1982; Wallerstein, 1979; Wallerstein and Hopkins, 1977), and I shall draw heavily on these in the discussion which follows. Wallerstein has argued that the modern world system emerged between 1450 and 1600 as a capitalist world economy (and capitalism) emerged as this world system. He does not claim that this world economy has included all areas of the globe at all times – large areas of world were not effectively incorporated in the system until the beginning of the nineteenth century (cf. Sokolovsky, 1985). Rather, it is argued that its logic entails continuous expansion towards that end, much as previous world systems, constituted as world empires, were based on expansion.

The capitalist world economy is characterized by several basic processes and structures. Of course, there is great variation across the globe and over time in the specific forms of large-scale social change, but these processes and structures, it is claimed, are sufficiently stereotyped and recurrent as to allow us to conceptualize the world economy as a system. The basic processes are of three types: cyclical processes, secular trends and state formation. Basic structural systemic features include the core–periphery division of labor, the inter-state system and unequal development (Chase-Dunn and Rubinson, 1979).

Wallerstein's argument is that the core areas of the world system have developed in the context of a set of economic exchanges and political relationships among actors located in different parts of the system, including countries of the periphery, the semi-periphery and core. Each core country is characterized by an active coalition of economic actors who are able to use their own state's apparatus to pursue their interests *vis-à-vis* nation-based actors in other core countries as well as less powerful and less well-organized groups in the periphery. Competition among core groups in the context of cycles of expansion and contraction and shifting international alliances tend to undermine any one national group's dominance in this system (e.g. Goldfrank, 1983; Bergesen, 1983). Wallerstein points out that there have thus been three hegemonic core powers since the modern world system emerged: the United Provinces in the sixteenth century, England in the nineteenth century, and the United States in the twentieth century.

The dependency theorists had already described the relationship between developed and underdeveloped countries for the nineteenth and twentieth centuries, espcially for Latin America, which world-system theorists then generalized to the capitalist world system since its inception. Core capitalists seek markets for manufactured goods, sources of raw materials and cheap labor in peripheral areas. These aims are achieved through a variety of means, including the market, military force and subtler political mechanisms such as core capitalist political alliances with internally repressive elites in the periphery (e.g. Galtung, 1971: Kentor, 1985). These relationships have 'underdeveloped' the peripheral areas, while core areas have benefited.

World-system and dependency theorists contend that peripheral countries continue to suffer from a number of disadvantages that are direct consequences of their relationship to the core. These include relatively slow economic growth, highly unequal distributions of income and wealth, highly repressive political regimes, underemployment and unemployment, and so on. There is a large and growing body of literature bearing out many of these theoretical claims (e.g. Fiala, 1983; Bornschier and Chase-Dunn, 1985; Williams and Timberlake, forthcoming).

World-system theory has not been without its critics, however. In this chapter I shall discuss briefly three criticisms. The first is that the perspective does not take sufficiently into account the fundamental nature of class conflict to social change (e.g. Brenner, 1977). Wallerstein, especially in the first volume of *The Modern World-System* (1974), is accused of having portrayed social relations as determined almost exclusively by the position of groups of actors with respect to the world market. The second criticism is that world-system theorists have paid insufficient attention to the role of states as institutions that are somewhat autonomous from world economic processes (Skocpol, 1977). Social change at the societal level, it is claimed, is shaped as much by the internal logic of state bureaucracies – especially in societies with strong states – as by world-economic processes. The third criticism comes from those who point out that we need to examine the way patriarchal relations interact with global social forces in reproducing the hierarchical world division of labor (cf. Ward, 1984). These three criticisms will be addressed in terms of how they might pertain to a world-system perspective of urbanization.

Among the most obvious manifestations of the global unevenness produced by world-system processes are those involved in the tremendous differences in the apparent nature of urbanization in the periphery compared to the core. Although there are vast differences throughout the Third World, observable in all are high rates of urbanization in the face of economic stagnation, imbalanced city systems, and over-employment in a labor-intensive service sector and the urban informal sector. Social scientists influenced by the paradigm have increasingly framed their research on comparative urbanization in terms of the world-system perspective (cf. Timberlake, 1985; Meyer, 1986), although there have been several prominent earlier efforts in theorizing about urbanization in terms of international political economy (e.g. Hardoy, 1975; Abu-Lughod and Hay, 1977). Recently, patterns of change experienced by core cities have also increasingly been discussing from the standpoint of global political economic processes (cf. Rodriguez and Feagin, 1986). The apparent 'deindustrialization' of certain cities in the United States has important implications for urban social formations. How various urban processes have been interpreted in these ways is discussed at length in the following sections.

GLOBAL UNEVENNESS IN MACRO-URBAN PATTERNS

Although the level of urbanization (defined as the percentage of a given population living in areas classified as urban) in LDCs is still far smaller, its sheer volume, in terms of numbers of people, and its tempo are much greater than has ever been the case in the core. Bairoch (1975) estimates that between 1850 and 1880 the average annual growth of urbanization in Europe was 1.2 per cent, raising the level of urbanization from 15 per cent to 22 per cent. On the other hand, between 1950 and 1985 the level of urbanization in less developed regions increased from 17 per cent to 32 per cent (United Nations, 1984b). Furthermore, this analysis of the numbers masks the fact that higher rates of overall natural increase in most of the Third World would contribute dramatically to the increasing population of key cities even if the urban proportion remained stable. Natural increase, together with the other key factors contributing to the growth of large cities – migration from rural areas and annexation of outlying areas not previously defined as urban – have caused the poulations of many key cities in LDCs to double or even treble over the last 30 years. Mexico City, for example increased from three million in 1950 to an estimated 15 million in 1980; during this same period Jakarta grew from 1.8 million to 7 million, Accra from 240,000 to 1.4 million, Manila from 1.6 million to 5.3 million, and Buenos Aires from 5.2 million to 10 million. During New York City's 25 years of most rapid growth, from 1850 to 1875, it increased by 1.2 million (Chase-Dunn, 1985b: 280–1).

Over-urbanization and imbalanced urban employment structure in the periphery of the world system

Many nations in the Third World are said to be 'over-urbanized'. This form was introduced to the development literature in the 1950s (cf. Hoselitz, 1955) and has had various meanings since then. It has also been seriously criticized for almost as long as it has been used (cf. Sovani, 1964). Originally it was based on the observation that the urban population of many LDCs has been a much larger proportion of the total population than expected from the extent of industrialization. Criticism of this observation comes from those who question the basis of the expected relationship between urbanization and industrialization (as indicated by such criteria as GNP per capita, or energy consumption per capita). The expectation seems to be rooted in a version of modernization theory that argued that 'normal' development would occur everywhere in much the same way as it did in Western Europe and the northern states of North America. In these regions people moved to cities as the manufacturing sector grew because industrialization required the geographic concentration of the general labor force and of the various functionally interdependent enterprises involved in manufacturing and services (Hawley, 1981: 71–2).

The pattern in LDCs is different because industrialization has been much slower, but urbanization has proceeded quite rapidly none the less. Thus, outsiders visiting Third World cities are usually struck by the apparent large numbers of urban residents who are unemployed or working at such seemingly unproductive jobs as car minders, peddlers, scavengers, and so on. Sovani's original criticism of the over-urbanization thesis was that the basis for the expected relationship between the relative size of the urban population and industrialization was theoretically untenable. He questioned the assumption that LDCs would follow the same path to modernization as the more developed countries and even whether the latter would not have been seen as 'over-urbanized' during their periods of most rapid urban growth.

It has also been noted that demographic trends are very different in the less developed countries of the post-World War II era than for nineteenth-century Western Europe. In poor countries today natural population growth remains very high in both rural and urban areas. It would be a mistake however to view overpopulation in rural areas as simply a demographic phenomenon. Many would point out that there has been pressure on the availability of land for political-economic reasons as well as for demographic ones. The 'agricultural revolution' in the Third World has often had the effect of forcing peasants off the land as capital-intensive agricultural technology has replaced labor-intensive methods and as corporate land-ownership has turned peasants into agricultural wage laborers or into migrants to the cities. In fact, urban migration may be the best alternative to massive rural poverty (Firebaugh, 1979).

In the last five years researchers employing world-system and dependency perspectives have interpreted the apparent over-urbanization in many Third World countries in terms of the global core–periphery division of labor. The theoretical argument is that various mechanisms that reproduce this division of labor serve to exacerbate aggregate over-urbanization because they both limit the spread of industrialization and encourage urban population growth. For example, some argue that foreign investment in manufacturing is often concentrated in export and luxury consumer products that are unlikely to stimulate dynamic, self-sustaining industrial development. Yet this limited industrialization creates the illusion of urban opportunity sufficient to stimulate migration from rural areas (cf. Todaro, 1981). This is especially true to the extent that rural opportunities are limited; international dependency relations are said to be involved here as well. Rural foreign investment in peripheral countries often displaces peasants, turning some of them into rural wage laborers. But other former peasants choose, or are forced, to move to cities to seek their livelihood. In the Philippines, Dole Pineapple operations have had this effect in a very direct manner. In Costa

Rica one also finds evidence of linkages between transnational corporate agriculture and rural poverty. There the short-run profitability of cattle-raising for the American fast-food industry has forced many small subsistence farmers off their land and undermined the ecological stability of the land through over-grazing.

There are also direct political reasons for associating dependency with over-urbanization. Sometimes with reluctance, often with exuberance, political leaders in most Third World nations actively seek to attract foreign investments, especially in modern industry. Because of this and many other factors to do with class relations and national politics, larger urban areas may often benefit from government expenditures in infrastructure and public services in an effort to attract these foreign investments. This constitutes what Guglar (1982), following Lipton (1977), calls the 'urban bias' that fuels even more city migration.

David Smith (1984) is more explicit about the exacerbating impact of world-system processes, through national class relations, on over-urbanization. He goes beyond Guglar's formulation of the urban bias theory, asking for clarity about the 'material class interests' of the urban elite and about their international economic and political alliances. Policy implications of viewing over-urbanization as a demographic feature or as mirroring only a rural versus urban public spending bias are misleading, he argues. It is more useful instead to interpret it as a manifestation of dependent development. This leads to an analysis that understands the overlapping interests of local elites and multinational firms (e.g. for cheap labor) and their influence on the policies of the state (see also D. Smith, 1985). Thus, over-urbanization is not a reflection of a simple 'urban bias' that pits the urban working class against the rural masses. Rather, it is part of a complex relationship pitting the interests of what Evans (1979) calls the 'triple alliance' against both urban and rural masses. Policies attempting to deal with over-urbanization that ignore its rootedness in international dependency relations and class conflict are thus doomed to failure according to Smith (1984: 20–3).

There is one more way in which some might argue that world-system processes serve indirectly to encourage over-urbanization. This argument assumes first that the linkage mentioned above between overall rapid population growth and over-urbanization is valid, and then rests on the contention that one reason for rapid population growth in the periphery is penetration by foreign capital.

Kathryn Ward is prominent among those who have forwarded this argument. Under conditions of dependent development a number of conditions are present which limit the fertility-supressing effects that demographers have associated with the economic growth of the developed countries. In the first place, the status of women may actually decline with penetration by foreign capital. For example, women workers are sometimes displaced from their traditional industries, and 'without the creation of new jobs in related industries this displacement should contribute to women's smaller share of industrial employment' (Ward, 1984: 40). Ward contends that this declining economic status corresponds to declining political status, and the increased subordination of women by present and new patriarchal social relations. One consequence is that women's control over their own fertility declines. 'Therefore, a major determinant of fertility is the structure of opportunities for women, i.e., whether or not women have access to the new educational, economic, and political resources generated by development' (Ward, 1984: 47). In addition to affecting fertility through its influence on the status of women, there are other effects of dependent development that are associated with high birth rates. One is that the fruits of economic growth are usually highly concentrated in the hands of a small elite, and, thus, absolute levels of poverty remain high. Poverty, and its concomitants, such as high rates of infant mortality, work against lowering birth rates. Thus, through its effects on fertility, world-system involvement may also be linked to over-urbanization.

Note that no one is arguing that world-system involvement alone causes high birthrates or even that it is the major direct cause of over-urbanization. Rather, the argument is that through a number of direct and indirect mechanisms, peripheralization in the world system is a major contributing factor to what has been termed over-urbanization. Most of the evidence in support of this interpretation comes from a small number of quantitative, cross-national studies that have documented the expected relationship between some indicator of penetration by foreign capital in less developed countries and an indicator of over-urbanization for the 1960s and 1970s (e.g. Bradshaw, 1985; Timberlake and Kentor, 1983). This research, and the theoretical arguments on which it is based, tend to see over-urbanization as only an outward manifestation of world-system processes and structures rather than reflecting a basic aspect or aspects of the system.

A second line of theorizing on over-urbanization focuses more explicitly on the employment patterns that characterize the phenomenon, and sees these as reflecting relationships for more fundamental to the global capitalist system. This argument begins with the observation that non-agricultural employment in peripheral countries is concentrated in tertiary occupations[2] – much more so than in the core countries now or at any time in the past. There is nothing inherently 'underdeveloped' about tertiary sector jobs. In fact, the best-paid occupations in the world are in this sector – e.g. doctors, research engineers and corporate managers. But there is good reason to believe that the tertiary sector in peripheral countries is composed largely of occupations at the other end of the pay-scale – the street hawkers, domestic workers and rag pickers. Many of these are jobs in the 'informal' urban sector. Such jobs tend to be very labor-intensive and they elude formal supervision and regulation by the state (Portes, 1985a, citing Roberts, 1976).

Field research in many different LDCs has indicated that it is in these jobs that migrants from rural areas most often find initial employment (e.g. Peattie, 1968; Perlman, 1976; Lobo, 1982); in many cases it is the only kind of employment they will ever find.

Developmentalist interpretations of this segment of the workforce often viewed it as either somehow 'traditional' or as 'marginal'. However, as Smith (1984) points out in his critique of Guglar's interpretation of over-urbanization (1982), it is not accurate to characterize this work as necessarily 'inefficient' or representing 'misemployment'. Anthropological fieldwork indicates that it is neither. In the first case, the work that at first glance may appear traditional because it is so labor-intensive, is often shown to have been non-existent before the expansion of modern capitalist market relationships into the area in question. In the second place, it is extremely doubtful that these jobs are in any sense marginal. Smith cites several examples of fieldwork which shows how apparently 'marginal' workers in Third World cities, such as garbage pickers, are inexorably linked to a system of modern production (e.g. Birbeck, 1978; Sethuraman, 1978). Such workers are often performing 'necessary labor very cheaply' (Smith, 1984). Smith points out that, in fact, informal work can benefit local elites and their multinational allies by providing them with cheap inputs, thus allowing them to realize greater profit. He interprets over-urbanization as an outward manifestation of exploitative social relations of labor that are best understood 'in the context of a society's place and changing role in the modern world-system and, more proximately, in the political and economic structures and struggles linked to these wider changes' (1984: 22).

Portes (1985a) effectively demolishes the argument that informal sector workers are marginal by pointing out that such work is crucial to the survival not only of the families in this sector, but also of families with workers in the formal sector. He argues that it is through informal sector labor that the low wages of formal sector workers in the Third World are subsidized. The subsidies take the form of the many services performed by informal sector workers for others at below market prices. Without these services formal sector labor would require higher wages in order to reproduce itself. But these low formal sector wages in the periphery, coupled with the fact that some of its labor is employed in enterprises owned by core capital producing commodities for the world market, are important ways in which surplus is extracted from the periphery to the core. Portes summarizes his argument by noting that:

Direct subsidies to consumption provided by informal to formal sector workers within a particular peripheral country are also indirect subsidies to core-nation workers and, hence, means to maintain the rate of profit. Thus through a series of mechanisms, well-hidden from public view, the apparently isolated labor of shantytown workers can be registered as gain in the financial houses of New York and London. (1985a: 61–2)

Thus, the core-periphery division of labor and the modern mechanisms that have reproduced it – notably the way trade and investments are structured – are linked to what had long been viewed as an aberration of 'normal' development in less developed countries. The global perspective suggests that, instead, the vast expansion of the tertiary and informal sectors *is* normal in the sense that it can be understood as stemming, in part, from systemic processes. Of course, the general way in which labor is employed in the core is also shaped by world-systemic processes.

The limited quantitative research that has attempted to test hypotheses relating world-system processes to national labor force structures has usually focused on the effects on non-core country labor force structures of core investments. Evans and Timberlake (1980) found that higher levels of foreign direct investments are associated with more rapidly growing tertiary labor sectors in the periphery, although Fiala's later research (1983) indicated that this effect may be indirect. Timberlake and Kentor (1983) present findings that indicate that core investments in the periphery increase 'imbalances' in the labor force structure in the ratio of service to manufacturing jobs. That is, countries with higher levels of investment have larger increases in the ratio of service jobs to manufacturing jobs. They also report positive effects of investments on a measure of over-urbanization that compares the size of a country's urban population to its level of industrialization. Bradshaw (1985) corroborated some of these findings in a sample of black African countries.

All these studies are limited by either their relatively small samples or their 1960s to 1970s time frame. However, Timberlake and Lunday (1985) found data indicating that the ratio of tertiary to secondary jobs in the periphery has been higher than in the core since at least 1900, when the ratio was 1.25 in the peripheral countries for which data could be found and 0.81 in the core. In 1970 the respective ratios were 1.76 and 1.24. It should be pointed out that the data involved in each of the studies leave much to be desired. For example, the most theoretically interesting labor force category from the point of view of world-system theory is that of the informal sector. Yet, its very nature of being work that is not regulated by the government means that it is unlikely to be enumerated in official statistics.

World-system processes and the changing structure of the urban labor force in the core

Relatively recent urban changes in core areas suggest the importance of structural and cyclical aspects of the capitalist world economy. The rise of the so-called 'post-industrial' labor force in the rich countries of the world is, no doubt, largely a function of technological developments, such as increased automation. From the developmentalist perspective in which the post-industrial concept was originally embedded, the growing predominance of the tertiary labor force and the dwindling size of the secondary (manufacturing) sector represented an evolutionary transformation dictated by the logic of modernization. But it certainly also has much to do with the role of core areas in the global division of labor. The core usually retains key financial, managerial and research and development functions even as manufacturing moves to the semi-pheriphery and periphery. In the United State, for example, headquarters of large firms usually remain in place (or at least in the country) as production shifts to sites outside the high-wage core. To take one example, in Akron, Ohio, once known as the rubber capital of the world, the last tire rolled off an assembly-line some five years ago. Nevertheless world headquarters for Goodyear, Firestone, Goodrich, and General have remained there, along with some research and development activities. Even when foreign investments from core areas establish *new* production jobs in the periphery (rather than merely shifting existing jobs out of the core), professional, managerial, financial and research jobs are likely to be created and retained in the core (e.g. Vernon, 1971).

The interpretation of urban labor patterns around the world are complicated further when we go beyond a simple discussion of the core–periphery division of labor to consider the effects of some of the other global processes that are central to the perspective. The recent restructuring of capital can be seen as a response to a cyclical feature of the system. It has been a response to the most recent phase of contraction and increase in intra-core competition (cf. Bergesen, 1982). During such phases intense competition in the market-place compels capitalists to adopt a number of strategies aimed at maintaining profit margins. Sassen-Koob's concept of 'peripheralization at the core' (1985) may be an exaggeration when we look at the actual conditions under which labor in the periphery is employed, but it seems justified when we turn our attention to the unemployed rubberworker in Akron, the former steelworker in Pittsburgh, and the nomadic workers who flooded, at least temporarily, into the trailer parks of the 'boomtowns' in the Sunbelt of the US when production was cut in Detroit. Sassen-Koob points out that the mobility of capital out of certain regions of the United States, and out of the country altogether, has contradictory effects on urban labor structures (1984; 1985). On one hand, there obviously is deindustrialization (cf. Bluestone and Harrison, 1982). On the other hand, the very changes that comprise this process require increased 'global control capability'.

Several trends have fed . . . the development of global control capability: (1) the decentralization of manufacturing, (2) the decentralization of office work, (3) the move of large corporations into the consumer services market, (4) the increasing size and product diversification of large corporations. These trends have intensified the importance of planning, marketing, internal administration and distribution, control over a wide variety of types of information, and other activities that entail centralization of management, control, and highly specialized services. (Sassen-Koob, 1985: 238)

Sassen-Koob points out that this has very important implications for several dimensions of core city social structure.

First, in certain key cities there is significant growth in the producer service sector. It is in producer services that one finds those financial and high-tech activities that provide direct inputs into the production sector. Included are activities such as banking and credit, insurance, engineering, accounting, and so on (Sassen-Koob, 1985: 247, citing Singelmann, 1978). Sassen-Koob shows that this sector has indeed grown considerably in the latter part of the 1970s in the 'global cities' of Los Angeles and New York (in which 1977–81 growth rates in employment in producer services were 30.4 per cent and 20.1 per cent respectively). She points out that these activities are relatively free of the need to be located close to their consumers because what they provide is relatively easily transmitted given modern means of communication and transportation. It might also be suggested that some of the recent decentralizing tendencies within corporations in terms of production would require a growth in such producer services without implying their decentralization. As Bluestone and Harrison point out, a major reason for the decentralization of production has been to give corporate management flexibility with respect to its ability to keep wages low by shifting production to different locations in response to wage levels and union activity (1982: chapter 6). This decentralization has often been international, involving agreements with existing foreign competitors to share production facilities and the development of new production sites. It seems reasonable to expect that these decentralizing production schemes have required even more elaborate production services, in terms of financial arrangements, management problems and marketing strategies, and have thus contributed to the overall growth of this sector in core areas of the world economy. Sassen-Koob's analysis even suggests that much of this global control capability is vested in specialized firms rather than being included in the activities of the manufacturing firms themselves. She points out that the producer service sector of New York City experienced the 20 per cent growth mentioned above during a time when there was significant movement of major corporate headquarters out of the city.

One of the most striking social structural changes associated with these shifting employment patterns in the core is the apparent increases in income inequality. The decline of employment opportunities in the relatively highly paid manufacturing sector, coupled with the growth of the producer service sector in some cities, has exacerbated income inequality. On the one hand, the middle-income category has contracted; on the other, growth in the relatively highly paid professional and managerial service sector demands growth in low-wage jobs for workers providing services to this group. Sassen-Koob points out that this low-wage sector is often filled by immigrant labor, at least in the global control cities of the United States (1985: 255–63):

Polarization in global cities is further fed by several trends that contribute to an additional expansion in the supply of low-wage jobs. First, the existence of a critical mass of very high-income workers has led to . . . [the need for] an army of low-wage workers: residential building attendants, dog walkers, housekeepers for the two-career family, workers in the gourmet restaurants and food shops, French hand laundries, and so on. (1985: 262)

Portes (1981) also interprets such patterns of migration more generally in terms of the global economic system. His interpretation of several specific cases of international migration supports the view that we must go far beyond mere comparison of economic advantages at the destination and disadvantages at the origin. Instead we must recognize the degree to which there has been 'penetration of economic and political institutions of peripheral areas by those of the core': the degree to which dominant class interests in the periphery favor 'labor release'; and the degree to which dominant class interests in the core can reduce or resist political restraints on using (cheap) immigrant labor. Portes thus interprets migration from peripheral to semiperipheral areas and from peripheral and semiperipheral areas to the core (also see Portes, 1985b). Of course, these international labor flows by no means always contribute to urbanization (e.g. many immigrants from Mexico to the US initially work in agriculture), but in many cases they do.

Urban primacy

Another aspect of urbanization that has been of interest to developmentalists and world-system researchers alike is that of urban primacy. Behind the concept of primacy lies the notion that there exist 'systems of cities' within economically interdependent regions. Such systems of cities, it is argued, are characterized by a uniform relative population size distribution in countries with healthy, mature economies. Some disagreement exists concerning the 'normal' shape of such distributions, but there is general agreement that something like a lognormal distribution describes a healthy system of cities. Hawley notes that:

This log-normal distribution represents an expected pattern in an area all localities of which are fully served by urban institutions. No pockets of rural isolation remain. It is opposed to what has been termed a primate city pattern, which characterizes a great many developing areas. The primate pattern is a situation in which one very large city is found in company with a multitude of villages or very small towns. (1981: 238)

Primacy is thus linked to the absence of regional (usually national) economic integration and balanced economic growth.

This perspective is rooted in dominant theories in human ecology and urban geography, and most of the early work on it was done by geographers and sociologists in human ecology. Berry (1971) points out that the lognormal distribution of cities can be predicted from 'Gibrat's law or proportionate effect'. Given a random distribution of city sizes (i.e. resulting in a normal distribution), this 'law' leads one to expect that the larger cities will tend to grow at faster rates than smaller population centers. Over time this will result in the transformation of the city size distribution to a lognormal distribution.

When such growth conditions obtain for a system or cities, their frequency distribution is lognormal, and . . . if the distribution by size is lognormal, the system of cities will form a 'rank-size distribution'. (1971: 118)

The rank-size rule (Zipf, 1941) implies that a city's rank in a system of cities when multiplied by its population will equal the population of the largest city.

Originally, the term 'primate city' referred simply to the largest city in a system (Jefferson, 1939). More recently it has come to refer to a city that is much larger than expected on the basis of the rank-size rule, and 'primacy' now refers to a system of cities in which the largest city is primate. Many different strategies have been devised for measuring urban primacy in countries. Recently Walters (1985) developed an index based on the lognormal distribution. Using any number of cities in a distribution, it produces an index that indicates relative primacy, with values increasing from zero indicating higher levels of urban primacy and values decreasing from zero indicating more 'flatness' in the city size distribution.

Many less developed countries appear to have city size distributions that appear highly primate. Using Walters' index, and data from Christopher Chase-Dunn's urbanization research project at Johns Hopkins University, this can readily be documented. For example, in the Philippines in 1975, Manila was twelve times larger than Ceba, the second largest city, and the index of primacy was 15.32. In 1975 Guatemala City was 16 times greater than Quezaltenago, and the primacy index was 19.91. For Senegal the primacy index was 6.32.

In spite of several prominent examples of primate city distributions in more developed countries and of lognormal distributions in less developed countries, one is left with the impression that city systems in industrialized countries are nearer to the expected lognormal pattern. Thus, urban primacy has been equated with underdevelopment, either as a concomitant or as a causal factor. That is, the primate city has been viewed by some as 'parasitic' with respect to economic growth (Hoselitz, 1955), and development planners have suggested strategies for reducing levels of primacy with the understanding that this would promote a more healthy economy (C. Smith, 1985a; 124; Sen, 1975). Attempting to understand the roots of urban primacy has thus come to be seen as useful in so far as this would also lead to understanding some of the causes of underdevelopment.

Hoselitz suggested that extreme primacy is more likely to persist in countries in which the leading city is not well integrated with its hinterland,

and he pointed out that this is more likely to be true of colonies, former colonies and of politically independent but economically dependent countries (1969: 283). Others have been more explicit in applying the dependency and world-system perspectives to the interpretation of urban primacy. The primate city in Third World countries is seen as an outpost of neocolonialism amid a 'passive periphery . . . integrated upon the basis of submissive dependence' (Freidmann, 1978: 330). While others might question just how passively submissive peripheral areas are, there *is* widespread agreement that international relations of economic and political dependence have incorporated Third World cities into an international urban hierarchy. According to Frank (1969), these large primate cities operate like 'suction pumps' through which resources are expropriated from the periphery and panned 'upwards' to the core, developed world.

In her review and critique of dependency theories of urban primacy, Carol Smith summarizes the 'export dependency' theory of primacy (1985b: 102–9). She lists four major aspects of export dependence that proponents of the perspective have suggested contribute to the growth of a single large city in peripheral areas according to this view. First, export economics require only one, 'major outlet from the producing region to its external markets'. Second, modern means of transportation, especially railways, funnel the export commodities from the hinterland to the dominant centers without contributing to the need for anything but very minor population centers in the hinterland. Third, local industry and trade are often destroyed by these relations of dependence, thus undermining the 'economic base of provisional cities in the periphery'. Finally, foreign investments in the export sector often support infrastructural development of the leading city, thus enhancing its advantages even more.

One might also question whether the shift to dependent industrialization will mitigate the primacy-inducing impetus of foreign investments. To the extent that multinational corporation production is for re-export to the core, it tends not to develop the backward linkages throughout a country that would lessen primacy by contributing to the growth of other cities. Furthermore, whether exports are in primary commodities or manufactures, they tend to be rather highly concentrated in only a few commodities. On the one hand, the concentration of either raw material commodities or industrial commodities should be seen as an immediate manifestation of the penetration of peripheral national economies by foreign capital; and on the other hand, this commodity concentration should be associated with the geographical concentration of export transportation facilities and industrial production sites. Thus commodity concentration, itself a hypothesized outcome of dependency, is likely to contribute to the persistence of primacy. Furthermore, foreign investments in industry may excerbate primacy by contributing to the 'city lights' effect, attracting migrants from rural areas and other smaller towns.

The recent research on urban primacy clearly indicates that world-system structure and processes need to be taken into account in interpreting variation in city size distributions, but not to the exclusion of more locally determined factors. In his study of Latin American city size distributions, Chase-Dunn (1985a) compares changes in degrees of primacy/lognormalcy to those of core countries. Generally he finds more stability and lognormalcy in the core. But this generalization is limited. In the nineteenth century Latin American city systems were not significantly more primate than the core nor was there more change in the degree of primacy. However, between 1900 and 1950 Latin American city systems became more primate and core city systems remained stable, and between 1950 and 1975 primacy continued to increase in Latin America but declined in the core. Admittedly there is wide variation among countries in both the core and in Latin American. Chase-Dunn concludes that no simple argument attributing primacy in Latin America to colonialism, to import-substitution development, or to level of economic development (e.g. El-Shaks, 1972) explains patterns found in his data. Instead there appears to be important contextual effects of position in the world-system hierarchy, the specific mechanisms of which are yet to be worked out. His urbanization project at The Johns Hopkins University continues to collect data that should lead to a clearer picture of how city size distributions respond to the action of world-system processes on more locally proximate institutional features.

In his study of regional primacy in pre-federation Australia (1850–1900), Clark (1985) rejects both 'internal development' and 'international relations' explanations of primacy as somewhat naive. Instead, his research leads him to conclude that 'it is necessary to consider the qualitative nature of internal development and how it is conditioned, in turn, by the nature of involvement of a region in the larger world-economy' (1985: 170). To take one of Clark's examples, in the Australian colony of Victoria the principal city, Melbourne, declined in size relative to the other towns in the region between 1850 and 1880. This decrease in urban primacy followed the discovery of gold in the hinterland. While most of the other colonies experienced relative stability in degrees of urban primacy, Victoria's declined because '[C]ompared to the wool-growing that was the mainstay of the other colonies, alluvial gold mining created a large demand for labor at the point of production and favored the growth of country towns near the mining areas' (1985: 177). Clark notes that both wool production and gold mining reflected the pronounced dependence of the colonies on England, but that they produced different patterns of city hierarchy because it was the *kinds* of production that primarily determined city size patterns. He thus concludes that it is the nature of interaction with the outside world rather than the intensity of interaction (as Vapnarsky (1975) had argued) that primarily shapes urban hierarchy in dependent regions.

In their comparative historical study of urban hierarchy in South Korea and the Philippines, Nemeth and Smith (1985) build the case that the articulation of world-system processes with local social formations are crucial to understanding urbanization patterns. Their analysis stresses the importance of a country's urban system at the time it is incorporated into the world system, the nature of production of export and home markets, and the centrality of politics in directly and intentionally shaping urban patterns. On this last point, they argue that both policies originating in the core and policies stemming from local politics have been crucial to the relative growth of various cities in these two national city systems. Thus the extreme primacy of Manila is explained by the lack of an urban system at the time the Philippines was incorporated into the world-system in the sixteenth century, Manila's importance as the major port for the Philippines' large primary product export trade, the location of new import-substitution industries in the capital, and 'the implementation of policies affecting the spatial distribution of infrastructure and production facilities congruent with the needs and interests of an entrenched Manila elite' (1985: 197). On the other hand, Korea already had a fairly well-developed system of cities at the time of its incorporation into the new world system, it is not as dependent on the export of primary products but instead has quite well-developed manufacturing production for export, and there are overt policies, particularly in relation to the location of transportation infrastructure, that have led to a more decentralized urban hierarchy.

Somewhat in contrast to this interpretation of urban primacy, Carol Smith (1985a: 121–67) has developed a persuasive interpretation of urban city size distribution in Guatemala that does not rely on world-system or dependency concepts. Her argument, in brief, is that class relations are crucial in shaping city size distributions. But her purpose in presenting this argument is to refute economically-based theories of urbanization. Her research shows that it is the social relations embodied in class conflict and class struggle that *directly* determine urban patterns. However, she does not deny that these social relations within peripheral areas are themselves shaped by world-system processes and relations of dependency. Thus her argument is not entirely opposed to the approach of Nemeth and Smith on Philippine and Korean urban hierarchies, and the approach of London (1985: 207–30) on Thai primacy. That is, these efforts are concerned with how 'local' policies shaping urbanization are embedded in global processes, to some extent.

A final example of research on urban hierarchy is Chase-Dunn's interpretation of changes in city size hierarchy for the world since 800 AD (1985b: 269–92). Using Walter's new method of measuring urban primacy (1985), he examines variation in degree of primacy in the world city distribution from 800 to 1970. Although we cannot go into the details here, he makes an interesting argument that shifts towards and away from lognormalcy are predicted by various global processes, including the original consolidation of the capitalist world system, its cycles of expansion, and cycles of core competition involving hegemone decline, war, and the emergence of a new hegemone. For example he argues that increasing 'flatness' in the European city hierarchy from the beginning of the decline of Paris in 1300 to the rise of London as the leading city in 1825 corresponds to a basic world-system process: 'This decline of one hierarchy and the rise of a new hierarchy ... was ... based on ... the fragmentation of political hegemony into a multicentric interstate system, and then the emergence of a new hegemonic core state, the United Kingdom ...' (Chase-Dunn, 1985: 285).

CRITIQUES OF WORLD-SYSTEM THEORY AND URBAN THEORY

Class conflict

World-system and dependency approaches have been criticized for not adequately conceptualizing class conflict. Wallerstein's work was rebuked on this basis by Brenner (1977). His argument focuses on Wallerstein's alleged omission of the role of class struggle in shaping the dominant mode of production. Instead, Brenner asserts, Wallerstein implies that capitalism emerged and reproduces itself according to the motivations and interests of capitalists: 'The rise of the world division of labour, based on the commercial expansion of Europe, both gives us the origins of capitalism *apart from any transition through class conflict*, and the form of its economic development *apart from any class structure of capital accumulation*' (Brenner, 1977: 802). Much of this sort of criticism draws attention to a problem common to most macro-structural theories, specifically the issue of how these theories are relevant to individual and group actions.

It is difficult to deal coherently with the relation between world-system structure and group action, but there are several promising leads. The anthropologist Sidney Mintz provides an excellent example of how careful attention to global processes can promote a more complete understanding of the day-to-day lives of ordinary people (1974). His work on the peasantry of Jamaica, Haiti and Puerto Rico indicates very clearly the diversity of cultural responses found in the face of generally similar global patterns of involvement. That is, these three areas have similar histories of incorporation into the world-system and continue to be similarly dependent on the core. They were each peripheralized in the initial expansion of European capitalism; they all combined capitalist agriculture with the forced labor of Africans who compromised a very large proportion of the population; and they each continue to be very dependent today. Yet, Mintz argues, the peasantry of these three areas did not passively submit to the exploitative conditions in which they found themselves. Rather they both resisted and accommodated themselves to these conditions in remarkably creative ways. In doing so each group fashioned for themselves unique sociocultural formations in the face of a uniform and oppressive set of global circumstances.

This kind of approach in relating world-system processes to people would seem to have great potential in community studies in both the core and the periphery. Other studies detailing the absence of a uniform response to similar globally structured constraints are increasingly forthcoming (e.g. Trouillot, 1985; Kincaid, 1985). There are other recent studies that document the tremendous influence of world-system processes on local communities, but, at least implicitly, acknowledge that the variation in local, historically determined conditions (including local class relations) results in a variety of local urban patterns (e.g. Hill and Indergaard, 1984; Feagin, 1985; Trachte and Ross, 1985). Indeed, in this period of global economic crisis and restructuring, more and more interpretations of this sort seem to have been produced. This is not to claim that there have been many systematic attempts to apply Wallersteinian world-system theory to the study of communities. This, in fact, has not been done, and it remains to be seen whether anyone will consider that to be worth while. What we do have are a few studies that are principally concerned with how local communities interact with global processes in a general way.

Autonomy of the state

Skocpol (1979) has persuasively argued that world-system theorists (as well as others) have not adequately conceptualized the state. Many proponents of world-system theory seem to view the state in largely instrumentalist terms. That is to say, the dominant economic groups are assumed to control the state and to use this control to further the economic interests of their own class. As Skocpol puts it, Wallerstein 'has managed to create a model that simultaneously gives a decisive role to international political domination and deprives politics of any independent efficacy, reducing it to the vulgar expressions of market-related interests' (1977: 1080). Her argument, and her comparative historical research, supports a different view of the state. States are not merely 'analytic aspects of abstractly conceived modes of production, or even political aspects of concrete class relations and struggles. Rather [they are] actual organizations controlling (or attempting to control) territories and people' (Skocpol, 1979: 31). State regimes operate in the context of an international system of states and 'class-divided socioeconomic structures' (31), but they also have a logic of their own.

Arguably, her case is overstated. States as organizations are certainly not completely autonomous from the workings of the world system. Even according to Skocpol's own analysis of real historical cases of social revolutions, state action was dramatically shaped by the operation of the interstate system of the capitalist world economy. Nevertheless, if we understand her argument to be that world-system approaches should not define the state as merely an instrument of powerful economic coalitions, then it is a good one. In terms of the present effort to outline a world-system perspective on urbanization, the implication is that such an effort must include a conceptualization of state organizations. David Smith's work (1984; 1985) hints at this by drawing attention to the fact that urban patterns in the Third World are shaped by a combination of core interests, local elite class interests and state policies. Feagin's work on Houston comes closer in conceptualizing the interplay between local capital, multinational capital and local and national state policies in fashioning socio-economic change there since the 1930s (Feagin, 1985).

Any efforts in the future to analyze urban change in terms of the interaction of world-system processes and the logic of the state as an organization will be very complex, if for no other reason than that the several layers of state organizations in which cities are embedded will complicate analysis. Work on deindustrialization and fiscal crisis in the United States (e.g. Squires, 1984; Kennedy, 1984) arguably comes closest to addressing urban issues from perspectives that begin adequately to acknowledge the world-economy, local and national 'states' and class strugle.

Patriarchy as a mechanism of unequal exchange

There is a feminist critique of theories describing the mechanisms through which surplus value is transferred from the periphery to the core. This critique accepts arguments such as those of Amin (1976) and Portes (1985a), that low wages in the periphery account for much of the surplus extraction to the core, and that these low wages are made possible by the laborers' reproductive costs being borne by subsistence enclaves or, more recently, the informal sector. As discussed above, goods and services can be acquired by formal sector workers at below market cost through transactions in the informal sector. In this way low wages in the periphery are subsidized. But the real subsidy accrues to global capital. To the extent that the reproductive costs of labor are borne outside of the formal market, wages can be kept low and profits correspondingly high.

However, what Portes, Amin and others have failed to note is that these reproductive costs are disproportionately borne by women:

[R]egardless of whether it is argued that the support structures for the maintenance of low wages are from rural subsistence enclaves or the informal market in urban areas, women's labor comprises a large portion of the production in each of these modes of subsistence. (Hammond and Lam, 1984)

Hammond and Lam cite Boserup (1970) in pointing out that when men are forced to migrate to find wage labor (e.g. seasonal agricultural work), women become directly involved in the production of subsistence goods for family consumption. (This is true in many other cases, too, but it is most obvious when large numbers of men are absent from communities for extended periods.) In many urban areas of the Third World women can be found working on the fringes of the formal economy, as household laborers, producing and selling petty commodities, and in many other such activities that contribute directly to the survival of their families.·

For our purposes, the importance of these observations concerns the nature of urban communities in the face of the global economy. The reproduction of the hierarchical core–periphery division of labor in the world-system depends, in large part, on mechanisms through which wages in the periphery are kept low. Recent feminist scholarship has pointed out that when existing forms of patriarchy are overlaid and exacerbated by the penetration of foreign capital, the super-exploitation of women in the periphery follows (cf. Bandarage, 1984). The various ways in which this dynamic is expressed across diverse economic and cultural regions inevitably affect the character of urbanization. For example, Ward notes differential rates of urbanization for men and women in different major world regions (1985). In Third World cities with industries that have a preference for female labor (e.g. electronics), we are likely to find a growing relative proportion of working-age women. Of course gender preferences in industries which draw on migrant labor effect the sex ratios of the communities of origin as well as those of destination. In some European cities that rely on guestworkers from semi-peripheral countries one finds legal barriers preventing the entry of whole families. Men must return to their home countries periodically in order to see their wives and children. The general point here is that a comprehensive discussion of how the world-system processes affect urbanization must be sensitive to important differences in the way these processes affect men and women in different zones of the system, in different cultural regions, and at different historical moments. The scholarship needed for such a task is still in its infancy.

CONCLUSION

This chapter has reviewed recent scholarship that has interpreted urban social change from global perspectives. The argument has been made that world-system theory provides useful insights into the nature of urbanization. This case has been made on the basis of a review of the major theoretical elements of the world-system perspective and a discussion of the ways in which urban phenomena are related to it. The primary focus has been on the macro-urban patterns of over-urbanization, urban labor force structure, and city-system hierarchy, but implications for lower-level community patterns have also been considered. I have tried to show the logical connections between the core–periphery division of labor and the various mechanisms that reproduce it and urban structural transformation. The growing body of empirical research that supports these theoretical claims was also reviewed.

In summary, there is evidence that the size relation of cities in regions or nations is partly a function of the economic role played by the region in the global economy. This is especially apparent in the periphery where cities have been created as outposts of colonial and neo-colonial expansion accompanying the growth of the world-system and the concomitant

TABLE 2.1   *Summary of relationships of types of urban change to world-system structures and processes*

Urban outcomes	Proximate mediating factors	Underlying world-system structures and processes
Over-urbanization in the periphery.	Rapid population growth. Rural land shortages. Slow urban labor absorption. Rural–urban migration. Rural land concentration.	Structure of foreign investments: industrial production for export; agricultural production for export; agriculture and industry capital intensive. Global class relations.
Urban employment structure.		
Hypertrophy of tertiary and informal labor sectors in periphery.	Reproduction of low-wage formal sector labor power. Patriarchal cultural patterns. Political repression.	Unequal exchange. Surplus extraction from periphery to core. Hierarchical world division of labor.
'Post-industrial' labor force and deindustriali-zation in core.	Growth of professional and managerial occupations. Relative cost of core labor.	Hierarchical world division of labor. Global capital accumu-lation. Cycles of core competition and hegemony. Transnational production with centralized control. Global class structure.
Urban primacy in periphery.	Local class relations. Level of development at time of colonial contact. Rural–urban migration. Poor spatial integration. Centralized state bureaucracy.	World-system expansion and peripheralization. Nature of production/ marketing for world market. Colonial heritage.

peripheralization of outlying areas. But it is important to note that the growth or decline of cities also involves the specific spatial requirements of what is being produced in a given region, the cyclical demand for the commodities in question, and many more proximate factors, such as local class relations favoring the growth of some cities at the expense of others. (See table 2.1 for a schematic presentation of this and the following discussion.)

Over-urbanization in the periphery is interpreted as stemming, in part, from the specific effects of the structure of core capital investments. Limited industrialization (mainly for export) and the capital-intensive nature of both industrial and agricultural investments exacerbate migration to the cities and slow urban labor force absorption. This is necessarily intimately related to the enormous growth of the urban informal labor sector in the third world. The global perspective advocated here analyzes this sector in terms of its general relation to low-wage labor in the periphery and to capital accumulation in the core. This sector serves simultaneously as a 'disguised form of wage labor' directly involved in the production of commodities for the world market – see Castells and Portes (1986) – as a large reserve army of labor, and as the modern equivalent of the subsistence enclave, in which goods and services required by the formal sector labor force are provided at below market value. In turn, the low wages in the periphery are an important source of profit for core-based transnational corporations.

Core urban patterns are also shaped by world-system processes. Growing inequality within many US cities may be a concomitant of declining hegemony in the world market and the global restructuring of capital that has simultaneously inflated the professional managerial class and the workers who service their consumption needs, and withered the size of the industrial working class. This relatively highly paid working class in the middle of the American stratification system has declined numerically as the size of the highly paid professional and low-paid service sectors have increased.

The contrasting labor force structures in the core and periphery and the link of both to the dynamic world system highlight the major conclusion to be drawn from this chapter. It is that a comprehensive analysis of urban transformation must be rooted at some point in an understanding of the global nature of the modern political economy. In this case, it is clear that there is a global stratification system. Changing labor force structures in both the core and the periphery are influenced by many of the same global processes. Yet academic discourse on urban problems and on descriptions of urban social structure rarely and only recently acknowledge this. Textbooks in urban sociology (e.g. Abrahamson, 1980; Schwab, 1982; Spates and Maciconis, 1982) typically limit their material on global urbanization to international comparisons of rates and levels of urbanization. A developmentalist perspective is invariably employed in which differences between more and less developed regions are interpreted in terms of the distinctiveness of the histories and cultures of different world regions. Their isolation and independence are often emphasized.

In contrast, scholarship informed by world-system theory shows that many of these differing patterns of urbanization are rooted in a *common* history. It is the history of the modern world system in which hierarchically structured political and economic interaction among global regions is fundamental and endemic. Having made this statement, it is important to distance ourselves somewhat. Clearly, there are many historically and culturally unique determinants of urban change. I do not want to initiate debate over whether these are more important than the global determinants discussed here. What I would like to stimulate is more scholarship on the relationships between global processes and more locally proximate determinants of urban social change.

Finally, the scholarship undertaken so far has rarely involved a systematic application of world-system theory to urban processes. No doubt this is because, in practice, this 'theory' is but a metaphor for any approach that gives prominence to global political-economic relations through which unequal development is reproduced. Nevertheless, the research efforts that have taken this theoretical tack have shed new light on urban change. Global approaches to social change are in a state of flux. Debate continues about what the fundamental processes of the world system are and how they articulate with social processes and social formations thought of as existing primarily at other, more local levels. Even without consensus on these issues, future efforts to understand urban change are unlikely to be useful without some conceptualization of the global structures and processes at work.

NOTES

1 The data on urbanization in the next few pages are from the United Nations (1984).
2 The primary sector refers mainly to agricultural occupations but also includes jobs in forestry and fishing, and sometimes in mining. The secondary sector includes jobs in manufacturing, electrical and other utilities; construction; and mining. Tertiary occupations are those in commerce; transportation, storage, and communications; personal services; and government and other services.

REFERENCES

Abrahamson, Mark (1980) *Urban Sociology*, 2nd edition, Englewood Cliffs, N.J.: Prentice Hall.

Abu-Lughod, Janet and Richard Hay (eds) (1977) *Third World Urbanization*, Chicago: Maaroufa Press.

Amin, Samir (1976) *Unequal Development: An Essay on the Social Formations of Peripheral Capitalism*, New York: Monthly Review Press.

Bairoch, Paul (1975) *Economic Development of the Third World Since 1900*, (Berkeley: University of California Press.

Bandarage, Asoka (1984) 'Women in development: liberalism, Marxism, and Marxist-feminism', *Development and Change*, 15: 495–515.

Bergesen, Albert (1982) 'Economic crisis and merger movements: 1880's Britain and 1980's United States'. In Edward Friedman (ed.), *Ascent and Decline in the World-System*, Beverly Hills, Calif.: Sage.

—— (1983) 'Modeling long waves of crisis in the world-system'. In A. Bergesen (ed.), *Crises in the World-System*, Beverly Hills, Calif.: Sage.

Berry, Brian J. L. (1971) 'City size and economic development'. In L. Jakobson and V. Prakash (eds), *Urbanization and National Development*, Beverly Hills, Calif.: Sage.

Birbeck, C. (1978) 'Garbage, industry and the "cultures" of Cali, Columbia' In R Bromley and C. Gerry (eds), *Casual Work and Poverty in Third World Cities*, New York: John Wiley and Sons.

Bluestone, Barry and Bennet Harrison (1982) *The Deindustrialization of America*, New York: Basic Books.

Bornschier, Volker and Christopher Chase-Dunn (1985) *Transnational Corporations and Underdevelopment*, New York: Prager.

Boserup, Ester (1970) *Women's Role in Economic Development*, New York: St Martin's Press.

Bradshaw, York (1985) 'Overurbanization and underdevelopment in black Africa: A cross-national study', *Studies in Comparative International Development*.

Brenner, Robert (1977) 'The origins of capitalist development: A critique of neo-Smithian Marxism', *New Left Review*, 104: 25–92.

Castells, Manuel (1984) *The City and the Grassroots: A Cross-Cultural Perspective*, Berkeley: University of California Press.

Castells, Manuel and Alejandro Portes (1986) 'The world underneath: The origins dynamics, and effects of the informal economy'. Paper presented at the Conference on the Comparative Study of the Informal Sector, Harper's Ferry, West Virginia.

Chase-Dunn, Christopher K. (1985a) 'The coming of urban primacy in Latin America'. *Comparative Urban Research*, XI (1–2): 14–31.

—— (1985b), 'The system of world cities, A.D. 800–1975'. In M. Timberlake (ed.), *Urbanization in the World-Economy*, Orlando: Academic Press.

Chase-Dunn, Christopher K. and Richard Rubinson (1977) 'Toward a structural perspective on the world-system', *Politics and Society*, 7 (4): 454–76.

—— (1979) 'Cycles, trends and new departures in world-system development'. In John Meyer and Michael Hannan (eds), *National Development in the World-System*, Chicago: University of Chicago Press.

Chirot, Daniel and Thomas D. Hall (1982) 'World-system theory'. *Annual Review of Sociology*, vol. 8.

Clark, Roger (1985) 'Urban primacy and incorporation into the world-economy: The case of Australia, 1850–1900'. In M. Timberlake (ed.), *Urbanization in the World-economy*, Orlando: Academic Press.

El-Shaks, Salah (1972) 'Development, primacy, and systems of cities', *The Journal of Developing Areas*, 7 (October): 11–36.

Evans, Peter (1979) *Dependent Development*, Princeton N.J.: Princeton University Press.

Evans, Peter and Michael Timberlake (1980) 'Dependence, inequality and the growth of the tertiary: A comparative analysis of less developed countries', *American Sociological Review*, 45: 531–52.

Feagin, Joe (1985) 'The state in the free enterprise city: the case of Houston', *American Journal of Sociology*, 90: 1209–30.

Fiala, Robert (1983) 'Inequality and the service sector in less developed countries: A reanalysis and respecification'. *American Sociological Review*, 48: 421–8.

Firebaugh, Glenn (1979) 'Structural determinants of urbanization in Asia and Latin America, 1950–1970'. *American Sociological Review*, 44: 199–215.

Frank, André Gunder (1969) *Latin America: Underdevelopment or Revolution*, New York: Monthly Review Press.

Friedmann, John (1978) 'The spatial organization of power in the development of urban systems'. In L. S. Bourne and J. W. Simmons (eds), *Systems of Cities*, New York: Oxford University Press.

Galtung, Johan (1971) 'A structural theory of imperialism', *Journal of Peace Research*, 2: 88–111.

Goldfrank, Walter (1983) 'The limits of analogy: Hegemonic decline in Great Britain and the United States'. In A. Bergesen (ed.), *Crises in the World-System*, Beverly Hills, Calif.: Sage.

Gugler, Josef (1982) 'Overurbanization reconsidered', *Economic Development and Cultural Change*, 31 (1): 173–89.

Hammond, Catherine and Julie Lam (1984) 'Women's subsistence labor and unequal exchange'. Paper presented at the annual meeting of the Society for the Study of Social Problems, San Antonio.

Harody, Jorge (ed.) (1975) *Urbanization in Latin America: Approaches and Issues*, Garden City, N.Y.: Anchor.

Hawley, Amos (1981) *Urban Society: An Ecological Approach*, New York: Ronald.

Hay, Richard (1977) 'Patterns of urbanization and socio-economic development in the Third World: An overview'. In J. Abu-Lughod and R. Hay (eds), *Third World Urbanization*, Chicago: Maaroufa Press.

Hill, Richard Child and Michael Indergaard (1984) 'Downriver: Deindustrialization in southwest Detroit'. Paper presented at annual meeting of the Society for the Study of Social Problems.

Hoselitz, Bert (1955) 'Generative and parasitic cities', *Economic Development and Cultural Change*, 3 (April): 278–94.

—— (1969) 'The role of cities in the economic growth of underdeveloped countries'. In G. Breese (ed.), *The City in Newly Developed Countries*, Englewood Cliffs, N.J.: Prentice-Hall.

Jefferson, Mark (1939) 'The laws of the primate city', *Geographical Review* 29 (April): 226–32.

Kennedy, Michael (1984) 'The fiscal crisis of the city'. In Michael P. Smith (ed.), *Cities in Transformation*, Beverly Hills, Calif.: Sage.

Kentor, Jeffrey (1985) 'Economic development and the world division of labor'. In M. Timberlake (ed.), *Urbanization in the World-Economy*, New York: Academic Press.

Kincaid, A. Douglas (1985) 'Peasant into rebels: Community and class in rural El Salvador'. Paper presented at the annual meeting of the International Studies Association, Washington, D.C.

Lipton, Michael (1977) *Why Poor People Stay Poor: Urban Bias in World Development*, Cambridge, Mass.: Harvard University Press.

Lobo, Susan (1982) *A House of My Own: Social Organization in the Squatter Settlements in Lima, Peru*, Tucson: University of Arizona Press.

London, Bruce (1985) 'Thai city–hinterland relationships in an international context: Development as social control in northern Thailand'. In M. Timberlake (ed.) *Urbanization in the World-Economy*, Orlando: Academic Press.

Meyer, David (1986) 'The world system of cities: relations between international financial metropolises and South American cities', *Social Forces*, vol. 64 (3): 553–81.

Mintz, Sidney (1974) *Caribbean Transformations*, Baltimore, Md.: The Johns Hopkins University Press.

Nemeth, Roger J. and David A. Smith (1985) 'The political economy of contrasting urban hierarchies in South Korea and the Philippines'. In M. Timberlake (ed.), *Urbanization in the World-Economy*, Orlando: Academic Press.

Peattie, Lisa R. (1968) *The View from the Barrio*, Ann Arbor: University of Michigan Press.

Perlman, Janice (1976) *The Myth of Marginality: Urban Poverty and Politics in Rio de Janeiro*, Berkeley: University of California Press.

Portes, Alejandro (1981) 'International migration: Conditions for the mobilization and use of migrant labor under world capitalism'. In A. Portes and J. Walton, *Class and the International System*, New York: Academic Press.

—— (1985a) 'The informal sector and the world-economy: Notes on the structure of subsidized labor'. In M. Timberlake (ed.), *Urbanization in the World-Economy*, Orlando: Academic Press.

—— (1985b) 'Urbanization, migration and models of development in Latin America'. In John Walton (ed.), *Capital and Labour in the Urbanized World*, Beverly Hills, Calif.: Sage.

Roberts, Bryan (1976) 'The provincial urban system and the process of dependency'. In A. Portes and H. Browning (eds), *Current Perspectives in Latin American Urban Research*, Austin, Texas: Institute of Latin American Studies and the University of Texas Press.

—— (1978) *Cities of Peasants*, Beverly Hills, Calif.: Sage.

Rodriguez, Nestor and Joe Feagin (1986) 'Urban specialization in the world-system: An investigation of historical cases', *Urban Affairs Quarterly*.

Sassen-Koob, Saskia (1984) 'The new labor demand in global cities'. In Michael P. Smith (ed.), *Cities in Transformation*, Beverly Hills, Calif.: Sage.

—— (1985) 'Capital mobility and labor migration: Their expression in core cities'. In M. Timberlake (ed.), *Urbanization in the World-Economy*, Orlando: Academic Press.

Schwab, William (1982) *Urban Sociology: A Human Ecological Perspective*, Reading, Mass.: Addison-Wesley.

Sen, Sudhir (1975) *Reaping the Green Revolution: Food and Jobs for All*, New York: Orbis Books.

Sethuraman, S. (1978) 'The urban informal sector in Africa', *International Labor Review*, 116 (3): 343–52.

Singelmann, Joachim (1978) *From Agriculture to Services: The Transformation of Industrial Employment*, Beverly Hills, Calif.: Sage.

Skocpol, Theda (1977) 'Wallerstein's world capitalist system: A theoretical and historical critique', *American Journal of Sociology*, 82: 1075–90.

—— (1979) *States and Social Revolutions*, New York: Cambridge University Press.

Smith, Carol A. (1985a) 'Class relations and urbanization in Guatemala: Toward an alternative theory of urban primacy'. In M. Timberlake (ed.), *Urbanization in the World-Economy*, Orlando: Academic Press.

—— (1985b) 'Theories and measures of urban primacy: A critique'. In M. Timberlake (ed.), *Urbanization in the World-Economy*, Orlando: Academic Press.

Smith, David A. (1984) 'Overurbanization reconceptualized: A political economy of the world system approach'. Unpublished paper.

—— (1985) 'International dependence and urbanization in East Asia: Implications for planning', *Population Research and Policy Review*, 4: 203–33.

Sokolovsky, Joan (1985) 'Logic, space, and time: The boundaries of the capitalist world-economy'. In M. Timberlake (ed.), *Urbanization in the World-Economy*, Orlando: Academic Press.

Sovani, N. W. (1964) 'The analysis of "overurbanization" ', *Economic Development and Cultural Change*, 12 (January): 113–22.

Spates, James and John Macionis (1982) *The Sociology of Cities*, New York: St Martin's Press.

Squires, Gregory (1984) 'Capital mobility versus upward mobility: The racially discriminatory consequences of plant closings and corporate relocations'. In L. Sawers and W. Tabb (eds), *Sunbelt and Snowbelt: Urban Development and Regional Restructuring*, New York: Oxford University Press.

Timberlake, Michael and Jeffrey Kentor (1983) 'Economic dependence, over-urbanization, and economic growth: A study of less developed countries', *The Sociological Quarterly*, 24 (Autumn): 489–507.

Timberlake, Michael and James Lunday (1985) 'Labor force structure in the zones of the world-economy, 1950–1970'. In M. Timberlake (ed.), *Urbanization in the World-Economy*, Orlando: Academic Press.

Todaro, M. (1981) *City Bias and Urban Neglect: The Dilemma of Urban Development*, New York: Population Council.

Trachte, Kent and Robert Ross (1985) 'The crisis of Detroit and the emergence of global capitalism', *International Journal of Urban and Regional Research*, 9 (2): 186–217.

Trouillot, Michel-Rolph (1985) ' "In the sweat of thy face". World-market and peasant diet: The bananas of Dominica'. Paper presented at the annual meeting of the International Studies Association. Washington, D.C.

United Nations (1984a) *Migration, Population Growth and Employment in Metropolitan Areas of Selected Developing Countries*. Population Division, Department of International Economic and Social Affairs, New York: United Nations.

—— (1984b) 'Urbanization, urban population growth and urban structure', Population Division. Paper contributed to conference, *The Urban Explosion: Chaos or Mastery*, Geneva (November).

Vapnarsky, Cesar A., (1975) 'The Argentine system of cities: Primacy and rank-size rule'. In J. Hardoy (ed.), *Urbanization in Latin America: Approaches and Issues*, Garden City, New York: Anchor.

Vernon, Raymond (1971) *Sovereignty at Bay: The Multinational Spread of U.S. Enterprises*, New York: Basic.

Wallerstein, Immanuel (1974) *The Modern World-System I: Capitalist Agriculture and the Origins of the European World-Economy in the Sixteenth Century*, New York: Academic Press.
—— (1979), *The Capitalist World-Economy*, New York: Cambridge University Press.
—— (1980) *The Modern World-System II: Mercantilism and the Consolidation of the European World-Economy, 1600–1750*, New York: Academic Press.
Wallerstein, Immanuel and Terrence Hopkins, (1977) 'Patterns of development of the modern world-system', *Review*, 1: 111–45.
Walters, Pamela Barnhouse (1985) 'Systems of cities and urban primacy: Problems of definition and measurement'. In M. Timberlake (ed.), *Urbanization in the World-Economy*, Orlando: Academic Press.
Ward, Kathryn, (1984) *Women in the World-System*, New York: Praeger.
—— (1985) 'Women and urbanization in the world system'. In M. Timberlake (ed.), *Urbanization in the World-Economy*, Orlando: Academic Press.
Williams, Kirk and Michael Timberlake (1986) 'Political violence and world-system position'. Unpublished paper.
Zipf, George K. (1941) *National Unity and Disunity*, Bloomington, Ind.: Principia Press.

3

Cities and the International Division of Labor

Norman J. Glickman

INTRODUCTION

In this chapter I shall set out some working hypotheses about the role of cities in today's changing international division of labor (IDOL), within the context of more general structural change.[1] In doing so, I shall examine the complex ways in which cities have evolved over time, how they are centers for political and economic struggle, and how metropolises are affected by public policies. I shall discuss the following four major points:

1 There has been a vast transformation of the world economy in that energy price increases, new investment and migration patterns, and the interpenetration of markets have had profound and uneven effects on national economies. In recent years, economic growth, profits and wages have stagnated in most developed countries, while there have been diverse impacts on industries, occupations and cities. There have been employment reductions in traditional manufacturing and shifts to the high-technology and service sectors.

2 The 'third industrial revolution' (involving electronics, biotechnology and, significantly, information processing) has helped produce two contradictory urban trends. First, it has encouraged deurbanization and the dispersion of the poulation. This is so because technology and the maturation of product lines have promoted both standardized work and dispersed job sites, and because changing business strategies and organization have allowed firms to seek less urbanized locations. Hence, decline has occured in traditional manufacturing regions and there has been a continuing

An earlier version of this paper was presented at the Second World Congress of Arts and Sciences, Rotterdam, The Netherlands, 10 June 1984. This research was supported by the Mike Hogg Research Support Fund of the University of Texas at Austin. I thank Douglas Woodward for excellent research assistance and Bennett Harrison and Marcia Van Wagner for helpful comments.

decentralization of jobs and population. At the same time, an opposite tendency has produced agglomerations of corporate headquarters functions in a few large cities. These centers of administrative activities maintain control over regions that specialize in production processes that are lower in the urban hierarchy.

3 As a result of economic change, there have been pressures by groups and classes (e.g. income, race, regional, industrial and occupational) who have suffered and who demand policies to cushion themselves from decline. In an era of slow growth, with many groups bringing simultaneous pressures on the state, fiscal problems result. For instance, firms petition the state to increase their profitability via tax cuts, deregulation of markets, relaxed enforcement of health and safety regulations, and reduced social welfare benefits. Corporations have attempted to roll back previously won wage and working conditions directly through bargaining and indirectly through appeals to the state on the grounds that high wages are the prime cause of inflation and low productivity. Workers, on the other hand, fight to maintain their living standards and economic security through the extension of social legislation and urban programs. With slow economic growth, the state cannot meet all of these demands simultaneously. These problems are made more difficult to solve in a more internationalized economy, as external pressures add new dimensions to political conflict.

4 Economic programs trying to re-establish faster growth have geographical side-effects that often aid growing areas and suburbs at the expense of declining regions and central cities. Urban policies, on the other hand, generally try to ameliorate the problems of large cities and declining areas. Therefore, a policy dilemma has resulted that the state cannot easily solve.

In what follows, I shall expand on these points, taking the United States as a case-study.

SOME PHENOMENA

National and international economic change

The world economy has changed significantly in the last twenty-five years (see table 3.1). The 1970s saw sharp decreases in economic growth rates and increases in inflation. In non-socialist industrialized countries, for example, the average annual Gross Domestic Product (GDP) growth fell from 5.1 per cent to 3 per cent from the 1960s to the 1970s, while inflation rates more than doubled. There have been extraordinary increases in international trade, with the world's exports increasing more than twelve times between 1963 and 1981 (Deardorff and Stern, 1983). The last two columns of table 3.1 show the marked increase in trade as a proportion of GDP (e.g. from 12 to 20 per cent developed countries between 1960 and 1981).

TABLE 3.1 Macroeconomic performances of major country groups, 1960–81

| | Average annual growth rate of GDP per capital ^{m} (%) | | Average annual rate of inflation ^{m} (%) | | Average annual growth rate of foreign trade | | | | Exports of goods and non-factor services as a percentage of GDP ^{w} | |
| | | | | | Exports ^{m,a} | | Imports ^{m,a} | | | |
	1960–70	1970–81	1960–70	1970–81	1960–70	1970–81	1960–70	1970–81	1960	1981
Low-income countries	4.60	4.50	3.50	11.20	4.90	−0.70	5.30	2.40	7	9
Middle-income countries	6.00	5.60	3.00	13.10	5.40	4.10	6.40	4.80	17	23
Low-middle-income	5.00	5.60	2.80	11.10	5.20	3.00	6.50	4.10	15	23
Upper middle-income	6.40	5.60	3.00	18.60	5.40	7.00	5.90	4.70	18	23
Industrialized countries	5.10	3.00	4.30	9.90	8.50	5.40	9.50	4.40	12	20
Capital-surplus oil exporters	13.00	5.30	1.20	18.20	11.00	−1.50	11.00	20.80	–	69
Centrally planned economies ^{b}	4.90 ^{b}	5.60 ^{b}	–	–	9.40	6.70	8.60	6.10	–	–

w = weighted average, nominal terms.
m = median, nominal terms.
a = real terms, measured from volume indices.
b = 1960–70 and 1970–81.

Source: World Bank (1980, 1983: tables, 1, 2, 5 and 9).

To understand changes in the IDOL, it is useful to divide the world into three types of country: (1) *core* countries that make up the leading industrial producers of the Organization for Economic Cooperation and Development (OECD) and that house most corporate centers; (2) *semi-periphery* nations, consisting of the middle-income OECD nations and newly industrializing countries (NICs) that are dependent on core- nation capital investment; and (3) the poor countries and oil exporters of the *periphery* (Wallerstein, 1974).[2]

Two stages of international trade, capital investment and migration patterns can be identified (Glickman and Petras, 1981). During the 1950s and 1960s, labor was imported from the periphery and semi-periphery to the core, capital-intensive exports were sent from the core to the semi-periphery and periphery, most trade and foreign investment was intra-core, and low-cost energy was imported into the core from the peripheral oil-producing nations. After about 1974, however, new trends emerged. As economic growth declined, most labor migration ended, foreign direct investment (FDI) increased from the core to a small number of NICs, more labor-intensive imports came from into the core from the NICs, and high-price energy was imported by the core countries. Although reductions of labor importation into the core were accompanied by capital exports to NICS, FDI went to a largely different set of countries from those that were previously labor exporters. Thus, a *triangular* relationship of labor–capital exchange took place: labor had been imported from one set of semi-periphery and periphery countries, but capital exports went to NICs, few of which had been labor exporters.[3] The search for cheap labor in the NICs was largely for assembly operations, especially in the semiconductor, textile, clothing and shoe industries. Relocation of auto, chemical, steel and rubber operations from developed nations were often for marketing purposes or to supply other overseas operations. Importantly, while assembly functions decentralized, control activity remained in the core.

A good example of worldwide industrial dispersion can be seen in the automobile industry. Hill (1983) describes the transition from a US-dominated industry in the 1960s to one now characterized by massive foreign investment by American carmakers and increasing competition from Japanese and European producers. As a result, fierce global competition emerged and the US share of sales dropped sharply. There has been integration of worldwide auto operations, efforts to penetrate European markets by American firms, and penetration of the US market by the Europeans and Japanese. The results have been dramatic: between 1978 and 1982, US firms' car sales declined by 32 per cent while imports rose from 18 to 28 per cent of the domestic market. Employment fell by nearly 300,000 workers. Most recently, there has been massive foreign investment by US car companies (about $80 billion was projected for the period 1980–86) and simultaneous demands for protectionism at home. Global integration of operation has been implemented, involving geographically separate engineering, design, production, assembly and other operations. Ford 'World Car' is an example of this strategy. Nearly identical cars are assembled at various sites using components produced in different countries.[4] Firms are thus able to take advantage of local production conditions to maximize worldwide profits.

Castells (1984) shows a similar globalization of the semiconductor industry. Research and management functions, which demand intellectual labor, are located near universities and cities where 'quality of life' factors are high. But the other processes – mask-making, wafer fabrication, assembly and testing – may have geographically distinct and separate patterns. Therefore, labor-intensive assembly functions have been locating in Hong Kong, Singapore and Korea, where wages are low. By 1976, 'offshore' assembly plants employed twice the number of people working in similar domestic operations. The same lines of geographic development can be seen in the assembly processes of many other industries.

These patterns emerged because of improvements in communications technology and changes in business organization, resulting in the establishment of a 'Global Factory' (Barnet, 1980). A larger number of people have been brought into this international system of production, exchange and finance. Assembly work can be done nearly anywhere in the world with low-skilled workers. Thus, firms have looked for sites with low-wage, stable and unorganized labor, both within developed nations and in 'safe' LDCs (usually those with totalitarian regimes).[5] Crucially, the speed of capital shifts has increased as firms have become better able to disperse production worldwide because of the information revolution (Bluestone and Harrison, 1982; Castells, 1984).

Two spatial phenomena are directly connected to recent global economic change. First, the evolving IDOL has meant that cities have developed new functions. In particular, a few 'world cities' (Friedmann and Wolff, 1982) have evolved to organize and manage the far-flung operations of multi-national corporations. Cities such as New York, Tokyo, London and Paris house concentrations of corporate headquarters, high-level corporate services (accountancy, law, etc.), banking, research and government. Supervision of production facilities lower in the urban hierarchy takes place in these conurbations. Smaller cities assume roles as production, service and consumer centers (Pred, 1977; Cohen, 1981; Noyelle and Stanback, 1984). The higher a city is in the hierarchy, the more control it will have over its own economic destiny. Therefore, we see both a *spatial diffusion* of economic activity and a pronounced *territorial hierarchy* (Castells, 1984).

Second, direct foreign investment has affected regional development. During the early postwar era, most investment was in the core regions of developed nations because of uncertainty about alternative sites and the desire to be near consumer markets. Later, multinational corporations

(MNCs) decentralized investment, particularly in assembly operations (Glickman and Woodward, 1984).[6]

International trade and the US economy

Within these global patterns, the US economy also changed. There evolved a stagnant economy, a fall in the rate of profit (Nordhaus, 1974; Lovell, 1978), more overseas investment (OECD, 1981), slower productivity growth (Denison, 1979), and stagflation (simultaneous high inflation and unemployment). For example, the GNP growth rate fell from 4.7 per cent per annum (1961–65) to 2.2 per cent (1973–81). On a per capita basis, GNP growth plummeted from 3.1 per cent (1960–73) to only 0.9 per cent (1973–81) (Reich, 1983). Inflation reached 13 per cent in 1980, declining only under President Reagan's deflationary measures of the early 1980s and the deepest postwar recession. After-tax profits fell from 13.7 per cent (1966) to 7.6 per cent (1979).

US investment abroad increased substantially, while direct foreign investment in the US exploded in the 1970s.[7] US assets abroad were $226 billion at the end of 1983, three times the 1970 level. There was also a major shift towards investment in the NICs: 7 per cent of US FDI went to these countries in 1960–68 compared to 19.4 per cent between 1973 and 1978. By 1977, production by US parent companies and majority-owned foreign affiliates overseas was $161 billion, more than one-twelfth of domestic GNP (Howenstine, 1983).[8] Inward FDI grew from $13 billion in 1970 to $134 billion in 1983; the annual growth rate was 8.4 per cent from 1963 to 1973, increasing to 20.5 per cent between 1974 and 1981 (Schoenberger, 1983). Following Dunning (1981), Shoenberger (1983) argues that much inward FDI was by oligopolistic firms seeking access to the large US market in order to exploit their 'ownership advantage'[9] in such high-technology sectors as machinery and chemicals.

Trade of US goods and services grew rapidly, as exports increased from $29 billion in 1960 to $348 billion in 1982 (Belli, 1983). Merchandise imports and exports were both about 14 per cent of production in 1970; however, exports rose to 23 per cent and imports increased to 31 per cent of domestic output by 1983. Most significant has been the penetration of US manufacturing goods markets and the decline of the US as a world trade leader.[10] By 1980, nearly three-quarters of all goods produced in the US were in active competition with imports from other countries (Reich, 1983). The US now exports some high-tech items,[11] corporate and financial services, and agricultural products. At the same time, imports are strong in traditional manufactured markets that were previously US-dominated. Major import industries are autos (21 per cent of domestic consumption), consumer electronics (52 per cent), calculators (43 per cent), textile machinery (46 per cent) and cutlery (90 per cent) (Magaziner and Reich,

1982). Significant balance-of-trade problems resulted from declining competitiveness and higher-priced oil.

Trade has had differential effects on occupations and segments of the labor force. Frank and Freeman (1979) shows that some 85 per cent of the job losses attributable to US investment abroad has been in blue-collar occupations. Sectors affected adversely by imports have had high union membership and have employed more blue-collar, female and ethnic minority workers. At the same time, export industries tend to have more highly educated, young and managerial employees. Thus, increased imports and outward DFI have adversely affected lower-skilled workers.

IDOL and US spatial change

Changes in the IDOL have produced a number of notable consequences for American cities and regions. First, the decline in sales of heavy manufacturing goods in international markets (e.g. transportation equipment, non-electrical and electrical machinery, chemicals) has exacerbated unemployment problems in the industrial heartland of the Northeast and Midwest. Simultaneously, other regions have gained from trade: agricultural sales abroad have helped farming regions in the 1970s, and some of the large cities that lost manufacturing jobs have gained service positions (particularly in corporate headquarters functions). These corporate service jobs are concentrated in the Northeast and other large metropolitan areas (Stanback and Noyelle, 1982).[12]

Second, there has been an uneven pattern of foreign direct investment among US regions. In 1981, employment in non-banking US affiliates of foreign firms was concentrated in the Mid-East (23.4 per cent), Southeast (24.9 per cent), and the Great Lakes (16.2 per cent).[13] But, the fastest employment growth between 1974 and 1981 was in the Southwest (20.1 per cent per year compounded), the Rocky Mountains (16.1 per cent) and Far West (12.8 per cent) regions. McConnell (1980) argued that locations outside the industrial heartland are fast becoming the choice of foreign multinationals. In this sense, foreign affiliates are following the decentralization patterns of US firms. Glickman and Woodward (1985) show that there was significant dispersion from regions with considerable inward FDI directed to those areas that had little in the early 1970s. Their analysis points out that the spatial distribution of foreign firms is becoming similar to that of domestic companies, increasingly favoring the South and West.

Third, international migration (illegal and legal) has had a distinct regional character. Most migrants come from the Caribbean Basin, Central America and (more recently) Asia. Many Hispanic workers (often employed in secondary agricultural and service jobs) reside in the Southwest (e.g. California) and parts of the Northwest (New York, New Jersey). In all, the greater openness of the US economy meant that international forces had more significant effects on urban and regional development than previously.

Returning to the automobile and semiconductor examples discussed earlier, the regional consequences of the industries' transformations have been important. Historically, car assembly and production have been regionally concentrated in Michigan. In 1963, for example, 36 per cent of auto employment was in that state. With the globalization of the car industry, that figure fell to 26 per cent by 1977.[14] Semiconductors have been concentrated in California, Arizona, Texas and Massachusetts, where three-quarters of employment is located. Areas such as Silicon Valley near San Jose and the Route 128 area around Boston dominate research and management locations. Assembly operations that have not been located abroad are in low-wage areas of western states.

Urban and regional change in the United States

In addition to the effects of the IDOL, there have been other important spatial ramifications of structural change. On an interregional basis, sharp reversals of long-term regional patterns took place during the 1970s: for the first time the growth of jobs and population was greater in non-metropolitan regions than in metropolitan areas. Cities with large manufacturing bases lost jobs and population[15] to the suburbs (first the inner suburbs, then the outer suburbs, and, finally, the 'exurbs' and other non-metropolitan areas) and to the Sunbelt.[16] These phenomena represent more than spillovers across metropolitan boundaries, but encompass growth far from metropolitan areas as well. Part of the non-metropolitan change is due to energy and resource development, and a portion is a result of recreation- and retirement-related employment. However, much non-metropolitan employment growth is also in assembly operations (often in branch plants of large companies) that have relocated from large cities. Most big cities have lost population, independent of region. There has been much continuing migration to the Sunbelt,[17] including the return of blacks who moved to the North two generations ago.[18] In the 1980s, however, long-run patterns were re-established mostly because of the shifts in the IDOL.

The relative importance of industrial location factors has changed. With the decline of manufacturing (particularly heavy manufacturing), the traditional location determinants (transportation availability and costs, agglomeration economies, energy and, to a lesser extent, labor) have less significance or have changed in character. Firms have become more communications- and technology-oriented. Both manufacturing and service firms, for example, are able to decentralize routine operations to low-wage regions (domestically and internationally) and need little unskilled labor near their headquarters. Technological advances in transportation and communications allow greater decentralization, as firms have become more footloose (Malecki, 1979; Markusen, 1982). At the same time, financial reorganization makes decentralization more feasible (Bluestone and Harrison, 1982). Firms, particularly those that hire many white-collar workers, increasingly demand 'quality of life' factors. These reasons help explain why many small and medium-sized cities with pleasant living conditions and low taxes have been growing rapidly.

There has been, as a result of these factors, a polarization of the urban system (Hanson, 1983). Cities with concentrations of corporate command functions have a large measure of independence from the rest of the urban system. At the same time, areas that specialize in traditional production or provide consumer services are dependent on corporate centers for investment and finance. Even within metropolitan areas, there is considerable economic segregation – what Friedmann and Wolff (1982) call the 'citadel and the ghetto'. The gleaming towers of Manhattan coexist with the poverty of nearby Harlem and Bedford-Stuyvesant, although there is little employment for these neighborhoods' residents on Wall Street. Economic and spatial segmentation can also be seen in Silicon Valley, where the homes of researchers and managers are located aay from production-line workers (Saxenian, 1984).

SOME TENTATIVE EXPLANATIONS OF ECONOMIC AND POLITICAL CHANGE

Having discussed the IDOL and its effects on the US, we need to tie a number of factors together: the economic slowdown and responses to it, the changing nature of the state, the role of people's movements and corporate initiatives, and fiscal problems at the local level. I provide some tentative explanations in this section.

Three elements of the international postwar corporate system that were put in place in the 1940s and 1950s came back, in a dialectical manner, to haunt the American economy in the 1960s. These were: (1) *Pax Americana*, consisting of the Bretton Woods Agreement and other economic and defense measures, aimed at maintaining American postwar hegemony; (2) *a limited capital–labor accord*, an informal agreement between 'Big Capital' and 'Big Labor', to share productivity gains in key industries and to pass on higher costs to others; and (3) *a limited capitalist–citizen accord* to provide economic security through social legislation (social security, medical care, etc.) and the reduction of cyclical unemployment through demand management (Bowles, Gordon and Weisskopf, 1983). All parts of this unwritten 'social contract' were confined to certain sectors, classes and interest groups. The whole arrangement was predicated on the ability to reward those inside (and, to a lesser degree, outside) the accords by distributing the fruits of economic growth. Wolfe (1981: 10) described the early postwar political situation as 'A bipartisan coalition . . . formed to pursue economic expansion at home through growth and overseas through empire. . . . Politics would concern itself with the means – growth – and the ends, or purpose, of social life would take care of themselves.'

However, there were exogenous and endogenous forces at play that destroyed this very delicate set of arrangements. Significantly, there came the decline in US economic dominance and the end of the *Pax Americana* in the 1960s. This occurred because of the drain put on the economy in the late 1960s by the support for the military in Vietnam and by competition with the countries that the US had been trying to build up both for markets and for geopolitical purposes (e.g. Germany, Japan and stable LDCs). The growth of social programs and the unwillingness to raise taxes to pay for both the war in Southeast Asia and the 'War on Poverty' strained the US fiscal and political capacity. The rise of OPEC and the greater strength of raw material producers also weakened US hegemony. The US economic leadership declined drastically as it was increasingly challenged in its own domestic markets as well as in world markets that it formerly dominated. As a result, stagflation set in, and latent problems in various strata of society surfaced – in production welfare lines and bottom lines. With fewer resources available to keep the accord together, the agreement disintegrated.

Many of America's problems were reinforced by federal policies. For instance, by encouraging the outflow of FDI through tax laws and by other means, domestic jobs were lost. In the 1970s, American firms were competing with their own foreign subsidiaries. Corporations began, as part of a conscious business strategy, to reduce (when practical) production in the United States in many processes and industries (e.g. the assembly operations in the auto industry). Tax and regulatory policy made these corporate strategies easier to carry out. Reagan era monetary policy, in trying to battle against inflation, created high real interest rates and many international trade problems. The resulting overvalued dollar has made foreign investment cheap and exports expensive for American firms.

The domestic 'growth coalitions' (Wolfe, 1981; Mollenkopf, 1983), formed to increase economic growth both nationally and locally, fell into disarray. These alignments of corporate, labor and community leaders failed, partly because so many people were not in the coalition to begin with: secondary workers, women, ethnic minorities, consumer groups, environmentalists, and others had been largely powerless from the outset. During the 1960s, these groups put pressure on the state for a bigger slice of the pie. Wage bargaining by workers became much more aggressive, since the cost of being unemployed was very low (due to unemployment benefit and tight labor markets). Women and ethnic minorities also become more important as economic and political forces. These internal factors, combined with the US decline in the international sphere, contributed to the fall in the profit rate and to some of the productivity growth rate decline. Also, even within the growth coalitions, primary workers began negotiating more aggressively on workplace issues (e.g. assembly 'speedups', work safety), thereby putting further pressure on profits. Workers were less willing to accept poor working conditions and began to revolt on the production line (Aronowitz, 1973). Finally, there were additional costs placed on the system by the pressures of environmentalists, consumers and others.

The profit squeeze of the late 1960s to early 1970s inevitably brought a counterattack by corporations. As a result, the 'people's movements' for greater social welfare (Piven and Cloward, 1971) of the 1960s were superseded by what can be called 'corporate movements' in the 1970s. Faced with low profits, businesses took the offensive at the negotiating table, mounted strong anti-union drives, and lobbied hard for restrictive macroeconomic policies in order to reduce wage pressure. At the local level, fiscal limitation efforts (such as California's Proposition 13) received strong corporate backing. Politically, the corporate movement reached its peak with Ronald Reagan's election in 1980 and the passage of the 1981 tax and domestic spending reductions. The deep recession of 1981–2 served to discipline the workforce and to gain wage and shopfloor 'give backs'; under this pressure, unions were forced to agree to lower wages and inferior working conditions.

In the light of this corporate offensive, much of the increased international and interregional mobility of capital can be seen both as a way to increase profits by relocating to lower-cost areas (in the conventional, neoclassical economist's view) and as a way of combating labor's gains; in the latter sense, this is a way of crippling the labor movement (Bluestone and Harrison, 1982). Therefore, the movement of branch plants to non-metropolitan areas in 1970s can also be seen part of an anti-labor strategy (since non-metropolitan areas generally have low union penetration). Relocation to low-wage areas is not only national but international, as indicated earlier.

At the same time, the work process has been changed to reduce the demand for skilled and semi-skilled labor. This has been accomplished by automation, the reorganization of work, and by other methods. Much of this 'deskilling' occurs when firms relocate operations to low-wage regions and take advantage of new (and non-union) employees to restructure work (Noble, 1977). This reduces the necessity of employing high-skilled, expensive and independent labor. It helps tip the bargaining scales in favor of management and to increase profits.

CHALLENGES TO THE STATE

In response to some of the effects of structural change, the state has been called upon to do several, often contradictory, things: to take measures to increase profits and fight stagflation; to institute class-based social policies to aid displaced workers; to initiate urban and spatial measures to help depressed areas, and so forth (Friedland, Piven and Alford, 1979; Glickman and Alford, 1982). Since all of these could not be accomplished simultaneously in a slow-growth era, several kinds of conflict resulted.

On one level, the state has been subject increasingly to *external* pressures as trade relations grow more complicated. Assaults have come from other nations (e.g. trade wars, protectionist pressures), multinational corporations (who exact subsidies by threatening to relocate offshore), migrant workers and their employers, and international organizations (the EEC, LAFTA, etc.). All of these groups petition the state to protect their interests.[19] Corporations seek to break down national boundaries and use their full power globally. National governments, as a result, find themselves bargaining with footloose MNCs and, as a result, are less able to formulate effective policy.[20] Pressures build to protect jobs and social services for workers displaced by global shifts. These tugs bring ideological conflicts between free trade and protectionism. We find the US government preaching free trade, yet engaging in protectionism (e.g. the 'voluntary quotas' for imported Japanese cars). International conflicts over a variety of products (e.g. steel, wine, pasta) give significant trouble to nation-states.

In addition to these external pressures, the state is faced with *internal* conflicts. These have taken several forms, most often over distributive shares. For example, the corporate ascendancy of the last decade has resulted in sharply lower business tax rates, an increasingly regressive tax code, and real reductions in social spending. This has led to greater tax burdens being placed on consumers and workers. Displaced car, steel and textile workers seek protectionism, retraining and social benefits. Geographically, there are alo inherent conflicts between economic policies (e.g. accelerated depreciation allowances) that help expanding areas and urban policies that try to cushion declining cities (Luger, 1983; Glickman, 1984). These conflicts are aggravated by stagflation: as the economy performs poorly, there is more competition among interest groups and classes to try to fight for their shares of the pie. Fiscal strains result from these internal pressures on the state, especially when the economic pie is growing slowly.[21]

In addition, *region*-based demands add another dimension to the problems of the state. That is, coalitions of capital and labor fight for preferences for localities; these groups often transcend class and other alignments, coming together for limited purposes when under threat. Examples include a coalition of the Chrysler Corporation, the United Auto Workers Union and the City of Detroit that brought pressure for the 1980 federal loan guarantee to Chrysler.

Just as firms put pressure on the state for tax concessions (accelerated depreciation allowances, etc.) to increase profitability at the national scale, they also do so to increase profitability at the local level. Ronald Reagan's New Federalism, the devolution of other federal programs to the states, enterprise zones and cuts in social spending, are ways of aiding corporate growth. For instance, dispersing the powers of the federal government to the states means that lobbyists for social causes must go to 50 state capitals, where their power is diluted and where corporate power is felt most strongly (Peterson, 1982). Also, one can view tax revolts at the state and local level as corporate/wealthy-led attacks on the social wage; this weakens local tax bases and makes localities more vulnerable to further pressure from firms that induce cities to give greater tax breaks.

These international and domestic pressures result in an increasingly impotent state, since governments cannot deal effectively with internal pressures that often lead to fiscal stress. Nor can the state effectively make successful arrangements with the many pressure groups negotiating with it. The combination of internal and external pressures make decision-making very difficult.

Several elements are important to recall at this juncture: (1) the decline in profitability; (2) pressures by corporations on the state to do something to restore profitability (e.g. tax concessions, engineered recessions, deregulation); (3) corporate strategies to increase profits, including speedups, increases in supervision, less workplace autonomy, mergers and, significantly, threats to relocate; and (4) pressures by labor, consumers and environmentalists to maintain social and quality of life programs. These factors make the state (at both national and local levels) less able to operate effectively. The international dimension reduces even more the effectiveness of state policy because firms can withdraw capital investment. Capital mobility is a tool used by firms to gain advantage over labor and to extract concessions from the state. And, as we shall see, it makes urban policy more difficult to carry out.

URBAN POLICY

Urban policy (UP) is formulated to correct for market failure brought about by spatial imbalances and to spur economic development. For example, in order to provide space and funds for urban revitalization, UP has consisted of programs such as urban renewal (in the 1950s and 1960s, particularly) and housing. Other things have been done by national governments to reduce the cost of conducting business in cities, including infrastructure grants, loans, small business development efforts, transportation, and water and sewerage programs. An increasing number of programs are undertaken by localities themselves: selling land below market value, infrastructure provision for business, subsidized loans and grants aimed at attracting firms in the spatially competitive environment, noted earlier.

Another flank of urban policy consists of income transfers and public services, including AFDC (Aid to Families with Dependent Children) housing allowances for low-income families, Supplemental Social Insurance, and other income and service programs. These programs are often not for towns but for people and certainly have important urban effects. Some urban programs come about through categorical grants to localities and states, others through less restrictive block grants. The trend since the Nixon Administration has been towards the latter.[22]

Most of the money for these urban programs goes to welfare payments rather than to places. In fact, about $18 is spent on welfare provision (including retirement pensions) for every $1 spent on urban programs. Funds for urban renewal programs have been cut sharply, by 27 per cent in real terms between 1978 and 1984 (Glickman, 1984). Means-tested social programs for the poor were cut by one-sixth during the Reagan administration, about $75 billion (Bawden and Palmer, 1984).

But, in addition to these nominal urban programs, what I call 'the *real* urban policy' includes the indirect urban consequences of economic policy: accelerated depreciation allowances, investment tax credits and so forth. (Glickman, 1984). The incentives started by these programs are very powerful aids to industrial relocation even though they are not intended for these purposes. For instance, these tax programs try to increase investment by lowering the cost of capital and increasing cash flow. However, in doing so, they also encourage investment in new assets rather than the replacement of existing assets and favor equipment in preference to structures. The result is that the investment that results from these tax write-offs takes place in growing (often Sunbelt) areas, rather than in declining regions. Moreover, there are other non-urban policies that affect the spatial division of labor: the allocation of R & D expenditures, defense appropriations and bases, and other spending to growing, non-union, low-wage areas (Luger, 1983). These non-urban portions of UP constitute the most important part of the real urban policy.

Therefore, we have three branches of urban policy: 'place programs', 'people programs', and non-urban tax/expenditure policies. Most of these programs are biased towards growth areas that have low wages and 'good business climates'. Regions that have strong unions, higher wages, and so forth are being left behind, especially by footloose assembly operations. Therefore, economic policy aimed at increasing investment and production also aids corporations in a spatial sense since capital movements disrupt efforts to organize by workers. As a corollary, the efficiency of most local or national urban development programs is compromised by the mobility of capital. In effect, cities have far less control over local business activity because firms are so easily able to move. Therefore, municipalities find it more difficult to formulate and implement development policies because of the capital mobility and the conflict of urban policies with national economic programs.

For localities, slower economic growth and a more internationalized economy have led to frantic attempt to attract industry through local tax incentives, particularly tax abatements and industrial development bonds for new factories.[23] These local programs have become fundamentally 'defensive' in nature: local economic development officers say, 'If we don't offer these benefits, our town will be perceived as having a bad business climate.' This is 'negative sum' game for communities, as subsidies are transferred from them to the corporate sector. As soon as the subsidies run out, or depreciation allowances are taken, firms are free to move on, since they have invested little capital in their plants. Firms can then pit one city against another to win more favourable tax arrangements and create a 'reserve army of places' (Walker, 1978). Increasingly, tax incentives are being given when there firms threaten to move elsewhere.[24]

Related is the 'capital versus community' theme of Bluestone and Harrison (1982): firms are able to exert their power over communities and impose other social costs related to plant closures. The role of conglomerates (which have a 'portfolio of firms' to maximize overall profits) has become more important in the movement of capital as a way of opening new markets, disciplining labor, and taking external control of regional activity.

Fiscal problems have been occurring at the local level, not just in New York and Cleveland, but in growing areas since older areas are 'stuck' with old private capital or old public infrastructure and because of conscious disinvestment decisions on the part of corporations. The New York Municipal Assistance Corporation ('BIGMAC') and other (unelected) agencies are instituted to force reductions in services and wage cuts on the public. However, fiscal problems in fast-growth areas (e.g. San Jose and Houston) are also due to the overextension of local capital infrastructure and the refusal of local firms to support public spending on infrastructure or services needed for social reproduction.

CONCLUSIONS

I want to close briefly with some conclusions about the relationship between the IDOL and cities. Despite the rise of conscious and concerted efforts to control and direct growth, the ability of cities to determine their own economic destinies has been sharply limited by increases in capital mobility and by the changes in trade and foreign investment patterns. The ability of firms to rapidly shift production globally makes cities' futures less secure.[25] Moreover, cities continue to be the focus of political struggle over the distribution of income, as they house both modern corporate headquarters and wretched slums. The urban growth coalitions, as Mollenkopf (1983) tells us, have become weaker as a result of the splits between citizens' groups and firms. The hypothesis put forward here is that firms have been using the possibility of international relocation to extract concessions from both workers and cities. In doing so, they are able to tilt economic and political power in their favor.

In the end, cities find themselves less able to deal with their economic problems. Friedmann and Wolff (1982: 327) describe the dilemma as follows:

A major loser is the local state. Small, isolated without financial power, and encapsulated within the world economy, it is barely able to provide for even the minimal services its population needs. And yet, instead of seeking alliances with neighbouring cities and organized labour, it leaves the real decisions to the higher powers on which it is itself dependent, or to the quasi-independent authorities created by state charter that manage the infrastructure of global capital-system-wide facilities such as ports, airports, rapid transit, water supply, communications, and electric power.

The internationalization of economies, then, poses a number of difficult questions for urban planners:

How can the economic restructuring taking place at the local level be controlled, when it is often directed by external forces?

How can local conflicts (over land use, job creation, and the environment) be mediated?

What new political strategies and institutions need to be developed to gain a measure of autonomy in this ever-changing environment?

These questions must be answered by planners and local activists if cities are to regain political power.

NOTES

1 Structural change (or economic restructuring) involves long-term shifts in the composition of demand, production and occupational patterns; new technology; a changing international division of labor; shifts in relative prices; and evolving location patterns (both migration and industrial spatial restructuring).
2 Core countries include North-west Europe, North America, Japan and Australia. The semi-periphery consists of lower-income OECD countries such as Ireland and the NICs (including the Republic of Korea, Taiwan, Brazil and Singapore). The NICs have specialized in labor-intensive goods such as clothing, shoes, toys and electronics; many, however, became more capital intensive in the late 1970s, increasing exports of items such as steel to core nations. These categories do not correspond precisely to the World Bank data presented in Table 3.1 since official data do not differentiate within broad country groupings.
3 Pre-1974 importation of labor to Northern Europe took place largely because of labor shortages in industries such as construction, textiles, metal working, health care and consumer services. The major labor exporters came from the southern

tier of Europe, North Africa and from the Caribbean basin. In Europe, a number of institutions were established to recruit and transport laborers for employers. After 1974, investment was directed to NICs such as Brazil, Hong Kong, Korea and Singapore, none of whom had been a major labor exporter previously.

4 For instance, by 1880, 12 per cent of US 'Big Three' (GM, Ford and Chrysler) cars were produced by their Latin American affiliates, up from 5.5 per cent only seven years earlier (Trachte and Ross, 1983, cited by Castells, 1984).

5 This industrialization of a few Third World countries has led to rapid urban growth in major cities of these NICs. Although this chapter will concentrate on the developed world, the impact on NICs must be kept in mind.

6 Among the studies of the regional location of direct foreign investment, see Blackbourne (1974: 1982), Dicken and Lloyd (1976), Howenstein (1983), McDermott (1977), McConnell (1980) and Little (1983).

7 Although investment abroad by American firms increased, other countries' investment grew even more quickly. Between 1961 and 1967, the US had 61 per cent of all FDI made by 13 major investing countries (OECD, 1981). By 1974–78, the US share dropped to 30 per cent, while Japan and West Germany increased their combined shares from 9.6 per cent to 29.9 per cent. The share of foreign direct investment by the 13 countries made in the US was only 1.4 per cent in 1961–67, but grew to 24.5 per cent by 1974–78. By 1983, inflows of capital to the US ($82 billion) were far greater than outflows ($50 billion).

8 Viewed in another way, foreign production was three times the value of exports in 1960; by 1977, it was more than five times exports. Twenty-five per cent of outward FDI was in petroleum; other major industries in which US firms had large foreign investment were paper, rubber, textiles, wholesale trade and finance.

9 'Ownership advantage' refers to the ability to exploit superior technology, innovation and product differentiation abroad.

10 The US share of exports of industrialized capitalist countries declined from 21 per cent in 1965 to 16 per cent in 1983. During the same period, the US absorbed an increasing share of the world's imports (20 per cent in 1983 compared to 17 per cent in 1965).

11 According to the 1977 *Annual Survey of Manufactures*, the most export-intensive manufacturing sectors were electrical and non-electrical machinery, instruments, transportation and tobacco products. All but the last (which is small absolutely) have high-technology characteristics.

12 Corporate headquarter activity has been greatest in New York, Los Angeles, Chicago, Cleveland and San Francisco. Cities gaining Fortune 500 corporate headquarters between 1959 and 1976 were Houston and Minneapolis (Noyelle and Stanback, 1984).

13 About a quarter of the book value of property, plant and equipment was in the Southeast, with Louisiana, Florida, South Carolina and Georgia being the largest in that region. Among the state, California, Texas and Alaska had the largest foreign investments (Belli, 1983).

14 Car production has been spatially concentrated in other countries as well. Regions such as Piedmont (Italy), Niedersachsen (FRG), Ile de France (France), and the West Midlands (UK) have been major centers of car production (Hill,

1983). The secondary effects of the decline in car production have been felt in related industries such as steel and tyres. This change in location has been a major factor in serious fiscal problems in car-dominated cities such as Detroit and Flint.

15 For example, between 1970 and 1980, population declined by 18 per cent in St Louis, 24 per cent in Cleveland, and 21 per cent in Detroit (Tabb, 1984).

16 Garnick (1983) reports that metropolitan area population grew at nearly four times the rate of non-metropolitan regions between 1959 and 1969. In the subsequent decade, non-metropolitan areas grew faster. But this reversal of long-term trends was not uniform; in the more urbanized parts of the country (New England, the Mideast, the Great Lakes and the Far West), non-metropolitan areas grew faster in the 1960s and slower in the 1970s compared to metropolitan areas. For less urbanized regions, metropolitan areas grew faster in both decades.

17 Houston and Phoenix grew by more than 25 per cent during the 1970s, for instance.

18 It is critical to understand that often-made 'Frostbelt-versus-Sunbelt' categorization is simplistic. There are sections of the Sunbelt that have continued to stagnate (e.g. Mississippi) at the same time that states such as Texas, Florida and Arizona boomed during the 1970s and early 1980s. Similarly, there has been good growth in parts of New England and other Frostbelt areas.

19 Or, at least, not to interfere with their self-perceived prerogatives.

20 Unions also cannot bargain effectively with MNCs because labor is rarely organized internationally. Therefore, firms can play off workers in different countries and reduce wage costs (Bluestone and Harrison, 1982).

21 Although states and localities in the aggregate have run budget surpluses (deficits are generally not permitted by law), there are fiscal problems in many large central cities, intensifying the battle among cities for jobs and tax bases. Fiscal stress is particularly severe in cities with traditional manufacturing bases and large minority populations. Infrastructure is decaying and services have been cut. Fiscal problems make attracting employment more difficult for cash-poor cities.

22 Reasons given for devolution are the desire for greater local autonomy and an interest in reducing federal social expenditures. In reality, the result has been considerably less money going to needy cities and the poor.

23 At the same time, there are moves to create a positive environment for research-based employment (e.g. ties with universities) in order to attract high-tech firms.

24 Essentially, location decisions that were formerly among the best-kept corporate secrets have become among the most public as firms await bids from hard-up cities. In recent years, International Harvester has played off Ohio and Indiana, the Microelectronic and Computer Technology Corporation considered bids from 57 cities, and there has been international bidding for auto plants (e.g. Austria vs. Spain). The implications of these tax losses for local fiscal crisis are obvious and serious (Harrison and Kanter, 1978).

25 This is not to say that cities ever had complete control over their own economic development. My argument is that increased capital mobility and internationalization of the economy result in more external influence.

REFERENCES

Aronowitz, Stanley (1973) *False Promises*, New York: McGraw-Hill.
Barnet, Richard E. (1980) *The Lean Years*, New York: Simon and Schuster.
Bawden, D. Lee, and John L. Palmer (1984) 'Social policy: Challenging the welfare state'. In John L. Palmer and Isabel V. Sawhill (eds), *The Reagan Record*, Cambridge, Mass.: Ballinger, pp. 177–215.
Belli, R. David (1983) 'Foreign direct investment in the United States: Highlights from the 1980 benchmark survey', *Survey of Current Business*, 63 (10): 25–35.
Blackbourn, A. (1972) 'The Location of foreign-owned manufacturing plants in the Republic of Ireland', *Tijdschrift voor Economische en Sociale Geografie*, 63 (6): 438–43.
—— (1974) 'The spatial behavior of American firms in Western Europe'. In Hamilton, F. G. (ed.), *Spatial Perspectives on Industrial Organization and Decision-Making* Chichester, Sussex: John Wiley, chapter 9.
—— (1978) 'Multinational enterprises and regional development: A comment'. *Regional Studies* 12: 125–7.
—— (1982) 'The impact of multinational corporations on the spatial organization of developed nations: a review', in Taylor, Michael and Thrift, Nigel (eds), *The Geography of Multinationals*, New York: St Martin's Press.
Bluestone, Barry and Bennett Harrison (1982) *The Deindustrialization of America*, New York: Basic Books.
Bowles, Samuel, David M. Gordon, and Thomas E. Weisskopf (1983) *Beyond the Wasteland* New York: Doubleday.
Castells, Manuel (1984) *Towards the Informational City? High Technology, Economic Change, and Spatial Structure: Some Exploratory Hypotheses*, Working Paper no. 430, Berkeley: Institute of Urban and Regional Development, University of California.
Cohen, Robert B. (1981) 'The new international division of labor, multinational corporations and urban hierarchy'. In Michael Dear and Allen J. Scott (eds), *Urbanization and Urban Planning in Capitalist Society*, London: Methuen, pp. 287–315.
Deardorff, Alan V. and Robert M. Stern (1983) 'Current issues in trade policy', mimeo, Ann Arbor, MI: University of Michigan.
Denison, Edward F. (1979) *Accounting for Slower Growth: The United States in the 1970s*, Washington, D.C.: Brookings Institution.
Dicken, Peter and Lloyd, Peter E. (1976) 'Geographical perspectives on United States investment in the United Kingdom', *Environment and Planning, A*, 8 (6): 685–705.
Dunning, John H. (1981) *Economic Analysis and the Multinational Enterprise*, London: George Allen and Unwin.
Frank, Robert F. and Richard T. Freeman (1979) 'The distributional consequences of direct foreign investment'. In William G. Dewald (ed.), *The Impact of International Trade and investment on Employment*, Washington, D.C.: US Government Printing Office.
Friedland, Roger, Frances Fox Piven and Robert R. Alford (1979) 'Political conflict, urban structure, and the fiscal crisis'. In Douglas E. Ashford (ed.), *Comparing*

Public Policies: New Concepts and Methods, Beverly Hills, Calif.: Sage, pp. 197–225.

Friedmann, John and Goetz Wolff (1982) 'World city formation: an agenda for research and action', *International Journal of Urban and Regional Research*, 6: 309–44.

Garnick, Daniel H. (1983) 'Shifting balances in metropolitan and nonmetropolitan area growth'. Paper presented at the 1983 Meeting of the Regional Science Association, Chicago, November.

Glickman, Norman J. (1984) *Economic Policy and the Cities: In Search of Reagan's 'Real' Urban Policy*, Working Paper no. 26, Austin: Lyndon B. Johnson School of Public Affairs, University of Texas at Austin, *Journal of the American Planning Association* 50; 471–78.

—— and Robert A. Alford (1982), 'The state in an internationalized economy', mimeo, Bellagio, Italy.

—— and Elizabeth M. Petras (1981) *International Capital and International Labor Flows: Implications for Public Policy*, Working Paper no. 53, Philadelphia: Department of Regional Science, University of Pennsylvania.

—— and Douglas F. Woodward (1985) *Direct Foreign Investment and Regional Development: Some Empirical Findings*, Working Paper no. 33, Austin: Lyndon B. Johnson School of Public Affairs, University of Texas at Austin.

Hanson, Royce (ed.) (1983) *Rethinking Urban Policy: Urban Development in an Advanced Economy*, Washington, D.C.: National Academy Press.

Harrison, Bennett and Sandra Kanter (1978) 'The political economy of states' job-creation business incentives', *Journal of the American Institute of Planners*, 44: 424–5.

Hill, Richard Child (1983) 'The auto-industry in global transition', mimeo, East Lansing, MI: Michigan State University.

Howenstine, Ned G. (1983), 'Gross product of US multinational companies, 1977', *Survey of Current Business*, 63 (2): 24–9.

Kemper, N. J. and De Smidt, M. (1980) 'Foreign manufacturing establishments in the Netherlands', *Tijdschrift voor Economische en Sociale Geografie*, 71: 21–40.

Law, C. M. (1980) 'The foreign company's location investment decision and its role in British regional development, *Tijdschrift voor Economische en Sociale Geografie*, 71: 15–20.

Little, Jane S. (1978), 'Locational decisions of foreign investors in the United States', *New England Economic Review* (July/August): 43–63.

Lovell, Michael C. (1978) 'The profit picture: trends and cycles', *Brookings Papers on Economic Activity*, no. 3: 769–88.

Luger, Michael (1983) 'Federal tax incentives as industrial and urban policy'. In William Tabb and Larry Sawers (eds), *Sunbelt–Frostbelt: Regional Change and Industrial Restructuring*, New York: Oxford University Press.

Magaziner, Ira C. and Robert B. Reich (1982) *Minding America's Business*, New York: Vintage.

Malecki, Edward (1979) 'Location trends in R & D by large US corporations, 1965–1977', *Economic Geography*, 55: 309–23.

Markusen, Ann R. (1982) 'Sectoral differentiation of regional economies'. Paper presented at the 1982 Meeting of the Regional Science Association, Pittsburgh.

McConnell, James E. (1980) 'Foreign direct investment in the United States', *Annals of the Association of American Geographers*, 70: 259–70.

McDermott, Phillip J. (1977) 'Overseas investment and the industrial geography of the United Kingdom', *Area*, 9 (3): 200–7.

Mieszkowski, Peter (1984) 'The differential effect of the foreign trade deficit on regions in the U.S.A.'. Paper presented at the Conference on the Agenda for Metropolitan America, Center for Real Estate and Urban Economics, University of California at Berkeley, September.

Mollenkopf, John H. (1983) *The Contested City*, Princeton: N.J.: Princeton University Press.

Noble, David F. (1977) *America By Design*, New York: Oxford University Press.

Nordhaus, William (1974) 'The falling share of profits', *Brookings Papers on Economic Activity*, no. 1: 169–208.

Noyelle, Thierry and Thomas M. Stanback (1984) *Economic Transformation of American Cities*, Totowa, N.J.: Allanheld and Rowman.

OECD (1981) *International and Multinational Enterprises: Recent Direct Investment Trends*, Paris: OECD.

Peterson, George E. (1982) 'The state and local sector'. In John L. Palmer and Isabel V. Sawhill (eds), *The Reagan Experiment* Washington, D.C.: Urban Institute Press.

Piven, Frances Fox and Richard Cloward (1971) *Regulating the Poor*, New York: Pantheon.

Pred, Alan (1977) *City Systems in Advanced Economies*, New York: John Wiley.

Reich, Robert M. (1983) *The Next American Frontier*, New York: Times Books.

Saxenian, Annalee (1984) 'Urban contradictions of Silicon Valley: Regional growth and the restructuring of the semiconductors industry'. In Larry Sawers and William K. Tabb (eds), *Sunbelt/Snowbelt: Urban Development and Regional Restructuring*, New York: Oxford University Press.

Schoenberger, Erica (1983) 'The logic of foreign manufacturing investment in the United States: Implications for the US economy', mimeo, Baltimore, MD: Johns Hopkins University Press.

Stanback, Thomas M. and Thierry Noyelle (1982) *Cities in Transition*, Totowa, N.J.: Allanheld, Osmun.

Tabb, William K. (1984) 'Urban development and regional restructuring, an overview'. In Larry Sawers and William K. Tabb (eds), *Sunbelt/Snowbelt: Urban Development and Regional Restructuring*, New York: Oxford University Press.

Trachte, Kenneth and Robert Ross (1983) 'The crisis of Detroit and the emergence of global capitalism', mimeo.

Walker, Richard (1978) 'Two sources of uneven development under advanced capitalism: Spatial differentiation and capital mobility', *Review of Radical Political Economics*, 10(3): 28–37.

Wallerstein, Immanuel (1974) *The Modern World System*, New York: Academic Press.

Watts, H. D. (1980) 'The location of European direct investment in the United Kingdom', *Tijdschrift voor Economische en Sociale Geografie*, 71(1): 3–14.

Wolfe, Alan (1981) *America's Impasse*, New York: Pantheon.

World Bank (1980; 1983) *World Development Report*, Washington, D.C.: World Bank.

4

Urban Theory Reconsidered: Production, Reproduction and Collective Action

Michael Peter Smith and Richard Tardanico

Writings in urban theory differ in how they conceptualize urban development. At one end of the spectrum are those that highlight the *intrasocietal* dynamics of such processes and structures as cultural modernization and class relations. At the other end are those that highlight the connections of processes and structures within given social formations to the wider *intersocietal* dynamics of production and exchange. The approaches of location theory and modernization theory as well as structuralist urban theory and the theory of urban praxis have each differently stressed the role of intrasocietal conditions in urbanization. Dependency theory and world-system theory have been the leading approaches to explaining urban development from an intersocietal point of view. The first sections of this chapter review both of these approaches to urban theory with a view to developing a theoretical synthesis to connect macro-level research on the dynamics of the global political economy to micro-level research on urban politics. The chapter then focuses more precisely on the collective action theory of 'urban social movements' developed by Castells (1983). This approach offers a promising but as yet underdeveloped perspective on the interplay of political-economic and socio-cultural dynamics at the local, national and global levels in producing urban change. By way of critique, we argue that in producing urban change the sphere of production is inexorably linked to the sphere of 'collective consumption' through the medium of the everyday activities of households. The household is the basic micro-structure through which work and community life, and their contradictions, are experienced as united in family life. In the final section we explore more fully the web of interconnections between household, economy and politics, arguing that the everyday practices of urban households are the missing link capable of connecting the global to the local level of analysis and individual experience to collective action in urban politics. We conclude by offering an agenda for future research on global economic restructuring and community politics, which has emerged from our reconsideration of urban theory.

LOCATION THEORY AND MODERNIZATION THEORY

Location theory analyzes urban development by underscoring the calculus of decisions involved in choosing optimal industrial sites. It assumes an environment of small, competitive industrial plants, and views access to 'input' and 'output' markets, as well as transportation, as key locational incentives (see Walker, 1980). In addressing economic integration within urban-based regions, the theory considers the industrialization of primate cities – but not that of their backward counterparts – as an autonomous process. The impetus to industrialization in backward areas is contact with the activities and values of primate cities (see Friedmann and Weaver, 1979); a notion that brings us to modernization theory.

In modernization theory analysis of urban development flows from a portrayal of the world as a set of basically self-contained regions and nations. It describes them as evolving along a uniform path of socioeconomic development, the same path chartered by the leading areas of Western Europe and the United States; and it attributes differents in the pace of regional and national evolution to internal conditions that facilitate or impede the diffusion of such values as rationality, cosmopolitanism and innovation. Paralleling location theory, the modernization approach regards the urban-industrial growth of leading zones as generated autonomously, but that of lagging zones as catalyzed by exposure to the 'progressive' ideas of dynamic regions and nations (see Portes, 1975; Wolf, 1982).

The critique of modernization theory and research is extensive. This literature has underlined the ethnocentrism of the theory, which by asserting the evolutionary pre-eminence of 'modern' western industrial values, demeans the 'traditional' values of newly-industrialized societies. Among other things, critics have observed: (a) that the modernization approach has ignored contradictory elements of culture, such as the continued importance of tradition, ethnicity and religion in 'individualistic' western industrial societies (Smith, 1979); and (b) that the modernization approach to development theory overlooks the historical and structural causes of inequality at the local, national and international levels. Consistent with these problems is the perspective's reification of the state as derived from societal values and evolving towards pluralism (see Frank, 1969; Portes, 1975; Wolf, 1982).

Location theory and research also neglect the historical-structural roots of inequality. With respect to interregional inequality, the approach does so by taking as given the geographic distribution of input and output markets, as well as by assuming an environment of small, competitive industrial plants whose locational decisions are rational responses to the distribution of such markets. Neither the state nor local politics ever enter the analysis of interregional inequality as significant entities. The approach's infrequent discussions of international inequality are similarly flawed. And, by not only neglecting both the state and local politics but at the same time regarding labor as merely another input and industrial plants as mere 'black boxes', location theory and research fail to address socioeconomic inequality and its political expression within regions (see Friedmann and Weaver, 1979; Walker, 1980; Smith, Ready and Judd, 1985).

STRUCTURALIST THEORY AND URBAN PRAXIS THEORY

The work of Harvey (1973, 1978, 1982) and the early writings of Castells (1977, 1978) embody the principles of Marxist structuralism, which, like the otherwise contrasting approaches of location theory and modernization theory, emphasize the intrasocietal dynamics of urbanization. Structuralists focus on the logic of capitalist accumulation. The logic of accumulation is grounded in the class relations of capitalist society, which both generate and unequally distribute material resources. In this way, class relations structure the conventional patterns of social, cultural and political practice that reproduce bourgeois hegemony. Essential to this process is the 'relative autonomy' of the state, whose policies are assumed to serve the long-term, collective interests of the bourgeoisie by attempting to offset capitalism's inherently self-destructive tendency towards the disunity of the bourgeoisie and unity of the proletariat. In sharp contrast to the proactive political stance of the state and capital is the reactive political stance of the working class, who mobilize primarily in defense against the capitalist agenda (see Gold et al., 1975; Perry, 1984; Smith and Judd, 1984).

Smith (1980, 1983, 1984) and Castells (1983, 1984) are among the urban theorists who have recently taken issue with the structuralist perspective. The criticisms of these 'urban praxis' theorists underscore structuralism's deterministic and functionalist slant, which reduces consciousness, politics and culture to the logic of accumulation. What these critics emphasize instead is the duality of social structure and human agency, which contrasts with the abstractness of structuralism by locating human consciousness and being in the space and time of living societies. The notion of duality directs attention not only to structural constraints but also to structural opportunities. By duality, then, the urban praxis theorists mean that social structures are simultaneously outcomes and channels of human consciousness and praxis (see also, Gottdiener, 1985). Thus, social structures are fluid and ever-changing; they both reflect and guide the flow of human agency, including the agency of popular classes. Hence, far from being mere epiphenomena of capitalism's structural logic, consciousness, politics and culture are essential forces in the construction and reconstruction of society and economy (see Giddens, 1981; Smith, 1983, 1984; Perry, 1984).

The urban praxis critics of structuralist urban theory have also emphasized that, given its high degree of abstraction, structuralism is unamenable to empirical research; and that, like other brands of functionalism, it relies on circular reasoning. For example, structuralists commonly cite the pro-capitalist outcomes of state policies to explain the institutional roots of such policies. Such functionalist explanations divert attention from situational contingencies as well as political consequences that may inhibit or even jeopardize capitalist development (see Skocpol, 1979, 1980). Recent theorizing and research further suggest that structuralists say much too little about the interconnections of local and national society with capital accumulation on a world scale (Portes and Walton, 1981; Wolf, 1982; Chase-Dunn, 1984 a and b; Sassen-Koob, 1984).

This last criticism similarly applies to some of the theory and research on urban praxis. Some such writings (e.g. Lefebvre, 1971, 1976) entirely overlook the interaction of urban life with the global web of capitalist production and exchange. Others (e.g. Gottdiener, 1985) do not overlook this web, but they deal with it incompletely. Though at times the global political economy becomes a significant part of the urban praxis analysis (see, for instance, Smith and Tardanico, 1985), it often fails to be integrated into the perspective in ways that effectively explore its ramifications for local sociopolitical processes. Thus, in reacting against the abstraction and determinism of structuralist theory, the literature on urban praxis often goes too far by minimizing the role of structural forces in the constitution and reconstitution of cities.

DEPENDENCY AND WORLD-SYSTEM THEORIES

In seeking to explain urban development by focusing on wider *inter*societal structures and processes, to varying degrees analyses by Friedmann (1956, 1973), Harvey (1973), Walton (1976a and b), and Castells (1977) have made use of the dependency approach. This approach takes issue with the fact that modernization theory and location theory ignore or relegate to secondary importance the dynamics of international and interregional exploitation. 'Dependency' is conceived of as a phenomenon politically organized on a global scale as a hierarchy of exploitative relations that channel surplus value not just socially from subordinate classes to dominant classes within given social formations, but geographically from periphery to core at the national and international levels. 'Dependent' regions and nations are defined as those whose conomy, politics and society are dominated and distorted by external interests. Regarding urban development processes, the basic issue in dependency theory is how patterns of urbanization vary according to the socioeconomic and political relations of locales to national and international hierarchies of core/periphery exploitation (see Frank, 1969; Portes, 1975; Roberts, 1978).

Friedmann (1980, 1982), Walton (1982) and Castells (1983, 1984) have recently expanded the dependency approach by incorporating ideas found in world-systems theory (see Wallerstein, 1974, 1977, 1980). This perspective regards the dependency school as not going far enough. It argues that, like previous theories, dependency analysis conceptualizes economic processes and class relations as essentially *intra*national phenomena, albeit ones which are powerfully conditioned by their international context. The world-system perspective differs by claiming that economic processes and class relations are elements of an evolving global structure of production and trade; it views national and subnational political-economic units as elements of this global structure (see Wallerstein, 1979; Bergesen, 1980; Wolf, 1982). Hence patterns of urbanization within given societies must be examined in terms of the developing processes of production, trade and sociopolitical struggle on a world scale (see Chase-Dunn, 1984a; Sassen-Koob, 1984).

While raising the level of analysis to the global scale, the dependency and world-system perspectives have also overlooked important structures and practices in the processes of urbanization and development. Most basically, dependency and world-system studies can be criticized for inadequately addressing class structure and its consequences for both the political-economic transformation of societies and their positions in the global capitalist order. By stressing exchange relations over production relations, many studies in this genre have dealt superficially or not at all with concrete social formations and their associated patterns of class conflict. This oversight, critics assert, is crucial. For class conflict is a key driving force not only in shaping the development of local and national institutions, but likewise in structuring the responses of newly-industrialized societies to metropolitan expansionism and in transforming capitalism on a global scale (Tardanico, 1986; see also Walton, chapter 17 below). It is therefore no surprise that dependency and world-system analyses typically present no convincing explanation for the past and present dynamics of international capitalist development. A related criticism is that such analyses often portray both the state and civil societies as passive instruments or direct reflections of capitalist interests and structures rather than as an active, partially independent force (see Skocpol, 1979; Portes and Walton, 1981; Aronowitz, 1982; Wolf, 1982; Smith, 1984).

URBAN DEVELOPMENT: THE GLOBAL–LOCAL INTERPLAY

In light of our review and critique of the major approaches to urban development, how do we conceptualize the socioeconomic transformation of cities in the contemporary global division of labor? How is this division of labor connected to the spheres of everyday life and local politics? First, we regard this transformation not as simply a contemporary, domestic phenomenon but as an aspect of the past and present dynamics of world capitalist development. From this standpoint we can think of interregional capital flows within any nation as a subset of *global capital flows*. The importance of doing so is clear from comparative-historical scholarship that cautions us against reifying national and sub-national boundaries. Not that *states* and their boundaries are inconsequential; they indeed are powerful forces in the creation – and at times the subversion – of the foundations of capitalist accumulation (e.g. Tilly 1975; Skocpol, 1979; Petras, 1981; Carnoy, 1984; Kraus and Vanneman, 1985). Yet comparative-historical research informs us that everyday socioeconomic relations have spanned long distances and transcended political boundaries since well before the consolidation of the contemporary global division of labor. Moreover, far from being rigid barriers, such boundaries are *fluid*; they are constantly challenged and redefined by the very activities and struggles of human agents that challenge and redefine other dimensions of sociopolitical power (e.g. Braudel, 1973; Wallerstein, 1974; Tilly, 1975, 1983; Giddens, 1981; Portes and Walton, 1981; Wolf, 1982; Smith, 1983, 1984; Tardanico, 1984, 1986).

That economy, society and politics are more transnational than ever is a commonplace observation. Nevertheless, the prevailing perspectives on urbanization often ignore, minimize or inadequately address the web of relations that increasingly synchronizes the lives of people on a global scale. As we have seen, writings grounded in location theory and modernization theory say nothing about the structural foundations of international, national and local inequality; in their view, inequality at all of these levels is based not on exploitative socioeconomic and political relations but on the failure of some people to embrace 'modern' values or to make 'rational' market decisions.

The writings that say most about the interplay between urban transformation and the global web of socioeconomic and political relations are those that focus on the insights of dependency theory and world-system theory. Not that this literature is without its problems. This literature's emphasis on international exploitation is not inherently flawed; in fact, it constitutes an essential corrective to perspectives on socioeconomic inequality that neglect extraregional and extranational structures and processes. Nevertheless, problems do arise in that this brand of scholarship commonly regards the twin driving forces of global capitalism as class conflict within and political-economic competition between, *advanced* industrial countries and regions. Thus the perspective often neglects or minimizes structures and processes in underdeveloped zones which themselves influence strategies of capitalist accumulation, flows of international investment and patterns of urbanization (see Tardanico, 1986).

In response to criticism of this kind, a growing number of dependency and world-system studies have become more sensitive to the importance of local dynamics in both advanced and underdeveloped zones. The trend, then, is towards convergence with the approaches of structuralism and urban praxis (e.g. Walton, 1976a and b, 1982; Roberts, 1978; Portes and Walton, 1981; Friedmann and Wolff, 1982; Sassen-Koob, 1982, 1984).

A related problem, however, has been ignored in the theoretical literature on international development and the global division of labor. This problem arises from the focus of dependency and world-system research on *vertically* integrated processes at the global and domestic levels. Again, the issue is not that this conceptualization is inherently flawed; we most certainly agree that, in underlining relations of domination and subordination, it captures the fundamental character of unequal development. What it leaves unexplored, however, are the ways in which socioeconomic and political transformations in any locale (see Urry, 1981; Giddens, 1981) may be connected with related changes in other locales not only in advanced economies but also in the Third World. In so doing, dependency and world-system scholarship ignores or slights the way conflicts within, and competition among, urban regions may influence the distribution of investments among implicitly competitive zones throughout both the newly industrialized world and emergent peripheral areas within the core (see Sassen-Koob, 1982; Tardanico, 1984, 1986; Smith and Tardanico, 1985).

URBANIZATION AND THE INTERNATIONAL SYSTEM

In this light, we begin our reconceptualization of the socioeconomic transformation of contemporary core and peripheral cities from the standpoint of the restructuring of the international division of labor since at least the 1960s. In the context of the rising costs and declining worldwide competitiveness of metropolitan industry, essential to this restructuring have been advanced technologies of production, communication and transportation; transnational networks of services; and vast reserves of cheap labor in underdeveloped countries. Advanced technologies have enabled transnational corporate leadership to replace many high-skilled, high-wage workers not only by introducing labor-saving automation but by compartmentalizing operations into detailed, deskilled tasks and dispersing these in sites across the world.

Coordinating this complex of decentralized activities is a global hierarchy of management whose headquarters are located in such 'world cities' as New York, Los Angeles, Tokyo and Paris, with such cities as Mexico City, Saõ Paolo and Hong Kong playing regional-international roles, and others like Denver and Houston playing regional-national roles. Reinforced by transnational circuits of banking, finance and other services, this functionally and spatially reorganized system of production takes full advantage of the most crucial element of all: the massive supply of low-wage, well-disciplined workers in the world's newly-industrialized zones. In Latin America, Asia and Africa, where many governments compete to attract footloose metropolitan industries, growing numbers of such workers are employed in the manufacture of products not for sale in domestic markets but for export to the United States, Europe and Japan. The heightened flow of migrant labor on the global scale is another vital feature of today's reorganized system of international production (Frobel, Gardels and Pennick, 1980; Portes and Walton, 1981; Nash and Fernandez-Kelly, 1983). The overall picture is clear: advanced capitalist development and the socioeconomic transformation of core and peripheral cities are becoming more and more interlaced with the worldwide fabric of capital flows, production and trade (Portes and Walton, 1981: 141–7; Sassen-Koob, 1982, 1984).

In what ways can this emergent global pattern of development inform our understanding of the dynamics of urban politics and the role of 'urban social movements' in the transformation of cities?

URBANIZATION, COLLECTIVE ACTION THEORY AND URBAN POLITICS

The role of grassroots movements in the process of urban change has been a central issue in urban theory. These movements have been conceptualized variously as displaced forms of class struggle from the workplace to the community (Harvey, 1973, 1978) and as coalitions which form on a multi-class or non-class basis to promote distinctively 'urban' issues such as defense of place, culture or urban social services (Katznelson, 1981, Castells, 1983; Mollenkopf, 1983). While this literature has generated interesting theoretical debates and impressive empirical case studies, it also is not without problems. For the most part, the richly detailed case studies have ignored the global level of analysis. There has been no effective specification of the concrete historical mechanisms that mediate the interplay between global economy and local culture. When it appears at all, the global economy is a mere backdrop against which local dramas are played out. Second, there has been little detailed analysis of the basic microstructures (i.e. households, networks of households and related informal social networks connecting the workplace and community life) which compromise the primary units of material and cultural reproduction. This is no small omission since these microstructures are the irreducible building blocks of people's practical awareness of their everyday life. It is out of this awareness that collective action, whatever its roots, springs.

The scholar who has come closest to recognizing both the significance of the global–local interplay and the importance of analyzing the dynamics of community social networks to shed light on this interplay is Manuel Castells

(1977, 1978, 1983, 1984). Accordingly, we shall now examine his contribution to this aspect of urban theory, identifying its strengths and limitations, in order to move down from the community level to the even more basic mediating mechanisms tying urban households to each other and, ultimately, to urban politics and the global economy.

Castells (1977: 15–19) has defined urbanization as the 'social production of spatial forms'; the social process by which activities and populations become not only concentrated in limited space but imbedded in a corresponding form of culture and ideology. Urbanization, he states, cannot be separated from another social process, development, by which structural transformations facilitate a society's capacity for capital accumulation. Spatial forms, then, are assumed to be material products of historically-specific patterns of social organization. The social forces that shape urban forms, and the local struggles that challenge the spatial forms and social fabric of cities, are focal points of Castells' evolving body of writing. Central to his recent analyses (1983, 1984) is the idea that local struggles over the collective consumption of goods and services, when combined with grassroots demands for cultural control over urban space through political control of local government jurisdictions, may alter and even redefine both urban space and the sociopolitical character of urban life.

Castells (1977; 1978: 16–19; 1983: 237–8) has argued that the social production of spatial forms under capitalism's 'industrial mode of development' emanated from its structural tendencies: the concentration and centralization of capital; the diminishing rate of profit; the growing power of organized labor; and, most important, large-scale state intervention in the economy. The basic spatial consequence of these tendencies has been the agglomeration of the social and physical infrastructure of production, marketing and consumption in sprawling metropolitan regions. As organized labor strengthened its bargaining power, the state's heightened presence in the economy came to revolve around management and the delivery of 'collective goods and services'. As an essential part of the social wage, such goods and services – public transport, housing, health care, education, recreational facilities, and so on – eased tensions between capital and labor. Nevertheless, the structural contradictions of industrial capitalism eventually provoked generalized urban crisis, including reductions in collective goods and services.

Compounding this crisis at present is the fact that dominant interests have responded in part by accelerating the 'informational mode of development' and its associated internationalization of production. This response further erodes the quality of urban life by relocating the processes of production, consumption and power, thereby dissociating 'the space of organizations and the space of experience' (1984: 236, 238–41). One crucial result has been multi-class, grassroots mobilization both in defense of collective consumption and local cultures, and towards the devolution of political power to small-scale, territorially-based communities. As noted above, Castells' (1983, 1984) more recent work departs from his previous structural determinism by arguing that such grassroots mobilizations do not merely reflect but may transform the spatial character of advanced capitalist societies.

When analyzing the urban process in the Third World countries of Latin America, Castells (1977: 49–63) has argued that several traits characterize its contemporary urbanization: the extreme dominance of one city within national urban networks; the accelerated population growth of cities; an inflated service sector; the increasing segregation of social classes; and a widening gap between the living standards of rich and poor. Castells' early analyses of this situation called attention to the region's economic and political subordination to North Atlantic interests. He underlined not the mere fact of foreign power but its historically changing forms and, above all, the way it was incorporated into the social fabric of Latin America. From this perspective, Latin America's 'dependent urbanization' was viewed as the spatial expression of the interplay between the forms of North Atlantic domination and local social structures since the epoch of Iberian expansionism.

Castells, (1977: 49–50, 58–61) therefore suggested that we study dependent urbanization by examining the pre-existing social structures of subordinate nations, the social structures of dominant nations, and their modes of articulation. He explained Latin America's general path of sociospatial development and its internal variations by referring to the destructive impact of colonialism on indigenous societies, the area's diverse regional interconnections with foreign interests, and the changing balance of power among metropolitan countries.

In his more recent analysis of urban social movements in Europe, the United States and Latin America in *The City and the Grassroots* (1983), Castells has focused on the role of consciousness and social action in transforming the conditions of everyday urban life. In the Latin American context, this new focus has led him to study the activities of local grassroots movements in the region's cities for the defense of territorially-based identities and assertion of community control over collective consumption. Castells (1983: 179–85) claims that these movements are multi-class struggles which should be analyzed in light of how local sociopolitical arrangements combine with the global division of labor to exclude a growing proportion of the Latin American urban masses from the private housing and services markets.

Several dialectically linked relationships are crucial to comprehending the underlying theory of urban change developed in *The City and The Grassroots*. These are presented in figure 4.1. The vertical arrows indicate antagonistic relations; horizontal arrows indicate compatible relationships.

Informal themes recurring in *Grassroots* set a tone which reinforces the plausibility of the relationships posited in figure 4.1. For our purposes, the two most important of these are: (1) discussions of 'the city'/civil society, feminist politics and urban self-management which are paired with the following dialectical oppositions: 'the state', patriarchal social and political relations, and centralized administration of everyday life; and (b) discussions of the role of women in seeking to overcome 'urban contradictions' embedded in *reproductive* relations (in the household and community) are juxtaposed against the role of men in waging class struggle in *productive* relations (at work and *vis-à-vis* the state).

FIGURE 4.1 *Antagonistic and compatible relationships in urban change*

'Urban social movements' are thus conceived as non-productivist forms of social struggle. These movements are depicted as capable of producing significant urban change if they combine in their practice three types of demands – collective consumption, cultural aspirations and political control of local government – and if they can enlist the support of crucial mediating institutional structures. Schematically, this process of urban change may be depicted as in figure 4.2.

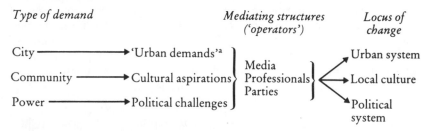

ᵃUrban space and services as use values.

FIGURE 4.2 *Social movements and urban change*

The dynamics of this process of unifying demands for services/space, cultural expression and political power are depicted, by means of a case study of the Madrid Citizens' Movement, as proceeding sequentially: shifting first from defensive demands (stop the bulldozer), to offensive ones (public redevelopment for neighborhood benefit), to the assertion of local culture (via networks and celebrations), and finally reaching the level of institutional reform (local self-government).

To understand Castells' consistent denial of the relevance of productive relations to the processes of urban change one must understand another theme found in *The City and the Grassroots*. The argument is made that when opposition to dominant social interests is based only upon the labor movement, this unites capitalist class factions against their basic antagonist. Thus, only when social groupings other than labor coalesce around a diversified range of 'urban' issues can the dominant class be divided into reformist and status quo elements, thus raising the possibility of creating conditions conducive to non-reformist reforms. In short, this occurs when, during the process of raising distinctively 'urban' demands, 'the citizenry', as a multi-class coalition, confronts dominant class interests and raises class issues, without provoking repression (see Castells, 1983: 263).

This theoretical reformulation, while expanding extensively upon Castells' collective consumption theory, by adding cultural, sociospatial, and political dimensions to the array of 'urban' contradictions, is fundamentally consistent with his initial effort to minimize the significance of production politics as a means to achieve social transformation under capitalism.

A close reading of the case studies presented in *Grassroots* reveals that Castells has succeeded in establishing these three axes of social conflict as central dimensions of urban politics. However, the facts contained in these richly detailed case studies do not fully support the proposition that reproductive relations (consumption, culture, political self-management) are clearly more central to our understanding of the dynamics of urban conflict than are changing productive relations stemming from capitalist domination of the production process and resistance to that domination. We argue instead that, in comparative historical perspective, the processes of production, reproduction and collective action are inexorably linked. Several interesting examples of the essential inseparability of the relations of production/consumption/reproduction and their relationship to grassroots mobilization can be found in Castells' own case studies. These serve to underline our argument. Consider the following illustrations.

The Glasgow rent strike   The mismatch between industrial growth and housing supply (collective consumption) *with* resistance to the proletarianization of skilled craft unions under wartime conditions (production) were the objective conditions that combined to foster a unification of work and community struggles in this case.

The Mission District   As described in this chapter, the issues which triggered social struggles were housing and urban renewal *and* the employment opportunity structure. 'Productivist' demands for jobs, employment for young people, and opposition to discrimination in the workplace all contributed to this grassroots neighborhood mobilization along with collective consumption demands (Castells, 1983: 113).

Gay power in San Francisco   The changing occupational structure of the city, with the expansion of opportunities for skilled, educated, professional financial and business services, was a key structural element, providing the economic base for the cultural demand for control of residential living space by young urban professionals, including the gay segment of the 'yuppie' (young professional) stratum. Furthermore, as Sassen-Koob (1984) has pointed out, in cities like Los Angeles, New York and San Francisco where large numbers of upper-income producer service workers are concentrated, employment demand is stimulated for low-paying domestic and household consumption service workers at the opposite end of a polarized employment opportunity structure. This, in turn, provides one of the economic 'pull' factors for new immigrants (from Central America in the case of San Francisco) thereby swelling demand for jobs, housing and public services in Hispanic neighborhoods like the Mission District, and perhaps intensifying the neighborhood-based social struggles there. Thus, in both instances of grassroots mobilization in San Francisco changing productive relations were inseparable from changing reproductive relations as determinants of popular action.

Val d'Yerres, France   The mobilizing issues here were enhanced quality of life, improved transport services and reduced traffic congestion. Why were these issues raised by the grassroots movement? Because of the profound mismatch between the location of residents' workplaces (production) and where the protesters were able to live (household reproduction).

1960s US/black urban rebellions   The issues predominant in this grassroots mobilization were housing, police brutality and employment. The employment dimension – a demand for more public service jobs for blacks – reflects, in part, the changing employment opportunity structure in older industrial metropolitan areas in the United States. These structural economic changes reduced the objective opportunities for absorbing black workers into the changing private sector industrial economy, making a demand for public service employment (arguably a collective consumption demand) necessary. In this case, people dealing with the opportunities and constraints of their everyday life acted where they could. Where social mobility was blocked by discrimination and segregation, economic opportunities were blocked by the early stages of urban employment restructuring, and state sector agencies were increasingly enmeshed in the body of public law ushered in by earlier civil rights protests, black demands focused on those options which appeared most potentially responsive to the needs and demands of black urban households: state policies to reduce discrimination, neighborhood control of state schools, and through this route, ultimately, hoped for better jobs and income to enable household survival and reproduction. Once again, it becomes impossible to separate work from the community, and productive from reproductive relations in those urban rebellions.

WORK, COMMUNITY AND COLLECTIVE ACTION: THE HOUSEHOLD AS
MISSING LINK

Most studies have portrayed households as bounded social units, drawing a
sharp distinction between the 'private life' of households and the 'public life'
of economy, politics, and so on (Zaretsky, 1976; Siltanen and Stanworth,
1984). Yet the household is the basic microstructure of social, economic and
political life in which working life and residential community life are
experienced as united in family life. The activities of people living in
households interact with the activities of people living in other households.
Some of these interactive processes of communication lead to the formation
of informal social networks within classes. Ultimately, household activities
are the basic elements of group and class formation in any social system (see
Przeworski, 1982). Furthermore there is a connection between the process
of capital accumulation and the social functions performed in households.
Households physically reproduce labor power by generating income through
a combination of formal and informal sector employment and state transfers
and services; the also are the primary unit engaged in socialization and
cultural reproduction, including socialization to the societal contradictions
which give rise to social movements.

A growing body of scholarship is redirecting attention to these connections.
This scholarship examines households – groups that share places of
residence and pool socioeconomic resources to ensure their maintenance
and reproduction – as a way of understanding the links between individual
behavior and collective action as people deal with the constraints and
opportunities of everyday life. Much research from this perspective focuses
on household and economy, underscoring their joint impact on patterns of
consumption, workforce participation, migration, and the like. Such patterns
both reflect and influence the organization of roles within households,
including the balance of relationships ·of households and their individual
members to production and exchange at the local, national and international
levels.

Although in a rudimentary and limited way, some of this literature has also
begun to focus on the points of intersection between domestic life and
politics. The minimal evidence suggests that, as political actors, the interests
of household members stem not just from the relationships of whole
domestic units to the larger division of labor, but also from the interaction of
group and individual roles in the microstructures of household, community
and workplace (see Safa, 1976; Nash, 1979; Bodnar, 1982; Kaplan, 1982;
Sanjek, 1982; Bolles, 1983).

The paucity of research on this topic is not solely attributable to the
conceptual underpinnings of most household studies; political research in
general has said little about households. This neglect is to be expected. Like

so much of the household literature, research on politics tends to compartmentalize private life and public life, with political issues being restricted to the latter sphere (Zaretsky, 1976; Siltanen and Stanworth, 1984). Such research revolves around two fundamental questions: whether values or material conditions shape political structures, and whether elites or masses are the driving force in politics. Attempts to answer these question do not always ignore households; for example, many scholars discuss the political relevance of childhood socialization. Nevertheless, the literature generally regards households as marginal to the political arena (Safa, 1976; Bodnar, 1982; Kaplan, 1982; Sanjek, 1982).

For several overlapping reasons, social scientists have increasingly argued that household, economy and politics should be considered not as separate pieces of institutional fabric, but as interwoven threads of a larger societal texture. The most basic reason is the growth of female participation in the wage labor force and politics, a trend which has challenged academicians to re-evaluate previous thinking about both the role of women in society and the links between households and other institutions (Nash and Safa, 1976; Fernandez-Kelly, 1983). Another reason is that, in the context of Third World upheavals and the expansion of transnational corporations, social scientists have reassessed theories of comparative economic development. As a result, rigid distinctions between 'traditional' and 'modern' economic sectors have given way to holistic perspectives that stress the interconnectedness of all varieties of production and exchange (Portes and Walton, 1981; Wallerstein et al., 1982; Wolf, 1982). Yet another reason is the growing attention being paid to the role of grassroots community mobilizations in urban politics throughout the world.

'Community' mobilizations for improvements in public services and neighborhood conditions have been especially prominent in the Third World, reflecting four features of Third World cities. First, dependent urbanization concentrates low-income workers in the informal economy, where, because of individualistic and precarious circumstances, labor is hard to organize. Second, conventional political associations, including trade unions, are unresponsive to the masses as a whole. Third, resource pooling networks, which center on households and neighborhoods, constitute the primary sources of social and political cohesion among low-income groups. Fourth, problems of inadequate public services and neighborhood conditions unite people of diverse socioeconomic standing (Portes and Walton, 1976, 1981; Roberts, 1977; Lomnitz, 1978; Nelson, 1979; Castells, 1983; Bienen, 1984; Portes, 1984).

When considering popular mobilizations the fact that workers in the formal and informal economies are not socially segregated should not be overlooked; individuals may work at any one time or over the course of their lives in both sectors, while those who work in only one sector or the other may nevertheless reside together in households and communities. The recent literature emphasizes that we know little about the political ramifications of the interplay between such work and residential arrangements. It suggests, however, that while those who work in large enterprises may be more politically active, political interests and movements among the urban popular classes depend on their relations not just to the workplace but to activities outside the workplace as well (e.g. Portes and Walton, 1976, 1981; Safa, 1976; Roberts, 1977; Sanjek, 1982; Castells, 1983).

It is therefore possible that, in spite of differing relations of individuals to the organization of production, members of the same household and neighborhood develop common political interests and engage in joint political action over communal conflicts with business and government officials. Another possibility is that, in spite of common relations to the organization of production, differing political interests and actions arise from the diversity of communal roles among members of the same household and neighborhood. A further possibility is that the web of relations to workplace, household and neighborhood unites labor and communal interests in one political bloc.

Even when popular movements are weak or non-existent, knowledge about the political significance of the interplay between work and residential arrangements is vital for evaluating the latent political interests and capacities of the urban working classes. Such interests and capacities must be taken into account as we consider the consequences of state and business policies; the options of powerful interests, such as government officials, party organizations, domestic entrepreneurs and foreign investors; and the potential outcomes of social, economic and political crises. For example, attempts by competing elites from the left, centre and right to co-opt the urban masses are a common feature of Third World politics. The results of such attempts stem in part from the political interests of the popular classes and their ability to negotiate with elite factions (Cornelius, 1975; Portes and Walton, 1976; Roberts, 1977; Nelson, 1979; Bienen, 1984). In light of the everyday networks of low-income people, their role in urban politics directs attention to this question: To what degree, and how, does the interplay of relations to workplace, household and neighborhood influence their political interests and capacity for political action?

A promising approach to research on the question focuses on the adaptive strategies of low-income households – the means by which they obtain and allocate socioeconomic resources to confront daily problems and achieve goals (see Mingione, chapter 14). As the most elementary sites of resource-pooling practices, households are situated within a broad field of income-producing activities (e.g. formal wage labor and such informal labor as direct subsistence production, domestic service and peddling), and socially-reproductive activities (e.g. food preparation, sexual relations, childcare and consumption). These activities include cooperative practices within and between households, as well as relations of household members to actors in other settings, such as markets, agencies and factories. In the context of low pay, high underemployment and unemployment, and inadequate welfare programs, the intra- and inter-household dynamics of obtaining and allocating resources are crucial to individual and collective well-being. None the less, interests within households are not necessarily homogeneous, as conflicts among members are structured according to sex, age, occupation and so on.

Further complicating matters are conflicting interests that arise from relations between households and relations of household members to actors in other spheres. Thus, we see that income-producing and socially reproductive activities are imbedded within social networks that encompass the organization of production and exchange *within, between and outside* households. At each of these levels, divisions of labor occur not merely within a locality; they likewise occur at the national and international level, as adaptive strategies scatter household members to different regions and countries (Roberts, 1977; Lomnitz, 1978; Portes and Walton, 1981; Sanjek, 1982; Wallerstein et al., 1982; Fernandez-Kelly, 1983; Schmink, 1984).

Adaptive strategies of households are not restricted to the socioeconomic arena, for the interests they engender often lead members to undertake political action – attempts to influence resource-controlling bodies within and outside government. These interests center on adequate provision of food, shelter, clothing and income; security of land titles; and access to such municipal services as drinking water, sewerage systems, electricity, paved streets, transportation, health care, markets and schools. The issue of income, which involves availability of work as well as amount of pay or profit, is the most fundamental point at which interests of household and community overlap with those of workplace (Cornelius, 1975; Portes and Walton, 1976, 1981; Nelson, 1979; Sanjek, 1982; Castells, 1983; Bienen, 1984).

Yet the interests engendered by adaptive strategies do not always lead to political action, and, where they do, such action may take a variety of forms. Among these are personal contact with patrons; mass land invasions; involvement in neighborhood associations and self-help activities; collective bargaining with outside groups; electoral participation; and formal affiliation with external bodies. Underlying the extent and forms of political action in any locale are the particular sources of conflict and solidarity within and between social classes and status groups, including the resources available to contenders; the organization and policies of government at the national, regional and municipal levels; and the availability of such alternative channels of action as changing jobs, moving to better neighborhoods and emigrating abroad (Leeds, 1974; Cornelius, 1975; Portes and Walton, 1976, 1981; Roberts, 1977; Nelson, 1979; Castells, 1983; Bienen, 1984). For example, disunity based on inequalities of property, skill, income, gender, and so on, is one of the factors that weakens the capacity of the popular classes to wrest concessions from capital and government. Organized labor, whose standards of living are subsidized by the cheap goods and services provided by informal workers, tends not to identify politically with their less privileged counterparts. The latter, meanwhile, are reluctant to engage in workplace militancy which, while promising better pay and conditions, jeopardizes both jobs and resource-sharing networks of household and community. In fact, self-employment and migration abroad are two common alternatives to labor protest. Unskilled female workers – above all, those who head households – are most vulnerable to low pay and bad conditions; their dual role makes labor militancy, as well as outmigration, particularly difficult and risky. Indeed, relatively well-educated young, single women, who reside with parents and siblings and merely supplement family income, are the most likely among female wage-earners to mobilize over workplace issues.

Interwoven with these lines of cleavage within the labor force are the profits that informal petty entrepreneurs, especially those who own small firms, derive from the cheap labor of informal workers. To this extent, the interests of informal petty entrepreneurs undercut the power of organized labor against modern industrial firms. But informal petty entrepreneurs do not form a monolithic bloc; among their numbers are traders, shopkeepers, artisans, and the like, whose precarious existence may align them politically more with informal workers than with formal merchants and manufacturers (Portes and Walton, 1976, 1981; Safa, 1976; Nelson, 1979; Peattie, 1979; Fernandez-Kelly, 1983; Portes, 1984).

In sum, such disuniting conditions, which revolve around the basic economic vulnerability of the urban popular classes, reduce the likelihood of work-based popular protest. So do other factors, including aspirations for personal and family advancement, spatial separation of workplace and residence, nationalism and anti-labor government policies. No wonder, then, that security and stability for low-paid workers hinge on family and community. Not uncommonly, governments accede, through either formal or personal channels, to neighborhood demands for land titles, services and facilities. Doing so legitimates government authority, co-opts beneficiaries and reinforces the *political* separation of interrelated residential and workplace interests (see Cornelius, 1975; Portes and Walton, 1976; Eckstein, 1977; Castells, 1983). The fact remains that not only the fluidity of income-producing roles, but also their intersection with roles of social reproduction in households and neighborhoods, may mitigate disuniting forces among the urban popular classes. How much, and to what political ends, is not clear (see Nelson, 1979; Sanjek, 1982; Castells, 1983; Bienen, 1984; Portes, 1984). It is clear that, to understand better the consequences of state policies and capital flows, the political and economic options of leading actors, and the possible outcomes of present-day crises, we must learn more about the political interests and capacities of the people. The relationship of their interests and capacities to resource-pooling networks is a prime research issue.

CONCLUSIONS

Attention to the interplay of local and global dynamics places in broader socio-spatial perspective such issues as competition for capital investment and labor flows among cities and regions as well as between core cities and peripheral export-processing zones (e.g. Portes and Walton, 1981; Friedmann and Wolff, 1982; Sassen-Koob, 1982, 1984; Hill, 1984). It places such issues in broader historical perspective too, since recent studies by Wolf (1982) and Tilly (1983) stress that today's global processes of indusrialization and deindustrialization are in essence nothing new; they have been an expanding and intensifying feature of the capitalist world system since capitalism's embryonic stages in early modern Europe (see also Chase-Dunn, 1984 a and b). Third, it places the study of core and peripheral urban transformations in broader theoretical perspective by promoting the kind of synthesis developed in this essay of insights drawn from structuralist, urban praxis, dependency, world system and collective action theories but concretely anchored in the study of the adaptive strategies of households.

Cities are shaped by the dynamic interplay of global, national and local conflicts over the organization and control of production and distribution, as well as over state structures and policies. The impact of the capital accumulation strategies of businesses and the state policies of governments have been frequently viewed as the central elements in the making, unmaking and remaking of cities. In our view, equally important, but more neglected, has been the impact of common people – their consciousness, intentionality, everyday practices, and collective action – on the planning and implementation of state and business policies as well as their consequences for the social production of cities.

Investigating the adaptive strategies of urban households offers a mechanism for connecting the individual to local community action, national level state policy-making, and the dynamics of the global political economy. Such an investigation need not focus only on the passive responses of households to externally imposed political-economic constraints. For the activities of households may constitute the social basis of local *initiatives* demanding wider political restructuring when the essential fabric of everyday family life is jeopardized by capital restructuring and state action or inaction. In addition to this voice option, the migration of people experiencing untenable economic and political conditions is a second way in which people make their own history. And it is the urban household that has often played an active and creative role in the social organization and channeling of migration flows on a global scale as a household survival strategy. Households may thus be seen as an initiating force in urban transformation. Just as they are constrained by the dynamics of the global economy, these forces from below constitute, in their turn, constraints on capital and the state.

In conclusion, to promote our broader theoretical, socio-spatial and historical conception of urban transformation we propose a two-stage research strategy. At the local level we propose the following research questions:

1 What social networks are created within, between and outside households by the income-producing and culturally reproductive activities of the urban popular classes?

2 What cooperative and conflicting social interests are generated by such networks, and what resources can be mobilized on behalf of the various interests?

3 How do such networks, interests and resources interact with the organization and control of production as well as with the structure and policies of the state to promote or impede work-based and community-based political action?

Complementing these questions at the local level, we propose the following global level research questions:

1 How have domestic institutional arrangements and conflicts interacted with the world historical development of capitalism to channel flows of capital both within nations and across international boundaries?

2 How have capital flows influenced class relations, state policies, and popular forms of political action locally, regionally, nationally and internationally?

3 What have been the consequences of class relations, state policies, and popular mobilizations for changes in the organization and control of production and trade at the domestic and international levels?

4 How have the changes in the organization and control of production and trade, in turn, fed back upon the social organization of everyday life in households at the level of the local community?

It is within this broad set of questions that we have sought to reconceptualize the present-day transformation of cities. Central to our reconceptualization has been an attempt to answer the more general question of how socio-cultural and political-economic forces interact at the local, national, and global levels to constitute and reconstitute urban space throughout the world.

REFERENCES

Aronowitz, Stanley (1981) 'A metatheoretical critique of Immanuel Wallerstein's *The Modern World System*', *Theory and Society*, vol. 10, no. 4: 503–20.
Bergesen, Albert (1980) 'From utilitarianism to globology: the shift from the individual to the world as a whole as the primordial unity of analysis'. In Albert Bergesen (ed.), *Studies in the Modern World System*, New York: Academic Press.
Bienen, H. (1984) 'Urbanization and Third World Stability', *World Development*, vol. 12, no. 7.
Bodnar, J. (1982) *Workers' World*, Baltimore, MD: Johns Hopkins University Press.
Bolles, L. (1983) 'Kitchens hit by priorities: Employed working class Jamaican women confront the IMF'. In June Nash and Maria Patricia Fernandez Kelly (eds), *Women, Men and the New International Division of Labor*, Albany: State University of New York Press.
Braudel, Fernand (1973) *The Mediterranean and the Mediterranean World in the Age of Philip II*. vols. 1 and 2, New York: Harper.
Carnoy Martin (1984) *The State and Political Theory*, Princeton, N.J.: Princeton University Press.
Castells, Manuel (1977), *The Urban Question*, Cambridge, Mass.: MIT Press.
—— (1978) *City, Class, and Power*, New York: St Martin's Press.
—— (1983) *The City and the Grassroots*, Berkeley: University of California Press.
—— (1984) 'Space and society: Managing the new historical relationships'. In Michael Peter Smith (ed.), *Cities in Transformation: Class, Capital, and the State*, Urban Affairs Annual Review 26, Beverly Hills: Sage, pp. 235–60.
Chase-Dunn, Christopher (1984a) 'Urbanization in the world-system: New directions for research'. In Michael Peter Smith (ed.), *Cities in Transformation: Class, Capital and the State*, Beverly Hills: Sage, pp. 111–20.
—— (1984b) 'The world system since 1950: What has really changed?'. In Charles Bergquist (ed.), *Labor in the Capitalist World Economy*, Political Economy of World-System Annual 7. Beverly Hills: Sage, pp. 75–106.
Cornelius, Wayne A. (1975) *Politics and the Migrant Poor in Mexico City*, Stanford: Stanford University Press.
Eckstein, Susan (1977), *The Poverty of Revolution*, Princeton, N.J.: Princeton University Press.
Fernandez-Kelly, Maria Patricia (1983) *For We Are Sold: I and My People*, Albany: State University of New York Press.
Frank, André Gunder (1969) *Capitalism and Underdevelopment in Latin America*, New York: Monthly Review Press.
Friedmann, John (1956) 'Locational aspects of economic development', *Land Economics*, vol. 32: 213–27.
—— (1961) 'Cities in social transformation', *Comparative Studies in Society and History*, vol. 4.

—— (1973) *Urbanization, Planning, and National Development*, Beverly Hills: Sage.
—— and Clyde Weaver (1979) *Territory and Function*, Berkeley: University of California Press.
——, Nathan Gardels and Adrian Pennick (1980) 'The politics of space: Five centuries of regional development in Mexico', *International Journal of Urban and Regional Research*, vol. 4, no. 3: 319–49.
—— and Goetz Wolff (1982) 'World city formation: an agenda for research and action', *International Journal of Urban and Regional Research*, vol. 6, no. 3: 309–44.
Frobel, Folker, et al. (1979) *The New International Division of Labor*. New York: Cambridge University Press.
Giddens, Anthony (1981) *A Contemporary Critique of Historical Materialism*, London: Macmillan.
Gold, David A. et al. (1975) 'Recent developments in Marxist theories of the capitalist state', *Monthly Review* (October): 29–43.
Gottdiener, M. (1985) *The Social Production of Urban Space*, Austin: University of Texas Press.
Harvey, David (1973) *Social Justice and the City*, Baltimore, MD: Johns Hopkins University Press.
—— (1978), 'The urban process under capitalism: a framework for analysis', *International Journal of Urban and Regional Research*, vol. 2, no. 1: 101–32.
—— (1982), *The Limits to Capital*, Oxford: Basil Blackwell.
Hill, Richard Child (1983) 'Crisis in the Motor City: the politics of economic development in Detroit'. In Susan S. Fainstein, et al., *Restructuring the City: The Political Economy of Urban Redevelopment*, New York: Longman.
Kaplan, Temma (1982) 'Female consciousness and collective action: the case of Barcelona, 1910–1918', *Signs*, vol. 7, no. 3.
Katznelson, Ira (1981), *City Trenches*, New York: Pantheon.
Kraus, Richard and Reeve Vanneman (1985) 'Bureaucrats versus the state in capitalist and socialist regimes', *Comparative Studies in Society and History*, vol. 27, no. 1: 111–22.
Leeds, A. (1974) 'Housing settlement types, arrangements for living, proletarianization, and the social structure of the City'. In Wayne Cornelius and F. Trueblood (eds), *Latin American Urban Research*, vol. 4, Beverly Hills: Sage.
Lefebvre, Henri (1971) *Everyday Life in the Modern World*, New York: Harper and Row.
—— (1976), *The Survival of Capitalism*, New York: St Martin's Press.
Lomnitz, L. (1978), *Networks and Marginality*, New York: Academic Press.
Mollenkopf, John (1983) *The Contested City*, Princeton, N.J.: Princeton University Press.
Nash, June (1979), *We Eat the Mines and the Mines Eat Us*, New York: Columbia University Press.
—— and Helen Safa (eds) (1976) *Sex and Class in Latin America*, New York: Praeger.
—— and Maria Patricia Fernandez-Kelly (eds) (1983) *Women, Men, and the New International Division of Labor*, Albany, NY: SUNY Press.
Nelson, Joan (1979) *Access to Power*, Princeton, N.J.: Princeton University Press.
Peattie, Lisa (1979) 'The organization of the "marginals"', *Comparative Urban Research*, vol. 7, no. 2: 5–21.

Perry, David C. (1984) 'Structuralism, class conflict, and urban reality'. In Michael Peter Smith (ed.), *Cities in Transformation*. Beverly Hills: Sage, pp. 219–34.

Portes, Alejandro (1975) 'The sociology of national development', *American Journal of Sociology*: 55–85.

—— (1984) 'Latin American class structures: Their composition and change during the last decades'. Occasional paper no. 3, SAIS, Washington, D.C.: Johns Hopkins University Press.

—— and John Walton (1976) *Urban Latin America*. Austin: University of Texas Press.

—— (1981) *Labor, Class and the International System*, New York: Academic Press.

Przeworski, Adam (1977) 'Proletariat into a class', *Politics & Society*, vol. 7, no. 4: 343–401.

Roberts, Bryan (1977) *Cities of Peasants*, Beverly Hills: Sage

Safa, Helen I. (1976) 'Class consciousness among working-class women in Puerto Rico'. In June Nash and Helen Safa (eds), *Sex and Class in Latin America*, New York: Praeger.

Sanjek, R. (1982) 'The organization of households in Adabraka', *Comparative Studies in Society and History*, vol. 24, no. 1.

Sassen-Koob, Saskia (1983) 'Recomposition and peripheralization at the Core'. In Marlene Dixon and Susanne Jonas (eds), *From Immigrant Labor to Transnational Working Class*, San Francisco: Synthesis Publications, pp. 88–100.

—— (1984) 'The new labor demand in global cities'. In Michael Peter Smith (ed.), *Cities in Transformation*. Beverly Hills: Sage, pp. 139–71.

Schmink, Marianne (1984) 'Household economic strategies: Review and research agenda'. *Latin American Research Review*, vol. 19, no. 3.

Siltanen, J. and M. Stanworth (1984) 'The politics of private woman and public man'. *Theory and Society*, vol. 13, no. 1.

Skocpol, Theda (1979) *States and Social Revolutions*, New York: Cambridge University Press.

—— (1980) 'Political response to capitalist crisis: neo-Marxist theories of the state and the case of the New Deal', *Politics and Society*, vol. 10, no. 2: 155–202.

Smith, Michael Peter (1979) *The City and Social Theory*, New York: St Martin's Press.

—— (1980) 'Critical theory and urban political theory', *Comparative Urban Research*, vol. 7, no. 3: 5–23.

—— (1983) 'Structuralist urban theory and the dialectics of power', *Comparative Urban Research*, vol. 9, no. 2: 5–12.

—— (1984) 'Urban structure, social theory, and political power'. In Michael Peter Smith (ed.), *Cities in Transformation*. Beverly Hills: Sage, pp. 9–27.

—— and Dennis R. Judd (1984) 'American cities: the production of ideology'. In Michael Peter Smith (ed.), *Cities in Transformation*, Beverly Hills: Sage, pp.173–96.

——, Randy Ready and Dennis R. Judd (1985) 'Capital flight, tax incentives, and the marginalization of American states and localities'. In Dennis R. Judd (ed.), *Public Policy Across States and Communities*, Greenwich, Conn.: JAI Press, pp.181–201.

—— and Richard Tardanico (1985) 'Reactions locales a la crise economique: les villes americaines et la nouvelle division internationale du travail', *Anthropologie et Societes*, vol. 9, no. 2: 7–23.

Tardanico, Richard (1984) 'Revolutionary Mexico and the world economy: The 1920's in theoretical perspective', *Theory and Society*, vol. 13, no. 6: 757–72.

—— (1986) 'Issues in the study of Caribbean crises'. In Richard Tardanico (ed.), *Crises in the Caribbean Basin: Past and Present*, Political Economy of the World-System Annual 9, Beverly Hills: Sage.

Tilly, Charles (ed.) (1975) *The Formation of National States in Western Europe*, Princeton, N.J.: Princeton University Press.

—— (1983) 'Flows of capital and forms of industry in Europe, 1500–1900', *Theory and Society*, vol. 12, no. 2: 123–42.

Urry, J. (1981) 'Localities, regions, and social class', *International Journal of Urban and Regional Research*, vol. 5, no. 4: 455–74.

Walker, Dick (1980) 'Industrial location policy: false premises, false conclusions', *Built Environment*, vol. 6, no. 2: 105–13.

Wallerstein, Immanuel (1974) *The Modern World-System*, vol. 1, New York: Academic Press.

—— (1977) *The Capitalist World Economy*, New York: Cambridge University Press.

—— (1980) *The Modern World System*. vol. 2, New York: Academic Press.

—— et al. (1984) 'Household structures and production processes: preliminary theses and findings', *Review*, vol. 5, no. 3.

Walton, John (1976a) 'Political economy of world urban systems: directions for future research'. In John Walton and Louis H. Masotti (eds), *The City in Comparative Perspective*. Beverly Hills: Sage, pp. 301–14.

—— (1976b) 'Urban hierarchies and patterns of dependence in Latin America: Theoretical bases for a new research agenda'. In Alejandro Portes and Harold Browning (eds), *Current Perspectives in Latin American Urban Research*, Austin: University of Texas Press, pp. 43–69.

—— (1982) 'The international economy and peripheral urbanization'. In Norman Fainstein and Susan Fainstein (eds) *Urban Policy Under Capitalism*, Beverly Hills: Sage, pp. 119–35.

Wolf, Eric (1982) *People Without History*, Berkeley: University of California Press.

Zaretsky, Eli (1976) *Capitalism, the Family, and Personal Life*, New York: Harper and Row.

PART III

Economic Restructuring in Cities: A Global Perspective

5

The Politics of Dependency in Deindustrializing America: The Case of Buffalo, New York

David C. Perry

Perhaps no industrial region in the United States has gone through as severe and economically debilitating an era of deindustrialization as the Buffalo region. Once an 'industrial giant' (Goldman, 1983), the region's fundamental industrial base is shattered. It remains in the mire of the structural crisis of the 1970s, a victim of transformations in the world economy when core industrial sectors were deskilled and decentralized, thus allowing the production process to spread out from the center to the Third World periphery, 'creating in effect global factories and a new international division of labor' (Fainstein and Fainstein, 1985; Cohen, 1981). Buffalo and the Western New York region are caught up in a downward spiral of deindustrialization – neither 'restructured' to compete as a prominent participant in the new round of technologically driven advances in information and communications, nor 'restructured' to compete as a leader in the sectoral shift of the United States into service production (Stanback and Noyelle, 1982; Noyelle and Stanback, 1984: Fainstein and Fainstein, 1985).

In a sense, the Western New York region is less evidence of global restructuring than it is an example of how a region can become the victim of global economic change. Hence, the relationship of the Buffalo region to the rest of the state, national and global political economy is one of essential powerlessness. The region, as the victim of global change and a limited participant in the new order, is increasingly *dependent* on outside market and state forces for its economic and social renewal. Without a healthy economic base, the region is unable to participate effectively in macro-level industrial

This article, in part, reflects the results of a series of research articles and papers developed by the staff of the Center for Regional Studies. I would like to thank in particular Robert Dimmig, Manoog Hadeshian, Robert Kraushaar, Jon Lines and Ellen Parker. I would also like to thank Joe Feagin and Michael Peter Smith for their support.

realignment, shifts in national and global competition and adjustments to the new era of limited economic expansion.

Recently, one Buffalo banker described the once industrially powerful region as: 'No more than a Third World country – to be used or ignored as the conditions of risk and profit dictate' (Perry et al., 1985). While the realities of investment can always be simplified by such a blunt statement, this is a fundamentally new way of viewing regions which have been historically at the center of the world economy.

If the Buffalo region is less a participant and more a victim of the present round of restructuring, then theories of dependency rather than restructuring may be more appropriate when describing the political economy of regional distress. Ultimately, the purpose of this paper is to recast notions of restructuring and dependency: (i) to start to develop a contemporary theory of 'distressed regions' in the center or advanced capitalist nations of the world economy; (ii) to clarify the notion of economic distress in the Buffalo region using this refined version of dependency; and (iii) to suggest an alternative agenda for economic development at the center, as well as the periphery, of the world economic system based on the notion of breaking the bonds of regional dependency.

RESTRUCTURING AND DEPENDENCE: APPLICATIONS IN DISTRESSED REGIONS OF ADVANCED CAPITALIST FORMATION

A fortuitous heuristic development of the past decade has been the introduction of a contemporary version of the concept of 'restructuring' into analysis of the world economy. 'Restructuring' is perhaps the most apt and complete of the terms which have been applied by a host of scholars wishing to describe and interpret the impact of the radical changes which have overturned the relations (economic, political, spatial and technological) of the world economy. In its most fundamental sense, restructuring, in the clear words of Edward Soja (1984):

is meant to convey a break in secular trends and a shift toward a significantly different order and configuration of social economic and political life. This evokes a sequence of *breaking down* and *building up* again, *deconstruction* and *attempted reconstitution*, arising from certain incapacities or weaknesses in the established order which preclude conventional adaptations and demand significant structural change instead.

At first glance, this conceptualization, by Soja and others, who have taken up the cause of restructuring, comes rather close to a revised but nevertheless orthodox reincarnation of the Shumpeterian notion of 'creative destruction'. Schumpeter (1942), eschewing the closed inevitability of a system driven by equilibrium, presents an open, entrepreneurial market-place, where the market, as it offered higher and higher opportunity costs in the present mechanism driving the mode of production, became the setting for the movement of capital away from the present inefficient means of production to alternative, new and profitable ones, hence generating a 'creative destruction' or a 'restructuring' of the mechanisms embodying the capitalist mode of production.

While such a definition fits well with the need to design a framework from which to view the global, and indeed even national, processes of spatial (or regional) reproduction of new technologies, leading to the building-up or rebuilding of regions internationally and nationally, such is not the case in regions such as Buffalo. Buffalo is a region long on structural 'destruction' and short on 'creativity' (or entrepreneurial reinvestment). Put another way, the crises of the 1970s still prevail in the region, and they have not been superseded by a technology-driven reconstitution of the mechanisms or means which are the structural core of the region's mode of production. As such the region, as I shall show, is far from 'restructured', 'reconstituted' or 'built up again'.

A further elaboration by Soja (1984) of the concept of restructuring is more apposite when discussing the political economic condition of distressed regions. He suggests that:

restructuring is rooted in crisis and a competitive conflict between the old and the new, between the 'inherited' and the 'projected' order. It is not a mechanical or automatic process, nor are its potential results pre-determined. In its hierarchy of contemporary manifestations, from the local to the global, the restructuring process must be seen as originating in and responding to severe shocks in pre-existing social conditions and configurations: and as triggering an intensification of competitive struggles to control the forces which shape material life.

While these starker terms allow us to come closer to describing the *impact* or the *'experience'* of 'restructuring' in the distressed regions of the capitalist center, such a conceptualization is not sufficient to encompass the aggregation of powerlessness which comes to characterize the social and economic relations of the regional political economy. Therefore, to the concept of restructuring, I would like to add the notion (if not the theory) of 'dependency' when discussing regional 'distress' at the center.

For classical scholars of 'dependency', the use of the concept to study regional economy development in center countries has not been appropriate because, until now, the *dependencia* scholars have been primarily concerned with the conditions of capitalist development at the periphery or semi-periphery (Wallerstein, 1979) of the world economic system. For such scholars, the source of center–periphery dependent relations is rooted in the imperialist 'relation' (Luxemburg, 1968; Fernandes and Ocampo, 1974; Amin, 1977). As such, Fernandes (1979), speaking for this tradition of scholarship, rejects most of what he terms 'theories of dependency' which have been applied to the center, especially the United States, because they are not rooted in a 'theory of imperialism' and have become 'vulgarized, sanitized, and sterilized'.

Dependency theory, or analysis of capitalism using the center–periphery dialectic, is a special inquiry in which the best of the scholars, through time, have posited a theory of the process of global capital formation in the scholarship of the 'imperialization' of peripheral nations in the world economic system. This process of capitalist development of the Third World is, for them, a process of 'dependent modernization' (Fernandes, 1979), or 'dependent development' (Evans, 1979). They have interpretively revealed evidence in the course of their work in the peripheral nations so that we have come to understand the Third World development process in terms of 'dependent capitalism'. This approach is so compelling for some that they conclude that 'the history of capitalism, in our times reveals itself more clearly in the periphery than in the center' (Fernandes and Ocampo, 1974; Fernandes, 1979).

The purpose of this essay is not to quarrel with either the essential intellectual logic or the roots of dependency analysis, as I have described it. Few movements in radical political-economic scholarship have been so rich at both the theoretical and interpretive level of essential Marxist thought, and the level of empirical application (Evans, 1979). I do dispute the notion that 'the history of capitalism in our time is revealed more clearly' in the periphery than the center. With their strong attachment to empirical and case analysis, dependency scholars have been very 'clear' in their application of center–periphery dialects to the conditions of the Third World (Evans, 1978). As such, the scholars of Latin America in particular, and the rest of the world periphery, have 'revealed' more than their structuralist and other centrally located counterparts the relations of dependency in the capitalist world economy. However, the present conditions of the center are evidence of 'dependency' as well. This is a dependency not rooted in classic imperialism but in the combined realities of regional distress which are the consequences of uneven economic development at the center (Castells, 1985). The difference between these distressed victims of 'restructuring' at the center, and the dependent states at the periphery and semi-periphery is the difference between the conditions of 'dependent modernization' (Evans, 1978) in the Third World, predicated on implicit and explicit imperialism rooted in the world system of monopoly capital (Frank, 1967; Baran, 1968; Fernandes and Ocampo, 1974; Evans, 1979), and a rising dialectical condition of 'dependent deindustrialization' in the center where distressed regions experience a destruction of the old industrial base with limited access to the conditions of growth for new, structure-altering means of practicing the mode of production.

For those studying the Third World, the concept of dependent development is characterized by a global pattern of vertical integration of the industrial process, where the product is the internationalization of the market.

'Dependent development' is a special instance of dependency characterized by the association or alliance of international (central or center-based multinational corporate capital) and local (Third World or peripheral or regional) capital. The state also joins the alliance as an active partner and the resulting triple alliance is a fundamental factor in the emergence of dependent development (Evans, 1979). The difference between local capital and international, or central, multinational capital is that multinationals make profit decisions in light of global strategies, while local capital is more prone to make regional strategies to accommodate regionally-based profit decisions.[1]

The third actor in the process of creating dependent relationships is the state. The national-state in the present condition of dependent development is a powerless, reactive actor which has at its heart an essentially aggregative or accumulative strategy of policy-making because, in the first instance, the very creation of 'development' is tied to cooperation with the external sources of capital, or the multinational investment corporation or bank. In spite of substantial evidence, especially in Latin America (Cardoso, 1972; Amin, 1977; Evans, 1979) of state repression of mass participation in the political process and an escalation of support for minority elite interests, the state becomes the dominant 'local' or 'regional' player in the process of 'dependent development' or 'modernization'.

Borrowing from the logic of this thesis, while not overturning the imperialist roots of the core–periphery relationship, I would now like to turn the discussion to the analysis of the center, and look at the effects of a restructured industrial sector of the world economy not as it affects the periphery but as it is experienced at the core. Here dependency is not meant to be wholly a discussion or elaboration of changes in the international division of labor and relations between the center and the periphery as played out in practice in the Third World relation to the capitalist center. Rather, this view of dependency looks at the impact of changes in the international division of labor and relations as evidenced in the 'deindustrializing (restructuring) center'. Such deindustrialization or 'deconstruction' of the social relations and detailed as well as structured division of labor in the distressed region of the center causes increased patterns of regional disintegration of the power resources of regional state and market capital. Put another way, deindustrialization at the center implies destruction of the locally controlled 'mechanisms' of the regional political economy and, more importantly, the destruction of the region's once prominent role in the center of multinational capital and the larger world economy.

A new role emerges for the region: its *relation* with other sectors and centers of capital in the United States and with other forms of state apparatus and resources become, decidedly, *dependent*. The local government, capital and division of labor became increasingly rationalized by *external* public and private sector resources and decisions, thereby rendering whatever growth there is in the industrial base increasingly to a new version of 'dependent deindustrialization'. The hyperbolic words of the local banker gain a clearer and more accurate meaning: the region at the center has achieved a comparatively dependent and powerless parity with regions at the periphery: it is 'no more than a Third World country – to be used or ignored as the conditions of risk and profit dictate.'

STRUCTURAL CHANGE AND CRISIS IN BUFFALO, NEW YORK

The economic decline of Buffalo and western New York did not coincide with the recent decline in heavy manufacturing industry. The present state of distress is the product of a long-term structural disintegration of the region's economic base or foundation. This trend in deindustrialization became the mode of the Buffalo region's[2] disengagement from the powerful center of multinational production and its increasingly dependent relation with the same centers of capital mobilization.

THE HISTORICAL TRANSFORMATION OF THE WESTERN NEW YORK ECONOMY

Buffalo's early history reads like a textbook example of classic restructuring[3] in the United States. For most of the nineteenth century, Buffalo, and its hinterland, enjoyed prominence as one of the true centers of the national economic empire. Dubbed 'the Lion of the West' because of its position at the mouth of the Great Lakes and the Erie Canal, the city, by 1850, was the largest inland port in America. It served as a major mercantile break-and-bulk point for the transport of most of the goods produced in the extraction outposts of the northern Midwest. Nascent manufacturing was based in food-processing activities which transformed the raw agricultural produce into the consumable goods of the rest of the northern and eastern cities. Tanneries, furniture factories, iron workshops and the nation's largest and most productive flour industry, grew up round this commercial base.

These home-grown manufacturing enterprises remained essentially local and did not penetrate markets beyond western New York. The commerce-dominated export base of nineteenth-century western New York mirrored the frontier/mercantile structure of the nation as a whole. This base was undermined in the latter half of the century by the development of the national railroad system. While Buffalo did have a well-developed rail system, the relocation of grain, wheat, wood and mining activities to the south, and the delays in shipping products to Buffalo by water or circuitous rail routes, diverted shipping lanes away from the lake steamers, the canal network, and even Buffalo's place in the rail network.

As this restructuring of the national commercial infrastructure took its toll on the western New York region, the area 'restructured' in classic Soja-type terms (1983) – it emerged as a growing industrial region for such activities as primary metal production. Thus the structural decline in the importance of commerce and grain milling was marked by the gradual transformation of the region's once insular manufacturing sector into a new economic base. Even with this change, between 1860 and the turn of the century, the city did not totally lose its commercial importance. The combination of the new industrial sector and the fact that, in 1900, the area was still the third largest port in the country and the second largest rail terminus, expanded the population of the central city of Buffalo to 350,000.

By the close of World War I, the region had become 'an industrial giant' producing a sizeable share of the nation's steel, railroad cars and engines, aeroplanes and automobiles. The industrial base was transformed through a specialization in heavy manufacturing and, led by the Lackawanna Iron and Steel Company (subsequently the Bethlehem Steel Co.), there were over 50,000 people working in the iron, steel and other primary industries by as early as 1880. By the end of the 1930s, the combined efforts of the Bethelehem Steel Co. and a new General Motors plant had made Buffalo a central producer of automobiles. Employment in central Buffalo reached its peak during World War II with 460,000 workers, nearly 50 per cent of whom (225,000) were in the heavy manufacturing sectors producing steel, aeroplanes, tanks and ships (Doolittle, 1986).

This shift in the structural base of the region's economy was accompanied by a subtle yet important change in the ownership structure of industry as well. In the first three decades of the twentieth century, trends in consolidation and absentee ownership were evident in the city's most powerful and national firms (Goldman, 1983). Briefly, in the early 1900s the largest oil transport companies, food processing companies, street car companies, graneries, theaters, department stores and newspapers in the region were bought by outside firms.[4] By 1930 all the region's largest steel companies and twelve major automobile factories were owned by multi-national companies.

This transformation of the local ownership structure was received as uncompromisingly 'natural' – a simple by-product of the region's economic growth. The growth of the auto industry in general and the Pierce Arrow Company in particular was the most dramatic example of this round of economic restructuring. The Pierce Arrow Company was a local firm which, unlike other auto manufacturers, eschewed the assembly-line for a production process in which a team of workers together made the complete auto. In the process, a 'virtually handmade' product emerged which was perceived to be one of the fastest, most durable and well-designed vehicles in America (Goldman, 1983). The car was so well received that the US government contracted with Pierce Arrow to build trucks for the war effort, thus netting Pierce Arrow over $5 million in 1916. Such a windfall and the offer of a group of New York City investors was enough to convince the owner, George Birge, to sell the plant for over $16 million. The investors, in tune with the changes in manufacturing which emphasized the factory assembly-line in preference to skilled craftsmen as the only way of competing productivity, dismissed all the local management and installed their own New York-based team along with assembly-line production. According to Goldman, by 1920, the company had lost $8 million and in 1928 it was sold again, this time to Studebaker. At the same time General Motors moved to Buffalo, followed soon after by Dunlop, the tire manufacturer.

Today, the old Pierce Arrow factory, standing on the edge of residential downtown Buffalo, lies empty except for a few pigeons and, ironically, horses – its only tenant being a riding stables. Pierce Arrow's experience can be viewed as a prophetic and tragic precursor of the plight of heavy industry in Buffalo, presaging by a few decades the process of structural crisis which would infect many sub-sectors of the regional industrial base. In the years following World War I the region's economy would boom as it became a center of steel, railroad, auto and other forms of machinery and heavy manufacturing. At the same time this increasingly industrialized economy was 'owned' by outsiders: 'By the end of the 1920's Buffalo had lost practically any ability to control its own economic destiny' (Goldman, 1983).

While the manufacturing economy, the twentieth-century economic base of the western New York region, peaked during World War II, the region suffered a precipitous drop of some 125,000 workers soon after the war ended. This was led by the close of the Curtiss Wright plant which employed over 40,000 workers during its wartime heyday. Concentrating for a moment on the industrial core of the region, the two-country Erie–Niagara area, Fred Doolittle (1986) identifies another important secular trend in the postwar period which amplifies the importance of heavy manufacturing controlled by outside ownership: with every recession of the postwar era, manufacturing employment has ratcheted down; that is to say, the region's post-recession recoveries have never been enough to compensate fully for the loss of employment incurred as a result of the recession (Doolittle, 1986) (see figure 5.1). Spurred by major retrenchment in the auto industry, especially at General Motors and Ford, coupled with corporate decisions which effectively close all the major steel industries in the region including Bethlehem and Republic, the region's economy has experienced a structural crisis from which it has been unable to fully recover.

As figure 5.1 indicates, and is further displayed for the entire region in table 5.1, the decline in manufacturing is a pervasive one, affecting all the 'active'[5] sectors of the region's industrial economy. When the St Lawrence Seaway opened in 1959 the final nail was hammered into the coffin of western New York's long-successful commercial base, making the region,

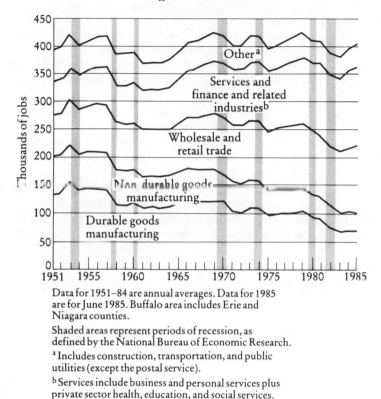

Data for 1951–84 are annual averages. Data for 1985
are for June 1985. Buffalo area includes Erie and
Niagara counties.

Shaded areas represent periods of recession, as
defined by the National Bureau of Economic Research.

[a] Includes construction, transportation, and public
utilities (except the postal service).

[b] Services include business and personal services plus
private sector health, education, and social services.

*FIGURE 5.1 Private non-agricultural employment in the Erie and Niagara Counties area
(from United States Department of Labor and New York State Department of Labor,
Doolittle, 1986)*

for most of the postwar period, even more dependent on its manufacturing
base. Initially, this dependence on manufacturing, especially heavy manufacturing, was masked by conditions of a world economy devastated by war. But
as the semi-periphery and periphery of the world economic system
restructured and subsequently captured a competitive share of the heavy
industrial base, the manufacturing sectors of Western New York were not
strong enough to pull the core of the region up to full recovery from cyclical
recessionary buffeting. The region's base was disintegrated in structural
terms: the manufacturing mechanism driving the mode of production in
Western New York had entered a period of long-term decline.

This pattern of structural crisis becomes all the more evident when we
compare the region to the rest of the nation. The shift of Buffalo's economy
away from manufacturng did not mean that the region had totally lost its
competitive edge in manufacturing. As we can see in table 5.1, the
manufacturing sectors generally retained greater than average national

employment rates in all key sectors of the manufacturing base. At the same time while in 1950 four out of the top of five of the region's employment leaders were in the manufacturing sector, by 1980 four out of the top five employment sectors were in the non-manufacturing or service sectors: education, health, retail trade and financial services. Therefore, at one level, the Chamber of Commerce approach to the region would say that the region was still competitive in manufacturing and growing in the new service sector. But again, table 5.1, when viewed more closely, provides a rather different picture. In manufacturing sectors of the US economy suffering absolute job losses as a result of international trends, the region suffered job losses two to twenty times the national rate. And in areas where the national economy grew (especially machinery, electrical manufacturing and printing) the region either suffered precipitous losses or grew significantly slower than the national average.

Regional growth in the rest of the non-manufacturing base is also suspect when compared to the rates of growth and change at the national level. As the data in table 5.1 indicate, the most dramatic growth occurs in these new sectors of the economy – mirroring changes nationally – but at rates (location quotients) that do not exhibit even marginally competitive (i.e. export base-generating) levels.

TABLE 5.1   *Employment data for the most active industrial sectors in the Western New York region 1977–82*

Sector	Employment		% change (US)	% change (region)	Location quotient[a] (1982)
	1977	1982			
Manufacturing					
20 Food and kindred products	13,395	12,081	−2.36	−9.81	−1.25
25 Furniture	3,774	3,254	−2.03	−13.78	1.13
26 Paper	4,870	4,473	−4.04	−8.15	1.12
27 Printing	8,736	9,571	15.11	9.56	1.12
20 Chemicals	9,500	8,632	0.68	−9.14	1.47
32 Stone, clay, glass	8,492	6,950	9.30	−18.16	1.93
34 Fabricated metals	18,484	15,380	−1.23	−16.79	1.56
35 Machinery, except electric	37,965	29,511	12.55	−22.27	1.91
36 Electric products	15,296	14,906	15.23	−6.40	1.15
37 Transportation equipment	20,375	15,609	−7.89	−23.39	1.43
38 Instruments and related product	4,185	3,689	12.12	−11.85	0.89
Wholesale trade					
50 Wholesale durable goods	16,848	17,973	16.53	6.68	0.94
51 Wholesale non-durable goods	11,041	11,399	12.50	3.24	0.85

TABLE 5.1 *(Continued)*

Sector	Employment		% change (US)	% change (region)	Location quotient[a] (1982)
	1977	1982			
FIRE[b]					
60 Banking	10,329	11,545	22.80	11.77	1.10
61 Credit	1,514	1,489	24.03	−1.65	0.37
62 Security	543	640	40.65	17.86	0.37
63 Insurance carriers	5,464	5,616	8.19	2.78	0.70
64 Insurance agents	2,946	3,472	26.65	17.85	1.08
65 Real estate	3,503	3,700	12.00	5.62	0.58
66 Combined real estate	175	136	−14.09	−22.29	0.82
67 Holding/other investments	274	809	−20.93	195.26	0.77
Services					
73 Business services	14,948	17,192	40.45	15.01	0.81
Tourism services					
70 Hotels	4,042	4,171	23.61	3.19	0.56
78 Motion pictures	715	749	11.15	4.76	0.57
79 Amusements	4,815	5,810	29.64	20.66	1.16
84 Museums	60	244	30.78	306.67	1.25
Other services					
60 Health services	33,758	43,535	33.77	28.96	1.14
82 Educational services	6,856	9,305	34.42	35.72	1.06
Total (all sectors)	489,235	489,268	14.35	0.0067	

[a] The location quotient is a ratio that measures the industrial concentration in a particular region or spatial setting. The numerator is employment in a given sector of the region divided by total regional employment, and the denominator is the national figures for the same sector and total. If the location quotient is greater than one then the region is assumed to have more employment in a given sector than does the nation.
[b] Finance, insurance and real estate sectors.

Source: US Department of Commerce, Bureau of the Census.

Looking at the most recent data for the industrial core for the region, the present upturn following the most recent recession has been no more successful than any in the past. As the nation recovered, the region's most promising and historically active sectors did not. With the exception of transportation equipment, all sectors have suffered a continued loss of jobs (see table 5.2).

In conclusion, the Buffalo region's original commercial structural base is dead, its manufacturing base, securely centered in heavy manufacturing, is

TABLE 5.2   Erie–Niagara County trends in manufacturing, 1983, 1984 and 1985 (total and most active sectors)

SIC	Sector	1983[a]	1984[a]	1985[b]	Net change 1983–4	Net change 1984–5
20–39	Total manu-facturing	103,700	104,700	103,900	+1,000	−800
20	Food process-ing	8,400	8,300	8,200	−100	−100
26	Paper	3,000	3,100	2,900	+100	−200
27	Printing	8,500	8,800	8,700	+300	−100
28	Chemicals	8,000	7,600	7,300	−400	−300
32	Stone, clay ceramics	4,300	4,200	4,100	−100	−100
34	Fabricated metals	9,800	10,600	10,400	+800	−200
35	Non-electrical machinery	9,900	10,600	10,100	+700	−500
36	Electrical products	9,200	9,500	9,200	+300	−300
37	Transport equipment	17,600	19,700	21,200	+2,100	+1,500

[a] 1983 and 1984 annual averages compiled by the New York State Department of Labor, Division of Research and Statistics.
[b] 1985 figures represent ten-month (January–October 1985) averages compiled from the New York State Department of Labor, Division of Research and Statistics by the Center for Regional Studies, SUNYAB.

substantially vitiated, and its growth in alternative sectors such as education, health, finance and the like has not been sufficient enough to make it competitive nationally much less internationally. In this recent round of long-term, deep-seated secular decline, there has been no dramatic 'reindustrialization' or 'reconstruction' (in Soja's terms) of the 'mechanism' or means of employing the mode of production at a regional level. The region is dependent on a heavy industrial base. This is owned by outside multinational capital, which has consistently disinvested in the regional factories as they became victims of a peripheralization of the productive activities they represent and now are essentially powerless to effect their own renewal. The evidence of the costs of such powerlessness are what I call dependent deindustrialization at the center of the world economic system.

DEPENDENT DEINDUSTRIALIZATION IN BUFFALO, NEW YORK

The epoch-defining changes in the national economy, as it evolved from a mercantile to an industrial and then a service economy have been reflected in the restructuring of the western New York economy. The region was able to participate in the commercial and industrial eras in relatively significant ways which added greatly to the population, job base and wage structure of the region. The latest round of secular decline in the industrial mechanism of the region has not been accompanied by a significant restructuring of the means of production – there have been only modest increases in the service economy and the technological revolution has in large part passed by the region.[6] At present, prospects for the region to regain its place at the center of the economy are doubtful. The population has suffered a precipitous decline and the sex and age structure of those who remain exhibits disturbing signs of long-term unemployment, welfare and age-based dependency and poverty.

POPULATION: THE DEMOGRAPHY OF DEPENDENCY AT THE CENTER

The Buffalo region experienced one of the most dramatic population losses between 1970 and 1980 of any major industrial region in the USA dropping 5.3 per cent (from 1,758,355 to 1,644,728). The core counties suffered most of this decline, losing 106,638 persons over the decade. Recent census data estimates show a further loss of 36,428 between 1980 and 1984. The future is not much more optimistic. By the year 2000, the population of western New York will have stagnated at 1,654,560; about 10,000 fewer than lived in the region in 1980.[7] But in some ways this future demographic stagnation is the good news. The more disturbing feature is the demographic realignment or 'restructuring' that will attend this continued decline in regional population. Using the same population projections, and breaking them down into age strata. I project that western New York will lose 107,384 of its population in the 15–24 age group by the year 2000 (Batutis and Scardamalia, 1985). If this is correct, this will leave the region with a serious shortage of people who represent the future labor force. Almost 60 per cent of the population will be over the age of 30. Those over the age of 65 will have risen from 207,168 in 1980 to 265,030 in the year 2000, an increase of 28 per cent. While this latter group compromised 12 per cent of the population in 1980 they will make up 16 per cent of the region's population by 2000, exceeding the absolute number of people aged between 15 and 24 by over 60,000.

These figures raise some rather important issues for the future of the region. Traditionally, a major resource of the region has been its pool of skilled labor. If Castells and others are correct, the future of a technologically restructured region, or the new 'center' rests in part on a 'large pool of well-trained, diverse and flexible workers'. The large outmigration of the region's young workers, as indicated by the data, leaves western New York with the wrong type of labor pool needed if the region is to participate in the latest round of economic restructuring in the center of the global economy.

Instead the demographic data suggest that the future labor pool in western New York will be characterized by older workers who will require massive public investments for retraining and who, by dint of their past experience, are less flexible and responsive to future technologies. The aging of the region's population also means larger amounts of structurally unemployed and increased dependence of the population on welfare payments. This is especially true when it is observed that the over 65 year olds will actually be a larger percentage of the region's population by 2000 than the 15 to 24 year olds.

These general demographic shifts are fuelled by two other patterns of economic disintegration: (1) a shift in the regional job structure from manufacturing to services, and (2) the increasing dependence of residents on long-term welfare assistance.

The decline in the skill of the labor force is closely linked to a decline in the attractiveness of the private sector jobs availale in the region. Employment figures for the four largest counties of western New York – Erie, Niagara, Chautauqua and Cattaraugus – comprise over 92 per cent of the region's private sector jobs. A study by Perry et al. (1985) of these counties reveals that a massive realignment of the job structure has accompanied the deindustrialization of the region.

TABLE 5.3   Ranked payroll and employment data for major SIC sectors for employed workforce in four County regions,[a] 1970–82

	Number employed		Change in number employed	Change in % employed	Mean payroll ranked
	1970	1982	1970–82	1970–82	1982
Total	467,529	452,149	−15,380	−3.29	15,287
Construction	18,911	15,376	−3,535	−18.69	23,284
Transportation and utlities	27,913	24,230	−3,675	−13.17	21,570
Manufacturing	200,265	141,144	−59,121	−29.52	21,414
Mining	371	977	606	163.34	19,133
Wholesale	28,461	29,010	549	1.93	18,252
FIRE[b]	22,696	26,490	3,794	16.72	16,694
Agriculture	870	1,017	147	16.90	13,769
Services	77,483	115,812	38,329	49.47	10,962
Retail	90,024	97,721	7,697	8.55	7,680

[a] Erie, Niagara, Chautauqua and Cattaraugus Counties.
[b] Finance, insurance and real estate sectors.

Source: United States Department of Commerce; Bureau of the Census: County Business Patterns, 1970–82.

Between 1970 and 1982, the manufacturing, transportation and construction sectors lost a total of 66,331 jobs (see table 5.3). These three sectors made up 53 per cent of the total employment for the four county areas in 1970, but by 1982, they comprised only 40 per cent of total employment. The average payroll per employee in these declining sectors was 21,582 or 141 per cent of the average payroll per employee across all sectors ($15,287).

The most rapidly growing sectors were services and retail, increasing by 46,026 employees, and comprising 47.2 per cent of the total regional workforce in 1982 as compared to 35.8 per cent in 1970. The average payroll of $9181 per employee, however, was only 60 per cent of the average payroll per employee across all sectors. Hence, the most dramatic growth in employment opportunities in the region was in those sectors of the economy with low-paid work while the highest income opportunities were shrinking, or, in many cases, shutting down.

The growth in low-paid service sector jobs was accompanied by historic growth in the region's unemployed. During the period 1976–82, the entire state of New York experienced a decline of 13.9 per cent in unemployment, while Western New York's percentage of unemployed went *up* by 18 per cent. In 1985, Western New York's unemployment rate, while substantially below the historic double figure rates of the early 1980s, continues to be the highest in the State.

All these trends combine to make poverty and low income a fact of life for increasing numbers of Western New York residents. In the eight counties 8.7 to 13.6 per cent of the population claim welfare assistance and these figures have increased every year since 1970. The data in table 5.4 shows

TABLE 5.4 *Percentage change in public assistance recipients and expenditure WNY and selected NYS Counties, 1970–85*

| | 1970–80 | | 1980–85 | |
	Recip. %	Expnd %	Recip. %	Expnd. %
New York State	−7.5	70.0	4.5	33.1
New York City	−15.3	58.6	4.3	40.3
Western New York	24.3	125.1	24.8	97.4
Erie	23.1	122.2	25.0	97.4
Niagara	20.0	98.3	41.6	123.9
Suffolk	27.0	103.6	−25.0	27.1
Monroe	13.8	96.8	42.4	108.1
Westchester	26.5	159.2	−11.7	28.1
Onondaga	−30.0	17.3	9.5	67.6
Nassau	−25.0	13.3	−36.6	−10.8
Albany	40.0	169.6	−42.9	−11.3

Source: New York State Department of Social Services, *Social Statistics*.

128 *Economic Restructuring in Cities*

consistently higher numbers of welfare recipients and expenditures in the region – higher than the State, New York City and other comparable areas. If the economic and demographic restructuring continues as it is projected, the poor, working poor, and aged will be characterized by increased dependence on state and federal income subsidies. A recent report by the New York State Comptroller similarly shows that the yearly percentage of payments to welfare recipients in western New York is rising more rapidly than other areas of the state. Indeed, while the patterns of public assistance dependency are dropping in other metropolitan regions, a rise is projected for the Buffalo area as it becomes the home of disproportionately large numbers of structurally unemployed and aged – a situation demanding increased shares of long-term assistance.

DEINDUSTRIALIZED DEPENDENCY AND THE STATE

As the economic decline drives increasing numbers out of the region or onto welfare or some other form of public assistance, the importance of transfer payments to the deindustrialized economy as a whole becomes even more pronounced. Sam Cole (1986), in a recent study of Buffalo, analyzed the relationship between economic growth in the region and social distribution and discovered that of the three types of economic development policy the state pursues in distressed regions (those which generate new economic activities, those which stimulate the retention of old activities and transfer payment policies) only increased welfare transfers effect a positive distributional equity between the rich and the poor. Using a social accounting matrix, which is a table that organizes the region's economic and social accounts into inputs and outputs. Cole discovered that the first two types of public policies reinforce the maldistributive and regionally unhealthy leakage of the lion's share of productive surplus out of the region: 'For some time the region has been a net exporter of surplus – hemorraging as its sluggish private sector exports from the local economy and as the public sector exports revenues. At the same time the region has become dependent on transfers from the outside economy which affect social distribution' (Cole, 1986).

More precisely, Cole discovers that the transfer of money from the federal and state government to 'lower income households (say the bottom 50 per cent by income) exhibits a relatively high multiplier in the local economy because lower income households have a relatively low propensity to save and pay fewer taxes than higher income households.' However, he also discovers that the consumption pattern in low-income households is such that, while the money is spent in the region, the surplus realized from such consumption (or wage income stimulated by such consumption) dispropor- tionately ends up as income for the rich. Therefore, the results of Cole's study suggest that dependence on the state for transfer payments in deindustrializing regions like Buffalo is a two-edged sword: On the one hand, it is (paradoxically) the most effective form of distributional public policy, yet on the other hand, the ' "downstream" effects supporting low-income households are gained predominantly by higher income households'.

Even with this productive effect of transfer payments, they are not seen in Buffalo (or elsewhere in the United States) as a part of 'formal' or avowed economic development planning and policy. Indeed, most forms of economic development policy and planning deliberately eschew any direct distributional or equity issues. The conditions of deindustrialization and economic distress are viewed as evidence in the United States of a lack of attention to the needs of capital. Profit, and not equity, is the issue of the day in contemporary urban America.

At present it is estimated that more than 80 federal, state and local government agencies are located in Western New York with a direct or indirect mandate to provide 'economic development policy' to the region. The bulk of these programs are directed to overcoming the structural realities which stand in the way of either regenerating the historical past or attracting a 'high technology' future, always with the goal of providing more jobs. This is a highly simplistic and, quite candidly, over-optimistic summary of the public agenda. More to the point is the fact that this entire amalgam of governmental agencies and programs has become integral to almost every facet of private sector reinvestment in the regional economy.[8]

The leaders of the major local economic development agencies were asked recently to estimate what percentage of business start-ups and expansions over $750,000 inaugurated in a manufacturing or production sector occurred without a governmental subsidy or support. The answers varied, but it was estimated that almost 90 per cent of all private sector initiatives in this category were no longer 'purely private'. In the Western New York region capital has come to depend upon – indeed expect – government subsidies to 'sweeten the development pie'. Put another way, the private economy does not work alone in Western New York. More ominously, the region is so substantially unattractive that regional planning must be decidedly accumulative in its approach if it expects to mount a 'successful approach' to 'restructuring' the region 'affirmatively'.

One example of this dependence on public sector subsidies is the recent history of leverage buyouts (LBOs) in the core industrial county of Erie. In the last ten years ten firms with over 100 employees have been bought out by local capital (table 5.5). All but one of these takeovers demanded state aid (financial subsidies and/or tax concessions: see last column of table 5.5). Only in the case of the Whiting Roll Up Door Co. did the buyout occur without direct local and/or state participation. In the cases of American Brass, and Dunlop, a review of the negotiations surrounding both suggest that the investors had significant investment capital and, it

TABLE 5.5　Erie County, locally bought-out firms' last 10 years: Manufacturing
firms with 100 or more employees

Firm	Local employment	Year locally bought	Local agencies
American Brass, Buffalo	850	1985	ECIDA[a] WNYEDC
Dunlop Tire & Rubber Corp, Grand Island	1,500	1985	ECIDA WNYEDC[b]
W & F. Manufacturing Co., Tonawanda	166	1984	ECIDA
F. N. Burt Co., Inc., Cheektowaga	260	1983	ECIDA
Globe International, Inc., Buffalo	144	1983	ECIDA
Buffalo Batt & Felt, Inc., Depew	115	1983	ECIDA
Barrister Information Systems, Buffalo	132	1982	split from Comptek
McDonald Products, Buffalo	103	1981	ECIDA
Hard Manufacturing Co., Buffalo	120	1980	ECIDA
Whiting Roll-Up Door Mfg, Akron	146	1977	
Total	3,536		

[a] Erie County Industrial Development Agency.
[b] Western New York Economic Development Corporation.

Sources: SUNY Center for Regional Studies, Buffalo; ECIDA.

would seem, could have been successful without an government subsidy. But
when it comes to investing in a deindustrialized region like Western New
York, the institutionalization of public subsidy has become so pervasive that
it is now expected. In a very real sense government participation is perceived
as part of the 'competitive advantage' of regions in structural crisis.

DEINDUSTRIAL DEPENDENCY AND EXTERNAL CAPITAL

Local capitalists and economic development planners have also come to
depend on outside capital, and the decisions made by outside capital, when
assessing and responding to economic change in the region. Of the 49
manufacturing firms employing more than 500 workers still in Western New
York, 15 remain locally-owned and these employ a little over 16,000

TABLE 5.6   *WNY large manufacturing firms (500+ employment) including General Motors*

	Organizational structure				
	Independent	Parent	Branch	Subsidiary	Row
Firms	1	2	3	4	total
Employing:					
	3	3	2	6	14
500–749	1,700	1,800	1,100	3,440	8,040
	1	2	7	2	12
750–999	900	1,610	5,897	1,517	9,924
	0	2	3	5	10
1,000–499	0	2,142	3,350	5,770	11,262
	0	4	5	4	13
1,500+	0	8,200	24,200	9,400	41,800
	4	11	17	17	49
Total	2,600	13,752	34,547	20,127	71,026

Source: SUNY Center for Regional Studies, Buffalo.

workers. The remaining 34 firms employ almost 55,000 workers (see table 5.6) and are all owned by outside capital.

Similarly, of manufacturing firms employing over 100 workers, more than 62 per cent of the workforce (77,775) were employed by firms owned by outside capital. The region's manufacturing base is now substantially owned by outside capital. By itself this fact is not important, but further analysis suggests that the majority of employment in what remains of the industrial base of the region is now effectively 'held hostage' to the decisions of outside capital, since our analysis of plant closures in New York State suggests that these subsidiaries are far more likely to be closed than independent or locally-owned firms. Analysis of the plants closed in the region's core counties of Erie and Niagara between 1965 and 1980 shows that companies with out-of-town headquarters were twice as likely to close as locally-owned companies. Conversely, if local planners could get local investors involved in a buyout of the firm, then the firm would be more likely to stay in the region and expand. The only problem has been that in distressed regions, buyouts have traditionally not been local. In western New York, the largest have been by outside capital employing six times as many workers as local capital employs.[9]

Once the firm is in the hands of outside investors, the decisions to relocate, expand, or close are made less on the basis of regional location advantages than on overall multinational corporate strategy. Local operations are frequently closed or reorganized because the parent corporation is divesting or rationalizing its operations. In some instances, the outside-based takeovers discussed above are engineered to make the local plant a 'cash cow', to be milked for capital investment and expansion elsewhere.

The effect of this outside ownership has been to encourage destabilization of the regional economy. Given the lack of local linkages and the tendency of these outside firms to close, the regional economy dependent on external capital cannot be said to have stabilized.

SETTING A REGIONAL AGENDA OF DISTRIBUTIONAL EQUITY IN A WORLD ECONOMIC SYSTEM

This section could alternatively be titled: 'Breaking the Bonds of Deindustrial Dependency'. In real terms this means setting a regionally-based strategy for planning for regional enpowerment of a dimension that at least establishes regional interdependence with the larger economic order, if not independence from the threatening vicissitudes of world capitalism and the present international division of labor.

Distributional policy at the center, especially the deindustrialized center, must be directed towards a refined notion of deindustrial dependency; namely, the conditions and issues of structural powerlessness that characterize regional *relations* with national and international capital. The second set of issues which need to be constantly specified by analysis of dependency at the center of the world economic order, are the *impacts* or *effects* of regional deindustrialization on the residents of the region. Hence, the foundation of contemporary distributional planning in distressed regions rests on breaking the relations of dependency and ameliorating the effects as experienced regionally of such relations.

Present patterns of state–capital relations suggest that such an assessment of the agenda for distributive economic development planning will not be received as legitimate by either state planners or regional centers of capital investment. As the banker said, regions at the center are like any other peripheral or semi-peripheral region, when it comes to consideration for capital investment. Realistically, present state–capital institutions cannot be viewed as sources of distributional planning: one can hardly expect the institutional architects of dependency at the core to alter radically their agendas and break the bonds of capitalism they have imposed, or perpetuate. At present, the sources of authentic distributional or equitable economic planning in regions such as Buffalo remain problematic. Therefore, while the following concluding thoughts may appear logical, they remain, realistically, quite speculative.

If there is a conclusion to be drawn from the case analysis of Buffalo, it is that these structural crises of deindustrialization at the center create a relation of dependency with multinational capital which keeps the region trapped in the non-competitive throes of the new international division of labor. Further, if there is a source for change and the initiation of distributional planning in the name of regional economic relief from dependency, it rests with labor. Organized labor has been almost totally unforthcoming in addressing the recent round of structural crisis. Caught almost exclusively in the mode of addressing issues of on-the-job retrenchment and benefits, labor unions in the region have been as powerless as any other regional body in the effectiveness of their response to the growing conditions of deindustrial dependency. At the same time, organized labor remains the most visible and important remaining *organized* unit of potential institutional response to the issues of equity raised by dependency at the advanced capitalist center. The agenda for labor is to organize *off* the job as much if not more than on the job. Local unions in the United States, and especially in Western New York area, could, because of their organizational history, be the focus of direction and mobilization of a distributional approach to deindustrial dependency.

A labor-directed agenda of distributional planning would be a two tiered approach, where labor directs its energies to a region-wide agenda of social and economic development and to an international agenda; thereby placing regional labor within the context of the world economy. The time for a substantial rethinking and redirection of the entire activity of labor is at hand. At a minimum the issues of dependency should force organized labor at the deindustrialized center to new *relations* with the community and new relations with world labor.

Secondly, the public sector at the regional level must wrest or otherwise capture 'state' power at the regional level. Put another way, if authentic region-based economic development is to occur in a way that breaks the inevitable relations and effects of dependency, then public sector power will have to be institutionalized at the regional level. Most immediately in Buffalo, this means re-organizing the number and modes of state–local relationships – stripping away many of the extraneous (to regional redevelopment) public agencies and reinvesting the considerable public financial resources and political legitimacy in a regional authority (Perry et al., 1985; Markusen, 1986) directly linked to the workers, capital and larger community of the region. The issue of regional empowerment in both political and institutional terms remains as strong and important in the era of economic restructuring as it has in past eras of contemporary urban change.

A third and equally important area of distributional debate is the re-organization of regional capital. Regions at the center, even those like Buffalo, have substantial amounts of capital owned by business labor and the state. The pattern of ownership and use of local capital must be placed in the hands and under the control of local investors, workers and the unemployed. Therefore, primary issues of regional planning include the application and mix of programs which increase the number of local LBOs, and worker takeovers. Local planning must also seek to mobilize local investment capital such as labor pension funds and transfer payment reforms. Finally, distributional planning must stimulate new relations between labor and capital through the implementation of local training programs and industrial effectiveness efforts.

The goal of this entire redirection of planning efforts is to enhance the power of regional labor, capital and government in an effort to break the bonds of industrial dependency, thereby establishing *new relationships* between the region and the center of state and capital. The *effects* of a new round of regional interdependence will create economic equity within the region and the rest of the world economic system. Quite obviously, the efforts outlined in this last section are not enough to accomplish all this by themselves. What is important is that efforts at regional economic development planning in these areas and elsewhere have as their primary goals the creation of *relations* with the rest of the economy which create neither a new round of dependency nor deepening strata of inequities in social relations.

NOTES

1 Evans (1978) enlists the work of Simon (1965) and March and Simon (1958) to explain the difference in local versus multinational decision-making as a function of the span of information each has at its disposal. Both decision structures are captured by 'bounded rationality' or imperfect information which serves as the boundaries within which decisions affecting the investment of capital and the organization of production are made.

2 The Buffalo region is comprised of the core county of Erie which is the location of the central City of Buffalo, the surrounding core counties of Niagara and Chautauqua which have, along with Erie, had a long and stormy industrial history and the more rural counties of Allegany, Genesee, Ontario, Wyoming and Cattaraugus. In all these eight counties make up the accepted western New York region of New York State.

3 As described by Schumpeter (1942) as 'creative destruction' and Soja (1984) as 'reconstitution' of the regional economy.

4 Standard Oil bought out one of Buffalo's largest oil transporting companies. In the early 1900s, processing and milling of grains, an activity which gained Buffalo the designation 'The Flour City', was substantially bought out by such firms as Washburn Company of Minneapolis and Quaker Oats. In 1905 the City's largest department store was bought out by the New York firm Associated Merchants, and the region's three largest streetcar manufacturing companies were purchased by a Morgan Bank affiliate which was then bought by the International Traction Company of Philadelphia (Goldman, 1983).

The pattern of consolidation and external control of the leading production firms of western New York only intensified in the next two decades. While the local newspapers and movie theaters were bought out by such firms as Scripps Howard and Fox Theaters, the steel industries and the twelve major automobile factories were all outside-owned. And whatever major grain and flour milling operations that had not been bought out in the previous era were overtaken during this period.

5 The SIC codes which embody the most productive industries in the region.

6 Manuel Castells (1985), in a comprehensive synthesis of the scholarship on the location of high-technology mechanism of the capitalist mode of production, gives five reasons for the location of significant new or agglomerated technological research, management and fabrication. High technology locates where there is (i) major universities, research units and a large pool of technical and scientific labor; (ii) a historically proven cluster of military/defense/related test units or sites; (iii) limited history of unionization not because of high wages but because union labor is slow to change and highly bureaucratizes; (iv) a high level of wealth which is socially organized in an entrepreneurial manner oriented to non-traditional finance and venture markets; (v) a good location in the advanced communication network of production (a process which is characterized by a highly discrete division of labor) which can be hierarchically divided spatially in regional, national even global terms. The Buffalo region as we shall see does not exhibit a substantial competitive advantage in any of these characteristics of Castell's synthetic model of the spatial location of high-technology production. Castells also draws heavily on the work of Glasmeier, et al. (1983), Storper (1982), Walker and Storper (1984), Markusen (1984) and Hall et al. (1984).

7 These demographic figures are all calculated for the eight-county western New York area by using New York State Department of Commerce demographic projections (Batutis and Scardamalia, 1985).

8 See Perry et al. (1985) for a more detailed discussion of this point.

9 See Perry et al. (1985) and the on-going data collection project conducted by Robert Kraushaar at the Center for Regional Studies.

REFERENCES

Amin, Samir (1977) 'Self-reliance and the New International Economic Order', *Monthly Review* (July–August), 29 (3): 1–21.

Baran, Paul (1968) *The Political Economy of Growth*, New York: Monthly Review Press.

Batutis, Michael J. and Robert Scardamalia (1985) *Official Population Projections for New York State Counties: 1980 to 2010*. Albany: New York State Department of Commerce.

Cardoso, Fernando Henrique (1972) 'Dependency and development in Latin America', *The New Left Review*, 74: 3–95.

Castells, Manuel (1985) 'High technology, economic restructuring, and the urban-regional process in the United States'. In M. Castells (ed.), *High Technology Pace and Society*, Beverly Hills, Caly: Sage, pp. 11–40.

Cohen, Robert (1981) 'The new international division of labor, multinational corporations and urban hierarchy'. In M. Dear and A. Scott, *Urbanization and Urban Planning in Capitalist Society*, New York: Methuen, pp. 287–315.

Cole, Sam (1986) 'Growth, equity and dependence in a deindustrializing city region', Working Paper, Center for Regional Studies, SUNY at Buffalo, New York.

Doolittle, Fred J. C. (1986) 'Adjustments in Buffalo's labor Market', *Federal Reserve Board of New York Quarterly Review* (Winter 1985/6).

Evans, Peter (1979) *Dependent Development and the Alliance of Multinational, State and Local Capital in Brazil*, Princeton, N.J.: Princeton University Press.

Fainstein, Norman I. and Susan S. Fainstein (1985) 'Economic restructuring and the politics of land use planning in New York City'. Presented at the Annual Meeting of the ACSP, Atlanta, November.

Fernandes, Florestan (1979) Foreword to P. Evans *Dependent Development, op. cit.*

Fernandes, Florestan and Jose F. Ocampo (1974) 'The Latin American revolution: A Theory of imperialism, not dependence', *Latin American Perspectives*, 1 (1): 30–61.

Frank, André Gundar (1967) *Capitalism and Underdevelopment in Latin America*, New York: Monthly Review Press.

Galsmeier, Amy (1985) 'The bifurcated occupational structure of high-tech industries: Implications for the regional division of labor'. Paper presented at the Annual Meeting of ACSP, Atlanta, Georgia.

Glasmeier, Amy, Peter Hall and Ann Markusen (1984) 'Can everyone have a slice of the high-tech pie?', *The Berkeley Planning Journal*, 1.

Goldman, Mark (1983) *High Hopes: The Rise and Decline of Buffalo, New York*, Albany, N.Y.: SUNY Press.

Luxemburg, Rosa (1968) *The Accumulation of Capital*, New York: Monthly Review Press.

March, James and Herbert Simon (1958) *Organizations*, New York: John Wiley and Sons.

Markusen, Ann (1984) *Profit Cycles, Oligopoly, and Regional Development*. Cambridge, Mass.: MIT Press.

Markusen, Ann (1986) *Steel and Southeast Chicago: Reasons and Opportunities for Industrial Renewal*, Evanston, Ill.: Center for Urban Affairs and Policy Research.

Noyelle, Thierry J. and Thomas M. Stanback (1984) *The Economic Transformation of American Cities*, Towota, N.J.: Rowman and Allanheld.

Perry, David, Robert Kraushaar, Jon Lines and Ellen Parker (1985) 'Ending regional economic dependency: Economic development policy for distressed regions', *Studies in Planning and Design*, Buffalo: Center for Regional Studies at SUNY, Buffalo.

Schumpeter, Joseph A. (1942) *Capitalism, Socialism, and Democracy*, New York: Harper.

Simon, Herbert (1965) *Administrative Behavior*, New York: The Free Press.

Soja, Edward, Rosalie Morales and Goetz Wolff (1983) 'Urban restructuring: an analysis of social and spatial changes in Los Angeles', *Economic Geography* 59 (2).

Soja, Edward (1984) 'LA is the place: economic restructuring and the inter-materialization of the Los Angeles region'. Presented at the Annual Meeting of the ASA, San Antonio, Texas.

Stanback, Thomas M. and Thierry J. Noyelle (1982) *Cities in Transition*, Towata, N.J.: Allanheld, Osmun & Co.

Walker, Richard and Michael Storper (1984) 'The spatial division of labor: Labor and the location of industry'. In Larry Sawers and William Tabb (eds), *Sunbelt/Snowbelt, Urban Development and Regional Restructuring*, New York: Oxford University Press, pp. 19–47.

Wallerstein, Immanuel (1979) *The Capitalist World-Economy*, Cambridge University Press.

6

Growth and Informalization at the Core: A Preliminary Report on New York City

Saskia Sassen-Koob

This chapter seeks to elucidate one particular aspect in the formation and expansion of informal sectors in major cities of highly industrialized countries. Does the increasing economic polarization brought about by new growth trends contain conditions that promote informalization in a wide range of activities? Linking informalization and growth takes the analysis beyond the notion that the emergence of informal sectors in cities like New York and Los Angeles is caused by the presence of large numbers of immigrants and their tendency to replicate survival strategies typical of Third World countries. Linking informalization and growth also takes the analysis beyond the notion that unemployment and recession generally may be the key factors promoting informalization in the current phase of highly industrialized economies.

Linking informalization and growth may point to characteristics of advanced capitalism that are not typically noted. It may also contribute yet another component to analyses of the informal sector in Third World cities that show its articulation with global capital accumulation. Finally, in so far as the existence of large immigrant communities mediates in the process of informalization, an analysis that links this process with structural conditions of advanced capitalism, should provide new variables for an understanding of the role of immigration in the current phase of such economies.

In order to identify systemic links between informalization and structural conditions in advanced capitalism I shall examine the effects of major growth trends in shaping a vast array of types of job, types of firms and subcontracting patterns that induce or are conducive to informalization. There is no precise measure of informalization and there is no exhaustive evidence. Juxtaposing these systemic trends with the available evidence should permit inferences about the patterns and scope of informalization. I shall focus on New York City, specifically the two major growth sectors which together with the general shift to services, define the current

Presented at the Symposium on the Informal Sector, Johns Hopkins University, 1984.

economic base of this city. These are the corporate services sector and what I call the downgraded manufacturing sector. While informalization can be seen as a probable development in a downgraded manufacturing sector, this is much less evident in the case of the corporate services. It is the strong tendency towards economic polarization that this sector brings about directly and indirectly which contributes to informalization of certain old and new activities.

The central hypothesis organizing the analysis is that the inducements to informalization result from the proliferation of small firms brought about by (a) the increased demand for highly-priced customized services and products by the expanding high-income population; (b) the increased demand for extremely low cost services and products by the expanding low-income population; and (c) the demand for customized services and goods by firms which are either final or intermediate buyers and the corresponding growth in subcontracting. This transformation of final and intermediate consumption is in large part associated with the economic polarization contained in major restructuring processes. Elsewhere I have discussed the evidence on economic polarization and the spatial distribution of the core economic sectors involved (Sassen-Koob, 1981; 1984; 1987). Here I shall focus on the growing economic polarization and what it entails regarding the organization of the labor process and the structures for social reproduction of high-income and low-income people. In the second half of the paper I shall discuss the preliminary findings from an investigation of informalization in New York City (Sassen-Koob and Grover, 1986).

ECONOMIC POLARIZATION: INDUCEMENT TO INFORMALIZATION? A PERSPECTIVE

Particular forms of economic growth promote informalization. In the post-World War II era, growth was characterized by the vast expansion of a middle class. The historical forms assumed by this expansion, notably capital intensity, standardization and suburbanization, deter informalization. And so did the cultural forms accompanying this process, particularly as they shaped the structures of everyday life. A major inference that can be drawn from this is that a large middle class contributes to patterns of consumption that promote standardization in production and hence, under certain conditions, are conducive to greater levels of unionization or other forms of workers' empowerment that can be derived from large plants – an empowerment which is, in turn, conducive to middle-income jobs. The patterns of economic polarization evident today work in the opposite direction, promoting small scales and non-standardized production.

When we compare the leading growth sectors of that period with today's, we can see pronounced differences in their occupational and income distributions. Today's leading sectors generate a higher share of both high-income and low-wage jobs. This polarization is further fed by the erosion of workers' gains in manufacturing and construction. To this should be added the high incidence of lay-offs and plant closures in unionized and well-paying jobs. Finally, the general shift to a service economy entails a much larger share of low-wage jobs than is the case with a strong manufacturing-based economy. The overall result is an increased income polarization. For example, I compared 1970 and 1980 census data on earnings (Sassen-Koob, 1987) and found the two highest earning classes increased their total share from 32 per cent to 37 per cent while the two lowest classes increased their share from 32 per cent to 38.5 per cent. Correspondingly, the two middle earnings classes reduced their share by 11 per cent.

This polarization assumes distinct forms in (a) its spatial organization, (b) the structures for social reproduction, and (c) the organization of the labor process. I shall discuss each of these in turn.

Locational patterns of polarization

For a number of reasons that can be grouped under the notion of agglomeration economies, economic polarization patterns seem to be particularly pronounced in major cities such as New York and Los Angeles. Indeed, I would tentatively argue that there is an even more pronounced discontinuity in the spatial organization of the economy in the current phase than in previous periods. That is to say, while many localities in the US shared in the economic expansion of the post-World War II period, this is less the case today. Today, certain locations, notably centers for the production of specialized services and research, account for a disproportionate share of the new growth. This share is even more pronounced in the case of global centers of production such as New York City. One consequence is that polarization tendencies are particularly strong in such major centers.

The high incidence of producer and other services in the employment structure of major cities contributes to general low- and high-income jobs. The data on earnings classes show a very high incidence of the next to lowest earning class in all services, except distributive services and public administration (Stanback et al., 1981). Almost half of all workers in the producer services are in the two highest earnings classes; but only 2.8 per cent are in the middle earnings class compared with half of all construction and manufacturing workers.

The greater economic polarization in large cities can be rooted in at least three conditions. First, the already mentioned locational concentration of major growth sectors with highly polarized income distributions in major cities. Second, the proliferation of small, low-cost service operations made possible by the massive concentration of people in large cities and the daily inflow of non-resident workers and of tourists. The ratio between the number of these service operations and resident population is most probably significantly higher than in an average city or town. Furthermore, the large concentration of people in major cities will tend to create intense inducements to open up such operations as well as intense competition and very marginal returns. Under such conditions the cost of labor is crucial and tends to the likelihood of a high concentration of low-wage jobs. Third, for these same reasons, together with other components of demand, the relative size of the downgraded manufacturing sector will tend to be larger than in average cities. Indeed, in many cities such a downgraded manufacturing sector is not a significant factor, if present at all.

Polarization in the consumption structure

Economic polarization in major cities has assumed distinct forms in the consumption structure which in turn has a feedback effect on the organization of work and the types of jobs being created. The expansion of the high-income workforce in conjunction with the emergence of new cultural forms has led to a process of high-income gentrification that rests, in the last analysis, on the availability of a vast supply of low-wage workers. As I have argued at greater length elsewhere (Sassen-Koob, 1981) high-income gentrification is labor-intensive, in contrast to the typical middle-class suburb that represents a capital-intensive process – tract-housing, road and highway construction, dependence on private automobile or commuter trains, marked reliance on appliances and household equipment of all sorts, large shopping malls with self-service operations. High-income gentrification replaces much of this capital intensity with workers, directly and indirectly. Behind the delicatessens and speciality boutiques that have replaced the self-service supermarket and department store lies a very different organization of work from that prevalent in the latter. Similarly, high-income residences in the city depend to a much larger extent on hired maintenance staff than the middle-class suburban home with its concentrated input of family labor and/or machinery, epitomized by the ever-running lawnmower.

The organization of work present both in the retail and in the production phase differs from that in large, standardized establishments. High-income gentrification generates a demand for goods and services that are typically not mass-produced or sold through mass outlets. Customized production, small runs, speciality items, fine food dishes are generally produced through labor-intensive methods and sold through small, full-service outlets. Subcontracting part of this production to low-cost operations, be they sweatshops or households, is common. The overall outcome for the job supply and the range of firms involved in this production and delivery is rather different from that characterizing the large department stores and supermarkets where mass production is prevalent and hence large, standardized factories located outside the city or the region are the norm. Distance from the stores is a different variable with customized producers.

Mass production and mass distribution outlets facilitate unionization both in production and in sales.

The expansion in the low-wage workforce has also contributed to the proliferation of small operations and the move away from large-scale standardized factories and stores. In large part the consumption needs of the low-wage workforce are met by manufacturing and retail establishments which are small, rely on family labor, and often fall below minimum safety and health standards. Locally-produced sweatshop garments, for example, have begun to replace cheap Asian imports. Hence the demand for low-cost products is increasingly met locally, which further expands a city's low-wage workforce.

The downgraded manufacturing sector

The social reorganization and technical transformation of the work process, and the new production jobs being created by high-technology industries, have all contributed to increase the share of jobs in manufacturing that pay very low wages. At the same time, industries with well-paying blue-collar jobs, such as auto and steel, are losing many jobs and degrading many others. One indication of this downgrading is the growth of sweatshops and industrial homework. Another indication is that one of the fastest growing industries, electronics, has characteristics of production that allow for the shifting of production and assembly jobs to low-wage countries where it employs mostly unskilled women (Safa, 1981; Nash and Fernandez Kelly, 1983). These same characteristics of production shape the job supply in electronics production and assembly in the US. Of interest here is the sharp drop in levels of unionization over the last decade in areas of rapid growth in high-technology industries, such as Los Angeles and Orange County (Wolff, 1984).

The consolidation and expansion of a downgraded manufacturing sector is well illustrated by the case of New York City. It is the result of several concrete developments besides the more general processes of social and technical transformation cited above. First, labor-intensive industries were affected differentially by capital flight from the city. In the case of the garment industry, the largest employer in the city's manufacturing sector, the bigger shops with mechanized production were the ones to move (NACLA, 1978; Waldinger, 1985). The less mechanized branches, specialized shops and the industry's marketing and design operations have remained in the city. Furthermore, the changing structure of consumption has also affected the garment industry; the greater demand for speciality items and limited edition garments has promoted the expansion of small shops and industrial homework in the city because small runs and proximity to design centers are important locational constraints (Sassen-Koob and Grover, 1986). A parallel argument can be made for other industries, notably furniture, furs and footwear.

Second, small-scale immigrant-owned plants have grown in number rapidly in view of easy access to cheap labor and, most importantly, a growing demand for their products in the immigrant communities and in the city at large. Probably the clearest illustration of this expansion is Chinatown (Wang, 1979). Capital from overseas Chinese has been flowing into New York City's Chinatown at a particularly accelerated rate since the middle of the 1970s. Besides real estate, the key growth factors in Chinatown's boom are the garment and restaurant industries. While overall recorded employment in New York City's garment industry has been declining throughout the 1970s, it actually increased in Chinatown's garment district. The number of unionized shops almost doubled from 1977 to 1981 (Abeles et al., 1983). Immigrants in New York City have set up small operations in food-processing, furniture, manufacture of a variety of consumer items, as well as, most importantly, garments. Many of these operations are part of the informal sector even though they produce for firms in the 'formal' sector. Indeed, subcontracting has emerged as a basic vehicle for lowering prices of production.

The expansion of a downgraded manufacturing sector partly involves the same industries that used to have largely organized plants and reasonably well-paid jobs but replaces these with different forms of production and organization of the work process, such as piecework and industrial homework. But it also involves new kinds of activity associated with the new major growth trends.

There seem to be three kinds of activity in this regard, that are not always mutually exclusive (Sassen-Koob, 1981). First, there is some evidence that an increasing component of manufacturing has a specific, narrow clientele: it ranges from the production of tools, through furniture to boxing gloves for particular firms (Port Authority, 1981; Conference Board, 1981). Second, there is the small-scale production for retailers selling to the growing high-income stratum whose numbers have increased sufficiently to promote the creation of a whole array of small businesses catering to their tastes, from gourmet restaurants to boutiques. What makes this production profitable is, undoubtedly, the possibility of gaining access to cheap labor and having huge mark-ups on final prices. Subcontracting to small plants willing to manufacture a small number of items is a key strategy to ensure the viability of this type of limited market production. Third, production for the newly expanded low-income mass market, much of it sold on the street, has partly replaced production for the middle-class market. The locational constraints on plants producing for middle-income markets are probably somewhat different since they have access to mass distribution and often have a nationwide market. This facilitates production through large plants. The low-income mass market that is emerging in large cities like New York and Los Angeles to a large extent is supplied by local or overseas sweatshops. The existence of a very large immigrant workforce facilitates sweatshop production close to the final market, something that is particularly desirable in the case of bulkier items such as pillows and of perishables. It is not possible to obtain measures of these three kinds of activities; this is merely a tentative organization of the fragmentary evidence available.

The possibility for manufacturers to develop alternatives to the organized shop becomes particularly significant in growth sectors. The consolidation of a downgraded manufacturing sector, whether through social or technical transformation, can be seen as a politico-economic response to a need for expanded production in a situation of growing average wages and militancy, as was the case in the 1960s. While it is true that average wages in production in New York City were never among the highest in the country given the absence of such key industries as steel, auto or aerospace, it is also true that average wages were increasing, and reached their highest level ever as recently as 1970: 101.2 per cent of the national average hourly wage in production. One indicator of the extent of downgrading is the decline of this wage level, which fell to 87.6 per cent of the national average in 1982. It would be significantly lower if sweatshops and industrial homework were included. This decline can also be seen in an area like Los Angeles whose economic base is radically different from New York City's, being dominated by aerospace and electronics: hourly production wages fell from 10 per cent of the national average in 1970 to 100.7 per cent in 1982.

A good part of what I am calling here the downgraded manufacturing sector is contained in the 'underground' economy. A small part of this production circulates internally and meets mostly the demand of insiders, i.e. the immigrant community. But most of it circulates through the formal sectors of the economy and represents not a survival strategy for its members but a profit-maximizing strategy for firms.

In sum, the argument is that the kinds of growth trends described above contain inducements towards the informalization of a whole range of activities. The intervening processes are the expansion of both a market for highly priced, and a market for extremely low-cost, goods and services. An additional intervening process is the downgrading of manufacturing, resulting partly from these changes in consumption, but more generally from technical and politico-economic pressures. The next section illustrates some of these trends with the preliminary results of our investigation of the informal sector in New York City.

NEW YORK CITY'S INFORMAL SECTOR:
PRELIMINARY FINDINGS

New York City appears to have a particularly developed underground economy. About 27 per cent of total personal income in New York in 1978 was estimated to be unregistered, as contrasted with 11.5 per cent for the rest of the US economy. This makes the underground economy in New York twice as large as it is nationally. Between 1969 and 1978, moreover, the underground economy in New York more than quadrupled from $3.87 billion to $16.2 billion (Spitznas, 1981). In our preliminary investigations, we found other indices to support the claim for the existence of a large and growing underground economy in New York. For example, income check mortgages, which provide loans without requiring the applicants to submit any information about their work or source of income (loans are based only on the value of the home purchased and a credit profile) more than doubled between 1984 and 1985. Total annual lending of this type increased from $61.1 million in 1980 to $684.5 million in 1984, or more than tenfold (Sassen-Koob and Grover, 1986).

The existence of a large and thriving underground economy in New York City has been the subject of much concern among state and local policymakers. Yet very little is known about the underground economy: its relation to existing forms of regulation, interlinkages with formal sectors of the economy and relation to broader societal developments. We suspect that much of this dearth of knowledge stems from the tendency to view the underground economy as a homogeneous unit for analysis rather than a diverse group of activities in need of diverse policy responses. Among other things, the underground economy encompasses illicit activities, tax evasion and sweatshop operations. The underground economy is generally distinguished from the formal economy in that it disregards existing governmental regulations such as occupational health and safety standards, minimum wage and overtime laws, and taxation and zoning regulations. Our investigation focuses on that portion of the underground economy which involves the production and/or sale of *licit* goods and services but taking place outside the regulatory apparatus. This is the sector we refer to as informal.

Modes of government regulation are particularly important to understanding the rise of informal production because of the costs that they impose on formal businesses through their various licensing fees, taxes and restrictions. Labor costs also have an effect on the formation and expansion of the informal sector: directly, in terms of the wage paid, and indirectly, in terms of various contributions demanded by law. One question is whether the importance of these inducements to informalization varies according to industry and location.

The objectives of the larger and ongoing research project are the following:

1 to assess the extent to which informal economic activities are growing in New York City and in which kinds of communities and industrial sectors;

2 to identify the linkages between these informal activities and formal sector

activities (in the communities, in the industries and in the wider city economy);

3 to identify whether there is, and if so, compare, the weight of demand that is internal to the communities in which informal goods are produced versus that which is external to the communities;

4 to identify the role that informal production plays in the spatial organization of particular industries in New York City;

5 to examine the importance of New York City as a location to informal producers;

6 to identify existing government policies towards, and those which implicitly impact, informal producers.

Information obtained through the fieldwork is being used to specify a relationship between the growth of informal activities in New York City and overall transformations in the economy. Individual motivations and diverse structural forces contribute to growth in New York's underground economy, among them illicit activities, business's and employees' desire to evade taxes and regulatory costs, and the growth in the immigrant population. However, our investigation primarily examines transformations in the organization of production and consumption structures which induce informalization.

The research involves a combination of secondary data analysis; ethnographic research in select communities and various kinds of workplaces; and interviews with informed individuals, including local planning officials, union officials, community members, etc. We used data on occupational safety and health administration violators, together with overtime and minimum wage legislation violators, to identify trends in informal production in New York City. On the basis of these data we targeted certain industries for more in-depth study of the informal component of their total production chain. We did fieldwork in communities identified by informed people as having a large informal sector or having a high density of immigrant population as an indicator for a high probability of informal activity. We used interviews with community boards and local development corporation representatives to target specific sites with violations. (Complaints of businesses in violation of legally defined uses of building or zoning ordinances are normally registered with local development corporations and community boards before being referred to the Department of Buildings.) Zoning maps and data from the Department of Buildings were used to obtain more detailed information on informal producers. Our site visits and interviews helped us to identify the extent and kinds of informal activities in these communities. They also helped us to assess how existing regulations influence informal producers and to determine if new modes of regulation are needed.

On the basis of our secondary data analysis, fieldwork and interviews, we found the following profile of the informal sector in the New York City area (Sassen-Koob and Grover, 1986):

a a rapid proliferation of informal operations (including industrial home-work);

b a rather wide range of industrial sectors with such operations: garments, general construction contractors and operative builders, heavy construction contractors, special trade contractors, footwear, toys and sporting goods, electronic components and accessories;

c such operations were also found in lesser measure in particular kinds of activities like packaging notions, making lampshades, artificial flowers and jewellery, distribution activities, photo engraving, manufacturing of explosives, etc.;

d a strong tendency for such operations to be located in densely populated areas with a high percentage of immigrants;

e an emergent tendency for 'traditional' sweatshop activity (notably garments) to be displaced in certain areas undergoing partial residential and commercial gentrification and in its stead new forms of unregistered work catering to the new clientele.

So far we have examined several industries and communities and completed interviews with 47 informants. The industries covered were: (1) construction, (2) garments, (3) footwear, (4) furniture, (5) retail activity, and (6) electronics. We did field visits in all the boroughs of New York City.

There follows a more detailed description of certain industries, much of it based on extensive interviews and field visits (Sassen-Koob and Grover, 1986).

Construction Based on several interviews with informed individuals, surveys and actual field visits, it is estimated that 90 per cent of all interior work in New York City is done without a building permit.[1] Although there is little underground activity in large public works projects, one interviewee noticed much illegal work in rehabilitation and small-scale store, apartment and commercial renovation. He also noted that most highly specialized craftsmen are immigrants, notably cutters, masons, plasterers, many of whom do not have residence or work permits.[2] In addition, there is widespread use of subcontractors (many of these not fully registered) for jobs that were once done through direct hiring of union labor. There is a growing number of Hispanics among subcontractors, in an industry where Hispanics were once excluded.[3] Subcontracting is the way large companies and large construction projects reduce their costs and avoid paying taxes on some earnings.[4]

Finally, unregistered work is common in renovations and alteration work in offices.[5]

Garments   Several studies document the rapid increase in the number of sweatshop (both union and non-union) and industrial homework since the early 1970s.[6] Overall, the following can be noted for the New York area: (a) it is estimated that there are about 3000 garment sweatshops; (b) they have been spreading to peripheral areas within the city and outside the city as rents have increased, e.g. out of the Chinatown area in Manhattan and into northern Manhattan, Brooklyn and Queens; (c) sweatshops and homework are most common in women's and children's clothes; (d) new branches in which sweatshops and homework are increasing rapidly are the so-called 'knitting-mills', furs, embroidery, stuffed toys and clothing for toys.

Footwear   Several informed people from city agencies and unions said that unregistered work is spreading both in standardized production and highly crafted production (sandals, moccasins). One estimate is that 10 per cent are unregistered; it is also increasing among union shops, via subcontracting and homework.[7] There is also growing evidence of unregistered work in handbags and other leather goods.[8]

Furniture   Both large, standardized factories and certain branches of furnishings (bedding, mattresses) have moved out of the area, to the south. There is new manufacturing activity in furniture and craftwork located in areas not zoned for this work. Examples are Ridgewood Astoria in Queens; Williamsburg, Sunset park in Brooklyn.[9] There are several new manufacturing shops, employing almost exclusively immigrants, making high-cost, crafted cabinets and other furniture in Jackson Heights (Queens) geared to the local, increasingly middle-income residents and fancy retail shops associated with commercial and residential gentrification.[10]

Retail activity   There is growing, piecemeal evidence of unregistered retail activity in more and more branches of industry, not only at fleamarkets and among peddlers, but also in the sale of such high price items as jewelry and furs.[11] Several of the other sources already mentioned cited evidence of informal buying and selling of inputs and outputs.

Electronics   There is growing evidence that unregistered work is increasing.[12] Despite the need for more fieldwork, certain aspects are emerging: (a) homework is also being done by native, white workers; (b) subcontracting is central to the electronics industry in the New York–New Jersey area among small firms with highly specialized kinds of production and specific customers[13]; (c) there are chains of subcontractors, and often at or 'neighbor' who is part of the subcontracting; these are often unregistered.[14]

POLICY IMPLICATIONS

Both the conceptual elaboration of the data on current economic trends and our preliminary findings point to the existence of strong inducements towards informalization of a wide array of economic activities, particularly in large cities. Both point, furthermore, to the existence of such inducements as a result of the characteristics of growth trends. While unemployment may also promote the expansion of an informal sector, it is the highly dynamic growth sectors (cf. Stepick, 1984) in the economies of large cities which are central to the existence of a highly dynamic expanding informal sector.

Linking informalization with growth trends in advanced capitalist economies raises a number of policy questions. Preliminary results from our investigation in New York City show differences in the locational constraints to which informal firms are subject. For one type of firm, access to cheap labor is the determining inducement for a New York City location. Access to the city's market – final consumers or firms – is clearly also significant, as is the massive scale which facilitates informalizationn. But it is ultimately access to low-wage immigrant workers which enables the firms to compete with shops located in other low-wage areas or foreign countries. Many of these sweatshops could easily be located elsewhere, mainly because extremely low labor costs can be found in a multiplicity of locations.

In contrast, many of the shops engaged in customized production evidence a whole host of locational dependencies on New York City. These firms are bound to New York City as a location because: (1) they respond to local demand of specific clients for products or services/product mixes; (2) proximity to design and specialized servicing is crucial; and (3) short turnaround time between completion of design and production is essential. Our evidence suggests that informalization among customized producers appear as a *combination* of: transformations in the economies of advanced industrialized countries that promote the expansion of small scales of production and locational dependencies on large cities; and policies rooted in an outdated view of the nature of manufacturing in advanced industrial economies, according to which large cities are no longer a desirable, necessary or feasible location for growing branches since large scales and standardization are the norm and hence access to abundant and low-cost land crucial locational criteria. According to such a view, whatever manufacturing remains in large cities is marginal, backward, and a remnant soon to disappear. However, these customized and small-scale producers represent one of the only sources of manufacturing job growth in the city. Since they face policies which discourage manufacturing in cities, they have strong inducements to produce informally. And the small size and labor-intensity of these firms makes them prone to informalization in any case. Similar constraints are at work in the production/sale of customized services. In short, New York City's large concentration of low-wage workers, many of whom are undocumented immigrants, may be crucial to some types of sweatshop operations, whereas supply–customer chains are more important to many customized producers.

If our community and industry case studies continue to show that the growth of customized production is one of the factors promoting the expansion of the informal sector in New York City, then policy making geared to controlling the spread of the underground economy will need to be reformulated in light of this new information. At present, fighting tax-evaders is a major concern of policy and regulatory efforts. But if a part of the growth of the underground economy is a result of new locational and organizational patterns of producers, in other words of structural transformations in the economy, then it becomes clear that such efforts are misguided.

CONCLUSION

Government policies, particularly those which aim to promote economic growth and community development, will need to incorporate a recognition of the multiple facets of the underground economy. They must distinguish between: (1) illicit work; (2) tax-evasion; (3) operations that exploit powerless immigrants to stay in business; and (4) operations that are not registered or up to code, in large part because they confront excessive regulatory burdens, tax burdens, and outmoded zoning restrictions.

We need to distinguish those components of the informal sector that are socially desirable from those which merely exploit powerless immigrants or evade taxes. We expect that the informal sector does, in some cases, act to strengthen New York City's manufacturing base. This is especially notable at a time when large scales of production and standardized manufacturing are no longer viable in most large cities. Policy-makers can then look to the informal sector as a source of employment, income and job training for low-income residents. The aim should be to formulate policies toward informal producers which promote local job retention and low-income neighborhood stabilization. This entails recognizing the ways in which certain local conditions promote informal activities. Our preliminary work shows that certain localities appear to attract and promote informalization of economic activities because of zoning regulations, pre-existing economic base or characteristics of the local labor force. Further investigation will be aimed at revealing the relative importance that local conditions and the production requirements of particular industries play in determining the strength of the informal sector in certain neigborhoods. In some cases we may find that local conditions induce informalization across a wide variety of industries; we also may find localities which provide for the labor force and spatial requirements of certain industries, and thereby specialize in a limited range of informal activities.

Policy-makers need to find ways to retain, and to capitalize on, the social benefits that New York City's thriving informal sector produces, perhaps through some modifications of existing regulatory policies, notably those that discourage manufacturing in cities and excessively burden small firms. They also need to respond to protect workers and residents from the undesirable aspects of unregulated employment, such as erosion of the tax base, health hazards and inadequate wages. Formal sector firms use the informal sector as a part of their overall strategies to minimize costs and maximize profits. By subcontracting a portion of their production to low-cost operations – be they sweatshops or individual households – firms need not employ unionized workers; and subcontractors can easily hire unlicensed firms and undocumented workers so as not to implicate the large contracting firm.

In sum, our conceptual elaboration of general economic trends and preliminary findings lead us to posit that the growth of informal activities in New York City is *not* primarily a result of individual survival strategies resulting from unemployment or illegal resident status. Rather, it is primarily an outcome of structural rearrangements in the overall economy to which people are responding. However, in order to respond individuals must be positioned in certain ways. Immigrant communities represent a 'favored' structural location to seize the opportunities for entrepreneurship as well as the most undesirable jobs being engendered by informalization.

NOTES

1 Report issued by Commissioner Fruchter. Additional information obtained from Stuart O'Brien, Inspector General, Buildings Department. According to information from the Union of Construction Contractors, 33 per cent of the $4 billion construction industry is non-union (1984–5) with a lot of unregistered work taking place either directly or indirectly through subcontracting. A recent accident in a mid-Manhattan construction site for a new high-rise building led to the discovery that one of the crane-operators was a subcontractor and unlicensed. This led to a city-wide inspection of major construction sites – that is to say, sites where general inspections are frequent, most labor is unionized and visibility high. It confirmed the widespread use of subcontractors for jobs that were once done through direct hiring of union labor. This took most policy makers and the press by surprise, in view of the intense public attention and frequent inspections accorded major sites.
2 Mr McGurtle of the General Trade Association for Union Contractors, NYC. Confirmed by many other sources: see Sassen-Koob and Grover (1986).
3 See Balmori (1983).
4 Paul Grazione, Director of the Enforcement Commission of the Department of Finance and Taxation.
5 Paul O'Brien of the Building Contractors Association of NYC.

6 See Abeles, et al. (1983); Waldinger (1985); Leichter (1982); Sassen-Koob with Benamou (1985); NY State Department of Labor (1982a, b); NJ State Department of Labor (1982).
7 Mr Figuaro, Director, Shoe Division of the ACTWU (Amalgamated Clothing and Textile Workers Union). This is a development of the last 5 to ten years. There are many 'fly-by-night' operations which stay open for 6 to 9 months.
8 Sassen-Koob and Grover, 1986 (interview no. 15). Data from the Department of Finance and Taxation show growing violations in footwear manufacturing in the city.
9 Sassen-Koob and Grover, 1986 (interview no. 3). Conversions of lofts and warehouses into elegant designer residences or shops and galleries has created a large demand for customized woodwork.
10 Bob Satzger of the Jackson Heights Community Development Corporation. As an area gentrifies there is a very localized demand for on-the-spot woodwork and installations.
11 Sassen-Koob and Grover, 1985 (interview no. 22). Also found was growth of homework in packaging notions, including name-brand cosmetics, e.g. Clinique, for Christmas.
12 New York State Department of Labor, 1982a, b; New Jersey Department of Labor, 1982; Sassen-Koob with Benamou (1985).
13 Sassen-Koob with Benamou (1985).

REFERENCES

Abeles, Schwartz, Hackel, and Silverblatt, Inc. (1983) *The Chinatown Garment Industry Study*. Report to the ILGWU, Local 23–25 and the New York Sportswear Association.
Balmori, D. (1983) 'Hispanic immigrants in the construction industry: New York City, 1960–1982', Occasional Papers No. 38, New York: Center for Latin American and Caribbean Studies, New York University.
City of New York (1982) *Report on Economic Conditions in New York City, July–December 1981*. New York Office of Management and Budget and Office of Economic Development.
Conference Board (1981) *Announcements of Foreign Investments in US Manufacturing Industries. (First Quarter and Third Quarter)*. New York: The Conference Board, Inc.
Feige, E. L. (1979) 'How big is the irregular economy?', *Challenge*, 22 (Nov.–Dec.): 5–13.
Gutmann, P. M. (1979) 'Statistical illusions, mistaken policies', *Challenge*, 22 (Nov.–Dec.): 14–17.
Leichter (1982) 'Sweatshops to shakedowns: Organized crime in New York's garment industry', New York: Office of the 29th District of the State of New York, Monthly Report.
Light, Ivan H. (1979) 'Disadvantaged minorities in self-employment', *International Journal of Comparative Sociology*, 20: 31–45.
Lomnitz, Larissa (1978) 'Mechanisms of articulation between shantytown settlers and the urban system', *Urban Anthropology* 7: 185–205.

Morales, Rick and Richard Mines (1985) 'San Diego's full service restaurants: a view from the back of the house'. Report, Center for US–Mexico Studies, University of California, San Diego.

NACLA (North American Congress on Latin America) (1978) *Capital's Flight: The Apparel Industry Moves South*, Latin America and Empire Report, vol. 11, 3 (Special Issue).

Nash, June and M. P. Fernandez Kelly (eds) (1983) *Women, Men and the International Division of Labor*, New York: State University of New York Press.

New Jersey Department of Labor (1982) 'Study of Industrial Homework', Trenton, N.J.: Office of Wage and Hour Compliance, Division of Workplace Standards.

New York State Department of Taxation and Finance (1982) *The Task Force on the Underground Economy: Preliminary Report*, Albany: State of New York.

New York State Department of Labor (1982a) *Study of state–federal employment standards for industrial homeworkers in New York City*, Albany: Division of Labor Standards.

—— (1982b) *Report to the Governor and the Legislature on the Garment Manufacturing Industry and Industrial Homework*, Albany: State of New York.

Port Authority of New York and New Jersey (1981) *Inventory of Foreign-Owned Firms in Manufacturing, by Major Industry in the New York–New Jersey Metropolitan Region*, New York: Planning and Development Department, Regional Research Section, Port Authority of New York and New Jersey.

—— (1982) *The New York Regional Economy: 1891 Review, 1982 Outlook*. New York: Planning and Development Department.

Portes, Alejandro and Lauren Benton (1984) 'Industrial development and labor absorption: a reinterpretation', *Population and Development Review*, 10 (December): 589–611.

Renooy, P. H. (1984) *Twilight Economy: A Survey of the Informal Economy in the Netherlands*, Research Report, Faculty of Economic Sciences, University of Amsterdam.

Safa, Helen I. (1981) 'Runaway shops and female employment: the search for cheap labor', *Signs*, 7 (Winter): 418–33.

Sassen-Koob, Saskia (1981) 'Exporting capital and importing labor: Caribbean migration to New York City', Occasional Papers No. 28, New York: Center For Latin American and Caribbean Studies, New York University.

—— (1984a) 'The new labor demand in global cities'. In M. P. Smith (ed.), *Cities in Transformation: Class, Capital and the State*, Beverly Hills, Calif.: Sage.

—— (1984b) Growth and informalization at the core: the case of New York City'. In *The Urban Informal Sector: Recent Trends in Research and Theory*, Conference Proceedings, Baltimore, MD: Department of Sociology, Johns Hopkins University, pp. 492–518.

—— (1987) *The Mobility of Labor and Capital*, New York: Cambridge University Press.

Sassen-Koob, Saskia with Catherine Benamou (1985), 'Hispanic women in the garment and electronics industries in the New York metropolitan area', Research Progress Report. Presented to the Revson Foundation, New York City.

Sassen-Koob, Saskia and S. Grover (1985) 'Unregistered work in the New York metropolitan area'. Working paper, Columbia University, Graduate School of Architecture and Planning.

Spitznas, Thomas (1981) 'Estimating the size of the underground economy in New York City', *The Regional Economic Digest* (A semi-annual publication of the New York Regional Economist's Society) (Fall), vol. 1, no. 1.

Stanback, Thomas M. Jr, Peter J. Bearse, Thierry J. Noyelle and Robert Karasek (1981) *Services: The New Economy*, New Jersey: Allenheld, Osmun.

Stepick, Alex (1984) 'The Haitian informal sector in Miami'. In *The Urban Informal Sector: Recent Trends in Research and Theory*, Conference Proceedings, Baltimore, MD: Department of Sociology, Johns Hopkins University, pp. 384–434.

Tanzi, Vito (1982) *The Underground Economy in the United States and Abroad*, Lexington, Mass.: D. C. Heath. ·

Waldinger, Roger (1985) 'Immigration and industrial change in the New York City apparel industry'. In G. J. Borjas and M. Tienda (eds), *Hispanics in the U.S. Economy*, New York: Academic Press, pp. 323–49.

Wang, John (1979) 'Behind the boom: power and economics in Chinatown', *New York Affairs*, 5, 3.

Wolff, Goetz (1984) 'The decline of unionization and the growth of employment in the Los Angeles region', Los Angeles: Graduate School of Architecture and Urban Planning.

7

Detroit and Houston:
Two Cities in Global Perspective

Richard Child Hill and Joe R. Feagin

INTRODUCTION

Detroit and Houston became urban archetypes in the United States in the 1970s. Detroit was the snowbelt city in decline; Houston, the booming sunbelt metropolis. Each city was held up as an object lesson for the other. It was commonly argued, for example, that if Detroit wanted to revitalize, the city should embrace something like Houston's freewheeling, boomtown philosophy with all that implied: aggressive business promotion, weak labor unions, social inequality, low taxes, few social services and unplanned urban sprawl.[1] Others thought that as Houston matured, the Motor City's brand of welfare state capitalism would take hold and chart the Oil City's future. If so, Houston would experience growth in worker organization, an institutional partnership between Big Business and Big Labor, more political power among minority groups, tax increases, expanded social services and eventually, business disinvestment and fiscal crisis. But the 1980s held something different in store from what is implied in these laissez-faire versus welfare state contrasts.

Houston, in fact, was to experience an economic crisis in the 1980s not unlike the one which began to confront Detroit a decade earlier. Ironically, by the mid-1980s, it was the two cities' similarities, not their differences, that were most obvious. This suggests that answers to questions about a city's political-economic future are to be found as much beyond as within its local boundaries. Cities are spatial locations in a globally interdependent system of production and exchange. That global system is in crisis and transition. So the path a city follows in the future will depend upon the niche it comes to occupy in a changing international division of labor. Our aim in this chapter is to compare Detroit and Houston in the light of a changing world economy.

A NOTE ON THEORY AND METHOD

The modern city, it has rightly been argued, is an arena for collective consumption, a spatial network of local institutions organized to sustain and reproduce a resident population (Castells, 1973). But the consumer city is also a producer city. As production sites, cities are bound together in translocal chains of economic production, distribution and exchange. The most daunting urban problems today stem precisely from this lack of spatial correspondence between systems of local consumption and translocal production. It seems fruitful, therefore, to conceptualize how the city as a 'localization of social forces' (Zukin, 1980) is articulated with the city as a nodal point in the world capitalist system (Friedmann and Wolff, 1982).

Global ecology

Efforts to view cities in a global context have an interesting academic history in the United States. Half a century ago, R. D. McKenzie put forward a global perspective on urban structure and change that still has a decidedly contemporary ring. McKenzie was an early Chicago School urbanist, and his writings, along with those of Robert Park, launched the field of urban ecology. In his seminal essay, 'The Concept of Dominance and World Organization' (1927). McKenzie conceptualized dominance and subordination, specialization and integration, as ecological properties of a spatially organized world order.

McKenzie was interested in the spatial distribution of people and institutions, and for him, spatial organization was not haphazard. It was the product of human evolution. McKenzie reasoned by way of an analogy between changing human settlement patterns and the evolution of living organisms, particularly the human body. All but the very simplest organisms, he noted, are composed of specialized parts. These parts are integrated to each other and to the whole organism through their relation to a center of dominance, the location charged with coordination and control. Thus, for example, organs and limbs are integrated in the human body through relations of information exchange with the brain via the central nervous system.

In human as in other forms of biological evolution, there is a tendency to increasing specialization of parts and greater centralization of control and coordination activities. It follows, McKenzie reasoned, that human ecological evolution brings a growing hierarchy of dominance and subordination among settlements. Most settlements become more specialized and subordinated to a few settlements where coordination and control functions are performed.

Transportation and communication lines form the central nervous system in McKenzie's model of human spatial evolution. With technical advances in transportation and communication – like the railroad, telegraph and wireless – world spatial organization undergoes a seismic shift. Centers and routes rather than boundaries and political areas give definition to human space. A world once patterned by bounded clusters of small, undifferentiated, symmetrically related villages and towns gives way to a world organized by a few vast hierarchies of dominant centers, more specialized sub-centers, and subordinated peripheries.

McKenzie's global bent did not inspire students of human ecology at the time. Then, as now, urban ecologists tended to study variations in community and metropolitan structure within regional or national contexts (Hawley, 1984: 913). When they did make cross-national comparisons, ecologists seldom did so through the global prism that characterized McKenzie's thinking (cf., for example, Hawley, 1971; Berry and Kasarda, 1977). Ironically, McKenzie's interest in global spatial organization was carried forward by scholars working in theoretical traditions with different premises from those that shaped the ideas of early Chicago School urbanists.

The capitalist world system

According to McKenzie, transportation and communication routes are the threads that weave the global urban web. We can visualize these routes as the nexus of a world market which connects human settlements through the exchange of information, goods and services. Because market exchange among human settlements is competitive and unequal, communities are lodged in hierarchies of dominance and subordination according to the places they occupy in an international division of labor. Developing McKenzie's ideas in this direction leads us to an image of global organization that resembles the political economy of the world system put forward by Immanuel Wallerstein (1973).

What most distinguishes Wallerstein's political economy from McKenzie's human ecology is Wallerstein's interest in *capitalism* as the system that has embraced the world since the sixteenth century. Then, too, McKenzie thought political boundaries were yielding in importance to cross-national routes, so he did not pay much attention to geopolitics. Wallerstein, on the other hand, emphasizes the contradictory logic of a capitalist world economy superimposed upon competing nation-states. Imperial from its origins, the capitalist world economy consists of dominant capitalist centers, distinguished by a wage labor system, and subordinant peripheries where several modes of production coexist. For Wallerstein, centers and peripheries are social formations defined by their modes of production. Social formations are conjoined by commodity exchange in a world encompassing vertical division of labor. Within the global economy, hegemonic core powers dominate regional blocks of center and periphery states through cycles of imperial expansion and decline.

Wallerstein's theory of the capitalist world system doesn't lend itself directly to theories about cities and urbanization. To make that connection requires locating cities within broader social formations classified according to Wallerstein's center, semi-periphery and periphery schema. That entails analyzing the history of a city's relationship with other cities, US social formations and the world system throught the commodities a city's producers exchange on the world market.

World system urbanists have conceptualized city systems formed by inter-urban networks of commodity exchange and an international distribution of economic functions (Chase-Dunn, 1984). City size hierarchies have been mapped, and levels and rates of urbanization in the world system have been traced over time (Timberlake, 1985). World system theory has also generated comparative research on differing patterns of urbanization in center and periphery formations according to a city's location in the international division of labor and its mode of integration into the global economy (Walton and Lubeck, 1977; Portes and Walton, 1981).

The global corporation

Stephen Hymer, a brilliant student of the multinational corporation, has also linked human ecology to the political economy in a way that is more institutionally specific and historically concrete than Wallerstein. In his remarkable essay, 'The Multinational Corporation and the Law of Uneven Development' (1971), Hymer connected McKenzie's theory of world spatial organization to Alfred Chandler's (1962) theory of the evolution of the business enterprise. Since stages in the evolution of the business firms are intimately related to phases in the development of capitalism, Hymer, like Wallerstein, laid the groundwork for an urban political economy; that is, for a theory of the relationships between capitalism and urban organization on a global scale.

Hymer traced the administrative evolution of the business enterprise from workshop to family firm, from family firm to regional and national corporation, and from national corporation to multidivisional and multi-national enterprise. Each step in the evolution of the enterprise brought an increase in specialization and administrative complexity. Each step brought greater centralization of coordination activities in a control center and greater decentralization of execution activities to peripheral branches. Each step further elongated the corporate hierarchy of dominance and subordina-tion. And each step was contingent upon advances in communication and transportation technology. Indeed, at various historical moments, transpor-tations and communication enterprises – railroads, motor cars, and computers – offered administrative models for other corporations to follow.

Hymer's reconstruction of Chandler's theory of business evolution is reminiscent of McKenzie's discussion of human spatial development. Only in this case it is the firm and not the human settlement that occupies center stage. Indeed, the parallel was not fortuitous since Hymer believed that the evolution of the business enterprise was the principal contemporary force behind changing settlement patterns. As the corporation evolves, its local operations come to be supervised by field offices, field offices are supervised by divisional head offices, and head offices are presided over by a general office or command center. Applying location theory to the administrative structure of the corporation, Hymer posited a global hierarchy of cities corresponding to the hierarchy of the transnational corporate enterprise.

Corporations locate their branch plants in specialized *production and marketing* cities according to the pull of labor power, markets and raw materials. So production and marketing cities proliferate across the globe.

Field offices, on the other hand, locate in *regional cities* where they serve as centers of coordination and control over the local operations lodged in production and marketing cities. Coordinating activities are more spatially centralized and concentrated than day-to-day production and marketing, so regional cities are fewer, larger and contain more social control activities, like communications and information processing.

But it is *world cities*, those which house the corporate headquarters, that stand at the apex of the ecological pyramid. It is in world cities that corporate nerve-centers set goals and plan global strategies. Corporate headquarters are drawn to world cities to be close to wealthy capital markets, high-level government bureaux, major media and those key business services which facilitate the movement of global capital.

In Hymer's model, the global urban web is a vast net cast by the multinational corporation. A city's wealth, occupational structure, educational level, cultural sophistication, tax base and capacity for economic development are largely determined by where its economic base activities are lodged in the transnational hierarchies of modern corporations. Hymer's work too has generated scholarly interest in global hierarchies of dominance and subordination and uneven development among human settlements (cf. Thrift and Taylor, 1979; Cohen, 1981; Noyelle and Stanback, 1984).

International production systems

Hymer's theory emphasizes a cardinal political-economic tendency of our time: the internationalization of markets within giant corporations. The transformation of market exchange among independent enterprises into bureaucratic administration among organs of a corporate totality produces a new international division of labor. Corporate administration becomes the strongest thread binding localities into a world system. Absentee control, the hypermobility of capital, and the social consequences of global investment decisions become pressing public issues everywhere.

In Hymer's model, companies expand by adding new operations and divisions and by penetrating new regions and international peripheries. Each firm spreads its production and marketing operations even further outward; each places its middle-level coordinating operations in similar regional locations, those that correspond to common marketing domains; and each concentrates its high-level command operations in a few world cities. As an increasing percentage of the world's resources come to be controlled by a small number of multinational corporations, the world's ecological geometry starts to look like a triangle: a few, very large and very wealthy cities are at the top, a global ring of regional cities are at the center, and a myriad of production and marketing cities are at the bottom.

The clarity and simplicity of the development logic that connects the evolution of the business enterprise to the evolution of human settlement patterns give great force to Hymer's argument. But the connections between corporate organization and world urbanization are more complicated than Hymer's argument implies. His theory leaves out too much that characterizes too many cities, and it needs to be elaborated in several directions.

First, Hymer's singular focus on the internal structure of the corporation is too narrow a foundation for a theory of urban development. In particular, Hymer ignores the forward and backward linkages *among* business enterprises that go into making a product. Take the auto industry, for example; thousands of parts go into sub-assembly and then into the final assembly of a car. This requires a *production system* consisting of a multitude of operating units, ranging from transnational corporations to small parts shops, all linked by technology and organization in the manufacture of a final product (Hamilton, 1981).

The spatial concentration and growth of operating units knit together in production systems is what generates urban growth. Some operating units are tied into a production system as sub-parts of a single corporate administration, as in Hymer's model; but others are 'independent' entities bound to the system by market exchange, as in Wallerstein's imagery; and still others are connected through subcontracting relations that do not quite fit bureaucratic or market categories.

Hymer also has too unilinear a view of corporate ecology. He assumes that corporations producing different commodities at different historical moments evolve similar spatial oranizations. This is often true, but it is often not true, too. For example, Hymer's world city concept seems to fit New York City very well; yet not all, nor even most, transnational corporations choose to locate their headquarters there. Why not? And how does Hymer make sense out of metropolises like Detroit and Houston? Neither has the scale, the number of corporate headquarters, nor the concentrated financial clout to qualify as world cities in Hymer's book, yet they are not regional cities, and they are not production and marketing cities, either.

Detroit and Houston are better viewed as world command centers for elaborately organized international production systems in automobiles and oil. Transnational auto and oil companies are headquartered in Detroit and Houston because they have chosen to stay close to where they grew up and to the concentrated industrial expertise and cluster of supporting companies, from small-scale suppliers to high-level finance and specialized business services, that grew up with them. This remained true even after they cast their nets across the globe. In fact, the kind of world city Hymer conceptualizes seems most hospitable to the head offices of giant holding companies, those no longer connected in any integral way to a production system, and to the upper reaches of companies in high finance and the media.

National governments also play a role in structuring corporate location and urban form but that is outside Hymer's frame of reference. Like McKenzie, Hymer thinks centers and routes are more important than boundaries and political areas. But that's as debatable today as it was when McKenzie argued it in the 1920s. Nation-states create, design and expand capital cities according to national interests that are not reducible to corporate interests; indeed, the two are not always compatible. Govenments build production systems too, as the military-industrial complex in the United States so amply illustrates; but the headquarters for the Pentagon's production system are located on the Potomac. Interests of state help explain why urban hierarchies occur within nations as well as across them. And that suggests the geometrical imagery for world ecological organization cannot be confined to one big triangle; instead, world urban form looks more like a hierarchy of national triangles within global triangles.

The idea of international production systems is a synthetic concept which retains an emphasis on internal corporate organization and relations of production while acknowledging the significance of nation-states and unequal relations of market exchange among producers within and across national borders. It is a concept that seems to leave us better equipped, than a singular emphasis on internal corporate organization, market exchange or the nation-state can do, to explore the complexities of urbanization in a global system.

Our aim in what follows is briefly to profile two major US cities and compare their evolution against a background of changes in world industrial organization. We are particularly interested in how each city's changing role in the international division of labor comes to shape its built environment. Typically, social scientists make urban comparisons through the statistical analysis of variables calculated across many cities. Each city is considered to be a discrete and relatively autonomous entity, and explanation refers to the statistical explanation of dependent variables by independent variables through multivariate analysis. Here, however, we take a holistic methodological approach. We assume that cities are not discrete and independent entities, but rather are interconnected parts of a world system of cities. Explanation, in this scheme of things, comes from locating parts within a larger whole in such a way as to render their complementary and contradictory relationships meaningful (Harvey, 1978: 33).

DETROIT: CRISIS IN THE MOTOR CITY

Specialization and growth

Detroit grew with the automobile industry. By importing raw materials and semi-finished products and converting them into durable finished goods to be exported throughout the world, Detroit's factories formed the heart of a vibrant international production system. Apart from auto-parts suppliers, three complementary industries have played a particularly salient role in Detroit's 'metal-bending' economy: non-electrical machinery, fabricated metals and primary metals. Transportation and communication arteries connected the Motor City's factories to rubber plants in Akron, metal foundries in Cleveland, machine-tool shops in Cincinnati, steel mills in Buffalo, New York, hydraulic research laboratories in Columbus, Ohio and a myriad of other industries and industrial cities in states bordering the Great Lakes. Because most of the commodities these industries produce – foundry products, metal stampings, machinery and sheet steel – are destined for automobile plants, the prosperity of those Great Lakes cities has followed that of the car producers, too. Center of a specialized world manufacturing empire, Detroit's center city population grew from 250,000 in 1900 to 1.9 million in 1930, and peaked at 1.85 million in 1951 (Hurley, 1959).

The Motor City's 'Big Three' – General Motors, Ford and Chrysler – came to number among the world's largest corporations. General Motors alone possesses 121 factories in 77 US cities and an additional 35 subsidiaries in 26 foreign countries. The United Auto Workers (UAW) became the nation's biggest industrial union. Confrontations between the 'Big Three' and the UAW ushered in a postwar era of collective bargaining. Productivity bargaining, cost-of-living adjustments and group insurance plans brought Detroit's industrial workers the highest standard of living to be found in any major North American metropolis. But it was also in Detroit that ethnic minority unemployment, inner city poverty, decaying neighborhoods and violent street unrest came to symbolize the urban crisis of the 1960s.

Crisis and reorganization

Suburbanization, institutionalized racism and uneven urban growth set the terms of political discourse in Detroit during the 1960s. By the early 1970s, however, it was capital flight to other regions and abroad that most focused public attention. The Great Lakes manufacturing empire was crumbling in the face of regional and international shifts in business investment and employment growth. In 1972, Detroit's civic elite commissioned a study of the exodus of capital from the Motor City. The study's conclusion was alarmingly simple: with outdated production facilities, a public infrastructure in poor condition, high taxes, and a strongly unionized and aggressive labor force, Detroit would be hard-pressed to retain business activity, let alone attract new investment (Mandell, 1975).

For the first time since the Great Depression, catastrophic levels of unemployment failed to dissipate with national economic expansion. Detroit's inner city lost nearly 250,000 jobs and 20 per cent of its population during the 1970s. With one-third of the city lacking any earned income and 60 per cent receiving some form of public assistance, with taxes rising, capital fleeing and property values stagnating, with municipal workers laid off and public services reduced, fiscal crisis became a routine event.

In 1980, the US auto industry experienced an economic slide unparalleled since the Great Depression. The car giants lost $3.5 billion, 250,000 were indefinitely laid off, and an additional 450,000 lost their jobs in supplier industries. Economic recession, rising energy prices, a saturated market for energy-inefficient cars, and increased foreign competition sent the Big Three's profits plummeting. The way the auto production system is laid out in the United States meant hardship piled upon hardship for people in Detroit and the industrial cities of the Great Lakes.

With their survival at stake, the auto giants mounted a reorganization strategy of a depth and scope unprecedented in the industry. Their plan included changes in product design; more global concentration and centralization of capital; redesign of the labor process in relation to new technologies; and transformation in the industry's international division of labor. To meet foreign competition, the Big Three have developed smaller more energy-efficient vehicles with standardized, interchangeable components designed to be manufactured and marketed in many sites in the world. More auto components are now built by computer-controlled machine tools and assembled by robots, while automation is being introduced into design studios, engine plants, warehouses, foundries and tool shops. It costs enormous sums to build a world car, to implement the new technologies and to enter expanding markets; so capital-short firms are pooling resources through joint ventures with international competitors. The auto transnationals are also working out a new international division of labor designed to maximize global profits by minimizing production costs through global resourcing: that is, by locating different segments of the production process in different regional and national locations according to the most favorable wage rates and government subsidies (Shaiken, 1984; ch. 6).

For the Motor City, global reorganization of the auto industry has meant massive job losses, substantial reductions in social services, major union concessions and a declining standard of living (Brazer, 1982). In 1978, auto companies employed 735,000 hourly workers in the United States; by the spring of 1984, that figure had dropped to 565,000 – a decline of 170,000 industrial jobs. About 105,000 of those auto workers were indefinitely laid off, while the remaining 65,000 had simply disappeared from the UAW's rolls (Luria, 1984).

A profitable US auto industry will not ameliorate the social crisis in the Motor City. Why not? Because making smaller automobiles means less machine work, cast iron, steel production and foundry work; because intense competition today will probably lead to overproduction tomorrow as companies attempt to maximize efficiencies from economies of scale, because more pervasive automation means production will outstrip employment growth at a more rapid rate, because continued global sourcing will mean further auto disinvestment, and finally, because the flexibility afforded by the corporate revitalization strategy – the increased centralization of capital in a few global firms, the new international division of labor, and the standardization of the production process on a global scale – will continue to undercut the collective bargaining and strike power of auto workers which augurs further losses in wages, benefits and working conditions.

Corporate stability and growth are premised upon the capacity to respond to changing national and international costs and conditions. The profit logic that once brought investment and growth to the city of Detroit now brings disinvestment, decline and decay. It seems as though the international production premises upon which the Motor City developed – cheap energy, a hegemonic corporate position in national and international auto markets, and expanding employment opportunities to industries linked to car production – have become a subject for study by economic historians.

Decentralization and uneven development

Viewed along the dimensions of time and space, the trajectory of economic development in metropolitan Detroit during this century can usefully be divided into three periods: (1) the era of city building, 1910–49; (2) the era of suburbanization, 1950–78; and (3) the era of regional competition, 1979 to the present. One era does not give way to the next so much as each new period forms a layer upon the ones that came before. The picture stays the same, even as it changes.

The era of city building in Detroit coincided with the creation of the assembly-line and mass production. When Henry Ford built his 'Crystal Palace' in Highland Park in 1913, the modern factory system was born. From then on the auto industry expanded according to a well-defined spatial logic: a factory, then complementary plants and residential development clustered along industrial corridors following railroad lines. Commercial districts emerged along highway arteries paralleling the industrial corridors. The Motor City grew in the wake of an expanding auto industry, outward from the Detroit River – north, west, south – into the hinterland. Development was unevenly distributed across the inner city, where housing was old and the poor were concentrated; the middle city, where land use was mixed and in transition; and the outer city, where urban gentry lived in large homes clustered around schools and parks according to a city plan. The era of city building was dominated by the spatial logic of industrial expansion (Sinclair, 1972).

The era of suburbanization can be dated from 1951, the year the central city's population peaked at 1.85 million residents. The United States experienced unparalleled economic growth during the early postwar years and the logic of industrial expansion stayed much the same, but now it extended beyond the city's limits. The Big Three built 20 new auto plants in the Detroit area during the decade following World War II, all beyond the boundaries of the central city. Complementary industries, commercial development and residential enclaves followed, like metal shavings drawn to a magnet, but this time it was the suburbs that boomed, not the central city. Between the late 1940s and the early 1970s, Detroit's share of the region's manufacturing employment dropped from 60 per cent to 33 per cent. Between 1958 and 1972, Detroit lost 60,000 jobs, mostly in manufacturing and retail trade. The suburbs, on the other hand, gained 247,000 new jobs.

Industrial organization did not change much, but two new development forces were at work during the era of suburbanization: federal policy and the reorganization of commercial capital. The federal government underwrote suburban growth by financing a massive motor system, and by providing mortgages, insurance and tax deductions for new home-buyers. Also critical to the suburban trajectory was the way commercial capitalists reorganized their business operations from downtown emporia and strips to regional shopping malls located on the periphery of the metropolis. Indeed, if the spatial logic of industrial expansion and mass production can be said to have dominated the era of city building, then the era of suburbanization was dominated as much by the reorganization of commercial capital, and federally subsidized mass consumption, as by anything else.

As industrial growth extended to the suburbs, and as commercial capital concentrated on the urban periphery, the principal axis of uneven development shifted from cities within the city to the line that divided the city from its suburbs. In Detroit that line became a racial barrier as the division between central city and suburb came to coincide all too closely with that between black and white.

The Detroit metropolitan area was a thriving economy, stimulated by high levels of capital investment. It contained nearly half of Michigan's population. Residents of this Detroit were mostly white; they lived in single-family houses located in the suburbs; and they earned an income above the state average. But the other Detroit, the central city, had become more and more like a segregated urban enclave during the decades following World War II. Home to hundreds of thousands of poor and unemployed people, the city was now pitted against the suburbs in a dual pattern of uneven urban development (Taylor and Peppard, 1976).

The era of regional competition can be dated from 1980, the year the auto industry experienced its worst depression since the 1930s. In the face of a sharply declining rate of profit brought on by world overproduction and increasing international competition, industrial corporations began shifting blue-collar production work abroad and automating it at home; and they targeted their domestic capital expenditures on administration, research and development, and high-value, high-technology operations. The upshot is a corresponding reorganization of the regional economy according to a new spatial logic.

Deindustrialization now spread out from the central city, and down river, into white suburban Detroit. Now residents in Detroit's industrial, working-class white suburbs came to share many problems with their central city neighbors. But even as capital flight and automation were dealing a hard blow to Detroit's industrial suburbs, a new type of regional growth pole was emerging. Epitomized by Silicon Valley outside of San Franciso, and Route 128 outside of Boston, it is the science city, or the technopolis, as the Japanese like to call it. At the core of the technopolis are universities with strong science and engineering faculties, government-subsidized research parks, and closely linked high-technology companies specializing in high-value production. Oakland County's Technology Park in suburban Detroit is billed as the 'workplace of the 21st Century', and fits this blueprint precisely. The era of regional competition is dominated neither by industrial nor by commercial capital. Rather, the driving force seems to be the creation of new information technologies and their application to all sectors of the economy.

For their part, Detroit officials have tried to revitalize the Motor City by following a corporate center redevelopment strategy. The linchpin in Detroit's redevelopment effort is the Renaissance Center (RenCen), a towering riverfront office, hotel and commercial complex meant to compete with outlying office centers and symoblize the city's corporate future. The Renaissance Center stands at the base of Detroit's central business district and extends along the Detroit Rier. RenCen phase 1 is composed of five towers – a 73 storey cylindrical, glass-walled hotel encircled by four 39-storey octagonal office buildings. In order to construct this massive project Henry Ford put together a 51-member Renaissance Center partnership – the largest private investment group ever assembled in the United States for an urban real estate project (Stark, 1973).

But this attempt to revitalize the central city into serious trouble from the beginning. The heart of the matter was Detroit's depressed downtown real estate market – the most salient indicator of the central city's weak position in the regional economy. The RenCen opened in the wake of the decision to close by three major retailers. The Renaissance Center started losing money immediately, and each year the deficit rose (Knecht, 1983). In April 1982, Henry Ford II announced that the RenCen would be sold at a loss to an investor group headed by a Chicago real estate tycoon. The buyers wanted the RenCen primarily for its tax advantages – depreciation allowances, investment credits and operating loss deductions. But the investor group could not raise sufficient capital to pay the negotiated price of $505 million. In 1983 RenCen's five major lenders, including four top US insurance companies, agreed to trade $220 million in debts for a 53 per cent share of ownership. But it is questionable whether anyone connected with RenCen will ever profit from ownership. It has been a big failure in the business coalition's quest for downtown revitalization.

The relationship between work and residence is changing in the Detroit metropolis, particularly among the Motor City's 'new class' of trend-setting professionals. Commuting is valued less; more people want to live nearer their place of work in planned 'new or old towns-in-town'. Detroit's suburbs are growing to number among Michigan's largest cities. Outlying suburban financial centers are surpassing Detroit's central business district in office space. And suburban industrial communities are hit as hard by disinvestment as any industrial area inside the Motor City. The very distinction between central city and suburbs is fading away.

Instead, a region of independent yet relatively autonomous cities is emerging. Knit together by a regional division of labor, these cities remain deeply divided along lines of race, class and municipal boundary. The principal fault line of uneven development no longer runs among areas within the city, nor between the city and its suburbs; rather it travels among competing cities within a region of cities. In the era of regional competition there is no longer one Detroit, nor two Detroits; there are many Detroits.

HOUSTON: THE CAPITAL OF THE SUNBELT

Specialization and growth

The discovery of oil 90 miles east of Houston in 1901 and subsequent discoveries closer to the city set the stage for Houston to become a major oil and gas center. By 1916 the larger oil corporations were beginning to dominate many sectors of the Texas oil industry; over the next decade they consolidated their control. Houston has since become the center of a world oil and petrochemical production system: 34 of the nation's 35 largest oil companies have located major administrative, research and production facilities in the metropolitan area. In addition to these corporate giants, there are 400 other major oil and gas companies there. Thousands of smaller oil-related companies have attached themselves to these major petroleum companies. About a quarter of US oil refining capacity and one quarter of the oil–gas transmission companies are located in the Houston–Gulf Coast area. One half of all petrochemicals made in the United States are manufactured there.

The expanded flow of profits to the oil–petrochemical sector over the last 20 years has provided the direct capital and borrowing capacity for other capital which lies behind much of Houston's industrial and real estate (spatial) growth. At the heart of investment decision-making by these companies is business leader concern for a 'good business climate', a codeword for an area with lower wages, weaker unions, lower taxes and conservative politics. Companies that function as locators, such as the Fantus Company, have advertised Houston as having one of the best business climates in the US. Houston has grown because of cheaper production costs (e.g. weaker unions, lower wages), weaker physical and structural barriers to new development (e.g. no ageing industrial foundation) and tremendous federal expenditures on infrastructure facilities (e.g. highways) and high-technology defense industries.

In 1973 the OPEC countries gained control over their oil, and once-dominant US companies became primarily suppliers of technology and marketing agents for OPEC oil. US company profits on Middle Eastern oil fell, but the sharp rise in world prices brought great increases in profits on oil controlled by US companies elsewhere. Between 1973 and the early 1980s the value of the oil and gas in Texas fields grew by 500 per cent, though the amount produced declined 28 per cent (Plaut, 1982: 203). In the 1973–5 recession employment in goods-producing industries dropped 6 per cent in cities such as Dallas, but grew by 18 per cent in Houston, because its manufacturing firms produce for the oil world's industry. The rise in OPEC oil prices in 1973–4 gave a boost to oil exploration and drilling, thus stimulating the Houston economy in a time of national recession. Between 1968 and 1980 the percentage of Houston employment in oil exploration, drilling and machinery expanded (Brock, 1981: 1–4).

Prior to the 1973–4 price rise an economic diversification trend was underway, with growing investment in non-oil projects. With the sharp rise in the oil price, oil companies and allied bankers moved away from diversification to a heavier emphasis on investments in oil projects. In the late 1970s there was yet another rise in the OPEC oil price, which further stimulated companies to invest in oil.

Crisis and reorganization

Yet, in 1982–7, Houston was looking a lot like Detroit. Job announcements brought long lines; tax revenues had plummeted; public sector workers were laid off; bond ratings had slipped; firms were going bankrupt in increasing numbers; and corporations were closing plants and shifting work overseas.

World-wide recession had led to an oil glut. The official price for a barrel of oil peaked in November 1981 at $34, then fell to $16 in 1985–1986. Falling oil prices do not motivate companies to drill for oil. The downturn rippled its way through drilling pipe and oil rig production; through construction and trucking; and eventually through retail stores and real estate. Industrial production declined in Houston more rapidly than the national average. The unemployment rate grew more rapidly in Houston than in the nation, reaching 9.7 per cent in 1983, up sharply from 1981. There was a decline in oil refinery use in Texas, from the 91 per cent capacity in the late 1970s to less than 70 per cent capacity in 1983 (Wright, 1982; Plaut, 1983: 16). Between June 1982 and June 1983 the Bayou City lost 75,600 jobs. In 1983, Houston had 952 business failures with $3.8 billion in assets – a substantial increase from 1982. Oil, real estate and retail industries suffered in the same period. In 1984, the number of bankruptcies continued to escalate.

By late 1984, Houston was showing signs of some economic recovery. Unemployment had dropped somewhat. But then there was another deep recession in 1985–87, with thousands of workers being laid off. This recession was due to OPEC dissension. A long-term economic recovery in Houston is contingent upon resurgence in the oil industry. And Texas oil is running out. Houston corporations have been pumping oil for eight decades. Oil production fell 33 per cent between 1972 and 1982, but this decline was obscured by a sixfold rise in oil prices during those years.

There is a question too, about whether Houston's economic base is broad enough to sustain the city in the face of declining oil production and oil prices. In the US, oil refining capacity grew at a 6.5 per cent annual rate in the 1940s and 1950s, while demand grew at just 7 per cent. From the 1960s to the early 1970s capacity grew at a 9.3 per cent rate, only a little less than consumption growth. There was little refinery overcapacity. However, between 1978 and 1982, the demand for crude oil dropped 45 per cent; and for gasoline, 12 per cent. Carmakers were forced to improve fuel-efficiency. Manufacturers and utilities switched from oil to coal and other fuels. This drop in usage resulted in overcapacity. In 1981–3, approximately 80 oil refineries were closed in the US, with a loss of 2.5 million barrels a day in capacity (Jankowski, 1983: 19–21). A number of major refineries in the Houston areas thus cut back production, some permanently. A wave of mergers signalled major reorganization in the oil industry in response to overproduction. Thousands were laid off in the Houston area as a result.

In the 1950s and 1960s, petrochemical manufacturers helped stimulate new uses for synthetic materials. The petrochemical markets grew at a 13–17 per cent annual rate. The industry's growth was based in part on cheap oil–gas feedstocks. These oil–gas feedstocks became much more expensive after the 1970s' price hikes. In the 1970s, according to a top executive at Exxon, petrochemical markets grew at only a 5 per cent annual increase. Overcapacity reached 16 per cent in the 1970s. By the 1980s, demand was dropping and overcapacity increasing. Overcapacity had increased to between 20 and 35 per cent, with Texas plants up to 40 per cent in 1982–3. Falling oil prices reduce the cost of materials for petrochemical firms, but they do not offset the large-scale overcapacity that exists. New petrochemical plants are under construction in Canada and in the Middle East. And the list of items for which plastics can be substituted has grown smaller as the years pass. Since 1980 the over-capacity has forced European petrochemical/ plastics manufacturers to shut down one-sixth of their capacity.

Over the last few decades petrochemical firms have been more concerned with what their competitors are doing than with the total market for petrochemicals. Competing with each other for market shares, they have in classical capitalist fashion created a situation where overproduction results in recession, shutdowns and cutbacks. In 1982 utilization rates in Diamond Shamrock's three large Houston petrochemical complexes had fallen to 60–5 per cent, down from 90–5 per cent three years before; and Exxon's Baytown plants suffered from falling utilization rates, which came just as a new plastics plant was opened. Several manufacturers, including Exxon, retired ageing plants instead of spending capital to upgrade them (Brubaker, 1982: 1,15).

US petrochemical companies have mounted a reorganization strategy to meet the overproduction crisis. They are cutting capacity and retrenching in basic petrochemical production, and they are concentrating on producing higher value speciality chemicals which are beyond the technological capacity of most Third World nations. This amounts to a structural realignment in the world petrochemical industry. A new dual, two-tiered international division of labor in the petrochemical industry is emerging which parallels tendencies at work in other US manufacturing industries. US companies will gradually reduce operations here, and focus on speciality chemicals. Third World countries are expanding into basic petrochemical production. By 1987, the Saudi Arabian Sabic complex is expected to produce 2 million tons of ethylene annually, mostly for export at prices below those of western producers because of access to cheap raw materials (Tagliabue, 1983).

This overseas expansion has involved US petrochemical companies, which have participated in overseas production through joint ventures – a distinctive type of global sourcing. By providing technical and financial support these companies gain a stake in petrochemical business that competes with their domestic operations. In 1983, Diamond Shamrock, for example, owned a petrochemical plant in Chile and joint-venture plants in Brazil and Korea. In 1983, Celanese had a plant in Mexico, while Exxon had plants in Scotland, Saudi Arabia and Canada. Shell's largest chemical complex was in Saudi Arabia. This global reorganization is bringing economic trouble to the greater Houston area.

Decentralization and uneven development

The oil industry has brought periods of rapid growth to Houston. Houston's population grew more than 100 per cent in the 1920s; the 1940s, 1950s, 1960s and 1970s also saw some of the more rapid spurts in US urban history. Coupled with the commitment of the local elite to auto-centered transit and private enterprise in housing – and a fierce opposition to mass transit and public housing – this rapid growth created a decentralized city. Houston is a very decentralized city, with builders and developers active in *seven* major business centers. Commercial and industrial corporations have commissioned or leased a vast array of megastructures (industrial parks, shopping malls, multiple-use projects and office towers built in these business centers). Between 1970 and 1981 a total of 361 large (more than 100,000 square feet) office buildings were built in the area, more than 80 per cent of all existing office buildings. Scattered between and beyond these business centers are residential areas, including condominium apartment buildings and sprawling suburban subdivisions, some of which are 25 or more miles from downtown.

Houston's developers have been pioneers in multiple-use developments (called MXDs in developers' publications), the newest type of megastructures added to urban development. Developers and allied powerful real estate actors see MXDs as the new wave of urban development. Take, for example, the Houston Center project. In 1968, Texas Eastern Corporation, a major Houston oil-gas company, bought 33 square blocks of downtown Houston for $40–50 million. At the time of purchase this was a mixed area of older commercial buildings, apartment blocks and houses. The development has been seen by its developers as remolding urban life. By 1982, Houston Center included a 44-story office tower and a 46-story office tower linked together by an 8-story street-spanning wing. Two blocks were sold to a major bank. A 30-story hotel was constructed as part of the project along with an exclusive athletic and dining club. In the mid-1970s, however, Texas Eastern ran into a problem with their development schedule and sold a half interest in major sections of the project to Canada's Cadillac Fairview Company, one of the world's largest development corporations. This multi-block Houston Center project, when completed, will be the largest private project in US urban history.

This and other megastructure projects illustrate the central role of oil and gas companies in Houston's physical development. The large office and MXD complexes scattered in the seven 'downtowns' in Houston are populated primarily by oil and gas companies and by the legal, accountancy and other business service firms serving the oil industry. Some of the capital for this real estate development has come, directly or indirectly, from the huge surplus profits won by oil and gas companies since 1970.

Not only development but also speculation helps to create sprawl in this low-density city. Oil and real estate corporations and old Houston oil families have bought up large areas of land in and around Houston, with the expectation that the land will apprenciate in value. Foreign corporations, from Germany to Canada, have done the same. Banks, syndicates of doctors, real estate people and large corporations have bought and held land waiting for its rapid appreciation. This has taken place in central areas and on the suburban fringe, where it has helped create a leapfrog pattern of development.

Yet, not all Houston residents profit from growth. Houston's low-income and minority homeowners and tenants have suffered greatly from market-oriented growth. The central city houses large numbers of black and Mexican-American, low- and middle-income families. Many areas of the central city have suffered from gentrification, the replacement of poorer families with better-off professional, technical and managerial families who wish to live near their jobs in the office towers. Gentrification has displaced residents of ethnic areas as well as elderly whites. The Fourth Ward is one of Houston's oldest black communities, with the misfortune of being in the path of expansion of the central business district. The area is populated by tenants living in single-family dwellings and in a major public housing project. Because of its proximity to downtown, developers have their eye on the area. A number of prominent consultant reports have suggested that the area should be redeveloped. The major public housing estate there is scheduled for demolition, significantly reducing the amount of housing for middle-income families.

Since 1982 Houston's booming real estate industry has experienced a dramatic decline, in large part because the energy industry is in a classic crisis of overproduction. Corporate expansion in the 1970s led to the proliferation of skyscrapers, to over-construction. Houston's housing market, for several years the national leader, comprised 10 per cent of all new US housing in the early 1980s. In 1974–74, about 100 million square feet of office space was built. Yet in 1983–4, the building boom collapsed. By mid-1984 Houston's office space glut was the *highest* among the top 25 cities in the US. About 25–30 per cent of the office space was vacant in Houston compared to 5–10 per cent in Chicago and New York. This glut was created by extreme overproduction by competing developers seeking profits in a booming oil town. When Houston's oil economy faltered, so did its office construction boom. Large inventories of new and used single-family homes were unsold; and large numbers of apartments were vacant. Houston's mostly new hotels and motels were 90 per cent full in 1981, but by 1984 they were less than half occupied. A major real crisis was on hand, one which is likely to continue as Houston faces the geographical consequences of slow oil–gas industry decline.

Houston is also facing a major infrastructure crisis. The hidden side of its 'good business climate', its low taxes and scaled-down government, has been a neglect of sewerage, water, flood prevention and other infrastructure facilities. This neglect has simply postponed the cost of paying for decaying or seriously inadequate facilities. Hundreds of billions of dollars will be required to meet Houston's escalating infrastructure costs. And that does not include the human costs of this neglect. Paying for infrastructure repair will require massive tax increases, which are even less likely in an era of slow economic decline. The 'free enterprise' city has cost, and will continue to cost, its citizenry heavily in monetary and social expenses not normally enumerated in promotional and news media accounts of Houston's growth.

CONCLUSION

Because Detroit and Houston are spatial locations in a global system of production and exchange, the forces shaping their convergent and divergent paths have not been bounded by municipal, regional or even national lines. Three themes have ordered our tale of these two cities: (1) specialization and growth; (2) crisis and reorganization; and (3) decentralization and uneven development. It is to these reference points that we turn to draw our concluding comparisons.

Specialization and growth

Detroit and Houston evolved as specialized nodes in internationally organized production systems, one centered on the auto industry, the other on oil and petrochemicals. The Motor City grew and prospered, expanded horizontally and vertically, all in time with the beat of plant, warehouse and office investment for the production of cars. Detroit developed as a one-industry town located near supplies of labor and raw materials. The mass production of automobiles spurred a vast and growing demand for fuel, and at the other end of an auto–oil 'pipeline', more than 1000 miles away, Houston began to prosper not long after Detroit's emergence as the Motor City. Experiencing a series of growth spurts, particularly in the 1920s, the 1940s and the 1960s, Houston became the oil capital of the world. It too expanded horizontally and vertically, with its seven business centers and hundreds of major plants, office towers and shopping centers. The Oil City too developed as a one-industry town located near crucial raw materials and labor pools.

Detroit's auto specialization generated a leapfrog logic of spatial development. Industry, commerce and residences decentralized into sub-urban rings, assisted by federal highway and housing finance programs. But even in the midst of postwar prosperity, large numbers of blacks were confined to blighted areas in the inner city. Houston's own distinctive specialization created a complex geographical network of oil–gas centers encircled by suburban belts. Houston's spatial brawl was assisted by the same federal highway and housing programs that conditioned suburbanization in the Motor City. The auto and housing industries played the most aggressive role in the postwar 'Highway Lobby' that pressured the federal government to support new highway and housing programs, while the oil companies remained more in the background. Yet Houston's oil interests were just as firmly committed to a low-density, decentralized urban environment. Black and Mexican-American workers and their families were a large island of poverty in a central city bordered by huge megastructures, like Houston Center.

Crisis and reorganization

The era of prosperity for the city of Detroit was temporary. Detroit's economic hegemony in world auto markets and its expanding employment in auto firms proved transitory. Global crisis and reorganization in the auto industry brought massive economic decline to the central city – a loss of 27 per cent of its population and 50 per cent of its auto subsidiary manufacturing companies. As its industry left town, its human problems grew.

Yet even the 'shining buckle of the Sunbelt', once thought to be immune to urban crisis, experienced the fundamental contradictions of a capitalist world system. The 1982–7 recession was Houston's worst ever; the Oil City had even boomed through most of the Great Depression. The 10 per cent unemployment, over 1000 bankruptcies, oil refinery and other oil company layoffs, and cutbacks in the petrochemical industry indicate that Houston too is showing the effects of crisis and reorganization in the world oil–gas industry. Global sourcing in oil, oil refining and petrochemicals is not as far along as the reorganization of the auto industry, but it is underway.

Capital moves on a world market stage, and with modern modes of transportation and communication, big businesses can accelerate investment at a high velocity (Bluestone and Harrison, 1983). Working people and their families, on the other hand, move in locally-bounded communities. They cannot chart a new course with capital's velocity. Corporation's investment space outdistances people's living space and that is the fundamental urban contradiction in the world capitalist system.

Decentralization and uneven development

Capitalists themselves are caught up in the investment–living space contradiction, as indicated by Henry Ford II's failed attempt to revitalize Detroit's central city with a multi-million dollar investment in the Renaissance Center. The same contradiction is revealed in Houston's over supply of office towers and residential blocks which now have record-setting vacancies. During the next two decades Houston may come to bask in the same light that is now refracted through the 'Rust Belt'. And given Houston's starved social services sectors, the human and monetary costs of Houston's decline could well surpass Detroit's own experience.

So, ironically, the declining center of a crumbling Great Lakes manufacturing empire and the booming buckle of the Sunbelt both turn out to be one-industry towns whose export industries are going through a global reorganization that bodes well for neither's economic future. Officials in Detroit and Houston recognize the need to restructure and diversify their local economies. And both are emphasizing hi-tech complexes and suburban office–commercial parks; but that development policy presages further inequality and uneven development along lines of race, class and territory.

The Reagan administration's New Federalism policy notwithstanding, the extent to which each city can muster new comparative advantages and revitalize its economic base will continue to be affected by the kind of relationship each etablishes with the federal government. And here another irony comes into play. For one big advantage Houston, the self-proclaimed bastion of free enterprise, retains over Detroit, a fading outpost of the welfare state, is Houston's greater ability to garner largesse from the federal government; not the kind distributed by the Department of Health, Education and Welfare; but the sort passed out by the Pentagon.[2] Today's massive defense spending on the Pentagon's production system, the military-industrial complex, is spawning new industries, setting the direction for future economic development, and enriching or impoverishing regions. Even so, the critical issues always seem to remain the same. New urban development continues to be targeted to the privileged few. Power over urban development continues to be concentrated among a handful of individuals and corporations whose reach spans far beyond the metropolis. And urban development continues to be uneven, unpredictable and precarious, since the most important development decisions are made in private offices not in publicly accountable places.

NOTES

1 One of the strongest advocates for a Houston-style solution for what ails Detroit are the editors of the Motor City's own largest circulation newspaper, the *Detroit News*. Cf., for example, the special issue of the *Detroit News* editorial page reprints entitled, *Wealth and Welfare* (Detroit: *Detroit News*, 1985).
2 While Michigan produces more manufactured goods than all but two states, it produces fewer defense goods than all but three. Texas, on the other hand, has ten times the number of defense jobs, seven times the defense payroll, twice the total federal procurement dollars, and twice as many federal jobs as does Michigan (Mazza and Hogan, 1981). Houston's own special prize is the National

Aeronautics and Space Administration's (NASA) Manned Space Craft Center won in the 1960s through the political clout of Lyndon Baines Johnson (then US Vice-President) and the private lobbying of Brown & Root and big landowning oil corporations, like Exxon. By 1983, NASA employed 10,000 people, two-thirds in private companies dependent upon military research and development and procurement; and NASA's $600 million a year budget sustained over 1200 Houston firms.

REFERENCES

Berry, Brian J. L. and John D. Kasarda (1977) *Contemporary Urban Ecology*, New York; Macmillan.

Bluestone, Barry and Bennett Harrison (1983) *The Deindustrialization of America*, New York: Basic Books.

Brazer, Harvey (ed.) (1982) *Michigan's Fiscal and Economic Structure*, Ann Arbor: University of Michigan Press.

Brock, Bronwyn (1981) 'Houston less vulnerable than Dallas-Fort Worth to impact of the recession', *Voice* (Dallas Federal Reserve Bank), (October): (1982) 1–5.

Brubaker, Laurel 'Petrochemicals: Pressures Push Area Industry to Breaking Point', *Houston Business Journal* (15 November: 1: 5.

Castells, Manuel (1973) *La Question Urbaine*, Paris: Maspero.

Chandler, Alfred Jr. (1962) *Strategy and Structure*, Boston: MIT Press.

Chase-Dunn, Christopher (1984) 'Urbanization in the world system: New directions for research'. In Michael Peter Smith (ed.), *Cities in Transformation*, Beverly Hills: Sage.

Detroit News editorial staff (1986) *Wealth and Welfare*, Detroit: *Detroit News*.

Friedmann, John and Goetz Wolff (1982) 'World city formation: an agenda for research and action', *International Journal of Urban and Regional Research*, vol. 6, no. 3 (September): 309–44.

Hamilton, F. E. (1982) 'Industrial systems: a dynamic force behind international trade', *Professional Geographer*, vol. 33, no. 1: 26–35.

Harvey, David (1978) 'On countering the Marxian myth – Chicago style', *Comparative Urban Research*, vol. 6, nos. 2 and 3: 28–45.

Hawley, Amos (1971) *Urban Society* New York: Ronald Press.

—— (1984) 'Human ecological and Marxian theories', *American Journal of Sociology*, vol. 89, no. 4 (January): 904–17.

Hurley, Neil P. (1959) 'The automotive industry: a study of industrial location', *Land Economics*, vol. 35, no. 1 (February): 1–14.

Hymer, Stephen (1971) 'The multinational corporation and the law of uneven development'. In J. W. Bhagwati (ed.), *Economics and World Order*, New York: Macmillan.

Janowski, Patrick (1983) 'Refining and the challenge of maturity', *Houston* (July): 19–21.

Knecht, Bruce G. (1983) 'Renaissance Center: Ford's costly and failing bid to revive Detroit', *New York Times*, 3 July.

Luria, Dan (1984) 'Deindustrialization and public policy: Labor'. Paper presented at the Midwest Sociological Society Meetings, Chicago, Illinois, 20 April.

McKenzie, R. J. (1972) 'The concept of dominance and world organization', *American Journal of Sociology*, vol. 33: 28–42.

Mandell, Lewis (1975) *Industrial Location Decisions: Detroit Compared with Atlanta and Chicago*, New York: Praeger.

Mazza, Jacqueling and Bill Hogan (1981) *The State of the Region 1981, Economic Trends in the Northeast and Midwest*, Washington, D.C.: Northeast Midwest Institute.

Plant, Tom (1983) The Texas Economy, *Texas Business Review*, January–February: 15–20.

Rheinhold, Robert (1983) 'Texas economy seems exempt from recovery', *New York Times*, 6 August.

Shaiken, Harley (1984) *Work Transformed: Automation and Labor in the Computer Age*, New York: Holt, Rheinehart & Winston.

Sinclair, Robert (1972) *The Face of Detroit: A Spatial Synthesis*, Detroit: Wayne State University, Department of Geography.

Taylor, Milton and Donald Peppard (1976) *Jobs for the Jobless: Detroit's Unresolved Dilemma*, East Lansing, Mich.: Institute for Community Development.

Stark, Al (1973) 'Renaissance Center: how a team of businessmen put it all together', *Detroit News*, 24 June.

Tagliabue, John (1983) 'Oversupply in petrochemicals', *New York Times*, 2 April.

Timberlake, Michael (ed.) (1986) *Urbanization in the World Economy*, New York: Academic Press.

Wallerstein, Immanuel (1974) 'The rise and future demise of the world capitalist system: Concepts for comparative analysis', *Comparative Studies in Society & History*, vol. 16: 389–415.

Wright, Mickey (1982) 'Texas industrial water use long-term projection'. Unpublished draft report, Texas Department of Water Resources, Austin, Texas.

Zukin, Sharon (1980) 'A decade of the new urban sociology', *Theory and Society*, vol. 9: 575–601.

8

Economic Restructuring and the Internationalization of the Los Angeles Region

Edward W. Soja

The concepts of restructuring and internationalization have proved effective in capturing the scope, quality and interpretive meaning of the profound changes which have been taking place throughout the world economy over the past twenty years. In its most general sense, *restructuring* is meant to convey a break in secular trends and a shift towards a significantly different order and configuration of social, economic and political life. It thus evokes a sequence of breaking down and building up again, deconstruction and attempted reconstitution, arising from certain incapacities or weaknesses in the established order which preclude conventional adaptations and demand significant structural change instead.

Although this connection is often blurred and buried under idealized evolutionary schema in which change just seems to happen or appears to punctuate some ineluctable march toward 'progress', restructuring is rooted in *crisis* and a competitive conflict between the old and the new, between an 'inherited' and a 'projected' order. It is not a mechanical or automatic process, nor are its potential results predetermined. In its hierarchy of contemporary manifestations, from the local to the global, the restructuring process must be seen as originating in and responding to severe shocks in pre-existing social conditions and configurations; and as triggering an intensification of competitive struggles to control the forces which shape material life. Restructuring thus implies flux and transition, offensive and defensive postures, a complex mix of continuity and change.

In conjunction with the restructuring hypothesis, *internationalization* refers to both a particular scale at which restructuring is taking place (i.e. the scale of the global, the world system, the organization of an international division of labor) and to a specific set of processes affecting economic restructuring at all scales. The first meaning directs attention to the changing structure and composition of the global political economy. The second makes these changes an integral (if not central) part of the restructuring process itself wherever it is taking place.

That we are currently in the midst of a period of extensive restructuring and an accelerated internationalization of local economies seems difficult to deny. There is also widespread agreement among those attempting to interpret these trends that they were sparked by a series of interrelated crises – from the urban riots of the mid-1960s to the deep worldwide recession of 1973–75 – which marked the end of the prolonged period of economic expansion following World War II. Although this is less widely agreed upon, it can also be argued that these crises arose primarily within the particular organizational structures and patterning of social and spatial relations which sustained and shaped the expansionary capitalist accumulation of the postwar boom years. They can thus be seen as crises in the established international division of labor and global distribution of political power; in the expanded and now clearly contradictory functions of the capitalist state; in the Keynesian welfare system of agreements between governments, corporations and organized labor; in the well-consolidated forms of exploitation of women, ethnic minorities and the environment; in the inherited regional divisions of labor within countries; in the spatial forms and financial functioning of cities and metropolitan areas; in the design and infrastructure of the urban built environment; in the extent to which capitalist production relations are imprinted into everyday life, in the workplace and in the home.

Each of these arenas of restructuring has become the focus for a growing literature and a context for critical interpretation and debate. Each restructuring process has also generated a constellation of catchphrases aimed at capturing and defining the new forms and patterns assumed to be emerging. The phrases are familiar: 'Post-Industrial Society' and the 'New Services Economy', a 'New International Economic Order' along with 'Newly Industrialized Countries' (NICs) and the 'Peripheralization of the Core', a 'Power Shift' between 'Sunbelt' and 'Snowbelt' and the 'Deindustrialization of America', the 'Computer Age' and the 'Information Society', the 'Post-Welfare State' and the 'New Austerity', the growth of 'World Cities' and 'Global Capitalism', 'Think Global – Act Local'.

Concurrent with empirical processes of global restructuring and the development of a hyperbolic vocabulary to describe them, there has been a significant restructuring taking place in the broad realm of social theory. Inherited paradigms of western social science as well as western Marxism have been experiencing an homologous period of crisis and attempted reconstruction, marked by a decomposition of many established modes of interpretation and prescription and an effort to create reconstituted forms and approaches better suited to understand and act upon contemporary social reality. This restructuring of theory and practice is also in a state of flux and is similarly beset with competitive conflicts between the old and the new, between an inherited and a projected order, between continuity and change.

The purpose of this paper is to view the contemporary restructuring process, both in its concrete manifestations within the world economy and in its implications for social theory, through the 'window' of the specific recent experience of the Los Angeles urban region. Most of the empirical information which is included has been drawn from an earlier work (Soja, Morales and Wolff, 1983), but it has been recast and updated to emphasize a series of more general arguments and to set the particular local experience more directly into a comparative framework of urban restructuring studies. The paper is best read, therefore, not as a detailed description of the recent history of the Los Angeles region but as an indicative essay on the theorization and interpretation of urban change in a global context.

The organization of the discussion of Los Angeles is thus in itself a suggested framework for examining the changes currently taking place in other major urban-industrial regions. Rather than selecting singular and discrete themes for describing the restructuring process, emphasis is given to three paired relationships which together depict the underlying and often contradictory dynamic of contemporary urban and regional restructuring: deindustrialization and reindustrialization, geographical decentralization and recentralization, the peripheralization of labor and the internationalization of capital. Los Angeles is presented as the place where these interactive processes converge, articulate and become peculiarly magnified in intensity. The paper ends with a brief retrospective epilogue on the theorization and retheorization of the urban, not so much as a definitive declaration but as an invitation to further debate.

IT ALL COMES TOGETHER IN LA

The heading to this section, adapted from the immodest slogan of the *Los Angeles Times*, aptly describes the degree to which the Los Angeles urban region has become a microcosm of the multiple forms of restructuring differentially affecting other major cities and regions throughout the world. The particular combination and interrelation of changes which have occurred over the past twenty years is unique, but condensed within them are concrete expressions and reflections of the recent experiences of Houston and Detroit, Lower Manhattan and the South Bronx, Miami and Boston, São Paulo and Singapore. There may be no other comparable region which presents so vividly such a composite assemblage and articulation of urban restructuring processes. Los Angeles is literally a paradigmatic case, a 'conjugation' of the recent history of capitalist urbanization in almost all its inflections.

The urban region referred to consists of a conglomeration of cities and built-up areas which almost fills a 60-mile-radius circle around its nominal urban nucleus (the civic center of the City of Los Angeles) and extends over all or part of five counties (Los Angeles, Orange, Riverside, San Bernardino and Ventura). The total population within this area is now nearly 12.5 million and its gross regional product would rank it fourteenth among all the countries in the world (just behind India and the Netherlands and just ahead of Australia and Mexico in GNP. Contrary to many popular images of the region, it is a major industrial metropolis which, since the 1930s, has been the premier growth pole of industrial capitalism. Over the past half-century, employment in manufacturing has grown by over 1.1 million as the region rode the crest not only of the war economy and the postwar boom, but also maintained its industrial expansion through the crisis led economic restructuring of the past two decades.

This apparent continuity of urban and industrial expansion, however, masks the significant changes which have been taking place during this period in the overall fabric of urban social and spatial relations: in the location of industry and the geographical distribution of jobs, in the organization of the labor process and the composition of the workforce, in the incidence and intensity of working-class organization and community struggles, in the scale and structure of external contacts and exchange. The inherited urban mosaic has almost been transformed into a kaleidoscope of changing forms and functions, juxtaposing and interconnecting what may initially appear to be opposing tendencies and contradictory trends.

The deindustrialization and reindustrialization of Los Angeles

'Frostbelt' and 'Sunbelt' regional attributes come together in the Los Angeles area, intermeshing to produce a complete mix of selective industrial decline and rapid industrial expansion. The result is a markedly different industrial geography from that which had developed by 1960. Earlier rounds of industrial growth had concentrated production and employment primarily within a broad zone stretching southward from the city center of Los Angeles to the twin ports of San Pedro and Long Beach, with important outliers in the San Fernando and San Gabriel valleys and the so-called 'Inland Empire' of San Bernardino County. Within this extensive urban industrial landscape, whole municipalities such as Vernon and the bluntly named City of Industry and City of Commerce became almost entirely devoted to manufacturing and related services, leaving little room for a resident population: almost 50,000 people worked in Vernon, for example, but less than 100 lived there. Other cities such as Southgate (next door to Watts and almost midway between downtown Los Angeles and the ports) mixed heavy industrial production with some of the most attractive working-class neighborhoods in the country. These were almost entirely white neighborhoods, it should be added, for running through this industrial zone was one of the most rigidly defined racial divides in any American city.

Today, these areas have become the Detroit of the Los Angeles region, with numerous plant closures, high unemployment, economically devastated neighborhoods, extensive outmigration, and deskilling and wage-reducing occupational shifts from industry to service jobs. What had once been the second largest automobile assembly industry in the country has been reduced to a single plant in Van Nuys, itself currently threatened with closure. A tyre manufacturing industry second only to Akron has entirely disappeared, along with most of the southern California steel industry. In the four years from 1978 to 1982, at least 75,000 jobs were lost due to plant closures and indefinite layoffs, affecting primarily a segment of the labor market which was highly unionized and contained an unusually large proportion of well-paid minority and female blue-collar workers.

In Southgate, since 1980, the closure of Firestone Rubber, General Motors and Norris Industries-Weiser Lock represented the loss of over 12,500 jobs, from their peak employment of earlier years. In adjacent Watts, economic conditions have deteriorated more rapidly than in any other community within the City of Los Angeles and are now worse than they were at the time of the black riots in Watts in 1965. In the fifteen years after the riots, the area of predominantly black south-central Los Angeles which contains Watts lost 40,000 in population, its labor force was reduced by 20,000, and median family income fell to $5,900, $2,500 below the city median for the black population. Only minimal improvements have occurred in the 1980s.

This selective deindustrialization and job loss has had a major effect on the overall strength of organized labor. During the 1970s, unionization rates in Los Angeles County dropped from over 30 per cent to about 23 per cent. In Orange County, the drop was even more pronounced and, in manufacturing, which was experiencing an extraordinary expansion of employment, unionization rates plummeted from 26.4 to 10.5 per cent. This represented an absolute decline of over one quarter of the union membership in 1971. Declining union membership in turn helped to strengthen management efforts to rescind many of the contractual gains achieved by organized labor in the two decades following World War II.

The deindustrialization and de-unioniation of Los Angeles has reflected national and global trends generated in response to the economic and political crises which shattered the postwar boom and the Keynesian 'productivity deal' that was so much part of the expansionary period. As occurred during similar periods of crisis and restructuring in the past, technological innovation, corporate-managerial strategies, and state policies became more directly and explicitly focused on two increasingly vital and closely related objectives: the restoration of expanding profits and the establishment of more effective control over the labor force. Under the rationale of 'rationalization', a renewed celebration of the 'creative destruction' supposed to underlie capitalist development, the economic landscape which became consolidated during the post-war years began to be selectively destroyed and equally selectively reconstructed.

This comprehensive attempt to discipline labor (along with less efficient capitals and major segments of the central and local state) has been the essential core of the contemporary restructuring process, a means through which 'new room' for accelerated accumulation is being opened up: through reduced labor costs, the breakdown of the most powerful working-class organizations, increasing centralization and concentration of capital, intensi-fied capital mobility to establish a constant threat of closure and relocation, induced technological innovation to cut costs and create improved instruments for labor control and efficiency, growing subsidization of large corporations by the state and local government, all wrapped up in ideological programs to justify sacrifice and austerity by some for the greater national good.

From this more general perspective, the deindustrialization of Los Angeles has not simply been the local expression of an innocent process of modernization and post-industrial evolution, or merely a minor sidelight to an otherwise booming urban region. It has been a critical fulcrum around which the other aspects of social and spatial restructuring revolve. It forms, for example, the necessary introduction and backdrop to the expansive reindustrialization which has been taking place since the 1960s.

The reindustrialization of Los Angeles has been impressive. From 1970 to 1980, when the entire country experienced a net increase of less than a million manufacturing jobs, the Los Angeles region expanded by over 225,000. This net addition was more than that of the next two leading urban growth regions (San Francisco and Houston) combined and contrasted sharply with the combined net loss of 650,000 jobs in New York, Chicago, Philadelphia and Detroit. Most of this employment growth was concentrated in two very different segments of the industrial economy, the first a cluster of technologically-advanced sectors based on electronics, aerospace and massive defense contracting, the second a booming garment industry. Employment growth in these and functionally-related sectors enabled Los Angeles to maintain its position as a pre-eminent center of industrial production despite both selective deindustrialization and an extensive switch to the tertiary labor market.

The combined employment growth in seven sectors specializing in high-technology production (Aircraft and Parts, Guided Missiles and Space Vehicles, Office and Computing Machines, Radio and TV Equipment, Communications Equipment, Electronic Components and Accessories, Measuring and Controlling Devices) was over 110,00 in the 1970s. This represented an expansion of over 50 per cent and a net addition greater than the total increment of manufacturing jobs in Houston over the same period. If one compares this job growth with the total employment in the same seven sectors in Santa Clara County for 1979 (about 147,000), it can be claimed that during the 1970s the Los Angeles region *added* a high-technology labor force almost the equivalent of the entire Silicon Valley. More recent data show that by 1985 Los Angeles County alone employed over 250,000 people in the Bureau of Labor Statistics 'Group 3' category, another widely used definition of high technology industry. The equivalent figure for Santa Clara County was 160,000.

The Los Angeles region is today reputed to contain the highest concentration of mathematicians, scientists, engineers, skilled technicians and high-security-cleared production workers in the country. It has also been a leading recipient of prime defense contracts since the 1940s. Indeed, what ties together the seven SIC sectors referred to earlier more than anything else has been their shared dependency upon technology arising out of Department of Defense and NASA research and the stimulus of military contracts. Much of the continued growth of high-technology industries into the 1980s can be attributed to the demand stimulation arising from the Reagan administration's Keynesian policy of military expansion.

The growth of the garment industry has been equally revealing of very different aspects of the changing regional economy. Employment in this sector grew by nearly 60 per cent between 1970 and 1980, representing 12 per cent of total manufacturing employment growth and a net addition of over 32,000 jobs. This growth was closely associated with the rapid expansion of another segment of the labor market. Not only has the 'high technocracy' settled in extraordinary numbers in Los Angeles, but so too has what is probably the largest pool of low-wage, weakly organized, easily disciplined immigrant labor in the country. This still growing labor pool has affected virtually every sector of the regional economy, including the aerospace and electronics industry. Its imprint has been most visible, however, in the production of garments, especially in the category of 'women's, misses' and juniors' outwear', which tends to be highly labor-intensive, difficult to mechanize, and organized around small shops to adapt more efficiently to rapidly changing fashion trends.

It has been estimated that of the approximately 125,000 jobs in the garment industry, about 80 per cent are held by undocumented workers and more than 90 per cent by women. Unionization rates are low and infringements of minimum wage, overtime, child labor and occupational safety laws are endemic. Sweatshops which provoke images of nineteenth-century London have become as much a part of the restructured landscape of Los Angeles as the abandoned factory site and the new printed circuits plant. And, as previously noted, the sweatshops appear not only in the garment industry but in other manufacturing sectors as well.

Both the deindustrialization and reindustrialization of Los Angeles are to some extent continuations of trends which began before the mid-1960s. Their acceleration, however, and their linkage to other changes, have resulted in a major transformation of the sectoral structure of the regional economy and the composition and segmentation of the regional labor market. Over the past twenty years, the Los Angeles labor market has become increasingly polarized as its middle segment of skilled and unionized blue-collar workers dwindles in size, a small number of its expelled workers trickle up to an expanded white-collar technocracy, and many more percolate down into a relatively lower-skilled and lower-wage reservoir of production and service workers, swollen by massive inmigration.

To consider only this three-part division, however, is not enough, for the new segmentation and recomposition of the labor market is much more finely grained and complex. Embedded in it is not only the juxtaposition of a Houston and a Detroit but also many of the characteristics of the Boston region, where a deep and prolonged process of labor disciplining, plant closures and capital flight produced the conditions for an economic recovery based in large part on rapidly expanding high technology and service sectors (Harrison, 1984). This occupational recycling of the labor market reinforces the polarization of wages and skills, while simultaneously increasing the number and variety of employment specializations at the top and bottom bulges of the labor market. Cutting across these occupational shifts and sectoral restructuring is a further segmentation based on race, ethnicity, immigration status and gender. The end-result in Los Angeles is a regional labor market more occupationally differentiated and socially fragmented than ever before in its history.

Geographical decentralization and recentralization

Sectoral restructuring and increasing labor market segmentation have been paralleled by an equally pronounced spatial restructuring and changes in the occupational geography of the region. As the increasingly polarized and fragmented labor market is settled into new residential patterns and the collection of workplaces is increased and redistributed, the spatial form of the region has been significantly modified. The resulting spatial restructuring of production and consumption patterns at first also appears paradoxical, much like the combination of deindustrialization and reindustrialization, for it has involved both a decentralization and recentralization in the structure of the urban space economy. The integral logic of these apparently opposing trends, however, begins to make more sense when seen in the larger context of the periodicity of crisis and restructuring in the historical geography of capitalist urbanization.

Major periods of economic crisis and restructuring in American history, such as the last several decades of the nineteenth century and the Great Depression, have been associated with significant modifications in urban form, each tending towards a greater decentralization of population and employment patterns, each reflecting the need for reinvigorated capital accumulation and labor control. The persistent formation and reformation of the urban geographical landscape has thus always been a vital part of the urbanization process, both as a product shaped by changing political economies and as a conditioning factor shaping the trajectory of change itself.

Towards the end of the nineteenth century, for example, the classic form of the competitive industrial capitalist city (with Chicago as one of its paradigmatic expressions) began to disintegrate. Its extraordinary concentration of economic production and employment around the central urban core, the product of a long period of expansive industrial capitalism, was partly reduced as factory production decentralized increasingly into the urban fringe and such new satellite industrial centers as Gary and East St Louis. Accompanying this industrial decentralization was a residential suburbanization led primarily by an expanding group of managers, supervisors and professionals. One of the many effects of these changes was an increasing fragmentation of organized labor and an associated intensification of residential segregation by occupation, class and race. The models of urban form constructed by the urban ecologists of the 1920s and 1930s captured the continuing imprint of an earlier and more orderly urban structure but missed many of the major changes which had been taking place in the previous fifty years.

A similar round of accelerated decentralization was stimulated by the political conditions and legislative programs of the Great Depression and the New Deal, leading to the even more extensive residential, industrial and commercial suburbanization of the postwar years. Again, a key part of this restructuring process was the opportunity it provided for renewed economic expansion (e.g. through the explosion of demand for goods and services by newly suburbanized populations) and more effective labor control (e.g. through still further segmentation of the labor market and the ideological ties of worker home-ownership). Expanding metropolitanization left in the now relatively smaller central cities a residual mix of competitive sector firms, older industries, some luxury shops and hotels, key governmental agencies and major banks, some remaining corporate headquarters, a growing 'underground' economy, the largest concentration of minorities and the poor, and a constant tension between deterioration and renewal.

The current period of crisis and restructuring appears also to be stimulating another round of accelerated and selective decentralization for many of the same reasons. It may be premature to generalize about these changes at this time, but certain patterns seem to have become well established. First of all, the boundaries of the decentralization process have become much broader than the metropolitan region itself. Both population and industry are now more than ever before in American history decentralizing into smaller towns and rural areas (rather than other large cities and suburbs), evoking the declaration of what some have called the 'great non-metropolitan turn-around'. In addition, decentralization has taken on an increasingly global context, as urban industrial production has to an historically unprecedented degree decentralized outside the United States. This has dramatically internationalized the scope of urban analysis and the context for understanding the urban restructuring process.

At the same time as this new round of decentralization has been taking place, there has been occurring in many large urban regions a distinctive recentralization of economic activities, providing yet another challenge to conventional urban analysis and an additional connection with the changing international division of labor. This recentralization is not confined to the renaissance of once deteriorating downtowns and the office-building booms which have constructed new skylines in the centers of Sunbelt cities. It is marked by two additional features. The first is a more pronounced geographical concentration of financial management and corporate control, especially over the increasingly global reach of productive and banking capital, and the information and communications systems associated with this internationalization process. Perhaps the leading example of this tendency towards increasing centralization and concentration has been the recent expansion of southern Manhattan into what *Business Week* has called the 'New York Colossus', the 'Capital of "Capital" ' (23 July 1984). It is also behind the emergence of Los Angeles as a 'World City' and the 'Capital of the Pacific Basin', an aspect of the urban restructuring of the region which will be discussed in the next section.

The second feature characterizing urban recentralization has been the development of large new territorial production complexes within metropolitan regions and the associated formation of what have been called 'outer cities' around them. The new outer cities cannot simply be seen as industrial satellites of the major metropolitan center or as conventional suburban complexes. These sprawling, science-based urban conglomerations draw together a dense cluster of highly interconnected and technologically advanced industry and supportive service activities, often with local financing capabilities and access to large pools of venture capital. Amalgamated around these new production complexes are high-income and expensively packaged residential developments, huge regional shopping centers, created and programmed environments for leisure and entertainment, localized pipelines to a major research university and the Department of Defense, and usually an enclave or two of cheap, manipulable labor being constantly replenished by in-migration of both foreign workers and those deindustrialized out of higher-paying jobs. There is rarely any clearly defined center to these amorphous outer cities and they confound normal data-gathering procedures by being neither central city nor suburban fringe. Silicon Valley in Santa Clara County is perhaps the best known example of outer city formation, but others can be found in the Texas 'Metroplex' between Dallas and Fort Worth, Florida's 'Gold Coast' between Fort Lauderdale and Palm

Beach, in Nassau and Suffolk countries outside New York City, and in the area around Route 128 near Boston.

This brief overview provides an appropriate and necessary perspective from which to view the combined spatial decentralization and recentralization of the Los Angeles urban region. In many ways, Los Angeles has supplanted Chicago as the exemplary model of the twentieth-century evolution of urban form in the United States. In its extensive metropolitanization, extraordinary jurisdictional fragmentation, state-fostered suburban expansion and industrial growth, partially renewed and partially deteriorated downtown, and heavy dependence upon government employment (especially for the black population), the Los Angeles urban region was the primary growth pole of the state-managed industrial capitalism which emerged out of the Great Depression and remained dominant into the 1960s. Since the 1960s and during the contemporary period of crisis and restructuring moving towards what some have called 'global capitalism', it has managed to maintain its leading position as a center of production (and consumption) through a complex and selective interweaving of deindustrialization and reindustrialization, decentralization and recentralization.

Part of the spatial restructuring of the Los Angeles region has involved an accelerated industrial and residential decentralization, marked by the decline of the older industrial sub-regions, widespread plant closures and relocations, and especially the rapid expansion of the peripheral counties of Orange, San Bernardino, Riverside and Ventura. Collectively, these four counties averaged close to a 40 per cent increase in population during the 1970s and an even higher rate of employment growth. All available evidence suggests this collective growth rate is being maintained in the 1980s. Similar expansion has been occurring in several fringe areas of Los Angeles County, accounting for a large part of its population increase of 450,000 in the 1970s and over 600,000 from 1980 to 1985 alone.

As previously argued, however, this decentralization can be deceiving in so far as it masks a significant recentralization of industrial production, employment patterns and corporate management both in the downtown nucleus of the City of Los Angeles and in a series of growing outer cities. After decades of public and private campaigns, there has developed in the past twenty years a visible and sizeable downtown core to the Los Angeles urban region. And if one takes this downtown area to include a twenty-mile linear extension along the Wilshire Corridor to the Pacific, it is an urban core almost commensurate with the size and scope of the regional economy. By the 1960s, downtown Los Angeles was already the site of the second largest concentration of government employment in the country (after Washington, D.C.) and was an important domestic banking and financial center (although clearly behind San Francisco). Since then, it has expanded dramatically as a governmental and corporate citadel and as a center for the administration and control of both domestic and international capital.

Equally dramatic has been the formation of a string of outer cities peaking in the remarkable development of Orange County, where at least 1400 high-technology firms have clustered since the mid-1960s. The internal morphology of this new production complex is still taking shape and defies easy description, but two primary industrial concentrations can be identified. The first encompasses Anaheim, Fullerton and parts of few adjacent municipalities; the second is around the John Wayne International Airport between the Latino barrio of Santa Ana and the luxury resorts of Newport Beach, with the University of California-Irvine as its eastern edge. Each of these concentrations is a dense nest of interfirm transactions and techno-logically advanced production and service systems (see Scott, 1983; 1986). Surrounding them are the representative residential, leisure and commercial complexes which, together with high-technology industry, define what has now come to be called the 'Silicon landscape', or the new urban 'technopolis'.

Another technopolis has taken shape in the sub-region around Los Angeles International Airport (LAX), stretching south from Santa Monica to Torrance. This is the heartland of the region's aerospace industry and defense contracting as well as a rapidly expanding center for electronics, major banks and insurance companies, and a wide range of business services. Figure 8.1 illustrates the extraordinary residential concentration of engineers which has grown up around LAX to serve the local high-technology industries, peaking just south of the airport in an almost entirely white racial and occupational enclave of the high technocracy. Rapid industrial growth and office building in the Ventura Freeway corridor, along the southern fringe of the San Fernando Valley and into Ventura County, has the potential of still another outer city. Its western section, straddling the Ventura–Los Angeles County boundary, has already emerged as the region's third major concentration of high-technology industry and services. Evidence of this technopolitan development is also visible in figure 8.1, just north of the shaded LAX cluster across the open space of the Santa Monica Mountains.

These outer cities directly reflect the reindustrialization (and expansion of industry-related services) that has accompanied the spatial restructuring of the Los Angeles region. As such, they have been an integral part of the increasing labor discipline that has been so central to the recent history of the American economy. Greater sectoral segmentation of the labor market has been accommodated and reinforced by an increasing spatial fragmenta-tion and segregation of the labor force at both the place of work and the place of residence. This changing urban geography vividly brings to mind some of Nicos Poulantzas's comments on the production and reproduction of capitalist spatiality:

the mould of social atomization and splintering, . . . embodiment of the labour process . . . . a cross-ruled, segmented and cellular space in which each fragment

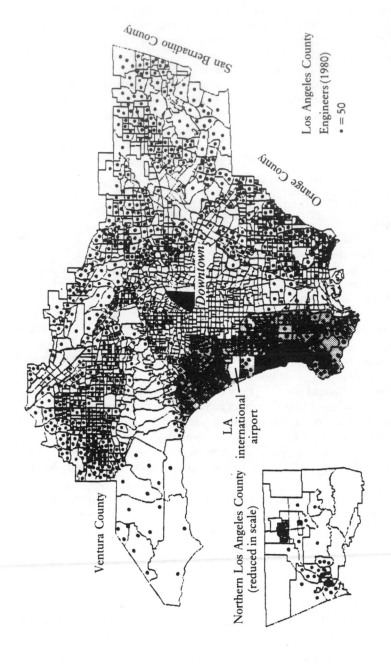

FIGURE 8.1 Residential location of engineers in Los Angeles County, 1980

Los Angeles County
Engineers (1980)

• = 50

San Bernadino County

Orange County

Ventura County

Downtown

LA
international
airport

Northern Los Angeles County
(reduced in scale)

(individual) has its place, and in which each emplacement . . . must present itself as homogeneous and uniform. (1978: 64)

Paradox and contradiction define the very nature of these manufactured spaces:

separation and division in order to unify; parcelling out in order to structure; atomization in order to encompass; segmentation in order to totalize; closure in order to homogenize; and individualization in order to obliterate differences and otherness. (p. 107)

Urban restructuring and the internationalization of labor and capital

As has already been noted several times, the restructuring of the Los Angeles urban region has been closely associated with an increasing internationalization of the local economy. Feeding off one another has been first a massive in-migration of almost two million people from Third World countries over the past twenty years; and second, an expansive internationalization of capital manifested in the emergence of Los Angeles as a World City, a production and control center for global banking, finance, trade and industry. This increasing internationalization of both labor and capital has been central to downtown redevelopment, from the new corporate towers to the thriving garment industry, and extends its influence into virtually every aspect of the changing urban structure.

Thirty years ago, Los Angeles County was 85 per cent non-Hispanic white, or 'Anglo'. Even then, however, there existed within the county one of the most rigidly defined black ghettoes in the country and the largest urban concentration of Mexicans outside their homeland. Moreover, this minority population had already been instrumental in an earlier round of industrial development as a source of exploitable labor and as a tool for more effective labor control. By the onset of the Great Depression, despite a vigorous past history of worker struggles, there had developed in Los Angeles an extraordinarily powerful organization of anti-union forces with sufficient economic and political influence to establish unequivocally the open shop and an extensive system of labor contracting. Reinforcing this power and helping to initiate what became a prototypical model of Sunbelt urban-industrialization, was a sizeable pool of cheap, manipulable, minority workers. Their presence served to squeeze the more established (and expanding) workforce both from 'below' (with respect to the vertical structure of the labor market) and from 'next door' (via the adjacency of the black ghetto and the *Latino barrio* to the major zones of industrial growth).

An intense episode of McCarthyist communist-baiting in the 1950s responded to the continued strength of the labor movement, which had pushed hard and appeared about to receive one of the largest public housing programs in the United States (Parson, 1982; 1985). But it also expressed the surpassing strength and domination of anti-labor forces. With organized labor under relative control, it was left to the minority populations to challenge the local regime of accumulation that had sustained fifty years of rapidly expanding industrial production in Los Angeles. As much as any other event, it was the Watts riots and Chicano (Mexican–American) protests of the 1960s and early 1970s which signalled the beginning of the restructuring process.

In this context, the contemporary restructuring of the Los Angeles region has many of the characteristics of a restoration, an attempted re-establishment and refurbishing of a system of labor relations which had proved successful in the past. Only in this round of restructuring, the reserve army of minority and migrant workers has grown to unprecedented levels and constitutes a pool of cheap, relatively docile labor that is not only locally competitive but also able to compete with the exploitative enclaves in the Newly Industrializing Countries (NICs) of the Third World.

The magnitude and diversity of immigration to Los Angeles since 1960 is comparable only to the New York-bound wave of migrants at the turn of the last century. A resurgence of migration from Mexico, both legal and illegal, has added at least a million residents to the existing population and the region has also become the primary overseas locus for a score of other countries as well. At least 200,000 Koreans have settled in Los Angeles since 1970 and have become a major influence in retail trade and the garment industry, with Korean family labor proving highly competitive with even the worst sweatshops. Filipinos, Thais, Vietnamese, Iranians, Guatemalans, Colombians and Cubans have arrived in very large numbers and several Pacific Island populations have grown almost as numerous as in their home areas. In what may be the record for in-migration from a single country, it has recently been estimated that the Salvadorean population of Los Angeles has grown by over 300,000 since 1980. Today the 'Anglo' population of the City and County of Los Angeles has probably dropped to well below 50 per cent.

This demographic transformation has produced within the region many of the labor conditions and corporate advantages of Third World Export Processing Zones. Under certain market conditions and wage rates, especially when added transport costs for similar goods produced overseas are sufficiently high, local shops in Los Angeles are producing automobile parts which are stamped 'Made in Brazil' and clothing marked 'Made in Hong Kong', enabling them to intervene in foreign delivery contracts. There is fierce competition in Los Angeles for the Free Enterprise Zones proposed by the Reagan administration, but it seems extremely unlikely that any which might be established will be able to attract manufacturing firms unless truly extraordinary subsidization is provided to compete with already existing opportunities.

Foreign capital as well as labor has been migrating into Los Angeles at an unusual rate, buying land, building office complexes, investing in industry, hotels, retail shops, restaurants and entertainment facilities. A growing proportion of the prime downtown properties – possibly more than a third – are currently owned by foreign corporations or by partnerships with foreign companies, led by Canada and Japan; and foreign capital is said to have helped finance over 90 per cent of recent multi-storey building construction. Japanese capital has directed the redevelopment of Little Tokyo and a rapidly growing inflow of Chinese capital, especially from Hong Kong, is likely to induce a similar transformation of Chinatown in the very near future. Several high-income residential districts are considered to be owned (if not occupied) primarily by Saudis and Iranians and, although it remains almost totally unexamined, it would not be surprising to find that the inflow of capital from Mexico outweighs the export from waged-workers and American corporations. Perhaps only in New York City has there been such a massive urban 'shopping spree' by international capital in so short a time and from so many different sources.

The internationalization of the Los Angeles economy has been produced not only by the inflow of labor and capital, but also by the expanding global reach of domestic economic interests. Large multinational firms head-quartered in Los Angeles, or with major local branch offices, have been an important factor in downtown development, and in the complex processes of industrial and spatial restructuring. One reflection of this internationalization of the local economy has been the growth of the Los Angeles port complex to the second largest in the country in dollar volume of overseas trade. Another has been the expansion of international banking and finance to a level surpassed again only by New York. And related to these concentrations has been the establishment in Los Angeles of an apparatus of capital management and control also second only to the so-called 'Capital of Capital' within the United States.

Downtown Los Angeles has become the anchor of a corporate and financial complex of headquarters, decision-making centers, and comple-mentary business services which stretches westward to the Pacific in Santa Monica. In this almost unbroken canyon of development, punctuated by such major nodes as Beverly Hills, Century City and Westwood, are over 60 major corporate headquarters, a dozen banks and savings and loan associations (building societies) each with assets over one billion dollars, at least half of the 180 million square feet of tower block office space in the region, five of the eight largest international accounting firms, and specialized clusters of lawyers, architects, engineers and developers. Overlying this citadel of corporate power, lest it be forgotten, are the axes of the 'Dream Machine': the television, motion picture and recording industries, which magnify and broadcast the cultural and ideological imagery and influence of Los Angeles around the world. Not only does 'it all come together' in Los Angeles, but it is all projected outward as well, appropriately mystified and depoliticized.

AN EPILOGUE ON THE THEORIZATION OF THE URBAN

Looking back at the recent history and changing geography of the Los Angeles urban region provokes questions which relate not only to the explanation of particular events and patterns but to a more general interpretation of the contemporary urbanization process. These broader conceptual, theoretical and political questions are linked to a series of debates and critiques which have been aimed at redefining the scope, direction and emphasis of contemporary urban studies in accord with the significant changes taking place in cities over the past twenty years. How then might the Los Angeles experience be interpreted within this more general framework, within the attempt to develop an appropriate and practical understanding of the specificity of the urban in the wider context of social theory?

The particular approach taken in this chapter already implies an answer and a choice. The explicit focus has been upon a complex composite of restructuring processes affecting the social and spatial organization of the urban labor market, industrial production and technology, and the relations between labor and capital. Underlying this restructuring are many different and often opposing forces. Primary among them has been the drive by business interests and the state to develop new sources for expanding corporate profits and restoring more effective means of disciplining and controlling labor. This contentious effort can easily be obfuscated by the descriptive detail of the many changes taking place. Alternatively, and perhaps equally deceptive, it can be treated as a determinant and invincible force, manipulating the landscape without resistance, contradiction or conflict. Approached as a continuous competitive political and economic struggle, however, the search for greater profitability and labor control must be placed at the center of attention in any analysis of urban restructuring.

Many of the new models and metaphors which have been offered in recent years to describe the presumed outcome of the contemporary restructuring process serve instead to obscure its fundamental origins and implications. Perhaps the most remarkable and misleading is the 'post-industrialism' hypothesis, with its implied end to the industrial era in advanced capitalist countries and the rise of a new service-based economy as an idealized conclusion, the top step in the climb through progressive stages of growth. To describe Los Angeles as a 'post-industrial city' is possibly the acme of mystification and misrepresentation. For almost 70 years (from the 1920s when the service sector accounted for a far greater share of total employment than it does today), the Los Angeles urban region has been one of the world's largest growth poles of industrial capitalism. It remains today an emphatically industrial metropolis, its social and spatial structure continuing to be shaped and reshaped by the changing demands of industrial production. As in other urban regions, the industrial structure is undergoing a pronounced transformation and a rapid expansion of service jobs has recently re-established the service sector as the largest in the regional economy by a small margin. These changes, however, do not represent a break with the fundamental labor processes of industrial capitalism, but rather a continuity marked by significant (and urgent) restructuring.

Throughout its history of periodic restructuring the capitalist city has remained a spatially organized 'social factory', an efficient ecological machine for the production of goods and services, the management and control of capital and labor, and the allocation of consumption and exchange. This does not mean that it has not changed significantly over time or that every capitalist city is precisely the same. Indeed, the central challenge of empirical urban analysis is to enrich our practical and theoretical understanding of the *differentiation* of urbanization processes over time and space, without losing sight of their underlying continuities. In some ways, the Chicago School of urban ecologists attempted to describe and theorize this mix of similarity and differentiation, but specified the urban in a set of causal mechanisms which emphasized natural processes and a transhistorical social dynamics. Seeing in this conceptualization an essentially ideological smokescreen, Marxist urban sociologists initially reacted by de-specifying the urban almost entirely and confining it within a more generalized causal framework of capital logic and class struggle (loosened only to allow attention to be given to collective consumption and the importance of distinctively *urban* social movements). Most of mainstream urban studies in geography, sociology, politics, economics, planning and anthropology remained either between these two poles or completely outside the debate, involved primarily with accurately describing the multidimensional empirical appearances of urban society and virtually ignoring causality and specificity altogether.

The accumulating evidence of major changes in the urbanization process over the past decade has increasingly revealed inadequacies in all these approaches and positions with respect to urban theory and analysis. At the same time, concepts of crisis formation and crisis-induced restructuring have become the catalysts for a new round of empirical and theoretical debate in urban studies and in the broader realm of social theory, often in connection with variants of a world systems approach to the internationalization of capitalist development. The interpretation of urban restructuring in Los Angeles presented here reflects this debate and indicates some preferred directions and emphases. Much further elaboration is necessary to make the underlying arguments clearer and more accessible, but the outlines of an explicit perspective can be identified.

The interpretive framework used in this paper can be described as a form of historico-geographical materialism exemplified in the changing political economy of contemporary Los Angeles. It is not an orthodox Marxist analysis, but is nevertheless materialist in its emphasis on the dynamics of capitalist development, the capitalist labor process, and the social relations of production and reproduction within the urban region. Its historicity is seriously incomplete but nevertheless indicative, especially in the interpretive emphasis given to the periodicity of crisis and restructuring. Implied here is the need to set the particular experience of urban restructuring within the long duration of capitalist development and its characteristic historical patterning into periods of accelerated expansion, emergent crisis and anticipatory restructuring. Whether placed within a long wave analysis following Mandel (1980), or described in terms of changing regimes of accumulation and modes of regulation (see Aglietta, 1979; Lipietz, 1984), the objective is to enhance empirical understanding and political action in the present through an appropriate interpretation of the past.

Restructuring in Los Angeles has thus been presented as part of a larger set of processes and strategies arising in response to the severe crises which occurred in the decade from 1965 to 1975. This accelerated and competitive struggle to restore and reconstitute the conditions for the expansive accumulation of capital has many similarities with at least two earlier periods, in the last several decades of the nineteenth century and through the Great Depression. There is much that is different in the current period of restructuring, but also much that is the same, as traced, for example, in the historical evolution of urban form. A beginning has been made by some urban scholars to describe and interpret the periodicity of capitalist urbanization in more detail than can possibly be given here, but much more work is both needed and anticipated in the future (see Gordon, 1977, 1978; Walker, 1981).

In addition to a materialist interpretation of history, there has also been running through this paper a closely associated materialist interpretation of spatial relationships, an historical *geography* of capitalist urbanization. Also indicative rather than definitive, this emphasis on the fundamental spatiality of social life may be the key new aspect both in an understanding of the specific forms and patterns of restructuring taking place in Los Angeles and in the wider retheorization of urban, regional and international political economy. Over the past decade, there has been occurring a notable convergence among a diverse group of scholars around a new critical theory of space and space–time relations (Soja, 1980; 1984). This reconceptualization of space and time relations, the social production of space linked to the social making of history, has created a much more spatially-explicit theorization of the political economy of urbanization, uneven regional development, and the international division of labor. More recently, the projection of social relations into their politicized spatial matrix (to use Poulantzas's term) and the recognition of a tense and problematic socio-spatial dialectic has forced a major rethinking of social theory itself.

The development of critical spatial theory has infused the social production of space with political meaning. Far from simply mirroring social relations, the spatial organization of society at multiple scales has been increasingly revealed as a dynamic field of social action, ideological confrontation and political struggle. Moreover, this politics of space is never more vividly manifested than during periods of crisis and restructuring, when inherited spatial structures become the arena for contending forces of preservation and destruction, adaptation and reconstitution, regeneration and transformation. The historical periodicity of capitalist development is thus associated with a sequence of changing geographical landscapes which consolidate during periods of accelerated growth only to be selectively destroyed and restructured in times of crisis and relative decline.

The restructuring and internationalization of Los Angeles and other major urban regions is part of this historical-geographical sequence representing another intensified confrontation between inherited and projected socio-spatial orders arising from the destabilizing and conflict-ridden effects of crisis stretching from the local to the global scales. The restructuring of urban spatiality in the United States is thus linked into related processes of regional restructuring (partly defined in terms of Sunbelt to Snowbelt shifts, the non-metropolitan turnaround, and other examples of the 'role reversal' of regions) and into changes in the larger world economy (e.g. the rise of the NICs, the peripheralization of the core countries, the expansion of global capital). All of these levels of spatial restructuring can be seen in the recent history of Los Angeles and effectively described under the same thematic headings used earlier: deindustrialization and reindustrialization, geographical decentralization and recentralization, and the internationalization of labor and capital. This adds still another meaning to the claim that 'it all comes together' in Los Angeles, now more insistently than ever presenting itself as the paradigmatic industrial metropolis of the late twentieth century.

REFERENCES

Aglietta, Michael (1979) *A Theory of Capitalist Regulation: The US Experience*, London: New Left Books.
Fainstein, Susan S., Fainstein, Norman I., Richard Child-Hill, Dennis Judd and Michael Peter Smith (1983) *Restructuring the City*, New York: Longman.
Gordon, David (1977) 'Class struggle and the stages of American urban development'. In David C. Perry and Alfred J. Watkins (eds), *The Rise of the Sunbelt Cities*, Beverly Hills: Sage.
—— (1978), 'Capitalist development and the history of American cities', in William Tabb and Larry Sawers (eds), *Marxism and the Metropolis*, New York: Oxford University Press.
Harrison, Bennett (1984) 'Regional restructuring and "good business climates": the economic transformation of New England since World War II', in Sawers and

Tabb (eds), *Sunbelt/Snowbelt: Urban Development and Regional Restructuring*, New York: Oxford University Press.

Lipietz, Alain (1984) 'Accumulation, crises et sorties de crise: quelques reflexions methodologiques de la notion de "Regulation" ', Publication no. 8409, Paris: CEDREMAP (Centre d'Etudes Prospectives d'Economie Mathématique Appliquées à la Planification).

Mandel, Ernest (1980) *Long Waves of Capitalist Development: The Marxist Interpretation*, Cambridge: Cambridge University Press.

O'Keefe, Phil (ed.) (1984) *Regional Restructuring Under Advanced Capitalism*, London: Croom Helm.

Parson, Don (1982) 'The development of redevelopment: Public housing and urban renewal in Los Angeles', *International Journal of Urban and Regional Research*, VI: 393–413.

—— (1985) *Urban Politics During the Cold War: Public Housing, Urban Renewal and Suburbanization in Los Angeles*, PhD Dissertation, Graduate School of Architecture and Urban Planning, University of California, Los Angeles.

Poulantzas, Nicos (1978) *State, Power, Socialism*, London: New Left Books.

Scott, Allen J. (1983) 'Industrial organization and the logic of intra-metropolitan location II: A case study of the printed circuits industry in the Greater Los Angeles region', *Economic Geography*, LIX: 343–67.

—— (1960), 'High-technology industry and territorial development: the rise of the Orange County Complex 1955–1984', *Urban Geography*, VII: 3–45.

Soja, Edward (1985) 'The spatiality of social life: Toward a transformative retheorization'. In Gregory and Urrry (eds), *Social Relations and Spatial Structures*, London: Macmillan.

—— (1980) 'The socio-spatial dialectic', *Annals of the Association of American Geographers*, LXX: 207–25.

Soja, Edward, Rebecca Morales and Goetz Wolff (1983) 'Urban restructuring: an analysis of social and spatial change in Los Angeles', *Economic Geography*, LIX: 195–230.

Walker, Richard (1981) 'A theory of suburbanization: Capitalism and the construction of urban space in the United States'. In Dear and Scott (eds), *Urbanization and Urban Planning in Capitalist Societies*, New York: Methuen.

9

Lima and the New International
Division of Labor

Patricia Ann Wilson

Once a pivotal city for global capital accumulation, Lima has been relegated to increasingly peripheral status by the changing international division of labor. With the recent globalized production and marketing strategies of multinational corporations, Lima's importance as a production and assembly site for the Peruvian market has waned. Rather than duplicating assembly plant facilities for each national market, multinational corporations are dividing the production process into discrete segments, each with its own set of cost-minimizing location criteria. Those cities receiving some of these production segments for the global market are the winners; those that do not are the losers. In Latin America São Paolo and Mexico City are winners; Lima is one of the losers. In Lima employment loss in assembly industry has not been compensated for by employment growth in so-called 'non-traditional exports'. The policy response of the conservative governments of the late 1970s, and early 1980s was to promote non-traditional exports in order to secure a niche in the new international division of labor. The policy of the current left of center government is to take advantage of Peru's backwater status in the international division of labor by pursuing internally-oriented development.

This paper begins with an historical overview of the impact of the changing international division of labor on Lima and the Peruvian system of cities, starting with the arrival of the Spaniards and the period of mercantile accumulation and ending in the early 1970s with the period of US dominated advanced capitalist accumulation. The following section is an empirical analysis of the impact of the new (post-1970) international division of labor on Lima, focusing on the local employment consequences of non-traditional export growth. The chapter concludes with a look at politics and public policy *vis-à-vis* the new international division of labor.

HISTORICAL OVERVIEW

The Spanish entered Latin America in the sixteenth century, during the rise of mercantile trading, in search of gold and silver, which were already used as a basis for exchange in the expanding mercantile trade of Europe. The Spaniards found the greatest sources of gold and silver in Mexico and Peru (Singer and Cardoso, 1972: 7–9). Since there was no existing productive organization for metal extraction, the Spanish developed a system of forced labor called the *mita*, in which peasants were forced to do the gruelling work in the mines using primitive technologies. The Spaniards used the indigenous agriculture production to provide the means of subsistence for the mineworkers. Since the Incan agriculture was already efficiently producing surpluses and channeling them to the Inca state in Cuzco, the Spaniards tried to take advantage of the existing productive structure. They kept its collective form but replaced the surplus appropriators – the Inca state – with their own representatives, the *encomenderos*, in a new form called the *encomienda*. The result was a sizeable surplus of gold and silver bullion for the royal coffers of Spain.

The next problem facing the colonizers was to channel the new mineral surplus safety and efficiently back to the Spanish Crown. To do so, they developed the Incan road system, particularly in the southern sierra, where the major mineral deposits were found (near Ayacucho, Arequipa and Postosi), in order to transport the precious metals from the sierra to the coast. The coastal cities established by the Spaniards for the purpose of conquest and control (Lima, Trujillo, Lambayeque and Tumbes) were given the new and very important function of serving as transhipment intermediaries to the Spanish metropolis. Some of the surplus was retained in the colonial cities to support the soldiers, functionaries, priests and merchants, but most of it was appropriated by the Crown.

Transferring surplus to the metropolis was not a peaceful process. The threat from smugglers, pirates and rival colonialists required vast military protection. To reduce this threat, most of the surplus from throughput Peru was brought together for shipment at one principal point, Lima, which was located at the maritime terminal of the Incan road to the mineral-rich southern sierra. Chosen as the capital, Lima became the principal link with the metropolis, not only as an intermediary for mineral surplus but also because of its administrative functions.

The system of cities in Peru in the sixteenth, seventeenth and eighteenth centuries clearly reflected the needs of mercantile Spain. Whereas Cuzco had been the geographically strategic focus of the Incan empire, Lima became the geographic focus of appropriated surplus under mercantilism, in a role completely subservient to the needs of the Spanish metropolis for gold and silver bullion. The Peruvian sierra – particularly the southern sierra, where the existing agricultural infrastructure and gold and silver deposits were most abundant – became the location of surplus production: agricultural surplus through the *encomiendas* to feed the mining sector and mineral surplus through the *mita* to fill the Spanish coffers. Jauja and Cuzco were developed as colonial cities, first to aid the conquest and later to circulate agricultural and mineral surplus. Some of the southern tribes fled to the isolated, infertile *altiplanos* (high plains) of the Andes to escape Spanish domination. Cajamarca and the northern sierra were relatively neglected by the Spaniards, as was the *selva* (jungle).

Late mercantilist period

In the eighteenth century a change in the needs of the metropolis was to have a significant impact on the Peruvian urban hierarchy. From the beginning of the eighteenth century, the labor force in Europe expanded sufficiently to create larger markets for new colonial products, particularly basic agricultural products. The new demand, and the fact that the Peruvian gold and silver mines were being depleted, put increasing pressure on the internal subsistence sector to produce an exportable agricultural surplus. The *encomiendas* were found to be incapable of producing more surplus, however; the peasants were already reduced to a minimum subsistence level, so that increased exploitation resulted in escalating death rates and epidemics (Singer and Cardoso, 1972: 13). This contradiction between the needs of the metropolis and the forces of production resulted in the creation of a new form of productive relations in the agricultural sector, called the *latifundios*. The *latifundios* were more productive than the *encomiendas*, despite the same primitive technology, mainly because they utilized economies of scale and a small degree of specialization of production. As on the *encomiendas*, the indigenous workers were kept at subsistence level to maximize the appropriable surplus. By the end of the eighteenth century, the forces of production on the *latifundios* were sufficiently developed to allow a regular exportable surplus.

The comercial function of the coastal cities grew rapidly in importance as a result of the new agricultural surplus. Although Lima was the principal beneficiary of the new surplus, other cities, such as Trujillo, Lambayeque-Chiclayo and Piura, also stepped up their commercial activities. Not only did the cities export the surplus directly to the Spanish metropolis, they also shipped the growing regional agricultural specialities between regions of Peru, using the coastal route as the main channel of international commerce.

One of the important consequences of the expanding commercial functions of the coastal cities was the development of a new class of merchants, financiers (usurers) and transporters. Some of the cities – particularly Lima, but also Trujillo, Lambayeque-Chiclayo and Piurra –

grew richer; and, as they did, they attracted more and more of the rural elite to the residential comforts and glitter of urban life. As a result, the urban service sector mushroomed. The cities – especially Lima – became the focal point of the cultural and political life of the colony and a center of increased demand for imported luxury goods from Europe. By the end of the eighteenth century, Spain recognized its American colonies not only as a source of monetary metals but also as a market for European goods. Despite this urban market, Peru was still a rural country; almost the entire population (90 per cent) lived in the rural areas, and nearly all the economic surplus was produced there.

The economic, political and cultural growth of the colonial cities harbored the collapse of colonial life itself – the movement for independence, led by the colonial mercantilists and supported by the *latifundistas*, who wanted more control over Peru's surplus. Because of the growing hegemony of English-dominated industrial capitalism over mercantilism, the Spanish could not prevent the declaration of Peruvian independence in 1821 and the substitution of English for Spanish hegemony over Peru.

The implications of late mercantilism for the urban development along Peru's coast are clear: growth of the *latifundio* system in the sierra to increase agricultural surplus for export; increasing commercial importance of the coastal cities for exporting the agricultural surplus and importing luxury goods for the growing *criolla* (Peruvian national) elite; reinforcement of the coastal axis for internal trade; and transformation of some of the coastal cities – with Lima at their head – into the colonial cultural and political centers for the Peruvian upper class and the breeding ground of the independence movement.

Industrial capitalism

The change from feudalism to industrial capitalism, and the concomitant change from Spanish domination to English domination, brought with it no fundamental alteration in Peru's internal productive structure or social relations. Peru retained its colonial mercantilist functions of channelling agricultural and mineral surplus to the metropolis (now English) through the commercial and financial intermediation of Lima and other coastal cities. The English bourgeoisie's needs for an increasing number of raw materials, with the onset of the Industrial Revolution, caused Peru to diversify its exports, adding first quano and nitrates and, after the 1870s, cotton and sugar from the new coastal plantations, but without changing its role of raw material exporter and luxury goods importer. This diversification integrated Peru more deeply into the European economy, making the new nation liable to the vicissitudes of European demand and business cycles.

MONOPOLY CAPITALISM

At the turn of the century, England's dominance and competitive industrial capitalism gave way to US dominance and monopoly capitalism. The US multinational corporations began investing directly in the extraction of Peru's minerals and plantation crops for export, thus reinforcing the development of extractive enclaves in the coast and the sierra and strengthening the financial and commercial (that is, non-productive) roles of Lima and the other coastal cities.

The period of advanced monopoly capitalism began in Peru after World War II, when multinational corporations spearheaded the country's industrialization process. Advanced monopoly capitalism represented a new international division of labor, in which the foreign appropriators (largely US multinational corporations) needed not only to continue extracting surplus in the form of mineral and agricultural products for export but also to use Peru as an additional market for their technology and capital goods. These needs translated spatially to (1) continuation of extractive enclaves (minerals in the sierra, plantation agriculture on the coast, and, later, oil in the *selva*), all with wage relations and advanced technology; and (2) urban–industrial growth along the coast, to create a market for manufactured goods and processed raw materials for export. The sierra, aside from the mineral enclaves, was needed only as a source of cheap wage goods (foodstuffs) to keep wages down in the industrial workforce. As a result, the 1950s and 1960s witnessed rapid urban growth and surplus accumulation in Lima and the coastal cities, and, in the sierra, continuation of labor-intensive technologies, largely non-wage relations, and price mechanisms favoring urban industrial products.

NON-TRADITIONAL EXPORTS AND THE NEW INTERNATIONAL DIVISION OF LABOR

The decline of US hegemony in the world market, represented by the dismantling of the dollar-backed gold standard in the early 1970s, opened up an era of intensified competition among multinational firms. Technological improvements in transportation and communication enabled firms to reduce costs by reorganizing the production process across national boundaries.

Two spatial strategies in particular have affected developing countries. Instead of investing directly in duplicated production facilities serving individual national markets, multinational firms are consolidating final assembly operations into fewer sites to take advantage of scale economies and exporting final goods to larger markets. At the same time they are dividing up the production process for many goods (e.g. electronics, textiles, automobiles) into discrete phases, with low-skilled assembly of components for re-export being concentrated in a few developing countries, and advanced manufacturing along with R & D going more to the industrialized countries. Both of these strategies have spawned a rise in manufactured exports from developing countries and intensified competition among them to garner a share of the manufactured export market. The competition resulted in a surge of tariff reductions and tax incentives in the late 1970s to promote these 'non-traditional' exports, as they came to be called.

Peru experienced spectacular growth rates in manufactured exports (as opposed to the traditional raw material exports) in the late 1970s. Non-traditional exports[1] multiplied eightfold from 1975 to 1980, increasing their share of total exports to over 25 per cent (see table 9.1). This growth is curious from the point of view of the international division of labor, since the real winners in the new spatial strategy in Latin America were Brazil for final assembly for the Latin American market, and Mexico, the Dominican Republic and Haiti for component assembly for re-export to manufacturers located elsewhere.

TABLE 9.1   Growth of non-traditional exports in Peru, 1970–82

Year	Amount (in millions, using current dollars)	% of total exports	% of GNP
1970	38	3.6	.4
1971	34	3.8	.3
1972	55	5.8	.5
1973	115	10.9	.8
1974	156	10.0	.8
1975	109	8.2	.5
1976	151	11.5	.8
1977	236	14.1	1.5
1978	349	19.1	2.1
1979	725	21.4	3.0
1980	845	25.5	2.9
1981	701	22.2	2.0
1982	759	23.5	n.a.

Source: ADEX (Association de Exportadores), using foreign trade data from the Andean Pact, the Peruvian Customs Office, and the Central Bank, and GNP data from the National Institute of Statistics' National Accounts, 1970–81.

What are the major non-traditional exports in Peru? Very few are either components for re-export or assembled goods for the Latin American market. Most are traditional local raw materials undergoing some industrial processing before export: for example, cotton processed into raw thread or cloth; fish canned, frozen or concentrated; copper processed into wires and cables, and chemicals processed into explosives. (See table 9.2.) The one notable exception is fishing boats, built by a state enterprise in Chimbote (the center of both Peru's fishing industry and its iron and steel industry) under contract to the Soviet Union. Thus, the rise of non-traditional exports added only slightly to Peru's role in the international division of labor: from exporter of raw materials to exporter of processed raw materials. At the same time Peru has lost much of its role as a final assembly point for the internal market.

TABLE 9.2   *The 20 principal non-traditional exports, 1979*

Product	Total NTE (%)
Raw cotton cloth	6.4
Canned fish	6.3
Cement	4.7
Fishing boats	4.7
Raw cotton thread	4.5
Frozen fish	3.9
Concentrated fish protein	3.5
Zamac (zinc alloy)	2.0
Copper wire	2.0
Copper cables	1.7
Baritena	1.6
Food supplements	1.3
Gold jewelry	1.2
Cacao paste	0.9
Cotton clothing	0.8
Explosives	0.7
Electric batteries (dry)	0.6
Silver jewelry	0.5
Cacao butter	0.4
Monosodium glutamate	0.4
Total	48.1

Source: Office of Foreign Trade and ADEX, compiled by Juan Aste, ECO.

What has been the impact of these changes on Lima? Within Peru, the rise in non-traditional exports in the late 1970s was felt most sharply in Lima. In fact, non-traditional export manufacturing is more concentrated in Lima than is manufacturing for the internal market.[2] While 66 per cent of the manufacturing establishments which do not export are located in the Lima metropolitan area, 73 per cent of those that do export are located there. There is a similar finding in the gross value of production: 58 per cent of gross product of industrial production by establishments that do not export was located in Lima, compared with 72 per cent of gross product by those that do export. As for the number of workers, the difference is smaller but in the same direction: 71 per cent of industrial workers in non-exporting establishments worked in Lima, compared with 74 per cent for the exporting establishments. (See table 9.3.)

TABLE 9.3   *Geographic concentration of manufacturing*

	Lima[a] (%)	Rest of country (%)	Total (%)	Total Abs. no.
Number of establishments				
Exporters	73.4	26.6	100.0	2,469.0
Non-exporters	65.5	34.5	100.0	7,162.0
Gross value of production				
Exporters	71.8	28.2	100.0	722.8[b]
Non-exporters	58.1	41.9	100.0	1,048.8
Number of employees				
Exporters	74.2	25.8	100.0	117,003.0
Non-exporters	70.6	29.4	100.0	149,879.0

[a] Lima defined as the metropolitan area, including the Port of Callao.
[b] In millions of soles.
Source: MITI (1979), author's compilation (see note 3).

This geographical concentration of non-traditional exports in Lima holds up across most sectors, as well. Two-thirds (67 per cent) of the non-traditional exports (in terms of FOB value[3] of gross product) are from sectors that are geographically concentrated in Lima – including those using raw materials from elsewhere in Peru, such as tobacco, petroleum, leather, chemicals and non-ferrous metal products. The only manufacturing sectors with a non-Lima geographic orientation are food, non-metallic mineral products, iron and steel, wood, paper, drinks and leather products, accounting for a total of one-third of non-traditional exports.[4]

Foreign capital has a greater presence in non-traditional export manufacturing than in manufacturing for the internal market, especially in Lima. Nevertheless foreign ownership is still not preponderant. For the country, exporting manufacturers average 17 per cent foreign stockholders, while non-exporting manufacturers average 11 per cent. In Lima the presence of foreign capital is slightly greater: 18 and 13 per cent, respectively. Of the principal fifteen non-traditional exporters, four are predominantly foreign-owned, one is state-owned, nine are owned by private national capital (one with minority foreign ownership), and one has mixed national–state capital. (See table 9.4.)

TABLE 9.4   *The 15 leading non-traditional export producers, 1979*

Firm	Ownership	Gross product (millions of dollars)	Principal product
Cemento Norte Pacasmayo	National	16.8	Portland cement
Bayer Industrial, S.A.	54% foreign 46% state	15.3	Acrylic fibers
Bahia	National	14.0	Frozen fish
Minpeco	State	13.5	Copper wire
Michel y Cia., S.A.	National	13.2	Alpaca tops
Concentrados Marinos, S.A.	National	12.8	Protein fish concentrate
Cia. Textil Peruano-Suiza	National	10.7	Fur tops
Fundicion Metales Bera	100% foreign	10.2	Zamac
Reiser y Curioni, S.A.	84% national 16% foreign	9.7	Gold jewelry
El Amazonas, S.A.	National	9.6	Raw cotton thread
Fundicion de Metales Sol, S.A.	National	9.3	n.a.
Cia. Estrella del Peru	Mixed state and national	9.2	Frozen fish
Ceper	80% foreign 20% national	9.1	Electric conductors
Perubar, S.A.	Foreign	8.8	Barite
Inversiones Navales, S.A.	National	8.7	n.a.

Source: See table 9.2.

Besides showing a somewhat stronger presence of foreign capital, non-traditional export producers are larger than manufacturers producing solely for the internal market. In fact, the export manufacturing estabishments average twice as many employees as the non-exporters, both in Lima and outside the capital. In terms of imported inputs, the export firms show the same percentages as for the non-exporters (about 21 per cent in Lima, 15 per cent for the provinces, and 20 per cent for the country as a whole).

The fact that most of the non-traditional exports are simply processed raw materials does not mean that they are a labor-intensive, low-productivity, low-wage activity. Quite the opposite is true. Because of the exigencies of competing on the international market, the presence of foreign capital, technology and inputs, and the large size of the firms, the majority of non-traditional exporters show higher capital : labor ratios, greater value added per worker, and higher earnings per worker than their counterparts producing exclusively for the domestic market.[5] (See table 9.5.) For example, while textile production for the internal market has a below-

TABLE 9.5 *Characteristics of non-traditional export manufacturers, for Lima and rest of Peru*

	Lima	Rest of country	National average
Capital/labor ratio[a]			
Exporters	1816	4907	2600
Non-exporters	1377	2337	1669
Value added per worker[b]			
Exporters	2396	2758	2489
Non-exporters	1874	3744[d]	2424
Earnings per worker[c]			
Exporters	534	539	535
Non-exporters	447	414	438
Foreign capital (%)			
Exporters	18.1	13.4	16.9
Non-exporters	10.5	10.9	10.6
Imported inputs (%)			
Exporters	21.2	15.3	19.2
Non-exproters	21.3	15.4	20.6
No. of workers per establishment			
Exporters	47.9	45.9	47.3
Non-exporters	22.6	17.8	20.9

[a] Fixed capital in thousands of soles (1979) divided by number of production workers.
[b] Value added per worker, in thousands of soles (1979) divided by number of production workers.
[c] Total wages and salaries in thousands of soles (1979) divided by total number of production and non-production employees.
[d] Without petroleum industries (SICs 353 and 354) the figure is reduced to 2763.

Source: Author's calculations using MITI data for manufacturing establishments in 1979 (see note 2).

average capital : labor ratio, textile production for export exhibits a higher than average ratio. Similarly, the value added per worker is twice as high among the textile exporters than among those producing for the internal market.

While non-traditional exports have been concentrated in Lima, the city has suffered from the decline in domestic industry. Since nearly three-quarters of Peru's manufacturing employment is concentrated in Lima, the decline in manufacturing production for the internal market has been sharply felt there. Despite the concentration of non-traditional export employment in Lima, total manufacturing employment there has stagnated: from 1975 to 1979 manufacturing employment grew at less than half of one per cent per year, which was less than the national manufacturing average.[6] Manufacturing in the secondary cities has been relatively buffered from this process.[7]

CONCLUSIONS AND PROSPECTS

The new international division of labor has largely left Peru in a backwater. The country has captured little re-export activity, either in components assembly or final goods assembly. The startling growth rate of manufactured exports in Lima during the 1970s was based largely on the processing of traditional raw materials. Moreover, even with a high growth rate, these so-called non-traditional exports represented only 3 per cent of GNP by 1980 (table 9.1). Since 1980 the growth of non-traditional exports has been unsteady.

Government development policy in the late 1970s and early 1980s was directed at gaining a foothold in the new international division of labor. Both the military government of Morales Bermudez and the constitutional government of Belaunde-Terry tried to attract international lenders and investors. They adopted IMF austerity measures, let the exchange rate float, lowered tariffs, and provided tax incentives for manufactured exports.

The strategy failed. In Lima the popular reaction to declining real income and rising unemployment and underemployment swept in a socialist mayor to office in 1983. In the countryside peasant agriculture continued in crisis and Sendero Luminoso increased its stronghold in some of the poorest areas. In 1985 the popular vote gave a first-round victory a left of center presidential candidate, Alan Garcia, of the Social Democratic APRA party.

The Apristas have proposed a new development strategy: *to take advantage of* the relative isolation that Peru's backwater status in the new international division of labor affords by focusing on internal development, particularly in long-neglected traditional agriculture. Garcia's unilateral declaration of very favorable terms for a slower repayment of Peru's foreign debt – successful so far largely because Peru's debt is too small for international lenders to worry about – has generated additional revenues that are being invested primarily in peasant agriculture. The objective is to promote greater national self-sufficiency in basic foods (i.e. reduce the need for food imports) and ultimately reduce the price of food to urban workers. Yet Garcia's acquiescence to urban workers' demands to keep food prices down in the short run have created supply bottlenecks among peasant producers.

The Apristas are trying to balance the conjunctural conflict between urban and rural popular sectors, rather than addressing the more structural conflict between the popular sectors and the interests of national and international capital. Whether the Apristas can turn peasant agriculture into the motor of national development without far-reaching structural reforms remains to be seen.

1 In Peru the official definition of non-traditional exports is sometimes arbitrary. For example, fishmeal is a traditional export (having been exported for years), but animal feed made from fishmeal is non-traditional. Fish oil is a traditional export except if it is hydrogenized, in which case it is considered a non-traditional export. Another difficulty with the NTE designation is that it is applied not only to manufactured exports (although more than three-quarters of the officially designated non-traditional exports are manufactured), but also to primary products which have only recently been exported, such as cacao. While figure 9.1 utilizes this expansive official definition, the subsequent empirical analysis uses data only on manufactured exports.

2 This analysis was based on original tabulations by the author using the statistical annual of the Ministry of Industry, Tourism and Integration (MITI), which is based on annual information on those manufacturing establishments with five or more employees. Using the MITI information, non-traditional exporters were identified by a dummy variable based on whether or not a firm received the tax rebate for non-traditional exports, called CERTEX. Nevertheless, there are two problems with this indicator. It does not reveal the percentage of export production, it only denotes whether or not a firm received CERTEX. Also, some non-traditional exporters do not receive CERTEX (approximately 15 per cent), so this variable is an underestimation of the actual number of non-traditional exporters.

   Another potential problem with the data from MITI was the methodology used in testimating omissions. The averages for businesses for each four-digit Standard Industrial Code (SIC) by size of establishment were assigned to all the omitted businesses with the same SIC in the same size range, without taking into account geographical location. Using the information for those concentrated in Lima, where there are also a disproportionately high number of exporters, it is possible that the MITI data overestimates substantially the amount of CERTEX paid. However, when checking the amount of total CERTEX paid by comparing the MITI figures with the sum from Customs, the two figures are close (that of MITI was 90 per cent that of Customs), reinforcing confidence in the MITI data.

   A series of 29 matrices (one for each three-digit SIC sector) were generated, contrasting establishments with and without CERTEX, in the Lima metropolitan area and outside Lima, with the following indicators: number of establishments, total CERTEX received, gross product, value added, number of production and non-production employees, total amount of wages paid, percentage of foreign capital, percentage of imported inputs, amount of fixed assets in machinery and equipment, and annual investment in fixed assets.

3 FOB or 'Freight on board value' refers to cargo value without the cost of transportation added in.

4 Those three-digit sectors with greater than 58 per cent of their establishments in

Lima (the national average for non-exporting manufacturers) are considered geographically concentrated in Lima.

5 Based on analysis of establishment level data aggregated by 3-digit SIC. (See note 2 above.)

6 Based on Ministry of Industry data for 1979, compiled by the author.

7 A shift-share analysis of manufacturing employment shows that a majority of industries fared worse in Lima (in terms of employment growth) than in the nation as a whole. Based on data by MITI for 1975 and 1979, the author carried out a shift-share analysis of 3-digit SICs in manufacturing in Lima compared to the rest of the country. Those industries with a zerio or negative value for differential growth (i.e. no comparative advantage in Lima) included all but petroleum refining, non-ferrous metal products, non-electric machinery, and transport equipment. Thus, most of Lima's lagging growth (i.e. below the national growth rate) in manufacturing employment from 1975 to 1979 was primarily due not to industry mix, but rather to less than average sectoral growth rates in Lima.

REFERENCES

MITI (Ministerio de Industria y Turismo) (1979) *Estadística Industrial, 1979*, Lima, Peru.

Singer, Paul Israel, and Cardoso, Fernando H. (1972) 'A Cidade E O Campo', Cadernos CEBRAP, no. 7, Sao Paolo.

PART IV

State Responses to Global Restructuring

10

The State, Capital and Urban Change in Britain

Desmond S. King

THE CONTEXT OF BRITISH URBANIZATION: STATE POLICY, UNEVEN GROWTH AND GLOBAL ECONOMIC DYNAMICS

One of the dominant themes in the new urban political economy literature (Zukin, 1980; Fainstein and Fainstein, 1983; Hill, 1984) is the importance of economic processes in the determination of both urbanization patterns and elements of internal municipal life (Katznelson, 1981). This work also emphasizes the significance of economic, political and social processes located *outside* the immediate terrain of any particular city to its internal structure. This includes regional, national and global economic patterns as well as the internationalization of capital. Cities and urban life are not only the product of national economic patterns, it is contended, but also of international ones (Tabb, 1984). However, what this new literature has neglected largely (with some exceptions – see below) is the key role of the state and state policies in the shaping of urban patterns – a factor arguably as significant as economic dynamics in the complex configuration of variables which determine collectively urban structures. By way of contrast, this paper takes as its main reference point the importance of *both* state *and* capital to an adequate analysis of British urban patterns, and attempts to construct an explanation combining the two factors. Thus the essay lies clearly in the perspective of the new urban political economy.

It will be argued that analysis of state urban policy is important for two main reasons. First, the flight of private capital from many formerly prosperous and industrial cities in advanced industrial countries, including Britain, necessitates a greater state presence if urban decline is to be controlled. Second, in the pursuit of certain interests which the state holds independently of societal interests, state managers have a concern with the condition of municipalities. While these latter objectives are pursued in the context of a private economy they are far from insignificant in shaping the contemporary form of cities.

Although this chapter will maintain the combined importance of state and capital in shaping British urban patterns, there is no denying the significant influence of economic forces. This is true especially given the nature of the economic system in Britain, which, as in most advanced capitalist societies, is a spatially and temporally uneven process. In market economies (which includes the British economy), where private investment decisions are dominant, economic activity tends to be uneven in locational distribution. The consequences of this are skewed regional and local patterns of economic activity, as Massey (1984: 67) observes in relation to employment patterns: 'the spatial distribution of employment . . . can be interpreted as the outcome of the way in which production is organised over space'. The same applies for patterns of urban growth and decline.

An additional issue is the increasing importance of the global economy, in which Britain occupies a weak position. This latter has coincided since the late 1970s with a neo-liberal administration disinclined to rely upon state intervention to resolve social problems or to arrest regional or locally-based economic decline. The British case is further complicated by the nature of the current administration's policies toward municipal and local authorities: increased centralization and central controls upon local budgetary allocations. Both measures restrict the ability of city authorities to formulate and implement effective policies to counter the erosion of their urban economies.

In what follows, an attempt is made to analyse British urbanization patterns as the outcome of state activity and the dynamics of capital. These are the two phenomena of principal interest and the focus of discussion. The serious problems of the British economy in the 1970s and 1980s have increased the importance of state policies aimed at relieving urban deprivation. And as already noted, there are important theoretical arguments about the state's interests in cities contributing to the formulation of these policies which require analysis. Thus this essay attempts to provide both a factual account of the major British urban patterns over the last few decades; and to analyse these patterns in terms of economic activity and state policy. The latter should contribute to research on the role of the state in shaping urbanization patterns in advanced capitalist societies.

The first section of the paper discusses the role of the state in shaping urban change by reference to recent work in the field of urban political economy. This relates both to the central and local state, and constitutes a framework for examining the impact of the British state on urban change. This is followed by an overview of the major urbanization trends in Britain and the differential role of state and capital in their determination.

THE STATE AND URBANIZATION

This essay concurs with the assumptions of urban political economy that urbanization and municipal behavior are the outcome, to a significant extent, of extra-local economic, political and social processes (see Harvey, 1973; Gordon, 1976; Castells, 1977; Hill, 1977; Smith, 1979; Katznelson, 1981). Cities and urban formations are not phenomena which can be satifactorily studied in isolation from the larger political and economic system of which they form a part. However, where urban political economy has brought successfully the influence of economic determinants into our understanding of urban patterns, it has neglected the role of the state. Referring to figure 10.1, the urban political economy literature has expanded our understanding of relationship 2 but in part at the expense of relationship 3. A cursory overview of some leading works will illustrate this point (which is changing as new work is done) and provide a background to the arguments about the state's interests in cities advanced here.

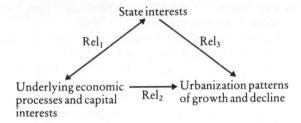

Rel₁   Economic processes constrain state action both by limiting the fiscal base for policy and by imposing certain preferences on state policy which diverge from state interests. Economic processes also stimulate state policy and intervention in market economies by requiring policy responses to temporally and spatially uneven economic development.

Rel₂   Economic processes and change are a central dynamic of urban growth and decline: shifting economic patterns have profound effects on municipal conditions.

Rel₃   According to the statist arguments (see text) the state has specific short- and long-term interests in cities reflecting both the state's own interests in survival and certain city needs.

FIGURE 10.1 Central relationships in contemporary urban political economy

The state in urban political economy

Scholars in the urban political economy tradition offer a continuum in their analysis of the importance of the state in influencing urban formations. Some like Gordon (1976) accord a minimal role to the state, regarding it as epiphenomenally derivative of economic processes; thus in relation to the corporate stage of American urbanization Gordon writes:

once this new urban form crystallized, of course, many additional influences affected urban growth ... All of these factors had secondary effects, however, in the sense that they tended to reproduce the structure of the Corporte City rather than change or undermine it. The foundations of that urban form was so strong that simple political influence could not change its basic shape. (Gordon, 1976: 55)

Clearly, Gordon considers all aspects of state policy concerned with urban issues to reinforce or support dominant economic interests. Harvey's (1973) study also minimizes the role of the state: he attributes a secondary function to the state as a channel of investment to cities where the market system is doing this inadequately: 'Harvey . . . gives . . . an imagery of capital being generated in production and allocated along these three circuits. However the allocation is not a smooth one . . . and thus capital has to be channelled by complex capital markets and by the state' (Procter, 1982: 84). Harvey's careful analysis of investment flows, mediating financial institutions and credit mechanisms results in a greater focus on economic processes and dynamics as an explanation of shifting urbanization patterns; and in a minimization of the role of state intervention.

Castells and Smith are two urban political economists (working within a neo-Marxist framework) who consider the state to occupy an important and distinctive role with respect to cities. Although the state's policies are still interpreted as essentially supportive of economic interests, the scope of these activities are substantially enlarged in these writers' arguments. Smith (1979: 245), for instance, draws the following conclusion about urban renewal in the United States: 'the most deliberate government effort to support advanced capitalist land-use priorities has been urban renewal. Instead of seeking to control the social costs of corporate development, urban renewal sought to subsidize the corporate structure's ability to redefine the form and the functions of our cities at minimal private cost.' Thus the state acts to promote and assist dominant private economic interests by subsidizing corporations and real estate developers in the form of providing infrastructural needs. In support of this type of argument Friedland's (1976; 1980; 1983) study of the distribution of urban renewal funds and Mollenkopf's (1975) large analysis of the pattern of postwar urban development, independently conclude that state policies promoted corporate and capitalist class interests at the expense of other less powerful societal interests. Even where current urban policy emphasizes private sector initiatives, this frequently necessitates substantial public investment: thus for Baltimore's Inner Harbour development the private sector invested $375 million between 1960 and 1982 but this was 'matched by $330 million from the city, state and federal governments. Moreover, the targeting of public monies in a relatively small area resulted in public disinvestment elsewhere in the city' (Boyle and Keating, 1985: 13). Public policy, and more importantly, public funds worked to support private investment and interests in Baltimore, which is in line with Smith's analysis. For Castells the state occupies a structural position in the entire political economy of each society in that it 'acts in the interests of the whole capitalist system' (1978: 19). For the state the city is both a location for capital to generate profit but also a 'coordinating agent particularly in relationship to the collective consumption of goods and services' (Procter, 1982: 93).

Complementing Smith and Castells's work are some urban scholars who have given the state's role in urban processes a more precise treatment, acknowledging its potential independence of economic constraints. Thus, Mollenkopf (1983), in his major study of postwar American federal urban programs, emphasizes the importance of initiatives within the state: 'the evolution of federal urban programs may be best understood as resulting from the competition among national political entrepreneurs to strengthen their political position by enacting new national programs which bolster their local constituencies (F)actors rooted within the political system itself, not the economy, have accounted for the actual design of the resulting federal programs' (1983: 48). In other words, political dynamics are at the forefront of federal urban policy according to Mollenkopf's analysis. A more systematic treatment of the state's capacity to affect urban change is provided by Feagin's (1984) study of Houston, Texas. Feagin develops a theoretically informed account of the relationship between state (national, regional and local) and capital (local and national/transnational) in the growth of Houston since the nineteenth century, concentrating on four time-periods. Substantively, Feagin concludes that the central state was of considerable importance to Houston's development: 'in every case cited here Houston demonstrates its dependence on the central state for public investment capital and market regulation, which enhance capital accumulation and consequent urban growth' (1984: 458). The central and local states, according to Feagin, have exercised significant influence upon Houston's urban patterns. While the aims of local capital and the central state overlapped, the former tended to seek out the latter's finances. A key issue in Feagin's analysis is the overlapping membership of local capital and the local state implying a state responsive to the needs of capital. Overall Feagin's study is an exemplary analysis of the intricate state–capital relationships underlying contemporary urban patterns. His Houston study strengthens Fainstein et al.'s (1983: 1) imperative that 'urban redevelopment cannot ... be explained through either a purely economic analysis or a study of local politics divorced from the economic relations that confine it'. It is the combination of economic dynamics and state policies which are crucial to the shaping of urban patterns. Feagin's study also highlights an important difference between theories of the state in their application to the United States and Britain. This concerns the background of key state or public officials. In Houston, Feagin finds a striking incidence of such officials coming directly from dominant economic groups; in Britain there is less incidence of state officials coming from the capitalist class. This is a general point, of course, about theories of the state and not one of exclusive concern to urban policy.

However, despite increased attention to the urban policy, for most urban scholars the state remains fundamentally rooted in the capitalist political economy and any relative autonomy it exercises is used exclusively for buttressing that system: the state acts as a regulator of the capitalist system in its totality. Thus Clark and Dear's (1984) explication of an explicitly state-centered theory conceives of state autonomy within the constraints of capitalist processes, this latter informing their analysis of state policy. The state does have a positive role, therefore, with regard to the capitalist system (the state provides social investment/social consumption and social expenses expenditures: O'Connor, 1973) but that role is quite explicitly based in the interests generated by its economic processes according to the assumptions of urban political economy. These assumptions provide the frame-work for the interpretation of urban public policy formulated by these scholars.

THE STATE'S INTERESTS IN CITIES

Such a view seems too limited, however, given not only the range of public policies affecting cities but also the needs of the state itself which are met at the urban level. This latter point underpins theoretical and empirical work I have done elsewhere (see Gurr and King, 1984; 1987; King, 1985) which is briefly summarized here. The state interests discussed here are distinct from those alluded to in the preceding section because there is no assumption that these necessarily derive from economic pressures.

The essential argument is that state managers have a certain autonomy from economic processes which allows them to pursue their own interests; at any given historical juncture the state may be dominated by capitalist economic interests but such domination does not necessarily hold. Over the long run state managers will attempt to increase their autonomy from economic interests. In relation to cities state managers *generally* pursue their own interests in the aggrandizement of power and resources and *specifically* have interests in the viability of cities which do not simply reflect the interests of private capital or any other societal group. Their general objectives derive from the concrete interests of public officials, elective and appointive, in maintaining the political institutions and relationships which underpin their power, status and privilege. A broad twofold distinction is made between those state activities concerned with the perpetuation of the central state (such as the maintenance of public order, legitimacy, durable political institutions, revenues) and those concerned with the perpetuation of cities (such as general and special collective goods, economic developmental policies, social service provision).

The first set of activities refers to those actions undertaken by the state in cities related to its own persistence: that is, failure to ensure a steady supply of revenue or to ensure public order, for example, has serious implications for the state's capacity to endure. Likewise, the state must maintain its legitimacy: preferably through voluntary compliance in advanced industrial democracies, and since these are preponderantly urban societies, cities are clearly the central location for this function. Cities are additionally the key location for the institutions of state authority which it seeks to make durable and effective. Referring to Eckstein's (1971) criteria (or what he terms dimensions) of effective political performance by governments or states – maintenance of civil order, legitimacy and durable political institutions of state authority – it is apparent that these are activities carried on by the state, to a considerable degree, in cities: states and state managers have basic interests in cities deriving from their presumed desire for perpetuation.

The second set of urban activities undertaken by the state refers to those actions and public policies necessary for the perpetuation and vitality of municipalities. However, these activities will be differentially distributed across cities since, for the central state, not all cities are perceived to be of equal importance: administratively important cities; economically important cities; and cities with large national public sector workforces are all likely to be favoured by the central state. Collective consumption goods refer to the basic, indispensable urban services which have become commonplace in contemporary urban environments: for example, fire protection, garbage collection, streets and lighting. The state's role in providing most such basic services has its origin in the nineteenth century: they have been augmented by more special types of collective goods such as educational facilities, public housing and transportation systems. The provision of special collective goods contribute to the legitimacy of the state, paralleling many other activities assumed by the state in the twentieth century.

The state undertakes two further types of activities at the municipal level relevant to the latter's effective continuance: first, developmental policies are initiated which aim to enhance local productivity levels and to promote entrepreneurial activity which in the long run build a sound local economy and expand the national revenue base. Social services for the disadvantaged are the last group of activities provided by the state at the municipal level which includes social welfare expenditures for the poor and unemployment benefits. As with general collective goods, these expenditues mirror the larger intervention of the state in the post-1945 period.

This is the theoretical backdrop to analyses of the state's role in urban patterning. On the one hand, the urban political economists acknowledge a certain autonomous capacity to the state but interpret state policy as fundamentally geared to the interests of capital. Contrasting with this, are the statist arguments, premised on the state's own needs and interests as constituting a not insignificant determinant of national urban policy. Both sets of theoretical arguments will be drawn on to interpret the urban policies of the British state since the mid-1960s. This distinction is perhaps drawn more sharply here than is fair to the relevant literature; this is simply to facilitate analysis of the British patterns of urbanization.

The British state's urban policy

Urban policy in Britain has never acquired the scale of its American counterpart either financially or in scope. The initial stimulus occurred in the mid-1960s when the concentration of large numbers of Commonwealth immigrants in inner cities were perceived as the source of inner city problems (McKay and Cox, 1979; Laurence and Hall, 1981). This led to the central grants to municipal authorities to address the specific needs of these immigrant groups. This initiative was followed by an Urban Aid Program in 1968 (expanded in 1975), the Community Development Projects from 1969 to 1976 (discontinued because of their radical analyses of the causes of urban deprivation), the Inner Area Studies 1927–7, the Inner Urban Area Act 1978, the Urban Development Corporations 1980, and the Enterprise Zone scheme of the present administration (see Gurr and King, 1987, Chapter 5 for fuller details of these and related policies).

Quantitatively, British urban programs have remained small compared to American programs even allowing for differences in national resources. Between 1968 and 1974 'only £1.7 million had been spent on the 146 different schemes' of the Urban Aid Program (Short, 1984: 158). However, this initial start gave way to more substantial expenditure: by 1979/80 the government was spending £165 million on urban programs (Laurence and Hall, 1981), and by 1984/5 the total urban budget was £413 million (Church of England, 1985: 182). In contrast, in the United States by 1978 federal outlays to cities amounted to £14,482 million (Anton, Cawley and Kramer, 1980: 83). While the trend under the Reagan administration has been to retrench federal urban aid it still remains significantly greater than its British counterpart.

Two sorts of rationale can be identified in the urban policies of the state. First, consistent with the importance of private capital, many of these policies represent efforts to encourage or facilitate investment by private economic interests. Thus the 1978 Act, initiated under a Labour government, created partnerships between the central and local government which attempted to harness private capital interests and investment for inner city economic revival. Likewise the Enterprise Zone schemes which have been the primary thrust of the 1979 Conservative government's policies work to remove state regulations on private capital investment and entrepreneurial activity. Butler (1982: 107–8) summarizes this urban policy: 'the primary aim of Britain's Enterprise Zones is to encourage industrial and commercial redevelopment in derelict or cleared areas of cities . . . The assumption is that by encouraging companies to develop these sites, a boost will be given to the entire local economy, leading to jobs and opportunities for the nearby residents.' The areas designated as Enterprise Zones have tended to be the most derelict inner city regions where factories and warehouses have been idle for years.

Enterprise Zones are very much ideologically compatible with the general free market and *laissez-faire* assumptions of the Thatcher government. By emphasizing the *removal* of state regulations on employment conditions, tax requirements and planning controls the Enterprise Zone policy also promotes the notion that too much state intervention in the past has contributed in no small part to the current economic crisis of the inner cities. The emphasis on renovating derelict Victorian inner city areas also ties in with the diagnosis reviewed below for the loss of manufacturing employment: that the old-fashioned nature of these building and plants are unsuitable for contemporary industrial and manufacturing purposes.

A second thrust or rationale of the British state's urban policy, however, has addressed the social and political consequences of urban decline. The dangers of public disorder and a weakening of the state's legitimacy have also informed urban policy in a way consistent with the theoretical arguments about the state's interests in cities outlined above. Thus the first urban programs (section 11 of the Local Government Act 1966) were responding to the arrival of Commonwealth immigrants. More recently, the current Thatcher government initially reduced urban aid on taking office but quickly reversed this policy in the wake of the 1981 urban riots (Short, 1984); however, this reversal itself proved to be temporary as the government's urban policy shifted to the Enterprise Zone schemes. Clearly, the current administration interprets urban decline and inner city economic crisis as a consequence of the natural working-out of market forces and accepts it as such. The policies it pursues, such as Enterprise Zones, attempt to work within the framework of market imperatives. But the state has been forced to respond to the social pressures and political alienation concentrated in the cities in the interests of its legitimacy and enduring capacity to rule. It is also the case that the current administration's electoral base lies in the more prosperous South of Britain and not in the old industrial cities concentrated in the North and Scotland. While both sorts of rationale inform urban policy at different times and to different degrees, it appears that the former is the more powerful long-term influence whereas the second is more visible for short periods: less influential over the long term but far from inconsequential. Limitations of space exclude a complete development of these points, especially in relation to the statist assumptions about the state's interests in municipalities (see King, 1985). Suffice it to observe that the state's policies towards cities reflect a series of influences, some of which emanate from within its own institutions and interests rather than being exclusively those of the economic system to which the state is related.

The local state and urban change

As already noted, central state urban policy since 1979 has been dominated by a neo-liberal and ideologically conservative administration. Substantively, the policy of this government has been informed by an overwhelming preference for market solutions to economic and social problems. In the long term such a policy has meant reduced national aid to distressed municipalities, and the pursuit of policies which attempt to activate market processes in the urban economy. However, this has proved less than effective in the context of national economic patterns which do not benefit directly formerly prosperous urban areas. At the local level, the consequence of central disengagement has been to encourage some local authorities (notably the new defunct Greater London Council) to establish their own locally-based economic initiatives. This, in turn, runs the danger of increased conflict with the central state whose economic priorities are national *not* regional or local. In the contemporary period this conflict is overtly political but as Young and Mills (1982: 99) note, it is a general problem for cities: 'different agencies and levels of government pursue different and often contradictory purposes. City governments must deploy policies against the tide, if only in the hope of reducing its rate of flow, so buying further time for adaptation.' The same authors suggest that 'the complex web of intergovernmental and multi-agency involvement impedes any strategic overview of the urban economy'. The interests of the central government in national patterns of economic activity necessitate their being responsive to market forces. In contrast, cities are responding to local fiscal and economic conditions. Thus, 'national and local responses to fiscal stress are likely to remain contradictory' (p. 99).

Local governments' concern with the weakness and vulnerability of their urban economies has intensified since the late 1970s and the policies of the current central administration. Thus the GLC established the Greater London Enterprise Board (GLEB) in 1983 to address the unremitting rise in unemployment within its jurisdiction while the six Metropolitan County Councils of the conurbations all became more interventionist in their local economies. While the policies pursued by these authorities was initially one of crisis-response they have evolved into more radical policy responses. For example, Sheffield City, the West Midlands County Council and the GLC all acquired 'a commitment not only to tackle job loss and the immediate crisis, but also to explore the possibility of developing socialist strategy in the economic and employment field in the longer term' (Boddy, 1984: 166). By the early 1980s all three were dominated by the Labour Party which has been developing and pursuing socialist strategy at the municipal level more systematically under the Thatcher administration than at any period in its history (Gyford, 1985). Inevitably the pursuit of such radical policies at the local state level has increased conflict with the central government given its fiscally conservative policy commitments. In fact, central–local relations have reached a level of conflict and salience in political consciousness unparalleled in British twentieth-century political experience (Newton and Karran, 1985). A major consequence of this conflict was the abolition (in April 1985) of the GLC and six Metropolitan County Councils which not only increased the state's centralization but also reduced the local governments' capacity to respond to economic decline. The central government has pursued *fiscal* (central control of local budgets) and *political* (abolition of a tier of local administration) policies which ineluctably diminish local autonomy and consequently the capacity for local policy reaction to urban and economic change.

However, those policies which have been formulated by the local state to counteract urban and economic change do not simply accord primacy to capital interests, as the references to Boddy indicate. The local government has its own interests to pursue independent of capitalist interests (Clark, 1984; King and Gurr, 1985). Thus Boddy (1984: 164–5) notes that analysis of the conventional economic policies of the local state must allow for the multiple sources of such policies, and not simply assume the dominance of capital interests:

the shared characteristics of mainstream local economic policy reflect more than simple need, necessity or the inevitably capitalist nature of the state. Although underpinned by the basically capitalist nature of the production system and of the state, explanation lies more in the combination of the ostensible aims of policy as it has emerged in particular local authorities, in response to, in particular, unemployment, the limitations of finance, powers and other resources.

Thus local government finds itself responding to the consequences of economic activity as much as attempting to encourage greater entrepreneurial activity in its economy. As such, the local government is clearly attempting to articulate a distinct role in the patterning of its urban formation and community. In the present economic and centralizing climate, this objective is pursued in a largely hostile environment but is none the less a key tenet of its policies.

It is important that the distinct roles of central and local government in urban change be understood and to realize that the priorities and interests of each can diverge significantly. This is certainly the case in the contemporary urban restructuring of Britain: the central state is concerned primarily with a national economic revival, a concern exacerbated by the ideological propensity of the current Thatcher administration. That this concern has been coupled with efforts to retrench municipal authorities' expenditures (the government proposed to cut financial aid totalling £138 million to depressed inner city areas in the three years after 1985) has highlighted the contrast with the objectives of city authorities. This has resulted in locally-based policies and agencies attempting to improve the local economy and hence encourage urban revival. Implementing this policy has been additionally hindered by the central state's attacks on local autonomy and increased control of local budgetary practice.

However, within this unlikely environment, genuine socialist strategies have been formulated and pursued by local government. This stands in contrast to the traditionally assumed role of local government in economic growth and urban change, as Fainstein and Fainstein (1983: 252) identify these: 'the economic objective of state action is to facilitate accumulation: in general terms, to implement programs which produce new investment in the built environment capable of generating private profit and of expanding the market value of real estate'. Some local governments in Britain have been able to alter these traditional objectives, as reported above, though they remain exceptions, if important ones. The success or at least potential for success of these local initiatives is indicated by the central state's determination to abolish a complete tier of local administration. These latter are put in terms of efficiency and revenue-saving, but as Flynn, Leach and Vielba (1985: 92) argue:

technical arguments about efficiency and economy mask profound ideological differences between central and local government about the proper response to a range of issues including economic decline . . . It is clear that central government has become seriously concerned about the alternative conceptions of economic policy espoused by the metropolitan counties and the Greater London Council.

There are, of course, problems with local government's attempts to influence its urban economy. In its efforts to attract new investment any one municipality is placed in competition with others chasing the same funds. Further, efforts to attract capital can lead the local government to develop as attractive environment as possible in terms of providing infrastructure, thus socializing production costs. The local state runs the traditional danger of financing private enterprises. Without doubt, this has been the dominant pattern in the past, and is the evidence from comparative experience in the United States. Arguably, this pattern has been dominant as a consequence of the capitalist system of economic organization, an issue considered further in the concluding section. Suffice it for now to note that local government does have a distinctive role in contemporary urban change in Britain but that the norm for this role is to be one supportive of capital interests and dynamics. Related to this point, the next section outlines the extent to which shifts in economic activity and capital have shaped urban patterns in Britain over the last few decades.

CAPITAL AND URBANIZATION

National economic activity and urban change

The decline of urban economies has been a harsh reality in Britain for at least the last fifteen years, and is arguably more pressing than in other industrial democracies, since certain regions and cities show little evidence of stabilizing or reversing their decline. The 1981 summer riots were, in part, an outgrowth of the tensions and social malaise concentrated in British cities, evidencing decline. These latter symptoms of urban decay have been developing since the 1960s in some of the worst affected British inner cities such as Liverpool and Glasgow. A journalistic account of Liverpool's decline sets the general tone of British urban decay in its most advanced stages:

No other city in Britain, and possibly in the world, has declined so steeply and absolutely in the last two decades. The docks have shrunk, factories close, wealth flees. In the past six years 50,000 manufacturing jobs, half the former total, have vanished. Liverpool faces out to old imperial trade routes and empty seas. At its back, the Lancashire textile industry has collapsed. The city undergoes a new British process: museumification. (*Sunday Times Magazine*, 1985: 20)

In other cities, such as Newcastle and Birmingham, the problems of economic stagnation, social decay and political alienation have also become commonplace in the 1970s and 1980s (Hall, 1981; Church of England, 1985). British cities are the victims of long-term economic structural trends which in the 1970s have meant significant economic hardship for vast parts of the economy and country. As Fothergill and Gudge (1982: 8) note: 'British cities are experiencing a rapid loss of manufacturing jobs while small towns and rural areas are quite successful in retaining and expanding their manufacturing base. As a general rule, the larger and more industrial a settlement the faster its decline.' This loss of manufacturing employment is mirrored by population decline. The key cause of urban decline is loss of manufacturing jobs (augmented by population loss), and it is precisely these which the urban areas have been losing:

the decline of cities and growth of small towns and rural areas is the dominant aspect of change in the location of manufacturing industry in Britain. The larger and more industrial its settlement, the faster its decline. At the two extremes, London lost nearly 40% of its manufacturing jobs between 1959 and 1979, while the most rural areas increased theirs by nearly 80% during the same period. (Fothergill and Gudge, 1982: 68)

Table 10.1 reports data on the decline of manufacturing employment in six types of areas: London, the six conurbations (Manchester, Tyneside, Clydeside, Merseyside, Birmingham and West Yorkshire); cities which are free-standing, that is, medium-sized industrial urban areas like Sheffield; industrial areas with smaller, principally industrial, towns located in them; county towns; and rural areas (see Fothergill and Gudge, 1982: 15–16). The evidence shows quite clearly that it is the more urbanized areas and London which have been losing the most manufacturing employment, trends confirmed by more recent data on manufacturing trends and population (Bentham, 1985).

TABLE 10.1   *Manufacturing employment by area type, 1959–75*

	Manufacturing employment as % of total employment in each area in 1952
London	−13.0
Conurbations	−7.9
Free-standing cities	+1.1
Industrial towns	+6.9
County towns	+7.5
Rural areas	+11.1

Source: Fothergill and Gudge, 1982: table 3.4, 31. See also OECD, 1983a; McKay and Cox, 1979: chapter 6; Short, 1984.

A recent study (ESRC, 1985) provides additional information on these main trends, suggesting that those trends highlighted in table 10.1 have persisted. Thus, the ESRC report that 'one million manufacturing jobs were lost in inner cities between 1951 and 1981 and a further one million from outer areas of the conurbations and from free-standing cities' (1984: 8). In inner cities there was a 36.8 per cent drop in manufacturing employment alone between 1971 and 1981 and a 32.6 per cent drop in the outer cities. Thus, the 1970s have seen no easing of the long-term decline in employment prospects for urban residents. Not unsurprisingly, these economic trends have had profound and serious social consequences (ESRC, 1985; Church of England, 1985; Gurr and King, 1987).

In the process of economic restructuring through which the British economy is currently passing, cities and conurbations stand as the most disadvantaged sites for industrial and manufacturing activity. The main cause of this disadvantage, Fothergill and Gudge argue, is the old-fashioned nature of municipal buildings and factories which severely limit the possibilities for expansion. This means that 'in cities investment in machinery displaces labour on the shop floor, and thus reduces employment' (Fothergill and Gudge, 1982: 68). Massey (1984: 135) concurs with this analysis: the cities have been affected most seriously because they 'tended to have the older and more labour-intensive capacity within any sector, and were therefore more liable to suffer from programs of capacity-cutting and technical change, and from the fact that what new investment was available sought out the attractions of less urban areas'. This process has been operating since the early 1960s, but has now spread to all major urban centers in Britain. The result is a serious decline of larger cities' manufacturing, and hence employment, base. This weakens the resources of the local economy while increasing the demands for social services provided by the local government/municipal authorities. Concurrent with these domestic trends in manufacturing activity is the impact of global economic patterns, to which we now turn.

Global economic activity and urban change

A key contextual factor to British urban patterns is the internationalization of capital and economic activity in the postwar period which has been especially detrimental for the British economy, as Massey (1984: 134) notes:

the decline in production industries is not, of course, peculiar to Britain . . . The fact that this generalised downturn took place rather earlier in Britain than elsewhere, and that it has been more severe, is a reflection of the longterm structural weaknesses in British economy and society. In the context of a shifting international division of labour and, later, a slowdown in the world capitalist economy as a whole, these structural weaknesses came home to roost.

Elsewhere Massey and Meegan (1978: 288) analyse the serious adverse impact of international competition on the electrical, electronics and aerospace equipment industries located in large cities. Profitability and international competition combined to undermine British cities as centers of production. Thus London, Manchester, Liverpool and Birmingham lost 36,106 jobs in these industries between 1966 and 1972. Global economic activity has thus contributed to British urban patterns, in a way comparable to the processes identified by Glickman (1982) in the American context. The internationalization of the world economy has eliminated the previous relative advantage for most advanced industrial countries including Britain: production is more efficient and profitable in newly industrialising countries. Consequently, 'multi-national corporations increasingly make production decisions on an international basis, rather than being limited to one country' (OECD, 1983a: 68). The outcome of this decisional process is decline and disinvestment for urban centers in advanced capitalist states:

The result of these developments in the last decade has been increased capital investment in the less industrialised countries relative to the highly industrialised ones. In particular, this process may result in disinvestment in declining areas of the highly industrialised world and investment instead of urbanising areas in less industrialised regions and countries . . . [C]apital investment in the United States has switched from the old industrial cities of the North East to the South and West and is now seeking even lower labour costs in the less industrialised countries of Mexico and the Caribbean. (OECD, 1983a: 69)

Those cities suffering disinvestment and manufacturing decline, which in Britain includes London and the major industrial urban centers, then assume the familiar economic, social and political traits of urban decline. While the unemployment and population loss increasingly characteristic of British inner cities did not necessarily cause the 1981 riotous behaviour located in these urban areas, they certainly constituted important contextual factors (Scarman, 1983; Kettle and Hodges, 1982). The cautious OECD report (1983a) is fully cognizant of this connection:

rising unemployment may initiate a self-perpetuating spiral of decline in certain urban areas. At the extreme, the increased unemployment of weak groups can lead to stress, alienation and increasingly serious social problems such as increasing rates of crime and vandalism. For example, Liverpool has experienced this phenomenon as the emergence of groups of people living in the social and economic margins of society become increasingly concentrated in areas of private and public sector rental housing. (OECD, 1983a: 71–2)

Liverpool's conditions find parallels in the other British conurbations and inner cities.

The picture of urbanization patterns in Britain is thus one of decline in both population and manufacturing employment in the old industrial urban areas. It is the older and most densely concentrated urban settlements which have been most adversely affected by these trends. The cursory overview here has emphasized the extent to which shifting global economic dynamics and industrial restructuring have underpinned these urban patterns; older industrial cities are less adaptable to the contemporary needs of capital. The role of urban systems in the process of capital accumulation has changed: the traditional industrial and commercial rationales, which were prevalent at the end of the last century and the first decades of this one, have dissipated. As Smith (1979: 236) observes: 'the tendency of capital is to concentrate and then to move globally to the least expensive points of production'. Although 'Western industrial cities emerged as a direct consequence of the growth of industrial capitalism as a dominant mode of economic organization' (p. 236), the shifting nature of capital interests and processes has made many old industrial cities redundant. This is as true of large British cities as of those in the north-east of the United States. What has not altered, but rather has intensified, is the role of cities as locational centers for the least privileged strata of society which has enduring implications for state policy as the previous section has attempted to demonstrate. The final section considers the interaction of state policy and capital interests in the process of urban change.

STATE AND CAPITAL IN THE DETERMINATION OF URBAN PATTERNS

The preceding sections have documented the major urban trends in Britain over the last three decades and located the source of economic difficulty for urban areas in their unsuitability to modern manufacturing needs as defined within the private, market-oriented dominant economic system. Attention has been drawn also to the importance of global economic patterns to urban, regional and national economic conditions, and the extent to which the British economy has been vulnerable within this global context. Two sorts of theoretical argument about the state's role in urban development have been explicated: those of urban political economy which emphasise the state's responsiveness to capital accumulation dynamics and needs; and those of the statist perspective which contends that the state is additionally attentive to its own interests in urban policy. The main thrusts of the British state's urban policies have been outlined, interpreted within these two types of theory and the responses of the local state to urban and economic change have been examined. Throughout, the neo-liberal economic principles of the present administration have been highlighted and the accompanying trend toward greater state centralization. In this final section, the main objective is to distinguish more systematically between the role of capital or economic interests and the role of the state in the determination of British urban change.

That the British urban system is undergoing substantial restructuring is quite plain from the broad trends outlined above. There is a marked trend away from older and larger industrial urban centers toward medium-sized towns and indeed rural areas. The evidence also suggests that the main dynamic in this process has been changes in the nature of economic activity and capital interests. Changes in manufacturing employment strikingly mirror the decline or growth of urban areas: where core manufacturing employment diminishes, population tends to decline, there is a concentration of unskilled workers, of welfare state dependants, and disadvantaged minorities. The opposite traits characterize the prospering rural areas and medium-sized towns. Thus the movement of capital and shifts in economic activity are at the kernel of British urban restructuring.

The state's role in this process of urban restructuring has altered. While it has been responsive to the needs of declining areas in the past, it is now fundamentally aligned with the dictates of market forces. This does not mean that the state's policies disregard depressed areas but its responsiveness to them is more transient (usually in the wake of social unrest) and less consistent than its support of capital. The state's policies toward distressed areas have emphasized market-based solutions. A recent example of this is the London Docklands Development Corporation, set up in 1981 with responsibility for developing 1000 acres of public land in London's depressed docklands. Its strategy is to sell off this land to private housebuilders and corporate developers, a strategy which is 'against the policies and wishes of local councils and local people' (*New Statesman*, 1986). More generally, the central state's commitment to national economic recovery based on private capital investment reinforces the traditional patterns of uneven economic development with their inevitable byproduct of abandoned and depressed urban areas and regions. As Lambert (1982: 114) notes, the operation of private capital sustains 'an overall pattern of *uneven* economic development within which phases of relative prosperity followed by impoverishment have been the fate of different regions and areas'. But the state's concerns with legitimation and self-maintenance broaden the scope of its urban policies to include concern with the conditions of urban decay. The evidence, however, suggests that in contemporary Britain these concerns have been subordinated to the larger objective of facilitating economic growth on the basis of private capital investment. The role of the state in influencing urban restructuring is far from insignificant, but the ideological composition of the present national administration has distinctly constrained that role. The same cannot be said of the local state where genuine concern about the all too visible consequences of urban decline have stimulated locally-based initiatives aimed at reviving the urban economy. But these efforts have suffered from insufficient resources and conflict with the central state, one consequence of which is the abolition of a tier of local authorities. They have also tended to support basic economic trends rather than successfully countering or controlling them.

This relates to a general point. If present trends continue the outcome of the current process of urban restructuring would clearly seem to depend on economic activity and the interests of capital. To date, the much heralded national recovery has failed to materialize while the symptoms of a depressed economy have increased, many situated in the economically most deprived urban areas. The persistence of these trends and their attendant manifestations is likely to increase the pressure on the state to assume a more active and positive role in the shaping of cities if they are to remain governable. Clearly the state has the potential to exercise a powerful and positive role in the structuring of urban formations but to date it has failed to carry this out other than on a short-term crisis-response basis. The efforts by some local states to influence their urban economy, and therefore urban formation, have been of limited affect, in part because of the power of capital and in part because of the opposition provoked within the central state to such local initiatives. The increasing diminution of local autonomy can only limit future attempts to realize this objective.

How do these sorts of conclusion relate to the theoretical issues raised earlier in the paper? A number of points can be made. In contrast to Feagin's (1984) case study of Houston, Texas where overlapping membership of local capital and the local state rendered the latter largely the instrument of the former some British local states are evidently seeking a more independent role in the restructuring of their urban economies. This is especially the case for Labour-controlled municipalities who have suffered most from the current national administration. The intensified conflict between the national and local state in declining urban areas provided support for Clark and Dear's (1984: 181) observation that 'the local state is in a very vulnerable position. It must respond to the strongest of local pressures, even if it is closely controlled by higher tiers'. But we can go beyond this by noting that the central state must itself act to maintain its position and derivative interests. This means, for example, that a national economic policy which neglects certain cities has to be balanced with other state interests, such as the maintenance of public order. It is these latter types of interest which have been insufficiently integrated into theoretical and empirical work on state–city relations in advanced industrial societies. In Britain, the national state's urban policy (in conjunction with certain economic policy objectives) has allowed the economic, social and political problems of some cities to intensify. But where this has been followed by outbreaks of public disorder and riotous behaviour the national state has rapidly resumed previous public expenditure commitments. Thus, as Clark and Dear (1984: 188) correctly note, 'autonomy requires legitimacy', and the bases of that legitimacy, lie in the interests which inform state policy, including that formulated toward municipalities. The state's own interests (and specifically its interests in cities), therefore, must be incorporated into any general explanation of urban restructuring or change (Gurr and King, 1987). Such an inclusion contributes to a more complete account of urban processes and one which is not solely based in economic dynamics.

We can conclude by noting two important trends which are likely to impact fundamentally on the future role of the state in urban structuring. First, the weakness of the national economy, reflected especially in the historically high unemployment level, will increase the pressures on the central state to intervene positively in the political economy and therefore in urban conditions. This may occur as a result of social disorder and concern for the state's legitimacy or more likely in the form of some effort to stimulate economic growth given the relative ineffectiveness of relying on private capital and investment. The second issue is that conditions are unlikely to improve in the short to medium term for the economies of large urban areas and the most severely affected parts of Greater London. Some may succeed in reviving their urban economy to a certain extent and in reversing or stabilizing the process of decline but it is difficult to imagine a large number succeeding in this, given the limited private investment available. It is also unlikely that market-based schemes like enterprize zones will prove sufficient to restore whole urban economies: they may have positive benefits in selected areas but there spillover affects remain imponderable. The main implication for the local state of these factors will be greater pressure to provide services and to pursue policies for economic revival. The problematic for the local state in this scenario is to meet these demands successfully in the context of diminished autonomy and resources. Its failure to do this will constitute a further pressure on the central state to intervene actively in the process of urban change. Complementing this pressure, will be the state's own perceptions about its continuing legitimacy. If these pressures are ignored, the social hardship, economic stagnation and urban decay concentrated in cities – the product of an uneven economic process based on private investment – will persist and probably worsen.

REFERENCES

Anton, T. J., Cawley, J. P. and Kramer, K. L. (1980) *Moving Money: An Empirical Analysis of Federal Expenditure Patterns*, Cambridge Mass.: Oelgeschlager, Gunn and Hain.

Bentham, C. C. (1985) 'Which areas have the worst urban problems?', *Urban Studies*, 22: 119–31.

Boddy, Martin (1984) 'Local economic and employment strategies'. In Martin Boddy and Colin Fudge (eds) *Local Socialism*, London: Macmillan.

Boyle, Robin and Michael Keating. (1985) 'Scotland and the brave new world', *The Times Higher Education Supplement*, 30 August.

Butler, Stuart M. (1982) *Enterprise Zones*, London: Heinemann.

Castells, Manuel (1977) *The Urban Question*, Cambridge, Mass.: MIT Press.

—— (1978) 'Collective consumption and urban contradiction in advanced capitalism'. In Castells, M. (ed.) *City, Class and Power*. London: Macmillan.

Church of England (1985) *Faith in the City*, London: Church House Publishing.

Clark, Gordon L. (1984) 'A theory of local autonomy', *Annals of the Association of American Geographers*, 74: 195–208.

Clark, Gordon L. and Michael Dear (1984) *State Apparatus*, London and Boston: Allen and Unwin.

Dunleavy, Patrick (1980) *Urban Political Analysis*. London: Macmillan.

Eckstein, Harry (1971) *The Evaluation of Political Performance: Problems and Dimensions*, Beverly Hills, Calif.: Sage.

Economic and Social Research Council (1985) *Changing Cities*, London: ESRC.

Fainstein, Norman I. and Susan I. Fainstein (eds) (1982) *Urban Policy Under Capitalism*, London and Beverly Hills: Sage.

Fainstein, Norman I. and Susan S. Fainstein (1983) 'Regime strategies, communal resistance, and economic forces'. In Susan S. Fainstein et al. (eds) *Restructuring the City*.

Fainstein, Susan S, Norman I. Fainstein, Richard Child Hill, Dennis Judd and Michael Peter Smith (1983) *Restructuring the City: The Political Economy of Urban Redevelopment*, New York and London: Longman.

Feagin, J. R. (1984) 'The role of the state in urban development: the case of Houston, Texas', *Environment and Planning D: Society and Space* 2: 44–60.

Flynn, Norman, Steve Leach and Carol Vielba (1985) *Abolition or Reform? The GLC and the Metropolitan County Councils*, London: George Allen and Unwin.

Fothergill, Stephen and Graham Gudge (1982) *Unequal Growth: Urban and Regional Employment Change in the UK*, London: Heinemann.

Friedland, Roger (1976) 'Class power and social control: the war on poverty'. *Politics and Society*, 6: 459–89.

—— (1980) 'Corporate power and urban growth: the case of urban renewal', *Politics and Society*, 10: 203–24.

—— (1983) *Power and Crisis in the City*, New York: Schoken.

Glickman, Norman J. (1982) 'Emerging urban policies in a slow-growth economy', *International Journal of Urban and Regional Research*, 4: 492–527.

Gordon, David (1976) 'Capitalism and the roots of urban crisis', in R. E. Alcahy and D. Mermelstein (eds), *The Fiscal Crisis of American Cities*, New York: Vintage Books.

Gurr, Ted Robert and Desmond S. King (1984) *The State and the City: The Political Economy of Urban Growth and Decline in Advanced Industrial Societies.* Evanston, Ill.: Center for Urban Affairs and Policy Research, Northwestern University, Working Paper no. WP84–3.

—— (1985) 'The postindustrial city in transition from private to public'. In Jan-Erik Lane (ed.) *State and Market: The Politics of the Public and the Private*, London and Beverly Hills: Sage.

—— (1987) *The State and the City*, London: Macmillan, and Chicago: University of Chicago Press.

Gyford, John (1985) *The Politics of Local Socialism*, London: George Allen and Unwin.

Hall, Peter (ed.) (1981) *The Inner City in Context*, London: Heinemann.

—— (1982) *Urban and Regional Planning*, 2nd edn. Harmondsworth: Penguin Books.

Harvey, David (1973) *Social Justice and the City*, Baltimore, MD: Johns Hopkins University Press.

Hill, Richard Child (1977) 'State capitalism and the urban fiscal crisis in the United States', *International Journal of Urban and Regional Research*, 1: 76–100.

—— (1984) 'Urban political economy: Emergence, consolidation, and development'. In Michael Peter Smith (ed.), *Cities in Transformation Class, Capital and the State*, Beverly Hills, Calif.: Sage.

Katznelson, Ira (1981) *City Trenches*. New York: Pantheon.

Kettle, Martin and Lucy Hodges (1982) *Uprising*, London: Pan.

King, Desmond S. (1982) 'The political economy of city systems in advanced capitalist states'. Unpublished paper, Dept of Political Science, Northwestern University.

—— (1985) 'A statist analysis of central state penetration of municipalities: State autonomy under advanced capitalism'. Unpublished PhD thesis, Northwestern University.

King, Desmond S. and Ted Robert Gurr (1985) 'The state and the city: economic transformation and the autonomy of the local state in advanced industrial societies'. In Paul Johnson and William Thompson (eds), *Rhythms in Politics and Economics*, New York: Praeger.

Lambert, John (1982) 'The inner city: Planned crisis or crisis of planning?'. In Chris Paris (ed.), *Critical Readings in Planning Theory*, New York and Oxford: Pergamon.

Laurence, Susan and Peter Hall (1981) 'British policy responses'. In Hall, Peter (ed.), *The Inner City in Context*, London: Heinemann.

McKay, David H. and Andrew W. Cox (1979) *The Politics of Urban Change*, London: Croom Helm.

Massey, Doreen (1981) 'The UK electrical engineering and electronics industries: the implications of the crisis for the restructuring of capital and locational change'. In Michael Dear and Allen J. Scott (eds), *Urbanization and Urban Planning in Capitalist Society*, New York and London: Methuen.

—— (1984) *Spatial Divisions of Labour: Social Structure and the Geography of Production*, London: Macmillan.

Massey, Doreen and Richard A. Meegan (1978) 'Industrial restructuring versus the cities', *Urban Studies*, 15: 273–88.

Mollenkopf, John (1975), 'The post-war politics of urban development', *Politics and Society*, 3: 247–95.

—— (1983) *The Contested City*, Princeton, N.J.: Princeton University Press.

New Statesman (1986) 'City stranglehold on local democracy', 3 January.

Newton, K. and T. Karran (1985) *The Politics of Local Expenditure*, London: Macmillan.

OECD (1983a) *Managing Urban Change*. Vol. 1, *Policies and Finance*, Paris: OECD.

—— *Managing Urban Change*. Vol. 2, *The Role of Government*, Paris: OECD.

O'Connor, James (1973) *The Fiscal Crisis of the State*, New York: St Martin's Press.

Procter, Ian (1982) 'Some political economies of urbanization and suggestions for a *research framework*', *International Journal of Urban and Regional Research*, 6: 83–97.

Scarman, Lord (1983) *The Brixton Disorders*, Harmondsworth: Penguin Books.

Short, John R. (1984) *The Urban Arena: Capital, State and Community in Contemporary Britain*, London: Macmillan.

Smith, Michael P. (1979) *The City and Social Theory*, New York: St Martin's Press.

Sunday Times Magazine (1985) 'The best of times . . . the worst of times', 25 August.

Tabb, William K. (1984) 'Economic democracy and regional restructuring: An internationalization perspective'. In Larry Sawers and William K. Tabb (eds), *Sunbelt/Snowbelt: Urban Development and Regional Restructuring*, New York and Oxford: Oxford University Press.

Young, Ken and Liz Mills (1982) 'The decline of urban economies'. In Richard Rose and Edward Page (eds), *Fiscal Stress in Cities*, New York: Cambridge University Press.

Zukin, Sharon (1980) 'A decade of urban sociology', *Theory and Society*, 9: 575–601.

11

Plant Closures in Socialist France

Sophie Body-Gendrot

When France's Socialists took power in 1981, one of the central planks on their platform was to fight unemployment and specifically to keep it below two million. Paradoxically, since their election there have been more job losses and plant closures in France than ever before. Restructuring the main sectors of French industry has proved an uphill struggle for the Socialist government and it has left its mark on declining industries and their labor force. While industry in France in 1986 is sounder than seven years ago, the benefits will take time to translate into new jobs and profitability. Consequently in March 1986 French voters did not give the Socialists the mandate they needed to see the course through. The aim of this paper is to demonstrate that although the Left thought it could implement its policy in effect from a clean slate, in reality it inherited a legacy which would prove to be a formidable obstacle to its efforts to modernize industry as painlessly as possible. The Left believed nationalization would hasten France's economic recovery. Unfortunately, the nationalized sectors were over manned and the management unenthusiastic, thus these expectations were not met. Faced with stark realities (i.e. plant closures) the Left radically changed its utopian vision. It had to promote free enterprise, market creativity and innovation. These changes turned out to be electorally costly.

THE HERITAGE

A dependent economy

The modernization of France was pursued with the goal that France should become independent. In one sense, it was an attempt to redress the humiliating defeat of 1940. 'Hit today by a mechanical force,' de Gaulle said in his famous address of 18 June, 1940, 'we will win in the future thanks to a

This chapter was originally presented at the Annual Meeting of the American Political Science Association in Washington, D.C., 30 August–21 September 1984.

superior force' (Stoffaës, 1981: 163). The French renaissance through industrialization was thus clearly expressed in Gaullist thought.

State intervention, nationalization and forward planning allowed France to achieve supremacy in advanced technologies such as weapons, trains, subways, nuclear energy, etc. The men who modernized France were anticipating an economically unified Europe and when trade barriers were lowered in 1957, nascent industry took the initiative and changed from a self-subsistence economy to an economy based on international trade. Exports grew from 10 to 22 per cent of GNP, investments increased by 25 per cent and the country experienced the international highest growth after Japan: 5.5 per cent a year between 1958 and 1973.

However, after the Gaullist era, in 1969, the situation underwent a disturbing change and France became less independent economically. For instance, while in 1957 France produced 82 per cent of its manufactured goods, 16 years later, that production had dropped by 8 per cent. In the meantime, France was exporting commodities like cars, etc. Less than half of its industrial infrastructure used to produce these goods was French, that is, less than half of the machines, computers, tools, which would, in turn, produce French tools and machinery. French industrialization therefore became vulnerable and subordinate to imports usually paid for in dollars.[1]

Since it did not produce essential commodities on a large scale, France's exports had to be cheap to be competitive. In the 1970s, it was able to do so for three reasons: (1) its industry was largely subsidized by the state which was taking financial and economic risks. Private companies too often relied on the state instead of using it as a springboard to pursue innovative adventures. (2) After decolonization, France took advantage of a large pool of available migrant workers. (3) Unlike France's other trading partners, profits were made at the expense of subcontractors. These factors would weigh heavily on its future (Lipietz, 1984).

The process of modernization in the second half of the 1970s was marked by a dual economy approach, with the state encouraging a small, modern, highly competitive sector leading the rest of the economy. But the former sector had become the victim of an internationalization of capital and processes, increasing its vulnerability and dependency.

However, while productivity had dropped to 1–2 per cent a year between 1966 and 1974 in the US, in France productivity continued to increase until 1974. But when it dropped, the fall was precipitous and France plunged into the world economic crisis which had already struck its partners.

Unemployment and inflation

After 1974, France was confronted by the new competitive countries of Southern Europe, South-East Asia and the Far East. Unemployment rose and small plants closed, but not as dramatically as in the 1930s. Social legislation prevented mass layoffs. As more people were layed off, more generous unemployment benefits were passed in 1974, allowing redundant workers to receive up to 90 per cent of their salary for the first year of unemployment (with a ceiling of $3000 a month).

At that time, the balance-sheet was mixed: production had decreased for the first time since the end of World War II by 10 per cent in 1975 and growth was maintained at 3 per cent a year. Inflation (as usual) was not under control. Companies like Philips in the Netherlands, ICI in UK, Olivetti and Fiat in Italy reduced their workforce and scaled down their business. After the second oil crisis in 1979, US firms did so on a great scale, and ruthlessly. In France, a dramatic restructuring of enterprises also started, with a fast decline of uncompetitive and traditional industries and the expansion of new ones.

Inadequate structures

French industry is plagued by unfavorable structural factors: the average plant is too small, in debt and family-owned. In 1982, only ten enterprises had a revenue of over 5 billion dollars, five of which were among the largest corporations in the world (Elf-Aquitaine; Cie Française des Pétroles: Electricité de France; Renault; and Peugeot-Citroën). Large mergers were too often financial and artificial conglomerates rather than large companies pursuing aggressive marketing strategies to dominate the world market. For a long time the financial approach had prevailed over the industrial one. However, reorientation in policies took place and concentrations became more frequent.

Another problem was the lack of concern paid to unskilled workers and the lack of technical skills which were needed in the new plants. Too often neglected, French workers have neither the status nor the qualifications they might expect in most industrial countries (Stoffaës, 1981; 171). Their numbers are not growing. According to a prospective study carried out by Professor Leontief, the trend is a secular one: and workers who represented 15.7 per cent of the workforce in 1978 will average 16.5 per cent in the year 2000 (*Le Monde*, 1985). In France, a gap separates technology, education and research.

SOCIALIST UTOPIA

It is in a context of economic dependency, falling profits, rising unemployment and inflation, that the victory for which the Left was unprepared took place. 'By a strange miracle,' as Lipietz points out, 'on a stormy night, [it] discovered it had picked the right number. What 9 million strikers in 1968, years of struggle, nights of endless talks and dawns of militancy had been unable to achieve, finally fell to them . . . an unconcerted victory, the result of thousands of individual actions, a wide array of sometimes hardly acknowledgeable motivations brought to power a Left which no longer wanted what it could get and still wanted what it could no longer get' (Lipietz, 1984: 110).

The Left believed that strong growth with no trade deficit and no increased economic dependency was possible if French industry could meet the new demands brought by an increase in purchasing power and a 'reconquest' of the domestic market. Its efforts were to bear both on capital goods where French dependency was important and on consumer durables (e.g. electric household appliances, electronic goods, furniture, textiles). More than 85 per cent of motorcycles, cameras and sewing machines, and more than 50 per cent of clocks, etc. were imported (Le Poing et la Rose, 1980: 54).

Nationalization

Nationalization was meant to help France change 'its direction' (*changer de cap*), as the Communist Party wrote in the autumn of 1971 or, more ambitiously, according to the Socialist Manifesto the following year: 'to change life'. An ambitious program!

The plan addressed three basic categories: a 'public services' composed of energy utilities, transportation and communications: this was the category that the provisional government under de Gaulle nationalized in 1945 and that the Socialists sought to expand by including the banking sector to give the country control of money creation, investments, credit and, in the long term, growth. The second sector included strategic industries such as electronics and petrochemicals, and 'lame ducks' such as steel which might have future growth in a favorable economic climate. The third was a hodgepodge of political causes (Renault) and national holdings (insurances), etc. (Delion, 1982).

Given the changes in the world economy and France's vulnerable position, nationalization appeared as the only alternative to 'multinationalization' (increased foreign penetration) and as the way to pursue extensive restructuring: 'Only a strategic state capitalism with the public sector giving a clear lead to the private in a re-equilibated mixed economy (not a non-market "command economy") and controlling what the British Left has called "the commanding mechanisms", was seen as capable of undertaking and coordinating the task' (Cerny, 1983: 17–18). As seen from New York, London or Bonn, the Socialist policy of nationalization to combat its economic woes appeared as a gamble and an experiment. It was a combination of Keynesian measures, 'pump-priming', stimulating demand and of planning policies acting on supplies in competitive industrial sectors. Profit was no longer the only aim but was coupled with a will to modernize and defend French industry (what Cerny calls the four r's: research, rationalization, retooling and risk capital, each of these elements as important as the others) (Cerny, 1983: 18, 19), to create jobs through public works programs and to increase the purchasing power of low-income groups.

Eventually, new social relationships in the plants and new responsibilities were to be given to the workers as their representation and participation increased. Information and training would be developed to bring the workforce into the decision-making process. It was the aim of the Auroux Laws to introduce more democracy in the workplace.

The public economic sector in France now employs 2,400,000 persons, (11 per cent of the workforce), 24 per cent of employees in firms with industrial activities and 48.4 per cent in firms of over 2000 employees versus 20 per cent before nationalization (Lipietz, 1984: 31). It represents 50 per cent of the revenue of large industrial firms (previously about 20 per cent (Cerny, 1983: 19) and one third of the national investments. Its qualitative importance is even greater since it covers strategically essential sectors of the French economy (e.g. aircraft, arms industries, computer technology, etc.).

THE STRUGGLE AGAINST UNEMPLOYMENT AND PLANT CLOSURES: BLIND ALLEYS

The Left thought it could make a fresh start. The poor would be taken care of and new income would be created which would contribute to the redistribution of wealth through taxation. An increase of 4.5 per cent in public expenditures, a 10 per cent rise of the minimum wage and the creation of jobs were supposed to trigger a 2.5 per cent growth of investments, a 5 per cent increase of exports and a 3.3 per cent production growth.

To contain unemployment at 2 million, the government, composed of Socialists and four Communists, tried several measures: 225,000 jobs were financed by the state (84,000 were provided directly by the government), 100,000 youths were offered job training schemes, 14,000 illegal migrant workers received work permits; the government encouraged the early retirement of 700,000 workers (some at age 55). Subsidies to industry doubled; the industrial research budget tripled.

Unemployment was under control until the end of 1983, but at an astronomical cost. Moreover, the problem of technological change and of industrial restructuring which was being experienced in most industrial countries was not solved.

At that time, the Socialists shared with the Communists the view that there were no condemned sectors, only condemned technologies. To modernize them, time and money were needed. How was the French approach to differ from Thatcherism or Reaganism? How was it to be financed? With the 3.3 per cent expected growth? With new taxes on profits and revenues? The case of the steel industry restructuring is a cogent example.

The case of steel

In many sectors, state subsidies allowed ailing industries such as steel to continue. Workers were paid to produce non-profitable goods on redundant machines paid for in dollars. For thirty years, the steel industry was managed by boards of directors preventing other industries from settling in their company towns or by government officials dreaming that France would produce an ever-increasing quantity of steel. In the 1960s and 1970s, a huge conversion took place, and a modern, competitive steel industry took shape alongside ports at Dunkirk in the North and Fos-sur-Mer near Marseilles. Enormous state-backed loans were provided, while one third of the expenses were borne by the state. French television reported recently that 10 billion francs in steel subsidies were spent in the last decade on plants that either never opened or were obsolete by the time they were completed. However, as long as the new plants were not fully operating, the old ones in the traditional regions were not closed. There were no cuts in the workplace, nor any retraining of the local work force. Yet productivity was very low: 75 tons a year per worker in 1974 compared to 240 in West Germany, 250 in the US, and 360 in Japan.

It was hoped that the old steel plants would meet the needs of the domestic market as long as necessary until the new industry was ready to conquer the world market. Unfortunately, before it was ready, the world economic crisis of 1974 crushed these hopes. The domestic market collapsed as well (down 16 per cent in 1974) with fewer demands and a car industry in recession. The losses came on top of existing debts and they exceeded the global revenue in 1977. Fifty thousand jobs were cut despite early retirement schemes and voluntary resignations, and violent demonstrations occurred in Lorraine and in the North in 1978/9. In 1982, when the new capacity of steel production was ready to conquer markets, it was too late: the American steel industry had obtained a return to protectionism and competition from Japan and South Korea was fierce. These were severe blows to the French industry and production dropped by one half. The state again had to cover a large part of the debts and the nationalization of the two largest plants appeared as a rational decision.

However, with the new austerity program of 1983, it was no longer possible to avoid plant closure in Lorraine and the loss of 100,000 jobs. In that region, one worker in two worked in the steel or a related industry. Consequently, a special program of retraining, early retirement and the option to quit with severance pay were introduced, led by an ex-union member. Moreover the industry received important financial help (5.75 billion francs in 1985). Is steel restructuring a success story? Is it obviously on its way to becoming one in 'structural adjustment' and if one considers the higher level (i.e. Europe), steel is the only industry truly European in the sense that the twelve countries of the EEC have agreed on a unified policy (with some loopholes) and they express themselves with one voice: the European steel cartel.

HARSH REALITIES

To succeed, the Socialist measures were relying on favorable or at least neutral international conditions. The second half of 1981 and 1982 were the worst. Under such circumstances, with rising US interest rates and a worsening of the crisis, Socialist philanthropy became untenable and the Left acknowledged its failure. But the failure was not an apocalyptic one, as the Right had predicted. The Socialist government did no worse in controlling prices than the previous one had; and it did better than its trade rivals in jobs, consumption and investments. The French standard of living even improved. No, it was a failure of objectives.

Unemployment, after stabilizing, rose again, foreign penetration increased, concurrent deflations weakened the franc and all those factors proved that the intertwining of world economies prevented an isolated country pursuing radically different reforms and policies. Investments and public expenditure only encouraged French industry to buy cheaper foreign products (machines, tools, computers and oil) to produce French goods. Imports increased by 14 per cent after 1981 as French production was unable to offer enough consumer goods consumption demands (i.e. for video recorders).

Spurred by the Communist-led union (Confédération Générale du Travail), workers rejected the reduction of the working week with reduced salary, which would have permitted the creation of 60,000 jobs in 1982. Had it been more clearly explained at the time it might have worked, according to experts. But unlike their opponents, the Socialists were doing poorly in communication skills.

Businessmen did not accept the idea of buying and expanding 'French'. They contested the Left's policies of expansion, having been used to former Prime Minister Barre's struggle against inflation. The high-tech competitive sector was interested in world growth, not especially in French growth. In fact, these businessmen looked for lower costs in France and with a Socialist government, it was also easier for them to lay workers off. In the fiercely competitive world, lay-offs and plant closures were often the only way to survive.

As for the large group of businessmen, they remained reactionary and suspicious of Socialist-inspired measures. It was indeed contradictory to have capital pay taxes as capital, while it was expected at the same time to expand and create jobs. Those who could have supported the Socialists' line, such as young, radical executives, were disappointed with the slow procedures of administrative bureaucracies. There were contradictions in the policies and the heads of the nationalized companies themselves had difficulties applying the directives of the Ministries. They sometimes found that they could not adjust their strategy to their own perception of the market (e.g. the chairman of a nationalized bank was replaced after he balked at granting 'soft capital' and loans to the troubled steel company Creusot-Loire, a private concern which a few months later went bankrupt).

In the spring of 1983, the failure of Keynesian policies led the Left to abandon the Communist policy of support to ailing industries. It adopted an alternative focusing on industrial competitiveness: 'More state intervention to help industries and less state action in favor of solidarity.' Those views were shared by the modern, managerial wing of the Socialist Party, led by men like Laurent Fabius, the former Minister of Budget who became Minister of Industry in March 1983. As some said at the time: 'it was better to be poor and healthy than rich and sick'. Plants thus had to be closed – 22,708 bankruptcies in 1983, an 11 per cent rise in one year (21.1 per cent for the industrial sector alone); the largest companies were as much threatened as the smaller ones: 7000 jobs cut in the government-owned telephone company; 4500 at Dunlop-France; 1500 at Chapelle-Darblay (the French paper production company); 2000 in the oil group Elf-Aquitaine; several thousands in the metallurgist Creusot-Loire and in shipbuilding; more than 10,000 in steel, chemicals, coal and refineries (Quatrepoint, 1983). The list of threatened or overmanned plants was growing every day.

Austerity brought about a deterioration of the social fabric: the defense of vested interests and privileges, what Lipietz (1984) calls 'social sadism': racism, demonstrations of workers against arbitrary decisions benefiting other workers, petty delinquency, etc. At the workplace, competition rose between two working classes: the aristocracy, with job security in well-paid competitive technologies and the rest: 60 per cent of the working class, vulnerable, dependent, alienated at the workplace by the machines and poor working conditions – young vs. old, white vs. non-white, men vs. women all fighting as the size of the pie was shrinking (Verret, 1981: 67). One of the areas of conflict was the automobile industry.[2]

The problems of the automobile industry

In the boom years, France imported cheap, unskilled foreign labor who received no promotion. Recently industry has been in trouble (foreign penetration is 40 per cent, the French models are not innovative enough, prices are high and firms have sought to expand instead of improving their products and modernizing their plants). The management has had to cut jobs. The domestic market suffers from a decrease in purchasing power. More than 7500 jobs have been lost at Peugeot-Talbot. Aid for migrant workers to return to their countries of origin (with training, cash and the guarantee by their home government that they will get a job) coupled with the reduction of the working week appear as a solution to reduce the potential explosiveness of strikes in Parisian plants. Another solution to avoid demonstrations has been to accept the notion of 'overstaffing' in certain plants. There were 18,000 underemployed employees at Renault in 1984. But the problems have been more acute at the Talbot plant at Poissy in the Paris region where large-scale strikes topped production. The plant was totally restructured and the name disappeared. A rescue plan was negotiated between the workers' unions, management and the government; 1900 laid-off workers were 'saved' (80 per cent of them were foreign): 1300 went into training programs paid for by the state, technological training centers were opened to take care of the laid-off workers, others retired or resigned. But these measures which often involve huge redundancy payments dent an already strained budget. The modernization of the auto industry calls for more automation and the shedding of 80,000 jobs between 1984 and 1988; that is, a good 10 per cent of the industry's workforce, including white-collar jobs, is forecast (IHT, 1984). Since 1985, Peugeot (taking into account Citroën and former Talbot) has returned to profitability but this implies paring the workforce and freezing wages).

'Retraining': such has been the panacea for dealing with overmanning and plant closures. In February 1984, Prime Minister Mauroy said: 'What is original in our plan compared to other countries is that we do not lay off. Our objective is to reconcile the economic imperative with the social.' Mergers, asset swaps (hasty government transfers of funds among budget categories), enterprise zones have been set in the most affected regions.

Besides the car industry, other economic areas such as coal, steel and shipbuilding are also feeling the pinch: it is estimated that 20,000 to 30,000 more jobs will come under the hammer in the steel industry, 17,000 to 27,000 in the coal industry, 4000 to 5000 in shipbuilding and an untold number in textiles and telecommunications. Between mid-1982 and mid-1983, 185,000 salaried industrial jobs were lost, much of them in construction and public works. Between mid-1983 and mid-1985, another 370,000 jobs disappeared. Job offers which have been created since 1985 do not compensate for the losses. When the Parliamentary elections were held in March 1986, 2.3 million people were looking for work – 10.5 per cent of the workforce, a slightly higher percentage than the West European average. (France's unemployment rate stood at 7.8 per cent in 1981 when the Socialists took office.)

The revolt of affected workers is just and predictable. There is not enough dynamism in the economy to help them get new jobs and there is virtually nothing governments, whether from the Left or from the Right, can do quickly to accelerate the 1 per cent or so economic growth (in 1986). 600,000 jobless workers benefited from retraining programs or community work projects in 1984 and 1985; the creation of public service works (a kind of CETA called TUC) reduced the number of unemployed young people; 360,000 of them volunteered to work 20 hours a week in hospitals, subways, museums, etc. The government paid them $170 a month, a little less than the unemployment benefit. The new Conservative government keeps the same approach but via privatization.

As for older workers (i.e. over 40) especially factory workers, either in Britain's Midlands, in Germany's Ruhr or in France's Lorraine, they are almost incapable of being retrained for a new kind of work. Despite conversions of old plants to new ones, the picture is grim. For many of those who experience economic, social and psychological dislocation, there are strong grounds for supporting the view that the pace of deindustrialization has been unacceptably rapid (Bluestone and Harrison, 1982: 48). Unemployment benefit at a cost of $15 billion annually and the repatriation of unemployed migrant workers have been emphasized to mitigate local discontent. But the poor take-up of the latter measure has fuelled Extreme Right racist and nationalist reactions.

The phenomenon of the Extreme Right breakthrough since 1983 – the National Front led by Jean Marie Le Pen – poses several questions:

1 Is there a connection between Le Pen's success and industrial restructuring at the local level?

2 Are migrant workers' movements illegitimate?

3 How do various local structures (political parties, unions) react politically to such changes as the 'new international division of labor'?

The National Front phenomenon

The speeches of Le Pen on the media revolve around one obsessional theme: immigration. Other topics, such as unemployment and instability are little developed and appear only in connection with immigration. Le Pen endlessly repeats that migrant workers should be kicked out of France and that the French should be the first to get the jobs and the benefits: 'The French must know that nothing, no juridical nor moral principle compels them to somehow accommodate all the people from the entire universe who "take the trouble" to come here and take advantage of social benefits which were at first conceived for the French on a solidarity basis' he emphasized in a TV speech in May 1985. 'France for the French', 'the French first' and 'we can't share our heritage with just anybody' all draw media attention. But do such assertations appeal to French workers who have been the victims of job losses? Who supports Le Pen?

Le Pen received 11 per cent of the votes and 10 of the 81 seats at the European Parliament elections in June 1984. His vote is heavily localized in regions of high immigration: 15 per cent in Paris, 17 per cent in Lyons, 21 per cent in Marseilles, almost 23 per cent in Nice and generally in the 36 cities of over 100,00 inhabitants. His electorate is mostly urbanized, male and older. But the socio-economic status of his electorate is *not* working-class; it is composed mostly of highly-educated residents of affluent neighborhoods. Only 6 per cent of those who had voted for François Mitterrand's and, 2 per cent of ex-Communists voted for him in 1984, in comparison with 18 per cent of the voters who had supported Jacques Chirac, the right-wing candidate, according to a poll performed immediately after the 1984 elections (Charlot, 1906, 10).

In 1966, S. M. Lipset in *Political Man* wrote that extremists appeal mostly to low-income categories because they offer easy and straightforward solutions. This assertion is not sustained in France. In the European elections or in recent polls, workers supporting Le Pen are under-represented and his highest score in a few declining cities like St Etienne (17%), Metz (16.9%) or Roubaix (19.3%) is an exception. It is a vote which is correlated to residential patterns and scarcely to workplace changes: 51 per cent of the French recognize that guest-workers have played a positive role in the economy in the last twenty years (Julliard, 1984).

Migrant workers' movements

Since 1974, the front door of immigration has officially been closed, but families and political refugees are authorized to sneak in by the back door. The presence of their families has given a high profile to Arab workers, especially after polls revealed that 70 per cent of them intended to stay in France.

Until 1979, the local level was a neutral arena of management but recently, conservative measures undertaken by left-wing mayors against North Africans in order to secure the working-class vote have increased the level of local politicization. Migrant workers' voting rights which are denied despite Mitterrand's campaign promises, have provoked hunger strikes. Such rights to vote at local elections would be granted to workers who are not French citizens but who are economic participants and taxpayers, but they are opposed by 74 per cent of the French (Julliard, 1984).

At the workplace, unions were embarrassed when wild-cat strikes were launched by migrant workers in the car industry. Such categorical fights of generally unskilled and non-unionized workers revealed the weakness of the workers' movement. The support brought by two major unions to these new social movements show that when trade unionism takes action in a socio-cultural milieu which is alien to its tradition, it loses strength: it deals with cultural problems which do not focus only on work or jobs. At Renault –

Flins, the strikes turned on the promotion question: to become skilled, one must reach level 180; but most migrant workers never go beyond 175 because their starting-level handicap is too important.[3] At Talbot and Citroën, in the spring of 1982, besides problems related to job level, qualification and technological change, striking migrant workers also claimed freedom of expression linked to their dignity: 'Not to be a lifelong unskilled Arab worker . . .'.

At the local level, unionism is in a disarray and as everywhere else, the victim of a crisis of militancy. Jobs which were traditional breeders of activism have disappeared while new ones do not generate a collective approach. Workers with status would lose more than they would gain by strikes; movements of revolt are intepreted as corporatist defense. The hot debate on time flexibility which took place in the spring of 1986 in Parliament revealed the limited role of trade unions and the Bill which favors employers was discussed as just another Bill.

LOCAL POLITICAL EFFECTS OF INDUSTRIAL CHANGES

One can only make assumptions on how the economic crisis and the Socialists' policy responses have been politically mediated at the level of local politics in areas most directly affected by plant closures. There is, amazingly, no study on the subject in France, a fact which is an interesting feature of social sciences in a centralized country.

Culturally, for centuries, the French mentality has been accustomed to a strong state which claims to be the motor of improvement. Unlike the US, state power is not fragmented by states, counties, cities or neighborhoods; the Parliament, the judicial system, the media hardly check its extensive power (Body-Gendrot, 1986). Traditionally, the state rather than private corporations takes investment risks in France and whereas in the US more than 50 per cent of the research is handled by private companies, in France, 63 per cent of research is funded by the state and in practice, it is even higher. This is to say, the blame levelled against local officials in the US who have been unable to prevent capital and human resources flight and decline is spared French local officials, who appear as mere executives of a centrally-determined policy. Besides, in the US, representatives of local government at various levels frequently intervene on behalf and at the request of private interests; the frontier between public and private is blurred; and industrial decline hurts public decision-makers directly. The situation is different in France. The top-down approach protects central government, the President, and their advisors are blamed, and not local officials who were never active entrepreneurs. It is too early to say if the new decentralization laws of 1982–4 which give more autonomy to the regions, departments and municipalities in matters of investments will alter that pattern. One does not change society by decree and so far the instinct is to turn to the central government for help.

Paradoxically, in France there is a high turnout at local elections. Is there a contradiction? Here, the phenomenon of cumulative elected positions (which the Left unsuccessfully tried to abolish) gives the bottom direct access to the top where most decisions are taken (Body-Gendrot, 1982). A mayor who is also an MP will plead for his city, a representative at the 'department' level who is also a Senator will ask his political friends to support a training program for young people. Partisan elections reinforce such mechanisms. It is under pressure from local Socialist officials that France required the EC Commission to be allowed to inject some eleventh-hour subsidies into steel against a secret commitment to eliminate several thousand more steelworkers' jobs after Parliamentary elections in March 1986.

An evaluation of the political effect of restructuring at the local level must adjust itself to national trends in France. The Lorraine region is a good example. Traditionally right-wing, its electorate swung to the left when the Socialist Party was appealing to a national audience in the 1970s. Lorraine returned 13 Socialist MPs out of 21 in 1981. Then when restructuring took place and a major industrial project was abandoned in March 1984, four Socialist MPs resigned and left the party. Today despite job creations, the Left is blamed for the 102,000 unemployed workers (10.7 per cent of the workforce). The creation of a Smurfs' Playland on former industrial sites appears as a good idea but other projects, such as a regional airport which might attract high-tech industries, are strongly criticized for their cost by political opponents in favor of an extension of the high-speed train. The Communist Party, a long-time defender of the working-class experiences a major crisis at the national level and it is not in a position to put forward viable local alternatives to unemployment. Le Pen has no impact in that traditional region where migrant workers do not exceed 8 per cent of the population.

CAN RESTRUCTURING – A NECESSITY – BE PAINLESS?

To help French industry get out of the crisis implies a clear vision of sectors to be aided. The Socialists' attitude has been ambiguous. To avoid social problems at first, they have heavily subsidized ailing industries, while new technologies were suffering from dwindling funds. For instance, in 1983–4, the state spent 40 billion francs to support the steel and coal industries (not counting social benefits) while electronics received 30 billion francs (Quatrepoint, 1983). The conservatives believe that France and Europe in general have wasted time and money trying to prop up troubled heavy industries which have the political power to demand subsidies because they are major employers in regions with few other jobs (IHT, 1986). They echo Lester Thurow's words: 'To have the labor and capital to move into new areas we must be able to withdraw labor and capital from old, low-productivity areas. But . . . disinvestment is what our economy does worst. Instead of adopting public policies to speed up the process of disinvestment, we act to slow it down with protection and subsidies for the inefficient' (Thurow, 1980: 77).

However, the measures which have been undertaken since the summer of 1984, when Laurent Fabius became Prime Minister and faced up to the harsh realities have been rigorous and supportive of competitive industries. As soon as the Communists left the government, the Fabius line stressed that the country could not afford too expensive social welfare systems.

Since May 1984, Prime Minister Chirac has opted for continuing austerity with an emphasis on the priority of production over distribution. He has rejected the solution of protectionism coupled with devaluation, which would help exports, as demanded by the Communist Party and the radical wing of the Socialist Party.

State intervention to aid industrial modernization is in line with the recognition of the private sector's dynamism. With the Fabius government's policy, (and now the Conservatives in government) the French have discovered the virtues of private companies and managerial skills. The emphasis is on a 'mixed economy', which can only please businessmen.

In the long run, the Fabius government's gamble was that restructuring would proceed at a swift enough pace to benefit from other Western countries' recovery. It was not a bad bet and for the first time in 1985, inflation was kept below 5 per cent, investments surged once more and, on the whole, the economy was sounder than it had been six years earlier. Many nationalized firms had been brought back into profit (Renault and the steel companies were major exceptions); more than 100,000 new firms were created in 1985. Yet the conservative opposition which won the March elections launched another round of privatization, deregulation and tax incentives in a program which looks much like Thatcherism or Reaganism.

One of the ironies of history is that socialism in power turned out to be, as N. Wahl commented, the period in which the French had to learn bitter and realistic lessons. Only the Socialists could proceed with such massive restructuring without causing revolutionary upheavals although they had to wrestle with their conscience to do so. An opinion poll showed that 56 per cent of the French now accept layoffs if the government has no other choice; they think that industrial modernization is vital, even if it causes layoffs. But the high rate of unemployment creates a deepening sense of insecurity. As they see the collapse all around them of the traditional economic base of their communities, the French may be tempted to follow any piper who, with his magic tune, will divert them from their fears.

1 This situation was not completely new: with expensive and difficult exploitation of its coal mines, France had always been highly dependent on outside supplies especially at the end of the nineteenth century during its steel revolution, when it lost the two provinces of Alsace and Lorraine. This situation worsened with the advent of oil as a major energy source in the last 30 years.

2 The automobile industry is a major industry in France; 270,000 persons work in construction; 560,000 in equipment and subcontracting; and 480,000 in related sectors. Despite difficulties, the industry is still profitable and represents 20 per cent of the state revenue (in taxes).

3 Levels 175 and 180 refer to labor categories established by contracts between unions and employees.

REFERENCES

Body Gendrot, Sophie (1982) 'Governmental responses to popular movements'. In N. and S. Fainstein (eds), *Urban Policy under Capitalism*, Beverly Hills, Sage.
—— (1986) 'Grass-roots mobilization in the 13th arrondissement of Paris. A cross-national view'. In H. Sanders and C. Stone (eds), *The Politics of Urban Development*, University Press of Kansas, 1987.
Bluestone, Barry and Bennett, Harrison (1982) *The Deindustrialization of America*. New York, Basic Books.
Cerny, Philip G. (1983) 'Dead ends and new possibilities: Mitterrand's economic policy between socialism and state capitalism', *Contemporary French Civilization* (Fall/Winter), 8, 1–2; 2–26.
Charlot, Monica (1986) 'L'émergence du Front National', *Revue Française de Science Politique*, 36, 1 (February): 30–45.
Delion, André and Durupty, Michel (1982) *Les Nationalisations en 1982*, Paris: Economica.
De Thomas, Bruno (1984) 'L'automobile, test du redéploiement industriel', *Le Monde*, 25 July.
Julliard, Jacques (1984) 'Immigrés. Les Arabes et vous', *Le Nouvel Observateur*, 30 November.
Le Poing et la Rose (1980) *Le Projet socialiste*, 12–13 January.
Lipietz, Alain (1984) *L'audace et l'enlisement*, Paris: La Découverte.
Mitchell, Leslie (1984) 'Rising unemployment slows restructuring of ailing industries', *International Herald Tribune*, 31 March.
Quatrepoint, J. M. (1983) 'La tente à oxygène de l'industrie', *Le Monde*, 9 November.
Schultz, Joseph (1980) *Regards sur la civilisation française*, Paris: Cle Internl.
Stoffaës, Christian (1980) 'Les talents industriels des Français'. In J. D. Reynaud and I. Grafmeyer (eds) *Français, qui êtes vous?*, Paris: 'La documentation française', pp. 157–74.
Thurow, Lester (1980), *The Zero-Sum Society*, New York: Basic Books.
Verret, Michel, 'Classe ouvrière, conscience ouvriere'. In Reynaud, op. cit.
Wahl, Nicholas (1983) 'Year three of Socialist France: Some impressions from the field'. *Contemporary French Civilization*, op. cit., pp. 106–45.

12

Urbanization, the Informal Economy and State Policy in Latin America

Helen I. Safa

Latin America has long been the most urbanized region of the developing world. By 1980, the urban population accounted for two-thirds of the total population, while agricultural occupations fell from 53.3 per cent in 1950 to 33.7 per cent in 1980, with secondary and tertiary occupations growing concomitantly (Rama and Faletto, 1985: 134). However, these aggregate figures also conceal wide disparities, with much higher (and older) levels of urbanization in Southern Cone countries like Uruguay and Argentina, and much lower levels in countries like Guatemala and Haiti. At the same time, urbanization, indusrialization and other indices of 'modernization' have not eliminated poverty and inequality. Though per capita GDP almost doubled from 1960 to 1980, the percentage of the population living in poverty was only reduced from 50 per cent to 35 per cent in the same period (Rama and Faletto, 1985: 134).

The persistence of poverty and inequality in rapidly urbanizing societies in Latin America is now generally explained by the dependent nature of capitalist development in the region. Starting with the colonial period, Latin America has been incorporated into a global capitalist economy, which has brought about fundamental changes in the organization and structure of production and exchange, and hence in the labor force. It has also led to changing patterns of urbanization and industrialization, and to the growth in importance of multinational corporations. While multinationals have accelerated the integration of the global capitalist economy, bringing about a 'new' international division of labor between advanced capitalist and developing countries, Latin America's incorporation into this global economy is not new, only the form has changed (cf. Walton, 1985: 3–4).

This chapter will attempt to review some of the recent research on the process of urbanization and industrialization in Latin America from the perspective of dependent capitalism, focusing on the relationship between the new international division of labour and the growth of the informal economy in the contemporary period. Although much debated and criticized, dependency theory helps us to move away from isolated, descriptive studies of cities and focus attention on the subordinate structural relationship imposed upon these countries by advanced capitalist countries through colonialism and unequal terms of exchange, resulting in very different forms of urbanization and industrialization. This subordination is reflected not only at the international level between nations, but also in the organization of production of the Latin American urban economy, that reveals a chain of subordinate relationships linking multinationals and larger domestic firms with smaller enterprises and independent producers in the informal sector. The economic crisis now facing Latin America has reinforced these subordinate forms of production and led to the increasing articulation between the formal and informal sectors.

The informal sector may be defined as unregulated small-scale manufacturing and service industries employing labor-intensive methods of production requiring a low level of skill and capital investment and often utilizing the labor of unpaid family members. While different forms of the informal economy have existed for a long time (including the period of competitive capitalism in advanced industrial countries), it has recently grown in importance in Latin America because of the cost advantages it represents to the dominant capitalist sector. The state has also played a critical role in supporting the growth of the informal sector, either as a means of cutting the cost of labor or, as we shall see, through regulatory policies which raise the cost of labor and increase the attractiveness of the informal sector.

In order to understand the importance of the informal sector in the urban economy of contemporary Latin American, this paper will start with a brief review of historical changes in the mode of production due to the nature of insertion into the capitalist world economy, which led to massive rural–urban migration and the increasing importance of industrialization and urbanization. We shall then examine the growth of the urban informal sector in terms of state policy and the contemporary economic crisis, focusing on the increasing articulation betwen the formal and informal sectors. Particular attention will be paid to the industrial sector, where changes in the organization of production are most apparent, and where the effects of dependent capitalism and the new international division of labor have brought about new forms of inequality in Latin American society.

THE URBANIZATION PROCESS AND HISTORICAL CHANGES IN THE MODE OF INCORPORATION INTO THE CAPITALIST WORLD ECONOMY

We can distinguish three broad periods in the mode of incorporation of Latin American societies into the world capitalist system: (1) the colonial period, during which Latin America served primarily as a source of raw materials and later as a market for manufactured goods; (2) the postwar period of import-substitution indusrialization; and (3) the contemporary period, dominated by export-led growth. We shall examine the first two periods here, leaving the contemporary period for the subsequent section. The attempt to generalize obscures many of the important differences among Latin American countries, particularly for countries like Argentina that industrialized much earlier. Nevertheless, in all cases, urbanization and industrialization are essentially the result of increasing incorporation into the world economy.

From the beginning, Latin America was geared toward an export economy, which in the colonial period consisted largely of primary products such as precious metals and sugar for sale to Spain and Portugal. Cities were small and centrifugal, serving primarily as centers of control and administration for rural areas and mining towns (Morse, 1971; 1974). Primacy was given to the fiscal and political needs of the mother country, rather than to internal development, leading to poor development of roads, communications and other forms of infrastructure. Due to the shortage of capital and labor, pre-capitalist relations of production were often retained, including forced labor in mines, and the *encomienda* system in agriculture. This tended to preserve ethnic and status differences between categories of the population, such as Indian, mestizo and white, which continue to serve as the basis of class differences to the present day.

In the nineteenth century, mercantilism gave way to commercial capitalism and the closer integration of Latin America into the European and North American economies. With independence from Spain and Portugal, British and US investments gained increasing importance, primarily for the promotion of export commodities such as cacao, coffee, cotton, wheat and non-precious metals. Latin America continued to serve as a source of raw materials, including foodstuffs, but also grew in importance as a market for the mass-produced manufactured goods made possible by the Industrial Revolution. This led, towards the end of the nineteenth century, to the increasing primacy of the urban system – the situation in which the largest city is many times larger than the second largest city. Roberts (1978: 47) maintains that the degree of primacy in different Latin American countries is directly linked to the extent of their incorporation within the world economy. By 1920, most Latin American countries had primate cities, led by Buenos Aires in Argentina and followed by Cuba, Mexico and Chile (Roberts, 1978: 47–8). However, despite early industrialization in Buenos Aires, most cities continued to serve primarily as commercial and administrative centers, with production focused in rural economic enclaves such as plantations and mines.

It is only in the postwar period (from the 1940s onwards) that industry assumes a significant role in the growth of urbanization in Latin America. Much of this is due to the populist policy of import substitution adopted by many Latin American countries in an attempt to break the historical dependence on imported manufactured goods and exported raw materials. Promoted by ECLA (The United Nations Economic Commission of Latin America) import-substitution industrialization was seen as a way of reducing dependence on advanced capitalist countries and spurring capital formation in Latin America. However, the development of domestic industry was hampered by the growth of multinationals and the continued dependence of Latin America on advanced capitalist countries for capital and technology. Despite attempts to create an internal market, much industrial development in Latin America is centered on the capital-intensive production of consumer durables destined primarily for the elite, since the majority of the population still lack the purchasing power to constitute a viable market.

Industrialization also led to increasing regional and class inequality. Pre-capitalist relations of production in the rural area were broken down with the disappearance of the hacienca and the increasing commercialization of agriculture. The peasant economy stagnated, resulting in heavy rural–urban migration. The class structure of Latin America cities changed dramatically in the postwar period with the growth of an industrial working class and indigenous bourgeoisie, as well as an administrative and commercial middle class. Nevertheless the service sector constitutes the fastest growing sector of the urban economy, due to the capital-intensive nature of industrialization, the growth of the public sector, and a vast reserve army of unemployed and underemployed workers in the informal sector.

RURAL-URBAN MIGRATION AND THE INFORMAL ECONOMY

With the shift in the Latin American economies from agro-mining to industry, the direction of migration shifted from temporary labor in mines and plantations to more permanent moves to the city. Initially, much of this migration occurred in stages, with moves from a village to a provincial town to the city, but with the growth of rural–urban migration, more movement has been directly to the primate city. The selectivity of migrants has also tended to decrease with the increase in numbers.

Earlier studies on migration focused on individual motivations, while the current emphasis on structural changes places these choices within a socio-economic context combining push and pull factors. Increased population growth combined with factors such as land fragmentation, soil erosion, diminished yields and lack of access to credits and technology have multiplied the pressures on the peasantry in Latin America, with migration often seen as the only alternative. Land fragmentation results principally from partible rules of inheritance which subdivides the land in each succeeding generation. Arizpe (1982) has shown how rural Mexican families are forced to combine agricultural work with other wage-earning opportunities, chiefly through a system of relay migration which sends successive members of the household into the city in search of jobs. The result in one village, Arizpe notes, is to convert a peasant community into a 'proletarian suburb,' utilizing urban wage labor as a subsidy for a declining peasant economy.

Despite the severe pressures on the peasantry, Roberts (1978: 90) maintains that areas of capitalist farming displace more people than do areas of peasant farming. Subsistence producers are squeezed out by increasing land concentration and commercialization of agriculture, leading to the formation of a rural proletariat of landless agricultural workers. Surplus labor is forced to the city, with older women and children often remaining behind in subsistence farming (Deere, 1979; Deere and de Leal, 1981). In many cases it is not the most impoverished sector of the rural population which leaves, but those from a better educated intermediate stratum who want to capitalize on their skills in the city.

It has been assumed that the maintenance of a rural subsistence sector in Third World countries lowers labor costs in the city by acting as a cheap labor reserve from which adult urban workers are drawn and can be returned when they become redundant. This has been described for Africa by Meillassoux (1972), Wolpe (1975) and others. However, with the distintegration of a viable subsistence sector in Latin America, it would seem, as Arizpe has shown, that the reverse is true, namely that urban wage labor remittances are increasingly a subsidy for a declining peasant economy (see Portes and Walton 1981: 73–7).

However, industry has not been able to absorb the surplus population expelled from the rural area in Latin America. Capital-intensive industrialization has tended to favor young skilled male laborers, creating a labor aristocracy with higher wages, social security and other fringe benefits (see Schmink, 1982: 31; Portes and Walton, 1981: 78–9). The number of these skilled workers has remained very small, even in highly industrialized cities such as São Paulo, where they are estimated at 23.8 per cent of the total workforce (Roberts, 1978: 124). Thus the great mass of rural migrants are absorbed into what has been called the 'informal sector' of Latin American cities.

Many studies have documented the way in which the informal sector enables the urban poor of Latin America to survive (Lomnitz, 1977; Arizpe, 1977; Scott, 1979; Peattie 1982; Schmink, 1986). A large percentage of workers in the informal economy are self-employed and recent rural migrants. Women form an important part of the informal economy, not only as unpaid family labor and domestic servants, but are increasingly, as we shall see, employed as disguised wage workers in small workshops or as domestic outworkers.

The whole strategy of families in the informal economy is geared toward maximizing income generation and minimizing the cost and level of consumption. Families often participate in a multiple wage-earning strategy, incorporating rural kin and sending as many members out into the labor force as possible, including women and young children. This heavy reliance on the sale of labor as a survival mechanism may help explain the continued maintenance of high birthrates in many areas of Latin America (Roberts, 1978: 91; Safa, 1982). Other income-generating activities may include petty commodity production, small-scale trade, and subsistence activities even in the city, such as gardening, food preserving and keeping small animals (Schmink, 1982). Costs are minimized through 'self-help' housing, illegal use of public utilities (such as tapping a neighbor's electricity or water line), use of networks to obtain cheaper goods and services, etc. It is estimated that between 25 to over 50 per cent of the population of Latin American cities live in squatter settlements, due largely to the phenomenal increase in urban land prices in recent years (Portes and Walton, 1981: 94–5).

The informal economy not only contributes to the survival of the urban poor in Latin America, it also cuts down the cost of goods and services for the formal modern sector. Many of the goods and services originating in the formal sector such as repair shops, transportation, construction, clothes, footwear and newer products such as electronics are sold at far lower cost than if they were produced in the formal modern sector. As we shall see, the formal sector also increasingly subcontracts production to the informal sector in areas such as garment and shoe manufacture, and construction, thereby reducing the number of workers paid the statutory minimum wage rate, social security and other fringe benefits. Thus, by decreasing the relative size of the formal sector and the costs of reproduction of these workers, the informal sector helps keep wages low in the entire urban economy (Portes and Walton, 1981: 85).

There has been considerable debate in Latin America regarding the degree and nature of articulation between the formal and informal economy, and the extent to which the informal sector may be considered residual, and liable to disappear with capitalist development. Contrary to earlier notions regarding the separate and marginal nature of the informal economy, it is now generally recognized as predominantly dependent upon the formal sector for capital, material and markets, thus contradicting the connotation of a dualist economy suggested in earlier studies. Workers move easily from one sector to another or simultaneously work in both, while urban poor households generally include workers in both sectors. It is now generally recognized that the informal economy does not develop simply in the interstices of the economy in traditional activities unprofitable by the formal modern sector. On the contrary, far from being a residual sector, it is a dynamic sector, constantly being recreated and reorganized in response to changing conditions in the formal sector. The rapid industrial growth in Latin America during the last 30 years has led to only a marginal decline in the size of the informal labor force, which stood, in 1980, at 42 per cent of the economically active population (Portes and Benton, 1984: 603).

Aggregate figures, however, mask changes in the nature of the informal economy which have been taking place in Latin America during this same period. The heterogeneity of the informal sector is now widely recognized, and there have been many attempts at creating a typology (e.g. Scott, 1979; Bromley and Gerry, 1979). However, most of these typologies tend to be static and do not fully recognize the dynamic, changing nature of the informal economy over time. We shall argue that much of this change is due to the increasing degree of articulation between the formal and informal sector with higher levels of capitalist development, in part stimulated by state policy, as we shall see in the next section.

ARTICULATION OF THE FORMAL AND INFORMAL ECONOMIES
AND STATE POLICY

Initially the informal economy was seen as a major deterrent to the modernization of the economy of developing countries. This assumption stemmed from dualist theories which tended to equate the informal sector with the traditional subsistence sector, marginality, and other forms of 'uproductive' labor (e.g. Geertz, 1963).

Recently, however, this dualist perspective has been severely criticized, to the point that many argue for abandoning the concept of the informal sector entirely. However, we must distinguish between those who continue to use the term from a dualist perspective, and those, like Portes and myself, who are well aware of the close articulation between the formal and informal sectors, and of the important functions the latter performs for the entire economy in terms of labor absorption, production and social reproduction.

As Portes (1983: 160) notes, the activities associated with the informal economy are not new, but were widely practised in the nineteenth century during the period of competitive capitalism in western Europe and the US. He distinguishes between three modes of production within the informal sector, then and now: direct subsistence (including subsistence agriculture and home production of animals, garden crops, and clothing for direct consumption); petty commodity production and exchange (based on the labor of the self-employed who produce goods and services for the market); and backward capitalist production, which includes small enterprises employing unprotected wage labor, and disguised wage workers (i.e. hired by larger firms on a casual or subcontracting basis). While each of these forms was common under nineteenth-century capitalism, what is new is the way in which the third form in particular has been recreated and reorganized under modern capitalism, as a way of assuring the supply of a cheaper and more flexible labor force.

Examples of the increasing use of backward forms of production now abound, both in developing countries and advanced capitalist countries. The basis of this increase appears to lie in a shift of the objectives of the informal sector during the contemporary period. The various forms of the informal economy originally served primarily the needs of the poor, by providing them with goods and services at lower cost than in the formal economy, and by assuring them of sources of income different from, or complementary to, cheap wage labor. In this earlier phase, direct subsistence and petty commodity production are particularly important, both as a substitute for and as a complement to cheap wage labor. These traditional forms of the informal economy persist, but today there has been an expansion in backward forms of production to serve the needs of the formal, modern sector; by subcontracting goods and services to small enterprises and casual laborers, firms in the formal sector have found a way of retarding or bypassing wage gains and state-enforced labor legislation.

Schmuckler (1979) describes the transformation of the informal sector in her analysis of the historical evolution of the clothing and textile industry in Argentina. She demonstrates how independent artisans ceased to produce an entire product and to serve the public directly (e.g. as seamstresses or tailors), and became increasingly dependent on larger commercial and industrial firms who supplied them with the necessary capital to continue producing in a highly competitive market. This form of subcontracting is far more developed and prevalent in the clothing industry, due to the greater seasonality of production and frequent changes in style. While similar to changes in the structure of production in England and other advanced industrial countries in the nineteenth century, the changes in Argentina have taken place in only two decades, spurred by the development of a mass market for ready-made clothing. Producers in the informal sector consist both of outworkers (mostly women working at home) and small workshops, which offer more opportunities for upward mobility. However, both are clearly subordinated to the capitalist production process, and can no longer be considered independent producers.

The informal sector benefits from subcontracting by being provided with capital and raw materials, which, as Peattie (1982) shows in her analysis of the shoe industry in Bogota, are major impediments to small firms. Here the growth of subcontracting can be attributed not only to an expanding and highly segmented market, but also to a desire by larger firms to avoid paying the fringe benefits required under labor legislation. Thus, the high cost of production in the formal sector is attributable not only to higher wages, but to fringe benefits such as health insurance, vacation pay, and redundancy payments.

As Joekes (1985) points out in her analysis of the growth of domestic outworkers in the clothing and textile industry, low wages are only one factor in the cost advantages of subcontracting as compared to formal industrial employment. Firms save money on fixed-asset costs such as buildings and utilities, and workers are often required to purchase or lease their own sewing machine and other materials such as thread and needles. However, the greatest advantage subcontracting offers is the flexibility of the labor force. Firms pay only for work produced, which can be scaled up or down with market fluctuations. Thus, the risks of market fluctuations are shifted on to the outworkers themselves. Joekes notes that the advantages of subcontracting are particularly critical in times of tight market competition and increased government intervention in the labor market, resulting in higher costs.

All of these factors influenced the development of the domestic *maquila* (or industrial homework) in Mexico City, described in a recent study by Benería and Roldán (in press). In their analysis, the *maquila* (outwork) appears as the last link in several stages of subcontracting reaching up through progressively larger firms and ultimately, in nearly 70 per cent of the firms studied, to multinationals. This demonstrates conclusively the direct integration of the informal sector, not only with the national but also the international economy. It would appear that the internationalization of production through multinationals has engendered such competition that firms are constantly searching for ways to cut costs, including the use of homework. Managers cited cost factors and labor flexibility as prime advantages in the use of subcontracting, which in this case included not only the garment industry, but plastics, toys, electronics and other forms of labor-intensive manufacture. Almost all of the homeworkers were married women with young children, who turned to this form of employment because of its compatibility with childcare and domestic responsibilities. A high percentage of women are also found in the small subcontracting firms, and the number appears to be increasing, especially in a non-traditional industries such as metal and electrical work. Thus, the decentralization, fragmentation and deskilling of production accompanying the growth of informal labor has tended to incorporate more vulnerable segments of the labor force such as married women. The growth of the informal sector thus may help to explain the increasing percentage of women in the labor force in Latin America during the past decade, a point to which we shall return later.

The domestic *maquila* in Mexico City operates without government sanction. In fact, much of this outwork is illegal, not because the *maquila per se* is outlawed, but because of its failure to meet legal labor requirements regarding minimum wages, fringe benefits, taxes and working conditions. Wages for homework, which are paid by the piece, fall far below the minimum wage and, according to Benería and Roldán, constitute a clear case of exploitation. Thus, this case appears to reinforce Portes' contention that government labor legislation, while designed to protect workers, may actually be stimulating the growth of the informal economy. Portes and Benton (1984: 615) note: 'In general, informal activities appear to expand most rapidly in those countries where state regulation of the econonomy is extensive and cost differentials between the two sectors are significant. On the other hand, in countries where the state has consistently adopted antilabor and deregulatory policies, the distinction between formal and informal sectors becomes blurred.' In short, according to Portes, the informal sector grows primarily in opposition to government regulated labor in the formal sector.

However, another case study by Truelove (1985) of rural mini-*maquilas* in Colombia shows increasing direct government support for this form of subcontracting and informalization of the labor process. Here again women play a control role, as disguised wage workers for the textile and shoe industry. In this case the women are organized into production cooperatives set up by the Valle branch of the Colombian Federation of Coffee Growers, who were attempting to prevent further decline in coffee production and the outmigration of laborers by improving the lives of small producers. The cooperatives provide the households of smaller producers and seasonal laborers with additional income through the women's wages, which now constitute a half to three-quarters of the total family income. At the same time, they aid the ailing textile and shoe industries by providing them with cheaper labor. The products reach both the national and international markets, and in fact the cooperative program has been so successful that it now ranks among the top five Colombian firms in terms of foreign exchange generated through off-shore assembly arrangements with multinationals. As a recognized non-profit-making organization involved in income-generation, the cooperative has received grants from international development assistance agencies as well as from the Inter-American Development Bank. Though workers receive limited benefits, these are deducted as overhead costs from their low wages. Thus, not only are the products of the informal sector reaching the international market, but the informal sector is being supported by national and international public funds.

Because of its capacity for labor absorption and cost advantages in a highly competitive international market, the informal economy is receiving increased support from both the private and public sector in terms of credit, access to raw materials and foreign exchange, and other privileges formerly reserved exclusively for the formal sector. This represents a clear change in attitude on the part of government agencies, who formerly tended to regard the informal sector as an obstacle to development and treated it with benign neglect or outright repression. Police raids on unlicensed street vendors or clandestine workshops are still common, particularly if they compete with firms in the modern sector. However, to the extent that their goods and services are channelled through the formal sector and benefit it with lower costs and greater flexibility, the more the activities of the informal sector are not only condoned but officially sanctioned.

A favorite mechanism for support of the informal sector is income-generation schemes of the type described above for Colombia. Similar schemes have been developed in the Dominican Republic and other Latin American countries with national and international support. A particularly successful program which has received special attention is the credit extension program of the Association for the Development of Microenterprises, Inc. (ADEMI), founded in 1983 as a private voluntary organization by a group of influential Dominican business leaders with support from the government and the Agency for International Development. The micro-enterprises are involved in a variety of manufacturing activities from making clothes, ceramics and bread, to the repair of refrigerators, and mattresses. Initial loans are small, but may become larger if the micro-entrepreneurs are successful in growing and repaying their loans. Wines (1985) has identified three stages in the growth of these micro-enterprises, starting with a small workshop dependent entirely on family labor and selling directly to the poor; to larger enterprises selling to shops and utilizing 'apprentice' labor which need not be paid the minimum wage or fringe benefits; to fully legalized firms employing a stable workforce and utilizing more imported raw materials (which requires licensing) and improved technology. The latter firms sell largely to boutiques catering to a middle- and upper-class clientele, for which they are paid more but must also produce goods of higher quality. Wines notes that penetrating this new market has been facilitated by IMF austerity measures which have hurt competitors such as large domestic producers and importers hampered by the removal of subsidized imports. Apparently the use of 'apprentice' labor at below minimum wages is no impediment to these micro-entrepreneurs receiving credit. Here we can see clearly how informal sector firms evolve from serving the needs of the low-income population to subcontracting relationships with larger firms in the formal sector servicing the larger economy.

Research on the ADEMI credit program by Blumberg (1985) notes that the economic crisis in the Dominican Republic has led to modifications which favor larger, more stable firms. Loans were formerly given to both individuals and solidarity groups composed of several individuals, including a high percentage of women. With the eroding economy, loans were suspended to the solidarity groups, thereby eliminating 77 per cent of the female beneficiaries. Although deemed a greater credit risk, these solidarity groups had not had higher rates of loan delinquency, and in fact had created more jobs than micro-enterprises run by men. Thus, loans appear increasingly restricted to fully established micro-entrepreneurs, who, as we have seen above, channel their products largely to the middle and upper classes. Here we see again how informal enterprises catering to the formal sector appear to receive special treatment from government-sponsored credit and other aid programs.

These examples tend to support Portes' (1983: 168) observation that 'the articulation of different modes of production, reflected in the formal, informal division, is ultimately a *political* process dependent on control of the state.' He argues that the importance of the informal sector varies in relation to three factors: costs imposed by the state on formal enterprises, the degree of enforcement of labor legislation, and the relative strength of organized labor. While all of these factors contribute to the higher cost of labor in the formal sector, it is also important to look at the direct support given to the informal sector by government and private sources. This support adds to the advantages of producing in the informal sector and widens the cost differentials between the two sectors. As we have seen, this support is not given indiscriminately, but responds to the interests of formal sector firms, who are increasingly utilizing the informal sector to reduce their production costs. This has led not only to an increase in the size and change in the nature of the informal sector in Latin America, but to a weakening of the collective bargaining power of labor, as we shall see in the next section.

LABOR AND THE ECONOMIC CRISIS

An important factor behind the growth of the informal sector is the economic crisis facing Latin American countries today. It has increased the drive to export, particularly manufactured goods, which, as we have seen, now figure importantly in the informal sector. Through subcontracting and the use of casual, unprotected labor, firms are able to produce more cheaply and to compete in an increasingly tight international market. The foreign exchange earned from exports helps to reduce the huge debt now facing most Latin American countries.

The economic crisis in Latin America was brought on by rising oil prices, unfavorable terms of trade, and a growing foreign debt and public sector deficit. It is characterized by high rates of inflation, increased consumer prices, and a decline in real wages and employment, placing an even greater burden on working-class families. For example, between 1973 and 1981 wages in the industrial sector in Argentina fell by around 21 per cent, while in Chile they contracted by over 41 per cent (Tokman, 1984: 16). In part, this was the result of stabilization models imposed by the International Monetary Fund, which mandated a freeze in wages with no control on prices. The IMF also required reduction in public expenditures in areas such as health, education and housing, in order to cut down on the pubic deficit.

Portes (1983: 166) argues that one of the principal goals of these stabilization policies are to roll back working-class gains by reducing the size of the protected formal sector, leading to rapid increases in unemployment and an increase in the size and nature of the informal sector. For example, in the period 1980–2, the Southern Cone countries, all then under military dictatorships, experienced drastic increases in unemployment, with figures close to 20 per cent of the economically active population in Chile and Uruguay and 10 per cent in Argentina (p. 167). Similar stabilization models with similar outcomes have now been imposed by the IMF in Mexico, Brazil, the Dominican Republic and other Latin American countries.

The increase in the informal sector in the Southern Cone can be seen in the growing number of self-employed and unpaid family workers, many of whom are women. Despite the traditionally high level of wage employment in these countries, from 1975 to 1978 the percentage of self-employed workers grew at a high rate, and in Chile included 20 per cent of the female labor force (Prates, 1981: 11). In the Southern Cone, most of the self-employed female workers are in commerce and services rather than in the manufacturing sector, which has suffered sharp declines due to IMF liberalization policies. Thus, while Southern Cone countries with an established domestic manufacturing sector have been deindustrialized, due chiefly to cheap imports, in other Latin American countries the manufacturing sector is expanding, principally through exports.

The informal sector in commerce has also expanded, and now includes the sale of non-traditional products such as perfume, digital watches and single cigarettes. In Brazil, this sector is now estimated to account for over 30 per cent of the GDP (*New York Times*, 1984: 11). In Colombia, employment in the informal sector is estimated at 45 per cent of total urban employment, and generated 40 per cent of all new urban employment between 1974–8 (Portes and Walton, 1981: 830). A large number of these informal sector workers are women, particularly in labor-intensive industries such as food processing, textiles and shoes. In one study, it was found that half of the Colombian women employed in these labor-intensive industries are working at home and being paid by piecework as independent workers; as in Mexico City, most of them are housewives who also bear onerous family responsibilities (Rey de Marulanda, 1982: 67). Although industrial homework may provide needed employment for these older married women, it is also an effective way of cutting wages and fringe benefits and weakening worker solidarity, particularly in a time of economic crisis. A similar restructuring and deskilling of the labor process is taking place in the US, and other advanced industrial countries, where women also constitute a cheaper source of labor than men (e.g. Nash and Fernandez Kelly, 1983; Redclift and Mingione, 1985).

The economic crisis in both advanced and developing countries also forces more women into the labor force. Faced with rising levels of male unemployment, higher prices, and falling wages, more women seek employment in order to enable their families and survive. This increases the supply of women seeking employment, while demand may be generated by structural changes in the economy. In Brazil, for example, the female economically active population almost doubled from 1970 to 1980, rising much faster than for men. Female participation in industry grew even faster, almost tripling in ten years, reversing the declining trend of previous decades. The reasons for this dramatic increase appear to be due to the growth in demand for female employment in certain non-traditional sectors such as metallurgy. However, a study by Humphrey (1985) of industrial employment in Sao Paulo indicates a clear pattern of gender discrimination, by allocating women to the worst jobs with no prospect of promotion or skill training. Humphrey (1985: 223) argues this is not due to their instability on the job, as dual labor theory has suggested, but to their greater stability in monotonous, menial assembly-line jobs, due presumably to a lack of suitable alternatives. Certainly this would appear to be the case among the long-term garment workers I have studied in the US and Puerto Rico (Safa, 1984). However, it is surprising that in large, modern firms such as electrical plants and factories making motor components, such a traditional sexual division of labor would have already taken place.

However, the increase in female labor in Sao Paulo appears to be taking place within the context of formal wage labor, without resorting to the massive form of subcontracting to the informal sector observed in other cities. Portes (1983: 167) argues that the apparent absence of a strong informal sector in the Sao Paulo industrial economy is due to the overwhelming advantage of capital over labor after two decades of military rule. This resulted in a weak and fragmented labor movement and industrial wages that are among the lowest in Latin America. These factors combined with the availability of cheap female labor undermined the need for an informal sector, at least in the manufacturing sector of Sao Paulo.

A recent study in Manaus of workers in both the formal and informal sectors tends to confirm Portes' hypothesis. Despres (1985) shows how the recent creation of a free trade zone led to a decline in self-employment, particularly among young women, who, as elsewhere, are the principal workers in these assembly line industries. However, Despres argues that the self-employed (most of whom are men) actually make more, because of the very low level of wages both in the free trade zone and in traditional industries. Again this is due to the state's minimum wage and benefit policies, which make it unnecessary to maintain a labor reserve to keep wages low.

It could be argued that cheap female labor in export processing fulfills the same functions as the informal sector in a number of ways. First, it reduces the cost of production, particularly in export manufacturing. This can be seen in the rapid increase since the 1960s in export processing industries in Latin America, Asia and other Third World countries. Though fostered by developing countries to support their export earnings and reduce unemployment, these export processing industries are often exempt from the need to observe minimum wages, fringe benefits, adequate working conditions, or the right to collective bargaining, even in countries where such labor legislation exists for domestic industries (Safa, 1981). Similar failures to observe labor legislation have been noted among young women working in the packing plants of Mexican agro-industry designed for export (Arizpe and Aranda, 1981).

Secondly, the integration of cheap female labor into paid employment fulfills much the same role in the social reproduction of the working class that the informal economy does. Both strategies (formal wage employment and informal sector activities) provide additional income for the family, and are often found within the same household (e.g. Bolles, 1983). In a recent study of women garment workers in Puerto Rico, I have shown how their wages constitute a principal source of income for the family, with the contribution varying according to whether the women are workers, single or female heads of household (Safa, 1984). Though most of the young women in this study lived in the rural area, their families no longer cultivated subsistence plots, but utilized their daughters' earnings (and transfer payments) to complement the family's income. Truelove's study (1986) of the mini-*maquilas* in rural Colombia suggests familiar findings.

Thirdly, both the use of cheap female wage labor and subcontracting to the informal economy weakens the strength of the organized labor movement in Latin America. The level of unionization is much lower among women, due to a variety of factors, including their concentration in certain industries, the recency of their entry to wage labor on a massive scale, the instability of their employment, and the neglect of unions. The informal sector is by definition not unionized, although there are isolated incidents of unions among domestic servants and other informal sector workers. Portes (1984: 608) argues that efforts by the state to increase unionization or enforce other forms of labor legislation may actually tend to increase the incidence of covert hiring and subcontracting in the formal sector.

Both the informal sector and export processing industries have been intensified in response to the economic crisis in Latin America. They both represent strategies by industries to reduce production costs at a time of intense international competition. However, labor recruitment for the two sectors differ, with young, single women preferred in export processing while older, married women are more likely to be found as industrial homeworkers or disguised wage laborers in the informal sector. There is a very small percentage of men in export processing industries, but they still predominate in other areas of manufacturing, and are also important in the informal sector. Several studies report that micrœntrepreneurs are often former wages laborers (Schmuckler, 1979; Wines, 1985). Since they draw on different labor markets, the presence of free trade zones does not necessarily preclude the formation of an informal sector; indeed, the added income in the community may enhance the development of a consumer market for goods and services produced in the informal sector.

CONCLUSION

Both the informal economy and export processing industries are manifestations of the new international division of labor, which represents the
newest stage in the incorporation of Latin American into the global capitalist
economy. As we have seen, incorporation is not new, but the form has
changed. In the colonial period, Latin America served primarily as a source
of raw materials and as a market for manufactured goods. The period of
import-substitution industrialization starting in the 1930s allowed for the
development of some domestic industry and an internal market, but was
rather quickly taken over by multinational corporations who controlled the
necessary capital and technology. The contemporary period has been
marked by economic crisis and foreign debt, increasing the vulnerability of
Latin American countries to foreign penetration, and resulting in the
weakening of organized labor and the increase in disguised wage labor
through the informal sector.

This weakening of labor occurs at a time when the level of state protection
for workers in Latin America is minimal, and where such labor legislation
exists, as social security, for example, it covers only a small percentage of
workers, the so-called labor aristocracy (Mesa-Lago, 1978). Most Latin
American workers still depend on the sale of their labor power for
reproduction, and cannot rely on the state to provide them with a social
wage. Now even these small gains are being eroded, as the informal sector
expands, and new, more vulnerable workers such as women enter the labor
force in greater numbers.

As Portes (1985: 29) notes, the evidence suggests 'that the informal
proletariat is not a class in a process of disintegration but a relatively stable
component of the Latin American class structure'. If the peasantry are
included, it constituted an absolute majority of the labor force during the
entire period of industrial development since 1950. The number of self-
employed workers, for example, has remained relatively constant at about
20 per cent of the industrial labor force between 1950 and 1980. In this same
period, however, the informal proletariat became increasingly urban,
reflecting the shift from agriculture to industry as the leading sector of most
Latin American economies. At the same time, its share of total income
declined relative to the top income sectors, pointing to increasing income
concentration and inequality (p. 25).

We have shown that the nature of the urban informal economy has also
changed during this period, with the increasing use of subcontracting to
unprotected labor in small workshops or in industrial homework. This has
contributed to the deteriorating position of the formal working class,
reflected both in a decline of wage levels and an expulsion of part of this
class into the informal sector (Portes, 1985: 35). What is even more alarming

is that in some countries this deterioration is taking place with full state support, at both the national and international levels. While government schemes to support the informal sector may be intended to reduce unemployment and enhance the mobility of individual entrepreneurs, they are also weakening the bargaining power of organized labor and reducing its small gains.

Ultimately, the fate of the informal sector in Latin America depends upon a political struggle between capital and labor for control of the regulatory role of the state. Burawoy (1983) documents this struggle in the history of advanced capitalist societies like the US or England, where the state intervened through social insurance legislation and state regulation to prevent the complete dependence of workers on wages for the reproduction of labor power. However, he points out that today the regulatory role of the state in advanced capitalist countries is being curtailed, not only by subcontracting to an informal sector, but more importantly by the vulnerability of collective labor to the national and international mobility of capital manifested in plant closures and relocation, often to the new export processing zones in Latin America, the Caribbean, Asia and other Third World countries. Thus, the international division of labor weakens the collective power of labor in both Third World and advanced industrial countries.

The new international division of labor makes possible the mobility of capital but weakens the solidarity of labor. It pits workers against each other, both at the national and international levels. This is manifested in the response of US workers to plant closures and relocation. The call has been primarily for increased protectionism, to stop the flow of cheap imports that have devastated industries like clothing, textiles and electronics, and even capital-intensive industries like automobiles and steel (Safa, 1981). For example, though as textile and garment imports increased by an average of 6 per cent per year during the decade ending in 1983, they increased 25 per cent in 1983 and 32 per cent in 1984. In 1984, imports accounted for 33 per cent of all apparel consumed in the US, resulting in the loss of nearly 250,000 jobs since 1980 (*GIST*, 1986).

In Latin America, however, the deteriorating economic situation of workers has led them into increasing conflict with the state. Not only have they been hurt by the decline in wage levels and the informalization of the economy, but they have suffered from the severe cuts in public services brought on by the economic crisis. Collective protest has centered less on jobs and working conditions, than on collective services like transportation, water and other public services, and housing (Safa, 1976). Most of these protests are organized on the basis of working-class neighborhoods and squatter settlements, like the cost of living movement in Sao Paulo where working-class women organized collectively to protest against the high cost of living and formed consumer cooperatives on their own behalf (Singer,

1982; Castells, 1982). As a consequence, these mobilizations tend to include much of the informal proletariat as well as members of the traditional working class. (Portes, 1985: 32). Left-wing political parties and labor unions, the traditional channels of political mobilization for the working class, reach only a fragment of the poor, and have been emasculated by the repression of military dictatorships. The state has thus become the most visible enemy of the urban poor, not private employers with whom workers still deal on a more individualistic, company basis.

It is no accident that, compared to other Third World areas, Latin America should show the most vigorous development of collective forms of urban protest, since it is there that the contradictions stemming from the process of dependent capitalism are most sharply defined. As we have noted, Latin America has experienced the longest and most extensive process of capitalist penetration, with the virtual dissolution of pre-capitalist modes of production in the rural area, thus placing a greater burden for survival on the urban informal economy. The concentration of low-income populations living in the city and facing an increasing deterioration in their living standards, accentuated by the economic crisis, gives rise to a very explosive political situation.

REFERENCES

Arizpe, Lourdes (1977) 'Women in the informal labor sector: The case of Mexico City'. In *Women and National Development*. Wellesley Editorial Committee. Chicago: University of Chicago Press, pp. 25–37.
—— 'Relay Migration and the survival of the peasant household'. In Helen I. Safa (ed.), *Towards a Political Economy of Urbanization In Third World Countries*, New Delhi: Oxford University Press. pp. 19–46.
Arizpe, Lourdes and Josefina Aranda (1981) 'The "comparative advantages" of women's disadvantages: Women workers in the strawberry export agribusiness in Mexico', *Signs, Journal of Women in Culture and Society*, 7, 2: 453–73.
Benería, Lources and Martha Roldán (in press) *The Crossroads of Class and Gender: Indusrial Homework, Subcontracting and Household Dynamics in Mexico City*, Chicago: University of Chicago Press.
Blumberg, Rae Lesser (1985) 'A walk on the "WID" side: Summary of field research on "Women in Development" in the Dominican Republic and Guatemala', Washington, D.C.: Agency for International Development (LAC and PP PPC/CDIE).
Bolles, Lynn (1983) 'Kitchens hit by priorities: Employed working-class women confront the IMF'. In June Nash and Maria Patricia Fernandez-Kelly (eds), *Women, Men and The International Division of Labor*, Albany: State University of New York Press, pp. 138–60.
Bromley, Ray and Chris Gerry (1979) 'Who are the casual poor?'. In R. Bromley and C. Gerry (eds), *Casual Work and Poverty in Third World Countries*, New York: John Wiley and Sons, 3–23.

Burawoy, Michael (1983) 'Between the labor process and the state: The changing face of factory regimes under advanced capitalism', *American Sociological Review*, 48 (October): 587–605.

Castells, Manuel (1982) 'Squatters and politics in Latin America: A comparative analysis of urban social movements in Chile, Peru and Mexico'. In Helén I. Safa (ed.), *Towards a Political Economy of Urbanization in Third World Countries*, Delhi, India: Oxford University Press, pp. 249–82.

Deere, Carmen Diana (1979) 'Changing social relations of production and Peruvian peasant women's work'. In *Women in Latin America: An Anthology from Latin American Perspectives*, Riverside, California: Latin American Perspectives, pp. 26–46.

Deere, Carmen Diana and Magdalena León de Leal (1981) 'Peasant production, proletarianization, and the sexual division of labor in the Andes', *Signs, Journal of Women in Culture and Society*, 7, 12 (Winter): 338–60.

Despres, Leo (1985) 'Industrialization, migration and the informal sector in Manaus'. Working paper 45, Helen Kellogg Institute for International Studies, University of Notre Dame, Notre Dame, Ind.

Geertz, Clifford (1963) *Peddlers and Princes, Social Change and Economic Modernization in Two Indonesian Towns*, Chicago: University of Chicago Press.

GIST (1986) 'Textile import control program'. Washington, D.C.: Bureau of Public Affairs, Dept of State.

Humphrey, John (1985) 'Gender, pay and skill: manual workers in Brazilian industry'. In Haleh Afsar (ed.), *Women, Work, and Ideology in the Third World*, London: Tavistock Publications, pp. 214–31.

Joekes, Susan P. (1985) 'Industrialization, trade and female employment in developing countries'. Santo Domingo, D.R.: United Nations International Research and Training Institute for the Advancement of Women (INSTRAW).

Lomnitz, Larissa (1977) *Networks and Marginality: Life in a Mexican Shantytown*, New York: Academic Press.

Meillassoux, Claude (1972) 'From reproduction to production', *Economy and Society*, 1 (February): 93–105.

Mesa-Lago, Carmelo (1978) *Social Security in Latin America*, Pittsburgh: University of Pittsburgh Press.

Morse, Richard M. (1971) 'Trends and issues in Latin American urban research, 1965–70', *Latin American Research Review*, 6, 1: 3–52 and 2: 19–75.

—— (1974) 'Trends and patterns of Latin American urbanization, 1750–1920', *Comparative Studies in Society and History*, 16, 4 (September): 416–47.

Nash, June and María Patricia Fernández Kelly (eds) (1983) *Women, Men and the International Division of Labor*, Albany: State University of New York Press.

New York Times (1984) 'On the streets of Brazil: Peddling up, sales down', 29 July: 9.

Peattie, Lisa R. (1982) 'What is to be done with the "informal sector"?: A case study of shoe manufacturers in Colombia'. In Helen I. Safa (ed.), *Towards a Political Economy of Urbanization in Third World Countries*, New Delhi: Oxford University Press, pp. 208–32.

Portes, Alejandro (1983) 'The informal sector: Definition, controversy, and relation to national development, *Review*, VII, 1 (Summer): 151–74.

—— (1985) 'Latin American class structures: their composition and change during the last decades', *Latin American Research Review*, XX, 3: 7–40.

Portes, A. and Lauren Benton (1984) 'Industrial development and labor absorption: a reinterpretation', *Population and Development Review*, 10, 4: 589–611.

Portes, Alejandro and John Walton (1981) *Labor, Class and the International System*, New York: Academic Press.

Prates, Susana (1981) 'Women's labour and family survival strategies under the "stabilization models" in Latin America', Vienna: Centre for Social Development and Humanitarian Affairs, United Nations.

Rama, German W. and Enzo Faletto (1985) 'Dependent societies and crisis in Latin America: the challenge of social and political transformation'. Santiago, Chile, *CEPAL Review*, 25: 129–48.

Redclift, Nanneke and Enzo Mingione (1985) *Beyond Employment: Household, Gender and Subsistence*, Oxford: Basil Blackwell.

Rey de Marulanda, Nohra (1982) 'La unidad de producción – reproducción en las mujeres del sector urbano en Colombia'. In Magdalena León (ed.), *La Realidad Colombiana. Debate Sobre la Mujer en América Latina*, Vol. I, Bogotá: ACEP, pp. 56–71.

Roberts, Bryan (1978) *Cities of Peasants*, Beverly Hills: Sage.

Safa, Helen I. (1976) 'Class consciousness among working-class women in Latin America: a case study in Puerto Rico'. In June Nash and Helen I. Safa (eds), *Sex and Class in Latin America*, New York: Praeger. pp. 69–89.

—— (1981) 'Runaway shops and female employment: The search for cheap labor', *Signs, Journal of Women in Society and Culture*, 7(2): 418–33.

—— (1982) *Towards a Political Economy of Urbanization in Third World Countries*, New Delhi: Oxford University Press.

—— (1984) 'Female employment and the social reproduction of the Puerto Rican working class', *International Migration Review*, 18, 4: 1168–87.

Schmink, Marianne (1982) 'Poor women in the urban economy in Latin America'. In Magdalena León (ed.), *Debate Sobre la Mujer en América Latina y el Caribe*, vol. III, Bogotá: ACEP (in Spanish), pp. 121–140.

—— (1985) 'Women and urban industrial development in Brazil'. In June Nash and Helen Safa (eds.), *Women and Change in Latin America*, South Hadley, Mass.: Bergin and Garvey, pp. 136–164.

Schmuckler, Beatriz (1979) 'Diversidad de formas de las relaciones capitalistas en la industria Argentina'. In Victor Tokman and Emilio Klein (eds.), *El Subempleo en América Latina*, Buenos Aires: El Cid Editores, 309–51.

Scott, Alison (1979) 'Who are the self-employed?'. In R. Bromley and C. Gerry (eds.), *Casual Work and Poverty in Third World Cities*, New York: John Wiley and Sons, pp. 105–129.

Singer, Paul (1982) 'Neighbourhood Movements in Sao Paulo'. In Helen I. Safa (ed.), *Towards a Political Economy of Urbanization in Third World Countries*, New Delhi: Oxford University Press, pp. 285–304.

Tokman, Victor E. (1984) 'Wages and employment in international recessions: recent Latin American experience'. Working Paper no. 11, The Helen Kellogg Institute for International Studies, University of Notre Dame, Ind.

Truelove, Cynthia (1985) 'The informal proletariat revisited: the case of the talleres rurales mini maquilas in Colombia'. Paper presented at the Political Economy of the World System Conference, 'Crisis in the Caribbean Basin: Past and Present', Tulane University.

Walton, John (1985) 'The third "new" international division of labor'. In J. Walton (ed.), *Capital and Labour in the Urbanized World*, London: Sage, 3–16.

Wines, Sarah W. (1985) 'Stages of microenterprise growth in the Dominican informal sector', *Grassroots Development*, 9, 2, Washington D.C.: Inter-American Foundation, pp. 33–42.

Wolpe, Harold (1975) 'The theory of internal colonialism: The South African case'. In I. Oxaal, T. Barnett and D. Booth (eds), *Beyond the Sociology of Development*, London: Routledge and Kegan Paul, pp. 229–52.

PART V

Local Responses to Global Restructuring: Community, Household and Urban Politics

13

Community and Corporations in the Restructuring of Industry

June Nash

The interdependence of community and industry is increasingly distorted by the changes occurring in the United States. The progressive integration of industry at the national and international levels has brought about the distancing of the local community from the seats of corporate decision-making. For the corporation, the ever-widening horizon of alternative opportunities for displacing specific contracts, whole manufacturing processes, or even entire plants to other parts of the United States, to other industrial countries or to new industrial centers in the Third World has increased managerial prerogatives and diminished the control exercised by city governments or a local workforce. This process, which began many decades ago with the rise of the great corporations at the turn of the century, has more recently intensified with the advances in communications enabling corporations to retain centralized control of distant branches, and with technology facilitating the transfer of production capability.

In the case of Pittsfield, Massachusetts, this process began with the purchase of the owner-operated Stanley Electric Works by the General Electric Corporation in 1903. The simple repressive control of the labor force exercised by the corporation in the first quarter century of its existence was gradually replaced by policies of welfare capitalism under the presidency of Bernard Swope in the 1920s and later by industrial unionism achieved in the 1930s. Each of these phases involved workers in corporate hegemonic control that structures the workplace and usurps the values and initiatives of workers. I shall argue that the incorporation of workers in to the US corporate hegemony was not simply the imposition of a dominant ideology

Research was supported by the National Science Foundation and the National Endowment for the Humanities. I am grateful to these funding bodies and to the many friends and supporters of this project in Pittsfield. I have benefited greatly from the assistance of Max Kirsch in the interviews of some of the informants. I am also thankful to him and to Judith-Maria Buechler, Hans Buechler and Herbert Menzel for suggestions that improved the clarity and strengthened the argument. I owe the quotation from Gramsci to Pamela Wright.

on workers but, rather, a negotiated process with labor initiating moves that ensured stable employment and wage levels. Although opposed by corporations, these moves proved beneficial to US industry. The current undermining of that hegemony is, similarly, being brought about by the corporations, aided by a pro-business government in the 1980s.

CORPORATE HEGEMONY AND COMMUNITY CONTROL

Where communities once served as the principal context for the reproduction of economic institutions, now corporations integrated at an international level generate the forms and beliefs transmitted in the production and circulation of goods. This cultural context is equivalent to what Gramsci (cited in Williams, 1960: 587) defined as hegemony:

> an order in which a certain way of life and thought is dominant, in which one concept of reality is diffused throughout society in all its institutional and private manifestations, informing with its spirit all taste, morality, customs, religious and political principles, and all social relations, particularly in their intellectual and moral connotations.

This definition is closely related to the configurational approach in anthropology. Ruth Benedict (1959: 46–7) was similarly concerned with what she called 'the interpenetration of different fields of experience, and the consequent modification of both of them' though she did not give priority to economic relations. This she would have considered to be the predilection of a particular society. What Benedict and Gramsci have in common is an understanding that the identity of a culture comes from the selection of traits that conform to one another in accord with a dominant configuration. From Gramsci, that configuration derived from a power structure controlled by the great corporations that persisted not through force but rather through consensual mechanisms that 'informed' behavior in all domains. He equated 'Americanism' with 'Fordism', the control exercised by large corporations during the period of 'welfare capitalism' in the 1920s when personnel relations took a 'trusteeship' approach to workers' lives beyond the workplace:

> it was relatively easy to rationalise production and labour by a skillful combination of force (destruction of working-class trade unionism on a territorial basis) and persuasion (high wages, various social benefits, extremely subtle ideological and political propaganda) and thus succeed in making the whole life of the nation revolve around production. (Gramsci, 1973: 285)

This replication of core cultural traits held by the society in the corporations identified them with Americanism and with the good of all those who upheld its central institutions.

Communities that hosted major branches of large corporations have ceded control over the welfare of their population and regulation of the environment to these enterprises as they became increasingly dependent on the jobs and tax revenues they bring. Cities like Pittsfield grew with the expansion of General Electric, drawing populations from throughout the United States and overseas. In order more effectively to assert its control over the labor force, General Electric used its power to limit the entry of other large corporations during its expansionist phase. Hegemonic control gained strength in so far as it was able to respond to and take into account the interests and needs of that population. In the present period of deindustrialization in the United States (Bluestone and Harrison, 1982) the decline of blue-collar work in power transformers production is correlated with outmigration.

The threat to corporate hegemony is brought about by the erosion of the preferential position of core industrial workers, as multinational corporations seek cheap labor sites for production overseas. It also stems from the attack by 'Reaganomics' (Reagan's economic program) on those programs that ensured social stability. The inability of most organized sectors of labor to confront this new threat reflects their failure to extend their organization to the secondary workforce and overseas. By mirroring male supremacist hierarchies and dominant white elitism of the corporations in trade unions, they diminish the political potential of workers in the present stage of restructuring American industry.

The restructuring of industry in Pittsfield is marked by a shift from blue-collar work in power transformer production to a highly trained and educated engineering and professional elite in research and design operations for plastics production and naval contracts. The loss of over 7000 production jobs since the peak activity years just after World War II has not been compensated by the increase of a few hundred technicians and design experts in the Ordnance and Plastics Divisions. The decline in production in the Power Transformer division was precipitous after each major strike. Following the wave of strikes in 1947, General Electric developed a policy of diverting production to satellite firms in the south to which they shifted production (Drucker, 1953). This policy was facilitated by the increased number of plants built during World War II at government expense. The Pittsfield plant lost small and medium-sized power transformer production in the mid-1950s, and, following the 101-day strike of 1969, in the early 1970s (Nash, 1984b). Ever since the recession of 1976, and particularly after 1982, the stagnation in the electrical machinery business resulted in massive layoffs and a demotion of the Power Transformer Division to departmental status. Pittsfield's population fell dramatically in the same period, from 57,000 in 1971 to 50,000 in the 1980 census. The 1985 city census shows a further drop to 48,000.

The restructuring of the Pittsfield General Electric plant follows national trends in the decline of consumer production and the increase in defense industry where there are much higher returns on investment. The electrical industry more than any other is in the forefront of the military expansion. This trend goes back to World War I when Gerard Swope, then an executive in the Western Electric Company, was appointed to the Department of War by the Secretary of War, Newton Baker. General Electric appointed him as president of the company after the war. Schatz (1983: 150–1) traces the movement back and forth between the electrical industry and the War Board up to the present day when a former public relations agent for the company is now President of the United States.

The questions I shall raise here are: How was corporate hegemony constructed, and how has it been affected by the current restructuring of industry? How have the community leaders and the unions responded to this challenge to the industrial accord that prevailed until the 1970s? What maintains consensual mechanisms supporting hegemonic control even after the corporations fail to fulfill their side of the social contract?

HOW CORPORATE HEGEMONY WORKS

Corporate capitalist hegemony in its peak years promoted values of rationality, individualism, competition, specialization, mobility and equal opportunity. Patriarchal in outlook, it was predicated on a male wage earner and a single-worker household. When women entered the workforce, it was considered a temporary expedient to pay for luxuries like restaurant meals or holiday travel. The values expressed in the home and community were found in the workplace. Work at home and in the factory was sex-segregated and ethnic separation was found in both neighborhoods and on the job.

Pittsfield embodies the blue-collar community. Chosen as one of the sample cities in surveys of consumer patterns, it is the battleground for discount chains and established catalogue retail outlets. During the Christmas shopping season, 'Zayres' stays open 24 hours a day to accommodate the three shifts of General Electric workers who are able to 'shop until you drop' (*New York Times*, December 1985). In business, production, family, sports and community affairs, the striving towards precision, technical know-how and one-upmanship defines the behavior that is exhibited, applauded and emulated. These values are manifested in the clipped hedges, mown lawns, polished and tuned automobiles. Sporting events provide a common meeting place for both management and workers where they project a universalized form of competition in games involving professionals, or their own children. The downtown shopping area has four sports shops that have continued in business when three clothing stores closed. The town's only bag lady wore a backpack. The best praise one can make of a game, a business, or an academic program in the community college is that it is 'competitive'. Equal opportunity and upward mobility are important validations for corporate hegemony. And if mobility is often translated into horizontal geographical mobility, that was blamed on individual failures. So long as one could assume equal opportunity, each individual was expected to maximize his or her potential. This was freedom: that is, what the US had and what was lacking in the Soviet Union. Patriotism and a willingness to fight for these ideals was recognized in preferential employment and ritual recognition accorded on Memorial Day, the Fourth of July, and Veterans' Day.

The construction and maintenance of this hegemony is based on inputs from labor and professionals as well as corporate managers. This was not always the case. Socialist ethics and communalistic activities coalesced around ethnic communities in the late nineteenth and early twentieth centuries (Gutman, 1976). In struggles marking the confrontation of labor and capital, the state and local police intervened on the side of corporations. In 1916 when the first plant-wide strike took place in Pittsfield, the local police force was reinforced by the Boston Metropolitan Park Police and, according to an eye-witness I interviewed, 'they beat up people on their own lawns' (Nash, 1984b). Even in peace time, the lines were drawn sharply between the owners and managers of production facilities and the workers dependent on them for a job. 'Welfare capitalism' of the 1920s stabilized the standard of living of workers, but did not eliminate poverty of the disabled or retired. Pensions amounted to $25 a month, one-third of the average monthly pay; credit unions enabled workers to buy consumer durables with instalment payments from savings accounts; and paid vacations were allowed after ten years of service. These provisions, limited as they were, overcame the high turnover rates in the industry.

What changed this picture were the labor struggles of the 1930s and the institutionalized processes of redistribution that labor leaders, together with some progressive representatives in the Roosevelt period, succeeded in establishing. With the onset of the Depression, corporate managers abandoned the stabilizing measures of the previous decade when production and profits were high. The Wagner Act legalized trade union organization, and the National Labor Relations Board provided the legal machinry to ensure its implementation. These changes affecting the workplace were combined with an opening-up of educational opportunities in state-funded schools and entry of working-class children into technical and managerial positions. Social security legislation passed in 1935 lessened the dependency of the elderly on adult children and ensured the right to live with dignity after retirement. Unemployment compensation that followed lessened the need to take any job in desperation.

The fruits of the 1930s organization were not realized until after World War II because of the wartime freeze on wages and the no-strike agreement. Following the war, a series of strikes hit the auto, steel and electrical machinery industries. Nationally organized trade unions confronted nationally integrated industries for the first time. War veterans marched on the picket line in their uniforms, the ethnic differences that divided them before the war overcome by their service to the country. The 10 per cent an hour average increase won by the strikers was not substantial, but the show of power startled management into devising new labor control mechanisms (Nash, 1984b).

While the labor movement enjoyed their success, the corporations forged a reinvigorated hegemonic control that united what President Eisenhower recognized as the 'military industrial compex'. In the Cold War climate that followed the allied victory, anti-communism directed against militant trade union leaders particularly in the United Electric and Radio Workers (UE) combined with the demand for high-profit, high-technology defense contracts. While the unions fought over ideological issues, the corporations expanded the control that they exercised in government. Extremely skilled 'relations' men, often selected from the trade union movement, presided over collective bargaining sessions that were weakened by the contest between the rival UE and IUE locals.

The General Electric approach to labor relations crystallized in a set of strategies devised by Lemuel C. Boulware who became vice-president during the 1960s. Taking full advantage of the divided workforce in bargaining sessions during the 1950s and early 1960s. Boulware's relations experts interviewed workers on the shop floor to discover what their minimum, irreducible demands were for forthcoming negotiations. The management negotiating team would then put forward a 'firm, fair offer' in the first session of a contract negotiation and never move from that. This offer would be widely distributed in the plant and even advertised in the local press (Boulware, 1969).

When, as often happened until the late 1960s when the divided unions agreed to coordinate bargaining sessions, the unions gave in and accepted the offer without any changes, the whole ritual of collective bargaining that validated their position was thrown into question. The 101-day strike of the electrical industry in 1969 required the united effort of AFL–CIO unions across the nation to force the corporation to modify its offer. Boulwarism exposed the social contract between organized labor and management that nearly led to the demise of the trade union movement.

The co-option of trade union goals by the company and the containment of political action in the union by the anti-communist crusade upset the power balance between labor and management that had resulted in the moves that forged corporate hegemonic control. Yet that upset has not undermined the support for corporations that have forced down real wages and diminished the employment levels in what are considered high-wage areas. I shall argue that the persistence of that control is related to the identification of the corporation with a broader cultural context that provides ideological validation despite the failure of the corporations to maintain their side of the bargain: high-wage jobs and security in employment. To paraphrase Gramsci, who linked Americanism with Fordism, Americanism is still linked with General Electricalism, although some are beginning to question that link.

AMERICANISM AND GENERAL ELECTRICALISM

The success of the Cold War and the isolation of political unionism in the post-war period is embedded in a broader context in which the benefits accruing from the presence of the corporations are accepted as the American way of life. Workers as well as managers accept the logic of the market as dictating public as well as corporate policies. The translation of most demands into economic terms, reducing political issues affecting planning and decision-making to cents per hour gains, was the path of labor peace. It yielded priority to the corporation in defining the broader goals of the society. We can summarize this leadership as 'good citizenship', 'good giving' and 'good living', to paraphrase the public relations phrases the corporation is fond of using.

Good citizenship

The corporation took the lead in 'harmonizing' the relations between labor and capital to borrow a phrase from Owen D. Young (cited in Schatz, 1983: 15), by encouraging their managers to participate in community affairs and serve on the boards of various charitable and welfare organizations. This was spelled out in the *General Electric Employee Relations News Letter* (3 June 1955) in a list called 'What the community will find General Electric trying to do'. In addition to providing good products, good jobs, good purchases, buying goods and services of local suppliers, they detail what it is to be a 'good citizen':

Good Citizenship. We will be found trying at all times in the community to be a good corporate citizen – such, for instance, as being a good taxpayer with no bargains asked; a good supporter of local charities (first, by generous contribution, and second, by our good pension, insurance and other employee benefit programs which insure that we will be chairing on these local charities); and a good worker in all other worth-while activities aimed at making the community a rewarding place in which to operate, work and live. Incidentally, besides our corporate activity, our individual managers and other employees are encouraged in their own desires to be useful individual citizens of the communities in which they live and work.

Good Loyalty. At all times we try to be warmly loyal to the good people, good institutions, and good projects in the community. Where it is a matter of our proper concern, we will carry this loyalty to the point of disagreeing publicly, as a matter of duty, with those who seem to be speaking or working contrary to the over-all community interest.

Good Profit. We try to maintain a profitable operation in the community in order to promote the strength and growth of our activity there and to reward properly the more than 300,000 share owners who risk their savings to supply us with the facilities and backing to make jobs possible there in the first place. All employees there have an opportunity to become share owners under our savings and stock bonus plan, and it has been gratifying to note the increasing number of our community-neighbors who have been choosing to invest their savings with us.

This was followed by a detailed summary of what General Electric needs from the community in order to stay in business. First of all, the costs of staying in business, including local and state taxes, must be kept favorable; second, union abuses in feather-bedding (requiring excessive numbers of workers in some jobs), walkouts, illegal strikes, and labor laws that 'either fail to protect the interests of employees, employers and the public' must not be tolerated by the community; and finally 'unfair and abusive treatment in politically-inspired investigations, inquiries, and hearings or from misguided support when given by the press, educators, clergy, public servants and others of influence to unwarranted attacks on local employers must cease'. Citing some of the 'old industrial communities' as having particular problems in all these areas, the newsletter stated that the community must perform brilliantly in other areas in order to retain their presence. They called upon community leaders to help their community obtain: cost-effective education to ensure that the right thing would be done in their own interests and 'in the balanced best interests of all'; a moral reawakening to help all concerned that 'the right thing is done voluntarily'; and finally 'political sophistication to guard all concerned against being bribed or fooled by demagogues'.

Good giving

Although the vocabulary has changed since the 1950s, promotion within the firm is still clearly tied to community service. The national Elfun Society makes this explicit to upper-level management. Founded in 1928 by Gerard Swope, the mission of the Elfun society was 'to promote leadership, enthusiasm, loyalty, and team spirit among company management'. Its contingent mission was to promote understanding of GE as a corporate citizen, serving 'as an important channel for mutual understanding with the community and within the company itself' (*GE Pittsfield News*, vol. 71, no. 24, 28 June 1985). The continuing mission of the Elfun Society to serve the community voluntarily and improve communications was endorsed by the present Chairman of the Board, John F. Welch.

One of the major activities of the Elfun Society is Project Business, 'a program conducted in cooperation with local schools across the nation to help young people develop a better understanding of business and the free enterprise system' (*GE Pittsfield News*, vol. 71, no. 24, 28 June 1985). The huge commitment to the program is shown by the 600 employees in the local plant who are members of the Society.

In addition to the ideological campaign carried out in educational institutions, the corporation makes an award named after its former president Gerard L. Philippe to employees with outstanding personal service to the community. In 1984 the award went to an employee who ran a sports program for the handicapped; a couple who pioneered a foster-care program for the mentally retarded; an engineer who served as scoutmaster, and others committed to a variety of different youth training programs. The target population is usually youths, and the idiom in which their development is couched is sports and scouting.

Closely linked to the service activities of GE Elfun Society is the Pittsfield GE Employee Good Neighbor Fund. Called 'the primary avenue through which local General Electric employees regularly support local charitable and social programs' (*GE Pittsfield News*, vol. 70, no. 32, 7 September, 1984) it promotes through employee contributions matched by company donations to the United Way and other major charities, a sense of the corporation as a good citizen. Since 1948 the IUE Local 255 has 'embraced' the concept of the fund as a means to make a single contribution in support of many agencies and organizations. With the theme 'Giving that Stays at Home', the Good Neighbor Fund sets up competing teams in each of their shops to meet the targets that rise each year even with the decline in employment. Ordnance team members were the clear winners in the 1984 campaign. The following year, when Ordnance was struggling to improve its image after the conviction on misconduct in contracts, their team was given the leadership position in the campaign. The $500,000 contribution raised that year included about $150,000 matching grant from the General Electric Foundation. In addition to the GNF drive, the General Electric Foundation has a gift-matching program that will enable employees and retirees to double the amount of their tax-deductible contributions to charitable organizations approved by the trustees. The top management of the local General Electric plant serve on the boards of community organizations with union leaders. One of the 'relations' men whom I shall call Herb gave some insight into the activities of the boards of the United Way, the Boys' Club, the YMCA, Girls' Club and other such groups:

We leave what happens over there [at the plant] out when we go to board meetings. I have seen representatives of management and unions meet on hospital boards of the United Way and the Good Neighbor Fund on which I served. The best part of it is that both parties [labor and management] work together.

This sense of the harmonious working together was expressed by a number of the directors of organizations mentioned by Herb as well as the Chamber of Commerce. The retiring director of the United Way spoke enthusiastically about the contributions made by GE, Berkshire Life Insurance, the banks, Sheaffer Eaton and other companies that gave an increase each year over their previous year's contributions. This enabled them to 'market our services more effectively', the director told us. Representatives of corporations and unions vie with each other to get a seat on the board. While we were interviewing him, he answered a call from the president of the Berkshire Council of the AFL/CIO. They were, he told us later, deciding when they would play golf: 'The links I have tried to establish with unions [no pun intended] are important in building a framework for meeting the real needs of working people,' he told us. His organization is expanding their services to go beyond the traditional outlets of the hospitals, the YMCA, the Boys' Club and the Girls' Club to include programs in alcoholism, child abuse and social problems dealt with by the women's center.

Business-like attitudes prevail in the agencies helped by the United Way along with state funding. In the case of the Berkshire Home Care, which started with a budget of $48,000 from the United Way in 1974 and now has a budget of $2,500,000, the agency quite consciously tries to help the elderly avoid welfare dependency by strategic intervention that enables their clients to help themelves with the help of volunteers and visits by the professional staff. The director of this program, like the director of the United Way, used the language of business to talk about the program:

We used to have to make out grant proposals each year. I waited until we had a product to get a sustaining grant. Now we have elderly housing in every major town in the county ... We provide each with mental health services, legal services, occupational services and geriatric health services. Visiting nurses do periodic checkups on our housing units. We have mini-clinics for nutrition and provide kosher as well as regular hot meals for many of the people. We run a monthly social for which we charge seventy-five cents. When you get them in, you educate them on their rights. This is part of a socialization process involving programs such as blood pressure checkups in which we catch health problems before they become difficult.

This energetic director has introduced a 'hot-line' that makes it possible for clients in need only to press a button to get help. Although these programs and the many voluntary organizations supported by the United Way are private voluntary services, they have depended on sustaining funds from the state and federal government. By 1983 CETA workers were no longer available to assist in staffing. In 1982 when I spoke to the director of Berkshire Home Care, he anticipated these cutbacks and was trying to work out ways of making the services self-supporting.

Good living

Sports events sponsored by a variety of organizations provide the matrix for cultural integration of class, sex and age segregated social groups. This was not always so. A half-century ago, baseball was the badge of blue-collar male workers' identity, and there were ethnically divided teams. In those days, men played hard ball (baseball), 'girls' played softball (a game like baseball played with a soft ball), and management played golf. It is not coincidental that the director of United Way saw his success in integrating the trade unions in the fund drive as related to his date on the golf links, nor that a retired shop steward identified Phillip Murray's decline as starting on the golf links. General Electric management and employees often use sports jargon to make their points. When they get down to the small print of a contract, either side might refer to it as the time for 'playing hard ball'.

Most of the factories had baseball teams. The woollen mills in the Polish quarter of town had one of the best teams. The reason for this, I was told, was that they were second-generation Americans and 'they are always very aggressive, you know'. Then there was an Italian team called the Wine Athletic Club. They didn't have to win since their social events were so highly esteemed. In the 1920s GE workers had organized their own baseball team. GE began to sponsor the team, even giving preferential recruitment to good ball players. Sam told me he quit when GE began to underwrite the teams' expenses. When I asked him why, he said that it was because they did not give compensation for injuries that occurred when playing. Of course, they did not receive such payment before, but then it was not considered to be part of the job. The engineers organized their own baseball team, but when they played games with other GE plants, they would include some of the production workers, I was told, to make sure they would win.

As ethnic subdivisions lost their significance after World War II, teams were organized on other criteria. Even the choice of sports changed. Soft ball is no longer considered a women's game and there are both male and female leagues that are considered to be very competitive. Soccer was organized in the high schools in the 1960s and now has both male and female teams that play throughout the county. Today sports events are organized by the Boys' Club, Girls' Club, YMCA, Catholic Youth Club, in addition to high school teams. The programs do not compete for membership I was told, but rather, provide a segmented division that raises competition to a community-wide base. The YMCA director explained the difference between their program and that of the Boys' Club: 'They shoot with a shotgun at their clientele; a shotgun makes a broad range. The YMCA is more of a rifle approach. We're after a concern, a task, and we aim for that group and we deal with it'. In their sports training, the directors try to instil values of sportsmanship, fair play and competitive aggression: 'We try to balance the most complete fitness center with the fact that you have to make a complete person. And that's our goal, to put the spirit, mind and body in one person and take him to the top,' the YMCA director told us.

The presence of three large and active organizations directed at inculcating sportsmanlike values in male youths is not fortuitous. It is the overt expression of deep underlying values supported by most members of the community, regardless of their class. Lower-class youths 'without guidance at home' were feared since it was felt that they would become delinquent or at best ruffians if they did not have such guidance. Alumni of the Boys' Club, that tended to serve more of the lower-class youths lacking what was felt to be the proper parental role-model, often attribute their success in life to the Boys' Club. The Girls' Club was not organized until a quarter century later and it does not have nearly the level of sports facilities of the boys. However their competitions and those of the girls in public schools sometimes make front-page headlines in the local press.

The emergence of leisure-time pursuits in the post-World War II period of relative affluence can be read in the landscape surrounding the city of Pittsfield. The two lakes that used to be the sites of tannery and textile mills are now the location of yaughting clubs and camps sponsored by the Boys' and Girls' Clubs as well as the Italian–American ITAM lodge, now run by a private concession for members. A ski resort operates all year with camping and hiking in the summer and fall attracting almost as many tourists and local people in both seasons. The General Electric Athletic Association is housed in an old stone farmhouse built in 1860 in the rolling hills that used to be part of a sheep farm where wool was produced for the textile factories of the last century. In addition to the nine-hole golf course, there are courts for tennis, softball and bocci ball (an Italian game, involving rolling balls on a lawn) as well as a picnic grove. The club, organized in 1939, now sponsors a rock and roll night on Tuesdays and Fridays as well as a Saturday night dance with music of the 1940s and 1950s. This attracts age-graded groups that are visible in many other public recreational centers. Both the company and the union use the GEAA's premises for kiddies' day once a year. A quarter-century picnic for employees with 25 years or more service is entirely financed by the company and is attended by well over 1000 people. A few years ago women of the Quarter Century Club decided they wanted their event in the evening at the ITAM Lodge where they could get dressed up and enjoy themselves away from the men.

Participation in sports, whether as a spectator or player, provides the idiom for being integrated in the culture. People of all social classes and ages wear sneakers and jogging suits or running shorts in many social settings that do not involve active sports. At the same time that it signifies identification with a sporting outlook, it negates identification with occupational or ideological movements that are not part of the mainstream. In a peace demonstration in June of 1982 a group of Buddhist activists from out of town stood in front of the GE defense works with placards proclaiming their support of peace. A teenager observing the demonstration commented that she supported their cause but did not want to be identified with them because of the way they dressed. The women had long hair and wore long full skirts like the hippies of the 1960s.

This complex network of service organizations and recreational institutions is a complementary part of an anarchic mode of production in which workers and their families bear the brunt of the troughs in the business cycle. The failure of a working-class party to develop in the US can be traced to these quasi-political and economic associations where workers and managers meet in collaborative action for community-wide concerns or for their own pleasure. In the nineteenth century, as Walkowitz (1978: 3) points out, the network of working-class associations and activities promoted organizational experience that 'provides some insight into the continuing process of adaptation by which the worker community became an effectual social and political unit in industrial society'. Better wages and a shorter working day provided the material basis for a different class alliance that became symbolized in the cultural activities. Just as in Worcester, where class alliances were obliterated with the shift from bars to movie theatres (Rosenzweig, 1983), so in Pittsfield we see in the popular culture centered on sports a blurring of class divisions.

Similarly the successful mix of public and privately-funded activities carried out by the new social welfare agencies such as the Berkshire Home Care, the Women's Center and the clubs minimizes the distinction between needy and self-sufficient citizens, in contrast to the state welfare agencies. In order to be accepted as a client in the latter, you become a category excluded from the hard-working, sports-loving privatized family life-style that characterizes the citizens of this city. Except for the hard core of welfare recipients, most members of the community would rather eat catfood than go through a supermarket check-out using food stamps. This final commitment to self-sufficiency and independence is the bottom line ensuring the hegemonic position of corporate capitalism. The question I shall now raise is how viable that hegemony is in a period of recession, unemployment and loss of population.

DEINDUSTRIALIZATION AND HEGEMONIC CONTROL

The decline in employment, combined with a loss in the younger and more productive population, is putting stress on the hegemony built up over the past century in Pittsfield. When I first started working on the project in 1978 there were 8000 working in the plant, with about 3500 in the Power Transformer Division. This represented a reduction to about half of the workforce that had worked in Power Transformers before the 1969 strike. By 1984 employment had dropped to 7000 with 2000 in Power Transformers. Women were harder hit than men, in part because their interrupted work histories meant that they had fewer years of service and consequently less seniority. In October 1986 the company announced that 600 of the remaining 1700 employees would be laid off immediately and that the remaining production would be transferred to their southern plants or sold.

The responses to these changes in the leadership of management, trade unions and city government were varied yet complementary. I shall summarize what we learned in interviews with leaders in these sectors.

General Electric management

Just as General Electric had institutionalized the role of labor relations as labor had formed a base for making claims, so had they institutionalized the role of community relations as public relations became more demanding. My requests for information were referred to this department. In the six-year period of my study, I perceived a change in the character and approach of the three successive community relations managers whom I interviewed.

In 1978 the manager of community relations was an affable, well-informed man who had come to the area in 1962 and decided to make it his home rather than seeking promotion outside. He occupied a two-room suite overlooking the Transformer Department and the slogan on the overpass, GE FIRST IN SAFETY. His secretary offered me a cup of coffee and we spent two hours talking about the industry's prospects. He spoke frankly about the uncertainty about the Power Transformer Division, given the lack of an energy program in the Carter administration and the continuing recession caused by the oil embargo. The city had already lost 7000 people, from the 60,000 population when he first came to the plant. He rejected my use of the term 'flight' to the south of middle-sized transformers, preferring to call it a 'spin-off' responding to 'the better business climate' in Shreveport, Louisiana and Rome, Georgia. This was not, he asserted, a result of lower wages – they tended to equalize over time. Rather, it was a combination of factors including lower electricity charges, fewer state regulations, and a more 'hospitable' state administration. He talked eloquently about the beauties of the Berkshires, the nature reservation near his home, and the Halloween parade in which he served as grand marshall. Started in the 1950s to avoid Halloween vandalism, it became the symbol for the presence of General Electric in the community. Hundreds of workers in Power Transformer worked for weeks making a dragon emblazoned with electric lights that stretched more than a block long.

During the summer of 1981 when Power Transformer was being written off as an unprofitable venture, 'headhunters' were invited into the GE plant during the July vacation. The director of community relations went to the highest corporate bidder, Westinghouse, along with his boss. The next time I visited the relations office, his successor was installed in a small side office. The new manager had had only one month to get acquainted with his work when I visited him and had to refer most questions to his secretary, who had 25 years' service in the company. He advised us that the firm had decided to 'limit their entry' into the transformer market since the three major producers, GE, Westinghouse and McGraw Edison, split a market which had declined from an annual growth rate of 7 or 8 per cent to 1.9 per cent. The strategy to 'scale down the business to take the fat out' was made so that a situation of 'three big guns fighting for the market' would not ensue. Unfortunately, he added, that meant reducing the number of employees. The plant then employed 7700 overall with 3000 in Power Transformer. He expected that 90 to 100 workers would leave in the next six months, and others would be moved to different departments. While salaried 'exempt' people (those who were hired on annual salaries rather than hourly wages and were not subject to government or union rules for hiring) would be found employment, he said that there was not much 'we' could do about union eligibles, adding that 'if we were to try to move them and settle them in other plants, it would be exorbitant, but we have been successful in placing a few in the transformer department of McGraw Edison.' Ordnance was expected to pick up some of the workers laid off, but that would take at least three years, he said, before Reagan's emphasis on defense would show up in the industry. The ageing workforce was a sign of attrition. In 1979 the 55 and over age group formed 29 per cent of the workforce, whereas in 1981 they formed 35.8 per cent.

When I questioned whether there had been a great deal of anxiety generated by the talk of shrinking the Power Transformer Division, he replied:

Oh sure, this is a most canny bunch of workers. At an employees meeting we laid out the whole situation. We had three meetings with questions. No one asked about management bungling. They seemed to accept the fact that when a market goes down you can't create a market when it is not there. You can't sell overseas nowadays or you're competing with other companies with lower costs of production. We have been losing a share of the market to outsiders who have come in. Our competitors have affiliated with Siemens and others who have gained a foothold in the United States.

Formerly, buyers used to favor one big supplier for all their equipment, but now they tended to spread their purchases and GE no longer benefited from the monopsonistic position they once held. This reasoning left out of the equation one of the factors that I had learned from union leaders. Power Transformer Division was making a profit, but not nearly at the level of other divisions, particularly Ordnance and other high-tech products favored by the Board of Directors.

I asked what plans GE had to ease the transition, and he replied:

I don't think the business is going out – just cutting down to a breakeven point . . . You will hear the mayor say that GE owes the city. We think the city owes GE. We had a payroll of $190 million. It was felt that it was more humane to place as many people as it could and try to trim the business to make it. Everyone describes the love-hate relationship with the community. Sometimes GE is described as a villain, but with the Good Neighbor Fund, GE gave $470,000 – 47 per cent of the million dollar drive.

A year later I returned to visit his successor who replaced him when he was sent to an overseas plant. Power Transformer was now down to 2200 employees. The laid-off workers we had interviewed were mostly young men and a few women with short service records. The new relations manager raised the issue we had heard discussed in the union about threats of withdrawal if productivity did not increase. He was very emphatic in denying this:

To my way of thinking, that would be unfair labor practices to say that if we can't get what we want, we will not operate the plant. It is not, however, illegal to state business realities. It is a fact that transformers are not doing well and that we have been losing money on them. But we are not Chrysler. They went to the other step, but GE would not be in that position.

The new director showed his mastery of 'rule number one' in co-opting the adversaries' position, asserting that the clause requiring at least six months' advance notice of plant closure won in the last contract was 'a positive gain made in open communication about the corporation's plant'. In fact, the corporation had fought that clause, according to the business agent of the local union. The relations director elaborated his point:

GE is not unwilling to communicate. Corporations are not human entities but they are entities none the less and do have moral responsibilities. GE has a high moral caliber; we would not simply close down over the weekend [this was an allusion to a statement I had made to a small electronic shop in the neighboring town that had left a sign on their door for the employees coming to work on a Monday morning reading, 'Gone to Jamaica.'] GE can't go to Jamaica and hide.

He summed up his view of community relations as follows:

Well, I'm looking at this through a one-year window, but I see the relations with the community are superb, especially with the political leadership and the human social sector leadership . . . I have heard stories of the fifties when GE lobbied against the other industries coming in to the community. I can tell you that now we spend money trying to get other industries in. We can no longer afford to be Daddy Warbucks. There is a need for other industry – tourism will not do it. The technology center will bring with it small plastics molders to the Berkshires . . . The Berkshires stand a chance of being the Silicon Valley of plastics.

His one-year window was already a window on the past, since over a dozen plastics firms, headed by GE-trained technicians, had sprung up when the local plant stopped producing plastic fixtures and casings for their products two decades earlier. Mostly non-unionized, these firms pay half the wage that GE workers receive. Subcontracting work from GE as well as other firms, they may well represent the future industrialization in the US: high-tech research and development centers surrounded by small unorganized production shops.

Trade union leadership

Union leaders were not nearly as sanguine as management about the future prospects for employment. The productivity drive launched by the company in 1982 in the interest of saving the Power Transformer Division, resulted in even greater attrition of the workforce. The district council leadership of the AFL-CIO recognized the problem in its 1982 Labor Day breakfast. The keynote speaker summed it up as follows:

Part of our problem has been, and will continue to be, the fact that this prosperous nation, the people that are the movers and shakers of our society, are trying to ship our work overseas. They're taking all our technology and giving it away to other nations. If you start saying that we've got to do something about the imports, you're called a protectionist. Well, if that's what they're calling them, start calling me one now. Because we've got to start moving.

He went on to ask for support of a bill in Congress calling for an increase in the percentage of component parts that are built by Americans in any product sold in the US. In fact, this district council leader's approach was to continue the same social contract with management. He concluded his speech looking backwards more than forwards:

As we all know, the ultimate goals of labor, the American Labor Movement, is and always has been, to help bring about the healthiest, best educated, productive society that is possible for humans to achieve. I don't see anything wrong with those goals, and I say for shame on any of our elected officials who do not rally behind us.

In summing up past victories of the labor movement, he mentioned Medicare (Government health care insurance for retirees), public education, OSHA (Occupational Safety and Health Administration) and Social Security. Significantly, he did not mention AFDC (Aid for families with Dependent Children), food stamps or Medicaid (Government health care insurance for independents): programs that are not based on the fiction of reciprocity towards employed workers but instead recognize and address the structural inequalities of the system.

The local business agent, noting that most of the jobs which moved out of Pittsfield to the South were the money-makers, added: 'I realize that the name of the game is profits, but I also contend that any company that plays a dominant role in the community, as General Electric does in Berkshire County, has a responsibility to the people and area both' (*Local 255 News*' 3 February 1977).

The greatest attrition in employment at the local plant has been in the ranks of union-eligible blue-collar workers, now only one-third as numerous as they were 15 years ago. The contract negotiated in July 1985 limited security coverage to paid-up members and failed to address the growing numbers of unemployed youths.

The illusion of a classless society, acted out in leisure-time pursuits and consumption, and sustained in the media, was never eradicated in the shops. Supervisory hierarchy was spelled out in numerous rituals carried out in daily routines, not the least of which was the punching of the time clock for each break from work. In the latest walkout at General Electric in June 1986, the production workers exprssed their outrage that they were selected for penalties for absenteeism, whereas engineers, supervisors and other 'ineligibles' for union membership (Nash, 1984a) were not penalized.

City officials

The proliferation of development commissions and private consulting firms in and around Pittsfield is an indication of the economic problems that the country is experiencing. Development agents within the county and city administration, as well as private organizations such as the Chamber of Commerce, are working with union and company representatives trying to attract new industries. They have developed several 'industrial parks' with state and local funds, and their target are the high-tech industries pioneered by small-scale entrepreneurs. The stated goals were those of internal growth, disbursement of state backed loans, or bonds, for existing manufacturing establishments and promotion of a diversified industrial base. Left unstated is the expectation that these industries will be small-scale unorganized shops. The owner of a small greetings card company that set up business in a renovated state school complained to the city council when his workers threatened to unionize that he could not stay in business if this happened. As for the unions, survival rather than growth dominates their outlook. There is no movement towards worker takeovers in divisions threatened with closure. Only one voice was raised in the City Council calling for employee operation of the GE Gynal Plastics Department when that was closed in December 1982, and no one took up the suggestion when 300 workers were laid off. When a state representative appealed to the Chairman of the Board of General Electric, John F. Welch, to bring in new consumer production lines to reverse the trend towards Ordnance production in 1985 when 600 layoffs were threatened, he was refused. Because of Pittsfield's relatively high wage levels, the presence of what is considered a strong union and an anti-business climate, the only growth at GE will be in the Ordnance Department on government defense contracts.

The mayor denied that reputation in his speech to the assembled trade union leaders on Labour Day:

One thing we have in Pittsfield is a stigma that we are anti-business. We have a great deal of difficulty bringing in new industry and expansion of business in Pittsfield.

When General Electric decided to build its new plastics technology research and development center in the city, he became more optimistic, anticipating that:

People will be coming from all over the United States, working with General Electric. They'll be spending their dollars here, they'll be staying here, they'll get news of our city out when they find out what a great place this is, and it may induce some other manufacturing concerns to decide to come up here too.

The mayor called for approval of an ordinance giving General Electric the right to build the plastics center, and there were few restrictions placed on their use of the site. People who lived in the vicinity of the plant and who raised questions about the potentially toxic waste discharges in the city council hearing were quickly silenced. Little effort has been made to assess the existing pollution to waterways and even the ground water in the city resulting from the years of accumulated polychlorinated biphenyls flushed into the lake bordering the General Electric main building (Nash and Kirsch, 1986). The mayor also succeeded in gaining a tax abatement for the Corporation, reducing their bill from $1.69 million to $874,000. This caused homeowners to bear 62.5 per cent of the total bill compared to 60 per cent formerly (*The Berkshire Eagle*, 14 March 1983). These actions follow national trends as corporations pay less and less of the tax bill while individuals pick up the balance. The tax reductions came in a year when GE's international after tax profits were at a record high of $438 million, up 10 per cent in 1982 over the previous year (*Fortune* 1983). In the same year, the chairman of the Board of General Electric was paid $1,018,330, an 18 per cent salary increase over the past year.

The decline in heavy industry (except for armaments) is taken as inevitable. In our interviews with 100 employed and laid-off workers at the General Electric plant, 16 claimed not to know what could be done to solve the problems of unemployment: 'If I knew, I'd be president,' one responded, implying that thinking about solutions was not the job of workers. Only six thought that government initiatives could bring about improvement and another three approved of training programs and public works. Eleven thought that increasing productivity on the job would make American products more competitive and six blamed inefficient management, calling for a reduction in their numbers: 'Too many chiefs and not enough Indians!' four people remarked independently when asked the source of the problem. Eight wanted to see a reduction in foreign imports, but only two saw the problem as a result of corporate investment overseas and felt that that should be restricted. Limited support for lower taxes, anti-inflation measures, increasing unemployment benefit was more than matched by nine calls for more industry with no attempt to state how that should be promoted. The feeling of hopelessness mentioned by six respondents was most poignantly expressed by one who said: 'I don't know what to think any more. Everything is in a turmoil. As an individual like myself, I can't do anything.' Only two expressed anything with a hint of class consciousness: 'Give the country back to the people! Big business runs the country and companies tell Reagan or Kennedy what to do.' And another said: 'They let the corporations gobble up one company after another. That's what's wrong!' But none sees unions as a counter to corporations, although several criticized the lack of local initiatives possible in the framework of union control.

CONCLUSIONS

Corporate hegemony is still a reference point for planning and development for the future. Workers are not yet completely disillusioned with corporate control nor do they entertain any illusions that they can take control of decision-making. The acceptance of market principles by workers as well as managers means that they accept the company's appeals to decreased demands for the product they make as justification for most decisions. None of the workers in this city has expressed any interest in worker control or ownership of production. The most striking effort in this direction has been the formation of small plastics companies by technicians who were laid off at General Electric. Far from being an alternative to corporate domination of production, these small, low-cost producers reinforce hegemony of monopoly producers and reproduce the commitment to private capital.

Community leaders have sought to make up for the loss of jobs in the corporation by 'selling' the town to new enterprises. This marketing effort has not been challenged by the unions despite the fact that most of the industries attracted have not been unionized. As yet, the unions have not offered a visible alternative to corporate and community programs for attracting new industries by offering tax rebates and free construction of access roads, sewerage and pipelines as well as electricity supply in the new industrial parks. A kind of welfare for capitalist enterprises has replaced welfare capitalism in reversing the public subsidies to maintain industry in the city.

The success of the corporations in 'harmonizing' their interests with those of the community has minimized the discontent in the present round of disinvestment in peacetime production. Yet this accommodation has a limited life span. The hegemony constructed out of the workers' own efforts to find a place for themselves in industrial society requires, on the part of corporations, at least a commitment to a place and to people who will work in production. With more lucrative investments overseas, and with the prospect of fully automated plants in the US, the corporation does not think they need consider any claims made on them. A 1982 Supreme Court ruling permitting corporations to ignore union contracts when they close down any one of their plants will accelerate their withdrawal from old industrial centers. Workers cling to these past commitments not out of false consciousness, but out of a sense of their own construction of that social contract. The 'harmonizing' (to borrow a term from Owen D. Young, Chairman of the Board of General Electric in the 1920s, cited in Schatz

1983: 15) of the relationship between labor and management was achieved through many cultural adaptations that equated General Electricalism with Americanism. These adaptations of sex segregation on and off the job, of preferential hiring of men at higher wages reinforcing patriarchy in the home, and of competitive vigor played out in sports competition and in the market-place are now beginning to break down. The negation of class division sustained in the sports arena and in the lifestyle associated with it is questioned as the gap between rich and poor grows. For the working people of the county, two wage-earners are needed to maintain the living standards they have grown accustomed to. It is the single heads of families – usually women in the secondary labor force – who are the most militant labor activists since they are unable to support a family on their wages.

By evading the labor unions that have succeeded in redistributing some of the gains from industry, and by eliminating jobs through overseas investment and automation, management is destroying the basis for their own hegemonic control, a control fashioned from the struggles of workers.

REFERENCES

Benedict, Ruth (1959) *Patterns of Culture*, New York: New York American Library.
Bluestone, Barry and Bennet Harrison (1982) *The Deindustrialization of America: Plant Closings, Community Abandonment, and the Dismantling of Basic Industry*, New York: Basic Books.
Boulware, Lemuel C. (1969) *The Truth about Boulwarism*, Washington, D.C.; Bureau of National Affairs.
Drucker, P. (1953) *The Practice of Management*, New York, Harper and Brothers.
Gramsci, Antonio (1973) *Selections from the Prison Notebooks of Antonio Gramsci*, edited and translated by Quintin Hoare and Geoffrey Nowell Smith, New York: International Publishers.
Gutman, Herbert (1976) *Work, Culture and Society in Industrializing America*, New York: Knopf.
Matles, J. J. and J. Higgins (1974) *Them and Us: Struggles of a Rank and File Union*, Englewood Cliffs, N.J.: Prentice-Hall.
Montgomery, David (1979) *Workers' Control in America*, Cambridge: Cambridge University Press.
Nash, June (1984a) 'Segmentation of the work process in the international division of labour'. In Steven E. Sanderson (ed.), *The Americas in the New International Division of Labor*, New York: Holmes and Meier.
—— (1984b) 'Impact of world-wide restructuring of industry on a New England industrial city'. In C. Bergquist (ed.), *Labor Systems and Labor Movements in the World Capitalist Economy*. Beverly Hills' Cal.; Sage.
Nash, June, and Max Kirsch (1986) 'Polychlorinated biphenyls in the electrical machinery industry: An ethnological study of community action and corporate responsibility', *Social Science and Medicine. An International Journal, Special Issue: Toward a Critical Medical Anthropology*, ed. P. J. M. McEwan.

Rosenzweig, Roy (1983) *Eight Hours for What We Will: Work and Leisure in an Industrial City 1870–1920*, New York: Cambridge University Press.

Schatz, Ronald (1975) 'The end of corporate liberalism, class struggle in the electrical manufacturing industry, 1933–1950', *Radical America* 9, 4–5: 187–205.

—— (1983) *The Electrical Workers: A History of General Electric and Westinghouse 1923–60*, Urbana and Chicago: University of Illinois Press.

Walkowitz, Daniel J. (1978) *Worker City, Company Town: Iron and Cotton Worker Protest in Troy and Cohoes, New York 1855–84*, Urbana: University of Illinois Press.

Williams, Gwynn A. 1960 'Gramsci's concept of egemonia', *Journal of the History of Ideas*, 21:586–99.

14

Urban Survival Strategies, Family Structure and Informal Practices

Enzo Mingione

INTRODUCTION

Since the mid-sixties there has been a long period of social transition characterized by major structural changes and by persistent socio-economic crisis. The greater attention paid to the latter has often limited the understanding of the former. The employment crisis, the fiscal crisis, and the growing political instability, even deindustrialization and industrial restructuring, have often been explained with exclusive reference to the economic recession. Even now, in the industrialized countries, expectations of a return to the halcyon day of the early sixties spring from every slight increase in the economic growth rate. We do not know if and for whom the future will be golden but what is certain is that the broad socio-economic and political consequences and characteristics of economic growth will be radically different from the fifties and sixties. Irreversible structural changes have taken place and must now be taken into account. Within this framework in the last decade many social scientists have begun to work on this hypothesis: they have critically discussed and renewed their methodologies; they have devoted increasing attention to forgotten or new aspects of industrial development in different socio-historical situations.[1] The purpose of this paper will be to analyse the possible consequences of the combination of two structural changes: the increasing importance even in the industrialized countries of non-formal market inputs to economic survival (which for simplicity I call *informalization*); and the increasing importance of *local* conditions, as they are reshaped and embedded in different rates and characteristics of the informalization process, among other structural changes.

To deal with such a complex problem either in general or in terms of specific surveys, it is necessary to discuss some important methodological criteria. Basically we need a theoretical/analytical framework in order to evaluate the different inputs for survival, combined with specific modes of reproduction of the labour force, and to link the different mixes to industrial development. I have already dealt with this problem in two previous papers (Mingione, 1983; 1985), and in consequence here I shall describe only the main lines of the solution adopted.

The starting point is to consider the different meanings of the wide range of resources which contribute to the survival of households, i.e. the reproduction mixes. We distinguish between internal resources – deriving from the households themselves – and external resources – contributed by the state, community, friends, churches and extended family network. In both classes we can distinguish between monetary resources gained in the formal market, monetary resources gained and contributed outside the formal market (informal in the strict sense or traditional monetary economies) and non-monetary resources in kind or activity for direct consumption. We arrive at the descriptive table proposed in table 14.1.

TABLE 14.1   *Classification of survival resources entering the reproduction mix of households*

	Internal: produced by the households themselves	External: contributed by the state extended family, friends, self-help networks
Formal market monetary resources	Income deriving from various forms of formal employment (1)	State income subsidies Inheritances Formal donations and gifts Other formal subsidies (2)
Monetary resources deriving from outside the formal market	Income deriving from various forms of informal or traditional employment activities (3)	Informal donations, loans, subsidies Gifts Exchanges of work (4)
Non-monetary resources	Domestic activities Work for self-consumption and do-it-yourself Self-service (5)	State services Donations in work for direct consumption or in kind directly produced by the donors Free communal assistance (6)

The main assumptions embedded in my interpretative approach are the following:

1 (1) may be the principal source of survival resources in an industrialized network, as it is considered by conventional economic or employment studies, but, as the other sources are complementary, they should also be taken into consideration and these are various cases where (1) does not appear or has a very minor impact in the mix.

2 Level (1) fixes the direct monetary cost of subsistence at formal market prices, i.e. it fixes the historical cost of labour and, *at the same time,* the capacity of expenditure of households (aggregate demand) which means that the higher the level of (1) the higher the cost of labour and the aggregate demand (market expansion).

3 Level (2) directly complements level (1) in terms of formal market monetary resources: it indirectly increases the cost of labour, through state expenditure for example, and directly increases the aggregate demand.

4 (3) and (4) contribute monetary resources so that they are both concerned in the formation of the costs of labour – (3) directly and (4) indirectly – and of the aggregate demand but they escape the control of the formal market and of the state with the result that prices, costs and taxation rates are different, and this gives rise to fundamental problem due to the fact that a process of informalization is now in motion.

5 (5) and (6) are the loci of unpaid work. Both, but principally (5), are fundamental survival resources and have been wrongly overlooked in traditional analysis. (5) mainly, complemented by (6), is to a certain extent related to (1) and (2) in the sense that insufficient income may be complemented by long hours of self-consumption/domestic activities or by contributions from the community, family, friends, state assistance, in kind or work. But this complementary relation varies a great deal in time and place and in different income groups. In fact the modes of provision of domestic and self-consumption goods and services can vary greatly according to the technologies available, their costs, the possibility of investment in durables which increase productivity, the quantity and quality of the output, the organization and division of labour within this section (see Mingione, 1985; Gershuny and Miles, 1983; Burns, 1977).

6 I have also assumed that the distinction between formal and informal is possible and applicable only when and where the economic organization is relatively regulated in terms of state, corporation and union control. In this sense we can note an historical process of regulation tending to register, standardize, tax, set professional standards and rules for an increasing number of human economic activities which has progressively involved every monetary transaction and tends to impose control also over an increasing number of non-monetary transactions (the contemporary

trends of family legislation, for instance). The historical process is not linear (the more a country is 'advanced' the more it is regulated) and many underdeveloped countries practise a relatively high level of regulation, but we can trace a clear demarcation between early industrialization in the now developed countris (very low level of regulation) and the later stages of industrial development on a world scale in which the level of regulation grows higher.

The term 'formalization' has been avoided in order to emphasize the fact that the regulation process is *not* the opposite of informalization: the two are closely connected and may easily proceed in the same direction, i.e. the more an economy is highly regulated the more it becomes convenient to practise informal patterns and, on the contrary, a deregulating pattern usually produces a certain degree of return to the formal sector of previously informal practices.[2]

7 The history of industrial development has been interpreted as a continuous shift towards the increase of (1) (which initially incorporated also (3)). But this shift has been far from simple and linear.[3]

The shift has involved tremendous social changes in terms of economic growth, patterns and rates of employment, distribution and levels of income, quality of life, but they have been unevenly distributed between the social classes and regions.

In this paper I shall not deal with the past transformations but shall assume that industrial development has been based also on fundamental changes in modes of survival and quality of life which had tremendous feedback effects on industrial development itself, even though these relationships have often been underestimated and relatively ignored.

RESTRUCTURING AND INFORMALIZATION: DIFFICULT INTERPRETATIONS OF A COMPLEX REALITY

The present social changes which run in the direction of more activities for direct self-consumption, more communal and more informal work, represent a wide range of activities taking place in different situations and, what is more important, they have been interpreted in different ways.

The most important distinction is whether informalization tendencies are interpreted as long-lasting transformations or as temporary consequences of the economic and social crisis. The first solution is more persuasive. It is true that long and deep-seated economic crises typically produce an increase in self-employment, and irregular or seasonal work, and a return to traditional/local market/extra-market activities as a consequence of high unemployment. But the present employment problems are not only a consequence of the economic downturn and slow growth. Automation and industrial restructuring and relocation appear to reduce, in the long run to an increasing degree, the levels (in terms either of duration or of number) of formal employment in industrialized areas; more so when the rate of investment in technological change and restructuring tends to increase (see Jallade, 1981; O'Connor, 1984).

There are a number of structural interpretations of the diffusion of informal activities and they differ according to differences of emphasis and with regard to particular or local aspects of a very complex phenomenon.

Four lines of interpretation are worth discussing.

First, the maximum emphasis on technological change in industrialized societies as the most important factor of a new wave of socio-economic development is represented by Gershuny's *social innovation* thesis (technological changes affecting the modes of provision of mass-consumption services) (Gershuny, 1978, 1983; Gershuny and Miles, 1983). This author argues that new technologies provide the means for increasing final self and informal provision of services (e.g. education through video tapes or computer terminals either individually or in informal community groups). This interpretation underestimates various aspects of the present social change: (1) the consequences of the uneven class and geographical diffusion of advanced technologies; (2) the exploitative use of informalization and technological change through corporation restructuring; (3) the critical feedback of this transformation in terms of underconsumption (through increased unemployment or underemployment or job shifts and restructuring). An opposite emphasis on technological changes (pessimistic/monitory instead of optimistic) has been put forward by Castells (1983, 1984, 1985). This author underlines the exploitative consequences and the loneliness, isolation and further individualization potentials of the technological transformation.

A second set of interpretations has been developed starting from Schumaker's thesis that 'small is beautiful' (1977). Informalization is seen as an alternative way of producing and surviving to the suffocating and alienating control of the corporations and the state (Heinze and Olk, 1982; Szelenyi, 1982). The potential innovative political character of some kinds of informalization is underlined but the possible 'exploitation' and indirect control relationships embodied in the expansion of the informal sector wherever it is found (Third World cities, industrializing regions, deindustrializing metropolitan areas) are underestimated.

A third set of interpretations concentrates mainly on the possibility of neodualistic *super-exploitation relations* between informalization and new developments of worldscale concentrated capitalism in terms of new forms of reproduction of cheap labour, of direct exploitation (either through the appropriation of unpaid work through self-service or through various forms of subcontracting) or of indirect exploitation (expansion of some privileged markets for do-it-yourself tools, electronic and information instruments, financial control, dismantling of state responsibility, etc.) (Bromley and Gerry, 1979; Portes and Walton, 1981). A different version of this approach can be found in authors who have studied the combination of high rates of exploitation of family work and of irregular employment (part-time, moonlighters, homework, etc.) in industrializing areas where small concerns are still prevalent (as in central and north-eastern Italy; see Bagnasco, 1977; Paci, 1980).

Finally some authors have interpreted the informal sector as a *new option of the survival strategies* of households in industrialized countries. Informalization appears to be one of the possible responses to inflation, the employment crisis, the rigidity of formal work and consumption (Ferman, Berndt and Selo, 1978; Pahl, 1980; Gershuny and Pahl, 1979). This interpretation underlines how, under certain conditions, do-it-yourself or informal solutions become not only advantageous from the economic point of view but are also the best option to get some goods or services quickly or of the required quality.

It can be easily assumed that none of these four ways of interpreting the current social transformation is wrong but that they are partial because they take into account only certain phenomena whereas the informalization process includes various different events. As Gallino points out, the informal sector is *at the same time*: '(a) a forced production of the development of late capitalist economy; (b) a free and creative social innovation choice; (c) a set of small recipes for survival; (d) a return to pre-modern social relations *with* the support of modern technologies' (1983: 87).

But it is also true that these and other structural interpretations of the present social pattern of change have a very important point in common. They express a radical change as a long-term tendency. It is no longer possible to accept the assumption that, in general, industrial development can be explained by means of an interpretative axis based on the ever-increasing importance of: (a) wage labour, differently graded and fragmented at different times; (b) organizational patterns of large manufacturing and tertiary concerns; (c) bureaucratic apparatuses pre-eminent among which is the nation–state. Informalization, peripheral or diffused industrialization (based on small and/or subcontracting concerns), the increase of chronic new forms of inactivity, unemployment and underemployment, the fiscal crisis of the state have dismantled the strongholds of practically every important interpretative approach of industrial development (with the exception of the one adopted by Polanyi, 1944, which for the same reasons has returned to fashion recently after having being nearly forgotten for three decades).

The collapse of this interpretative axis (which had worked quite well as an approximate reducer of social complexities) gives rise to interpretative difficulties but also to the discovery or rediscovery of important characteristics of current societies.

Apart from the question of the variety of working and survival strategies, among which the problem of the informal sector is crucial, this interpretative revision has other important consequences. For instance in our field it is interesting to mention two positions. Pahl (1984, 1985, 1986) stresses the importance of basing the sociological evaluation of stratification, political and social behaviour, marginalization processes, structuring of diversified life-styles on household/family structure and strategies, rather than on the profession and income of the breadwinner.[4] Dagnasoo (1985, 1986) stresses that the recent processes of diffused/peripheral industrialization (based mainly on small concerns and on subcontracting) and economic restructuring have meant an important reshaping of the equilibrium between different criteria of resource distribution. He identifies the four most important: reciprocity, the invisible hand of the market, organization of large concerns, and political exchange. The tendency of the last two to prevail has been weakened by a rigidity crisis and the first two have gained renewed importance, although in very different conditions to the historical ones where these criteria were dominant in the past. Informalization in a broad sense can be seen as an important symptom of this redefinition of the criteria of redistribution of resources both on a local and general scale.

It is now clearer that our problem has two themes. The first relates to the current real processes of social change, and the second to the capacity of social scientists to understand and make sense of these changes in complex societies where the interpretative reduction of complexities is at the same time extremely difficult and necessary.

As to the first aspect, it is clear that various kinds of informalization constitute only partial aspects of the global face of social change. Consequently they can only be explained by starting from an understanding of the more general logic of the new international division of labour, of working and economic restructuring processes – the combination of new patterns of financial concentration with decentralization, segmentation, subcontracting of working processes; the persistence and increase of unequal distribution of work, both in quantitative and qualitative terms, between age, gender, ethnic, social/geographical/professional groups, of new forms of marginalization and social promotion of different social strata. This connection explains both the variety of informalization processes and the possibility of interpreting them differently from different angles. From the opposite point of view it also explains why the debate on the informal sector and activities has become so fashionable and important, as this is a crucial aspect of the global restructuring of societies in different ways.

The second theme can be synthesized in the following way. Social scientists are having great difficulty in interpreting current social change as they have had to abandon the theoretical axis used with some success in the last 200 years. Among other phenomena, the informalization tendencies do not fit the interpretative models traditionally used to explain industrial development (for instance, the Weberian model of 'rationalization'; or the Marxist model of capital accumulation and concentration).

To schematize this interpretative difficulty, I have constructed figure 14.1 to stress both the complexity and variety of social networks where broadly

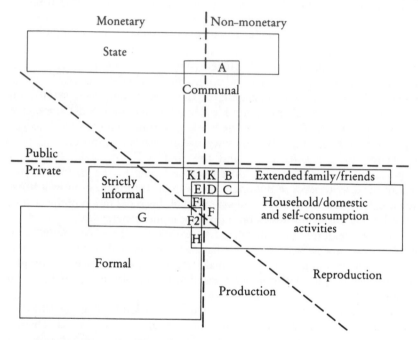

A = The state provide resources to promote communal activities; i.e. money, seats, capital to organize cultural or welfare voluntary local activities.
B = The base for communal activities is implemented by extended families or groups of friends.
C = Example: Childcare organized on a communal basis, where parents contribute to a rota of voluntary work.
D = As C, but some parents do not contribute their time but exchange with others in kind.
E = As C, but parents pay cash to some non-formally employed to look after their children.
F = Example: part of the production of an allotment is sold for cash to neighbors (F1), or to a shop (F2), or is exchanged for other services or goods (F).
G = Moonlighting or irregular work in a formal unit; unregistered income deriving from formal activities; subcontracting between a formal unit and an informal one, etc.
H = As F, but the production is sold officially (registered sale).
K = Communal activities utilizing informal work either paid in cash (K1) or in kind (K).

FIGURE 14.1 Subsistence resources network: overlapping areas; dualist interpretation intersections; broad informal areas

informal activities take place, and the fact that the most important dualistic reductions utilized to explain and simplify social reality no longer serve to explain the informalization processes.

Figure 14.1 hypothesizes three assumptions:

1 That there are approximately four areas of social relations which are involved in the informal sector broadly considered: the communal, the extended family and friends; the household; the strictly informal sector (irregular or illegal activities carried out to earn a cash income or other advantages); of which only the last is totally included in the broad informal concept;

2 that there are large areas in which the different networks overlap;

3 that the broad informal area is divided into two parts by the three most important dual interpretative differentiations of modern socities; monetary/non-monetary (commodification versus decommodification); public/private; production/reproduction.

Points 1 and 2 reflect the variety and complexity of the diffusion of the so-called informal activities. Point 3 expresses the difficulty of giving a clearcut meaning to a generally identified informalization process at least with regard to these three important dual divisions. The point is that the expansion of the broad informal system cannot be interpreted immediately as a decommodi-fication process (transformation from monetary to less monetary or non-monetary) or as a privatization process (shift from public to private concerns), or as an expansion of the reproduction area as opposed to the production area.

Starting with the acknowledgement that it is practically impossible to understand the informalization processes with the help of traditional binary/dualistic interpretative schema, it seems useful to deal with the problem using a totally different selection approach, that is to say, by successfully isolating limited sub-problems where it is relatively easy to make a reasonably acceptable point concerning the current social transformations. The problematic area selected in this paper relates to the social impact of various kinds of informalization, broadly intended, on life-style and the division of labour of different types of families/households in the industrial-ized world. The working hypothesis used here is that new important social handicaps are emerging to penalize social groups which are already weak and marginalized. The cross-analysis of the main restructuring trends of the economy and of the working processes and strategies with the most important changes in the family/household structure also reveals that these penalized areas are tending to increase.

This approach is deliberately intended to be limited and ignores crucial problems concerning the informalization processes. There are two main areas which are insufficiently considered. The first concerns the change in the economic cycle, i.e. the relation between formal and informal activities, the detailed impact of the restructuring of the working processes in different sectors and localities, the relation between financial concentration tendencies and segmented structuring of productive activities, broadly intended, and so on. The second relates to political balances and to the reshaping of the welfare state programs, i.e. the specific combination of provision of social services by the state and local authorities, the official market and various forms of self- and informal provisions, the last including new and old solidarity networks. Due to space limitation it has been necessary to postpone to future contributions the direct specific analysis of these problems using the same interpretative selective approach.

INFORMALIZATION AND THE FAMILY

It is necessary, first, to clarify the use I shall make of three terms: household, family and extended family. It is quite clear what I mean by household. While a family is always a household, a household can also consist of unrelated persons living together, or people living alone. Thus by family I mean two or more related people living together. By extended family, I mean two or more related people living in different households. It is also important to mention preliminarily some important current characteristics, and changes relating to the present households, family and extended family structure, in part independently of the informalization process. A first group of events relates to the number and demographic structure of families and households and consequently to a different access to resources and different internal divisions of labour. A second group of events relates to the access to the formal labour market of the different sexes, ethnic and age groups. Finally, the geographical mobility of families/households and its character also influence access to certain survival resources. Some important changes in the social structure of households and families are taking place in industrialized countries, although with different intensities and at different rates. The following points are largely confirmed by recent data.[5] Moreover, these trends are more radical in more advanced countries and regions and in large cities where it is likely that technological do-it-yourself and informal activities are becoming diffused faster.

1 An increase of single person or couple households: this tendency is occurring at different rates and times in practically every industrialized country in consequence of various factors, whether demographic (mainly the increased percentage of old people and aged females surviving their husbands, and the decline of the birth-rate), sociological (possible

increase of the divorce rate and decrease of the marriage rate), economic (increased economic opportunities for working females, increase in the minimum pension and welfare provisions). This tendency may in part be counterbalanced by 5, below.

2 Decrease of very large households due to the dismantling of inter-generational households and to the decreased birth-rate.

3 Increase in the number of households and families headed by a female with or, more often, without the presence of an adult male for the reasons given in 1, above.

4 Increase of the participation rate of women in the formal employment structure, particularly of married women. This process is very differently distributed geographically because it depends on the local labour markets and on the local culture and traditions, which makes it difficult to draw general conclusions.

5 Decrease in the employment rate of the younger age groups due to high unemployment and to a longer education period. As to the latter, this tendency will have a negligible effect on the household family structure (except as regards the amount of resources needed) in countries where a residential tertiary educational system exists, and a great effect where it does not exist.

6 Finally, the increasing geographic mobility of family households creates a number of handicaps in both emigration and immigration areas as it reduces some survival resources (mainly communal, extended family, friends networks) from the instable groups to various degrees.

From these six points it can be argued that the picture from the point of view of the household/family is becoming more articulated and differentiated with the result that it is difficult to grasp clearly the interplay of various handicaps and advantages. This can be explained by means of some simple illustrations. While it may be true that single or couple households need fewer total resources to survive, it is also true that they need greater per capita resources, and that often they are penalized as regards access to certain resources. If they have additional handicaps due to gender, age, physical disability, lack of support from extended family or community (because e.g. they have moved recently) they may face very serious survival difficulties. As small households either do not or are unlikely to find positive or negative counterbalances to handicaps or advantages, they tend to be polarized into very poor and very rich depending mainly on the income level of the wage-earner.

The family/household structure, as modified by the various events described above, as well as by the secular commodification process (dismantling of the internal productive capacities of the household) and by the more recent crisis of the welfare state (decrease of the quality/quantity of per capita services offered by the state) is especially affected by the impact of informalization in two directions: the development of self-service/do-it-yourself activities; the reproductive needs created by the diffusion of different forms of informal (strictly speaking) and neo-communal activities. Both developments affect the household/family structure in two ways: they modify the survival strategies, perspectives, potentials and they affect the internal division of labour (where this is the case) between sexes and age groups.

The first general impression is that the broad informalization process, by pushing exactly in the opposite direction to the tendencies mentioned above, creates tremendous incongruences and difficulties in the family/households system. This impression is often confirmed by more specific considerations and special surveys.

Let us first consider briefly the consequences of informalization as far as the survival strategies of the households are concerned. The spread of strictly informal and neo-communal activities will be considered under two different headings: the possibilities of being active in and the consequences of informal consumption. Activities in the informal/neo-communal complex system have consequences in the household/family relations (reproduction/ survival strategies) in general for two reasons: (1) problems caused by the time/income ratio: (2) intra-household organizational problems caused by the possible discontinuity or other special characteristics of informal/neo-communal activities.

If we assume that, in general, the working time/income ratio in the informal sector is lower than average and may be totally uncontrolled by the legal system, so that the working time may reach very high maximum limits, we have to concede that, in order to survive either partially or totally at the same historical average level as formal workers' households, survival strategies would have to be based either on long hours in informal activities, on additional contributions of self-consumption activities, complementary contributions of extra-household income either in kind or in work, or, as is often the case, on a mix of these three conditions. For this reason active involvement in the informal sector is easier for relatively large households and for households which are sociologically and geographically stable. Stability is also called for by the fact that informal activities are often connected with a solid network (neighbourhood, networks of friends, communal, large, extended family) which fails to be established when the local society is characterized by high turnover and mobility (Foudi et al., 1981).

In any case, the survival strategy of the family becomes very complicated and difficult, either based on very long hours of informal work or on very long hours of domestic work. The surveys on southern (Mingione, 1985) and central north-eastern Italy (Paci, 1980) tend to confirm this point: the informal workers with above-average income work more than 60 hours per week; the others survive with a very low and irregular cash income because domestic work exceeds 60 hours per week in medium-sized households (3 persons) and 75 hours in large households (more than 5 persons).

Often the problem becomes more complicated because of the irregularity of informal activities. Seasonal or other periodical downturns or upturns complicate the organizational patterns of households actively involved in the informal sector. This possibility creates greater difficulties for households with only one wage-earner involved in irregular informal work.

The neo-communal informalization creates similar problems. It works in favour of stable, medium-sized and standard households, to the disadvantage of outsiders, latecomers, small, unstable or unorthodox households. We can give a very simple example: a group of parents organize a communal system of child-minding. Single householders and others without children will be excluded and may eventually suffer from not being involved in the network developed by the initiative. Newcomers may find it difficult to gain admittance as the activities have been organized without their contribution. Departing families will suffer if, as is likely, they have to reorganize themselves completely in the new place of residence. Large households with other problems (aged or handicapped members, for instance) will find it difficult to be involved to the same extent as the other participants and may eventually find themselves isolated.

Similar problems can easily be found with regard to informal consumption. Newcomers, unstable and small households will not have the necessary information and easy access to the network (Ferman, Berndt and Selo, 1978; Mingione, 1985). If and where informal consumption signifies a considerable saving, ease or difficulty of access can constitute an important source of discrimination. There is some evidence that on the consumption front middle- and high-income groups benefit more than low- income groups, which are more unstable and have less time and resources to enable them to become involved in the informal network (Pahl, 1984).

The expansion of self-service, do-it-yourself and other work for self-consumption have even more paradoxical effects on the household/family structure. This kind of informalization is generally based on the capacity of a household to invest an increasing part of its income in the purchase of durables which increase marginal productivity (and consequently decrease the cost and/or increase the quality of some services and goods, which are then produced for the direct consumption of the household). This activity is both time- and money-consuming, although it can make for savings in the long run. It is evident that this transformation is to the advantage of relatively large (and to the disadvantage of small) households. The latter will be involved much more for symbolic/status reasons than for economic convenience, and only when they have a sufficient income to enter into the game. The idea that the 'innovation' of self-service based on relatively advanced technological domestic equipment also helps the poor or long-term unemployed manual workers to survive is often mistaken (evidence from various surveys: Foudi et al., 1981; Pahl, 1984; Wallace and Pahl, 1985; Mingione, 1985).

The overall picture is that survival strategies become more varied and complex as a result of broad informalization transformations, which probably also discriminate against some social groups and some forms of households. Furthermore, they transfer to the household/family structure responsibilities which they themselves, at least in the form into which they were transformed by other recent events, are not prepared to bear. But the picture becomes even more problematic if we take into account the internal division of labour within the household.

From this point of view it is important to understand how informal, neo-communal and self-consumption activities are divided in terms of gender and age, compared with the formal employment divisions, in the context of household/family organization. The general assumption that strictly informal jobs are done mainly by women, the young and the aged is often mistaken. On the contrary, there are kinds of informal work which are done almost exclusively by adult males; as in the case of moonlighting (at least in Italy and the United States, for which we have sufficient evidence: Miller, 1972; Michelotti, 1975; Clutterbuck, 1979; Gallino, 1982; Ragone, 1983; Reyneri, 1984; Paci, 1985). There are other kinds of informal activities which are carried out almost exclusively by females, such as out-work; others again which are commonly carried out by young or aged persons and some which involve every household member, including the children and old people. Due to these differences it is possible to establish only an open and simplified set of typologies.

1 Formally employed male 'moonlighters' + various numbers of non-employed (for various reasons moonlighter household are less likely to include other employed members unless the household is relatively large).

2 Formally employed males + informally employed females and (older) children.

3 Formally employed males + informally employed young or aged persons and (sometimes) other members. The presence (A) or absence of a full-time housewife may constitute an important distinction.

4 Informally employed males or females (A) and other non-employed members where, especially in the case of informally employed males, it may be important to distinguish between the presence (B) or absence of a full-time housewife.

5 Two or more informally employed members involved in the same informal business (the presence of a full-time housewife completely uninvolved in the family informal business is unlikely).

6 Two or more informally employed members involved in different non-family informal businesses. Here again the presence (A) or absence of a full-time housewife makes a difference.

The types generally considered more common, although with variations according to area, are 1, 2, 3(A), 4(A and B), 5 (particularly common in areas of peripheral industrialization) and 6(A). The range of the gender division of labour goes from the extremely radical division of 1, where the male is subject to long hours of formal and second employment while the housewife is absorbed by long hours of domestic/supportive work, to the relatively pre-modern, possibly not very discriminative but extremely time-consuming, organization of a family informal business in 5.

Two points should be made to complete the picture:

1 The lower working time/income ratio of informal activities is likely to be additional to the discriminative time/income ratio of women, young and aged so that 4(A) and 4(B) households, where the informal worker is young or a recent migrant or a member of a repressed minority or aged without a regular pension, are likely to fall below the poverty line.

2 Domestic work is largely carried out by women, even when they are employed part- or full-time or informally employed. As time consumed in household domestic activities does not substantially decrease with technical innovation and household capital investments, partly because of the increased qualitative requirements of the family (see also Gershuny, 1983), the time pressure on women tends in some cases to become very great (in our typology 2, 4 and 6). In general it can be easily argued that the renegotiations of gender divisions of domestic work are slow, complicated and evade too easy rational assumptions. For instance, there is evidence that adult unemployed males are among the least likely to increase their share of domestic activities, even when their wives are in full-time employment (see Pahl, 1984; Mingione, 1985).

With the exception of case 5, which has to be studied more carefully from the point of view of the household internal organization and division of labour in the areas where it is expanding and with regard to which accurate surveys are not yet available, informalization appears to increase the discriminative patterns of the intra-household division of labour.

Type 1 households have not been studied from the point of view of the internal division of labour, but we can suggest some hypotheses. The moonlighter is usually male, middle-aged (30–50) and the only 'breadwinner' of an above-average size nuclear family – at least this is the picture given by regular surveys in the USA and by Italian empirical research. The moonlighter would thus be totally unable to help with the heavy burden of domestic activities, which are borne solely by the wife. This type appears to be a reflection of one of the present paradoxes of labour market segmentation and of unequal distribution of employment. It may be easier for a middle-aged worker to find an informal second job to complement household income than for his wife or for his adult children to find any form of formal employment. So it is not very unusual today to find in the moonlighter household, a full-time housewife and one or more unemployed persons.

The situation can be even more difficult and discriminatory in types 4 and 6, as revealed by my survey in southern Italian cities (Mingione, 1985). The housewife is oppressed by the burden of very long hours of domestic work due to the fact that the informal worker (or workers) is occupied elsewhere, either working or looking for work.

We also have evidence from studies on outworking women (Roldan, 1985) that the division of labour and household survival organization is extremely difficult in type 2. The working hours of women are very long (always more than 60 hours per week) and the family organization creates enormous tensions and internal conflicts. Although informal work (outwork in particular) and eventually part-time formal employment for women are more flexible as regards combination with daily domestic requirements, the results appear far from satisfactory and do not eliminate the gender discrimination.

Let us consider, finally, some internal division of labour changes, presumably produced by the extension of neo-communal activities and self-service of the do-it-yourself type. Most of the burden of neo-communal activities tends to fall on women, especially when they relate to care of children and the disabled and aged. This creates a very difficult situation for households in which women are already burdened by an onerous time-budget, because they are the main or the only 'breadwinner', or have the dual responsibility of domestic work and formal or informal employment, or are absorbed by exceptionally long hours of domestic work.

If we assume that there is evidence that these kinds of household are increasing fast, we can understand how problematic the expansion of neo-communal initiatives may be. In fact, either these households have to give up access to neo-communal activities or, more likely, the women accept an additional burden which makes their life nearly unbearable. The situation may become acute where neo-communal initiatives develop as a substitute for previously existing welfare state provisions, as recently suggested by Gershuny (1983). Let us give an example. A public nursery is replaced by a communal service where parents look after babies in turns of two half-days per week. In most cases the mothers will have to work eight or more additional hours per week. For the majority it will create great difficulties.

While for some (full-time formally or informally employed because they are the breadwinner or because their husbands' income is insufficient) it may be impossible. The latter will have to pay for a substitute, if possible, or look for a different solution to the baby-sitting problem. Some may be able to rely on the extended family (grandmothers) but nevertheless the change discriminates against recent migrants and mobile groups, who are in any case very likely to be the weakest or worst-off.

Self-service and do-it-yourself activities are more difficult to consider under this aspect because they transcend gender and age divisions. If anything, we tend to assume that they are carried out mostly by middle-aged males. Probably this is true for some activities: (durables, furniture, car repairs, builing and carpentry, etc.) but not in every case, and not for other services, such as clothing manufacture and repairs, gardening, food preserving, etc. Here again there is discrimination against households in which males, females, or both are overemployed in other activities (moonlighting or working long hours: full-time poor housewives, full-time employed women, etc.). Once again we find a paradox of contemporary societies: those who have the greatest need of access to do-it-yourself and self-service facilities lack the money or time. (This was very clearly revealed at various levels in my survey of southern Italian cities: Mingione, 1985.)

I should like to conclude this section with a final observation: informalization produces many difficulties in the family/household structure and does not solve the problem of poverty or insufficient income because it is combined with a persistently discriminative division of labour in society and in the household. As such, it is likely to increase the probability of family crises and to render the management of the family more difficult. Only if it is combined with radical and progressive changes in the division of labour – a decrease in formal working hours of adult men and an increase of acceptable employment opportunities for the young and women – and within the household – an increase of the contribution of adult men, improvement of some important welfare state provisions to diminish the domestic burden – could it become an acceptable way of solving survival difficulties.

INFORMALIZATION AND LOCAL DIVERSITIES

In a sense, nearly everything I have said in the previous sections points to the fact that the informalization process has served to re-evaluate some local characteristic as opposed to general and universal patterns, and that specific local conditions are becoming increasingly important. Paradoxically, this is occurring at the very time when technological progress, one of the most important factors of the informalization process, both directly and indirectly, appears to be increasingly free of local restrictions. An educated human being, shelter, a computer, a telephone line and an electricity supply are, in theory, in any place the requisites for survival perfectly integrated with the 'world society'. But what is true in theory, and also in practice for a small group of households, is not true in reality for the everyday life of billions. The 'delocalization' potential of advanced technologies combined with broad informalization can work only in one direction: the diminution of the importance of metropolitan cores in industrialized countries. And this specific use of advanced technology for 'delocalization' continues a pattern initiated not so much by technological change itself but mainly by the increasing disadvantages and high costs of congestion and concentration. With specific regard to broad informalization, it becomes more or less widespread and develops different characteristics in different localities.

Perhaps the most important condition is the relative stability of local communities. In fact, neo-communal activities, strictly informal networks and even some forms of self-help and do-it-yourself activities find a more congenial ground for expansion in stable/compact communities or eventually in new communities composed of migrants from one region or village or belonging to a specific and concentrated ethnic group. This condition has been only recently rediscovered as one of the favourable factors of the recent wave of peripheral industrialization (also based on the spread of broad informal savings) in central and north-eastern Italian regions (Bagnasco, 1977; Paci, 1980). This condition may be found in small and medium cities and in regions which have not been too deeply involved in the radical transformations of the fast industrial growth period; but also in some areas of industrial cities and metropolitan regions where the recent or earlier settlers are relatively homogeneous socially and ethnically and by regional origin. The advantages of stability in this respect – the possibility of recourse to the extended family, the persistence and continuity of neighborhood relations, community solidarity and cooperation – can be defined only by means of careful local sociological studies and can be expected to be irregularly distributed. For specific historical reasons a town may be hit by waves of outmigration while another not far distant may remain stable: a neighborhood of a large city may remain untouched by redevelopment and so relatively homogeneous while another becomes a strange mix of old and new disparate settlers. Thus, in this respect local realities may react very differently to the informalization process.

Other kinds of informalization may become more or less widespread for other socio-historical reasons, which again can be identified only by a study of the local characteristics. For example, a single-industry textile and clothing area may have been characterized, from the early industrial period until the present, by a certain degree of persistence of out-work activities, and be revitalized, also with the use of new technologies, by the impact of informalization. Old single-industry areas abandoned by the corporations may be transformed into service/tourism areas with a very high degree of informal and do-it-yourself activities.

The variety of informal developments is such that many other examples could be given. But two important points have been sufficiently demonstrated; that the degree and character of informal developments can be exemplified clearly only on a local scale. This means that the task of constructing a social geography of the expansion of various forms of informal activities on different city-scales, in different economic regions and in different urban areas is an extremely difficult one. It is, however, a task which will have to be done if we wish to understand the advantages and disadvantages of these developments for the various social groups and, more generally, to assess the socio-economic prospects of survival in 'post-industrial' (?) societies.

The very important question of how the informalization process relates to the restructuring of the state beyond the welfare age, and to government policies, has not been taken into consideration in this essay for lack of space. Here it is worth mentioning two points relating to the subject which have emerged in the course of the present analysis and may constitute the working hypothesis for its development in the direction of state/informal relations.

Informalization, broadly intended, due to its uneven diffusion, incongruencies, contradictions and potential exploitative content, cannot be considered a substitute for welfare state provisions. Thus, the neo-conservative claims can be criticized on the grounds that the combination of partial welfare dismantling and informal diffusion ends in an increasingly unevenly stratified society where a growing section of the population is marginalized and deprived even of the possibility of obtaining satisfaction with regard to their basic survival needs and citizenship rights.

Furthermore – and this is the second basic point – the uneven and exploitative nature of the informalization requires careful attention and intervention from the state to respond to its negative distributional consequences. This response, even if we assume that in the future some governments will become conscious of its importance, and be politically ready to intervene, and have the financial resources needed, is bound to be extremely difficult owing to the very nature of the informalization process (so differentiated, elusive, difficult to stimulate and control, etc.). Consequently, the confrontation between state restructuring and the requirements/contradictions of the informalization process is likely to become a very important issue in the political arena and in the research agenda of social scientists.

NOTES

1 The origins of the present interest in non-monetary or informal activities are particularly difficult to reconstruct because they are complex and non-homogeneous. The emergence of this problem has been accompanied by a renewed interest in the work of Karl Polanyi (1944, 1977). Polanyi insisted on the evidence that market/monetary transactions have only partially taken the place of

pre-industrial relations, in various ways and at different times. The 'great transformation' has not negated the 'social economy' and a large number of extra-mainstream market relations remain important for an understanding of the everyday life and economy in different situations. The recent attention dedicated to 'the social economy' (see Lowenthal, 1975; 1981) has been directly inspired by Polanyi's seminal contribution.

The form 'informal sector' was first used in anthropological or socio-economic studies on Third World cities. For a critical review of this literature, see Bromley and Gerry (1979).

Later in the late seventies (with the important anticipation of Ferman and Ferman, 1973), increasing attention was devoted to the presence of 'irregular' or 'informal' economies in the industrialized countries (Ferman et al., 1978; Gershuny and Pahl, 1979; Cornuel, 1980; Ferman and Berndt, 1981; Mingione, 1981; Bagnasco, 1981; Heinze and Olk, 1982; etc.). At the same time, increasing attention was dedicated to the expansion of the 'underground' or 'subterranean' economy (*Business Week*, 1978, 1982; Feige, 1979; Gutmann, 1977, 1978 a and b, 1979 a and b, 1980; Heertje, Allen and Cohen, 1982).

But the critical origins and background of the present wave of studies are very broad. They include the vast feminist literature on the historically changing role of women's domestic work (for the Italian case see, among others: Balbo, 1976, 1980; Bianchi, 1981; del Boca and Turvani, 1979; Ingrosso, 1979; Saraceno, 1980), the work inspired by Schumacher's (1973) idea that 'small is beautiful', the various studies on 'household economy' (for instance: Burns, 1975, 1977), and the vast literature on labour market segmentation (for instance: Edwards, Gordon and Reich, 1976, 1982; Edwards, 1979; Wilkinson, 1982).

We can find a reflection of this wave of studies in a number of international meetings (for instance the Symposium on Informal and Peripheral Activities at the Xth World Congress of Sociology, Mexico City, 1982; the European Meeting in Frascati (Rome) in November 1982) and collective publications (among which: Henry, 1981; *Inchiesta*, 1983; Redclift and Mingione, 1985).

It is important, finally, to underline the fact that this approach is connected with and leading to new interpretations of the post-industrial societies in general (for instance: Gershuny, 1978, 1983; Rosanvallon, 1981; Minc, 1982; Illich, 1981) and of class stratification, political strategies, working/surviving strategies (for instance: Accornero, 1980; Gorz, 1980, 1983; Paci, 1981; Roustang, 1982; Mingione, 1983a; Capecchi and Pesce, 1983; Pahl, 1984).

2 In this respect deregulation policies may not produce automatically the revitalization of market expansion expected by neo-conservative policy-makers but only the appearance of previously hidden but existing parts of the economy. Whether or not they flourish depends on conditions independent of the regulative system.

3 Gershuny (1983: 38), using an approach little concerned with the historical aspect of the problem, describes twelve possible transformations of the mode of provision of goods or services, i.e. changes from one to the other of the four most important productive networks: formal; household; communal; underground. If we add the state as a fifth productive pole, the possible transformations increase to twenty. I would prefer, in the context of an historical approach (also inspired by Polanyi's suggestions), to consider the twelve transformations of figure 14.2

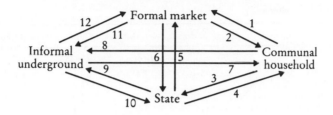

FIGURE 14.2 Twelve possible historical transformations

1 Pahl (1984, 1985, 1986) argues that social differentiation tends to become polarized in two opposite family types. The first cumulates more than one source of monetary income, various potential informal, do-it-yourself, self-service resources, the possibility of community and neighborhood solidarity. Consequently these families succeed in improving their standard of living even at difficult times of high inflation and unemployment. (The author argues that here it is also more likely that regularly employed and well-connected parents find the best possible jobs for their children.)

The opposite type accumulates all the disadvantages. Casual, poorly paid work, unemployment, underemployment, high social and geographical mobility also preclude access to the informal and community networks and leave insufficient money for the property and tools needed for do-it-yourself, self-help and new self-employed ventures. This is the group which increasingly suffers the effect of the crisis and of retrenchment of the welfare state.

5 Selective data available on Great Britain, Italy and USA confirm the trends towards a more fragmented household structure (see table 14.2). The rate of female activity increased in every country of the European Community, with the exception of Ireland (1975–7), between 1973 and 1977, as shown by Eurostat data (in Italy, France, Belgium, Great Britain and Denmark the increase was consistent: more than 4 per cent in only five years): 'The proportion of married women working increased throughout the 1970s from 49% in 1971 to 52% in 1978' (Harris, 1983: 218).

TABLE 14.2   Recent changes in the household distribution in Great Britain, Italy and USA

			% change
Great Britain	*1961*	*1979*	
	(%)	*(%)*	
Households with children	54	46	
Households with no children present	26	27	
2 or more families	3	1	
Single persons and non-family households	16	26	
Italy	*1971*	*1981*	
Households with 1–2 members	34.7	41.7	+39
Households with 3–5 members	55.2	53.0	+11.3
Households with 6 or more members	9.6	5.0	−39.9

TABLE 14.2   (Continued)

	1971	1983	% change
Milan			
Single households	19.4	36.1	+105.5
Households with 2 members	27.4	23.8	−3.7
Households with 3–5 members	50.2	38.9	−14.3
Households with 6 or more members	3.0	1.1	−58.3
USA	1970	1982	
	(in 000s)	*(in 000s)*	
Married couple family with own children under 18	40.3	29.3	−4.2
Married couples without own children under 18	30.2	30.1	+31.1
Other family male householder	1.9	2.4	+61.7
Other family female householder	8.7	11.3	+71.0
Total non-family households	18.8	26.9	+88.4
of which single persons	17.1	23.2	+78.3
Total households	63.401	83.527	+31.7

Sources: Great Britain: Harris, 1983: 218–19; Italy: population census; Milan: demographical prospects; USA: Norton, 1983: 20.

REFERENCES

Accornero, A. (1980) *Lavoro e non lavoro*, Bologna: Cappelli.
Amin, S. (1980) *Classe et nation*, Paris: Editions de Minuit.
Bagnasco, A. (1977) *Le Tre Italie*, Bologna: 11 Mulino.
—— (1981a) 'Labour market, class structure and regional formations in Italy', *International Journal of Urban and Regional Research*, 5, no 1: 40–4.
—— (1981b) 'La questione dell'economia informale', *Stato e Mercato*, vol. 1, no. 1, Bologna.
—— (1985) 'La costruzione sociale del mercato, strategie di impresa e esperimenti di scala in Italia', *Stato e Mercato*, no. 13: 9–45, Bologna.
—— (1986) 'Introduction' to A. Bagnasco (ed.), *L'altra metà dell'Economia*, Napoli: Liguori.
Balbo, L. (1976) *Stato di famiglia*, Milano: Etas Libri.
—— 1980, 'Riparliamo del welfare state: . . .', *Inchiesta*, nos. 46–7: 1–20.
Bawly, D. (1982) *The Subterranean Economy*, New York: McGraw Hill.
Bianchi, M. (1981) *I Servizi Sociali*, Bari: De Donato.
Blackaby, F. (ed.) (1978) *De-Industrialization*, London: Heinemann.
Braghin, P., Mingione, E. and Trivellato, P. (1978) 'Per una analisi della struttura di classe dell'Italia Contemporanea'. In M. Paci (ed.), *Capitalismo e classi sociali in Italia*, Bologna: 11 Mulino.

Braverman, H. (1974) *Labor and Monopoly Capital*, New York and London: Monthly Review Press.

Bromley, R. and Gerry, C. (eds) (1979) *Casual Work and Poverty in Third World Cities*, New York: John Wiley.

Bruno, S. (1979) 'The industrial reserve army, segementation and the Italian labour market', *Cambridge Journal of Economics*, 3: 31–51.

Brusco, S. and Sabel, C., 1982, 'Artisan production and economic growth'. In F. Wilkinson (ed.), *The Dynamics of Labour Market Segmentation*, London: Academic Press.

Burns, S. (1975) *Home Inc. The Hidden Wealth and Power of the American Household*, Garden City, New York: Doubleday.

—— (1977) *The Household Economy*, Boston: Beacon Press. *Business Week* (1978) 'The fast growth of the underground economy', 13 March: 73 74 77,

—— (1982) 'The underground economy's hidden force', 5 April. 64–70.

Capecchi, V. and Pesce, A (1983) 'Se la diversità è un valore', *Inchiesta*, nos 46–7: 1–25.

Castells, M. (1983) *The City and the Grassroots*, London: Edward Arnold.

—— (1984) 'New technologies and spatial structure in the United States'. Unpublished paper given at the International workshop 'Cities and their Environment', Bratsk-Irkutsk, USSR.

—— 1985 'High-technology, economic restructuring, and the urban–regional process in the United States'. In M. Castells (ed.), *High Technology, Space, and Society*, Beverly Hills and London: Sage.

Censis Isfol Cnel (1976) *L'occupazione occulta*, Roma: Censis.

Clutterbuk, D. (1979) 'Moonlighting comes out of shadows', *International Management* (June): 27–31.

Cornuel, D. (1980) 'Propositions pour une théorie duale de l'économie informelle', mimeo, University of Lille.

Dale Tussing, A. (1975) *Poverty in a Dual Economy*, New York: St Martin's Press.

Deiter, J. C. (1966) 'Moonlighting and the short work week', *Southwestern Social Science Quarterly*, 47: 308–14.

Del Boca, D. and Turvani, M. (1979) *Famiglia e mercāto del lavoro*, Bologna: 11 Mulino.

Donolo, C. and Fichera, F. (1981) *11 governo debole*, Bari: De Donato.

Edwards, R. C. (1979) *Contested Terrain*, New York: Basic Books.

Edwards, R., Gordon, D. and Reich, M. (eds) (1976) *Labor Market Segmentation*, Lexington, Mass.: Lexington Books.

—— (1982) *Segmented Work, Divided Workers*, Cambridge: Cambridge University Press.

Feige, E. L. (1979) 'How big is the irregular economy?', *Challenge* (November/December): 5–13.

Ferman, L. A. and Ferman, P. R. (1973) 'The structural underpinnings of irregular economy', *Poverty and Human Resources Abstracts*, 9 (March): 13–17.

Ferman, L. A., Ferman, P. R., Berndt, L. and Selo, E. (1978) 'Analysis of the irregular economy: cash flow in the informal sector', *Mimeo; a Report to the Bureau of Employment and Training*, Michigan, Department of Labor and Industrial Relations, The University of Michigan-wayne State University, Ann Arbor, Michigan.

Ferman, L. A., Ferman, P. R. and Berndt, L. (1981) 'The irregular economy'. In S. Henry (ed.), *Can I Have it in Cash?*, London: Astragel Books.

Foudi, R., Stankievicz, F. and Vaneecloo, N. (1981) 'Les chomers et l'économie informelle'. Duplicated paper, University of Lille.

Fröbel, F., Heinrichs, J. and Kreye, O. (1980) *The New International Division of Labour*, Cambridge: Cambridge University Press.

Gallino, L. (ed.) (1982) *Occupati e bioccupati*, Bologna: 11 Mulino.

—— (1983), 'Ripensare l'economia', *Inchiesta*, nos 46–7: 1–25.

Gappert, G. and Ross, H. (eds) (1975) *The Social Economy of Cities*, Beverly Hills and London: Sage.

Gershuny, J. I. (1978) *After Industrial Society*, London: Macmillan.

—— (1982), 'Social innovation: change in the mode of provision of services'. Duplicated paper, Xth World Congress of Sociology, Mexico City.

—— (1983) *Social Innovation and the Division of Labour*, Oxford: Oxford University Press.

Gershuny, J. I. and Miles, I. (1983) *The New Service Economy*, London: Frances Pinter.

Gershuny, J. I. and Pahl, R., (1979), 'Work outside employment: some preliminary speculations', *New University Quarterly*, 34.

Gilbert, A. and Gugler, J. (1982) *Cities, Poverty and Development*, Oxford: Oxford University Press.

Gorz, A. (1980) *Adieux au proletariat*, Paris: Editions Galilée.

—— (1983) *Les Chemins du paradis*, Paris: Editions Galilée.

Graziani, A. (1978) 'The Mezzogiorno in the Italian economy', *Cambridge Journal of Economics*, 2: 355–72.

Gutmann, P. (1977) 'The subterranean economy', *Financial Analysts Journal* (November/December): 26, 27, 34.

—— (1978a) 'Are the unemployed, unemployed?', *Financial Analysts Journal* (September/October): 26–9.

—— (1978b) 'Professor Gutmann replies', *Financial Anlysts Journal* (November/December): 67–9.

—— (1979a) 'The subterranean economy', *Taxing and Spending* (April): 4–8.

—— (1979b) 'Statistical illusions, mistaken policies', *Challenge* (November/December): 14–17.

—— (1980) 'Latest notes from the subterranean economy', *Business and Society Review* (Summer): 25–30.

Harris, C. C. (1983) *The Family and Industrial Society*, London: Allen and Unwin.

Heertje, A., Allen, M. and Cohen, H. (1982) *The Black Economy*, London: Pan Books.

Heinze, R. and Olk, T., 1982, 'Development on the informal economy', *Futures* (June): 189–204.

Henry, S. (ed.) (1981) *Can I Have it in Cash?*, London: Astragel Books.

Hirsch, F. (1976) *Social Limits to Growth*, Cambridge, Mass.: Havard University Press.

Humphries, J. (1977) 'Class struggle and the persistence of the working-class family', *Cambridge Journal of Economics*, 1: 241–58.

Illich, I. (1981) *Shadow Work*, Boston and London: Marion Boyars.

Inchiesta (1983) Numero speciale sulla economia informale, Anno XIII, nos. 59–60 (January–June).

Ingrosso, M. (1979) *Produzione sociale e lavoro domestico*, Milano: F. Angeli.

Irer (1983) *L'offerta di lavoro delle donne sposate*, Milano: duplicated IRER.

Jallade, J. P. (ed.) (1981) *Employment and Unemployment in Europe*, Staffordshire: Trentham Books.

Litwak, E. (1960) 'Occupational mobility and extended family cohesion', *American Sociological Review*, XXV: 1.

Long, L. and de Are, D. (1983) 'The slowing of urbanization in the US', *Scientific American*, vol. 249, no. 1: 31–9.

Lowenthal, M. (1975) 'The social economy in urban working-class communities'. In G. Gappert and N. Ross (eds), *The Social Economy of Cities*, Beverly Hills and London: Sage, pp. 447–69.

—— (1981) 'Non-market transactions in an urban community'. In S. Henry (ed.), *Can I Have It In Cash?*, London: Antragol, pp. 90–104

Michelotti, K. (1975) 'Multiple jobholders in May 1975', *Monthly Labor Review* (November): 56–61.

Miller, G. W. (1972) *Multiple jobholding in Wichita*, Wichita, Kansas: Western State University.

Minc, A. (1982) *L'apres crise est commencé*, Paris: Gallimard.

Mingione, E. (1978) 'Capitalist crisis, neo-dualism and marginalization', *International Journal of Urban and Regional Research*, vol. II, no. 2: 213–21.

—— (1981) *Mercato del lavoro e occupazione in Italia dal 1945 ad oggi*, Milano: Celuc.

—— (1981a) 'Nuovo ordine economico e divisione territoriale del lavoro', *Sociologia Urbana e Rurale*, no. 6: 189–216.

—— (1983) 'Informalization, restructuring and the survival strategies of the working class' *International Journal of Urban and Regional Research*, vol. 7, no. 3: 331–9.

—— (1983a) *Urbanizzazione, classi sociali e lavoro informale*, Milano: F. Angeli.

—— (1985) 'Social reproduction of the surplus labour force: the case of southern Italy'. In N. Redclift and E. Mingione (eds), *Beyond Employment: Household, Gender and Subsistence*, Oxford: Basil Blackwell.

Mottura, G. and Pugliese, E. (1975) *Agricoltura, Mezzagiorno e mercato del lavoro*, Bologna: 11 Mulino.

Norton, A. J. (1983) 'Keeping up with households', *American Demographics*, vol. 5 (February): 17–21.

O'Connor, J. (1973) *The Fiscal Crisis of the State*, New York: St Martin's Press.

—— (1984) *Accumulation Crisis*, Oxford: Basil Blackwell.

Paci, M. (1973) *Mercato del lavoro e classi sociali in Italia*, Bologna: Il Mulino.

—— (1979) 'Lo studio del mercato del lavoro in Italia: una sintesi delle principali ricerche e interpretazioni' *Quaderni di sociologia*. nos 2/3.

—— (1980) *Famiglia e mercato del lavoro in una economia periferica*, Milano: F. Angeli.

—— (1982) *La struttura sociale italiana*, Bologna: 11 Mulino, (ed.) (1985) *Stato, mercato, occupazione*, Bologna: Il Mulino.

Pahl, R. (1980) 'Employment, work and the domestic division of labour', *International Journal of Urban and regional Research*, vol. no. 1, London: Edward Arnold.

—— (1984) *Divisions of Labour*, Oxford, Basil Blackwell.

—— (1985) 'The politics of work', *Political Quarterly*, no. 13 (Autumn).

—— (1986) 'Social polarization and the economic crisis', mimeo, University of Kent, Canterbury.

Pahl, R. and Wallace, C. (1985) 'Household work strategies in economic recession'.

In N. Redclift and E. Mingione (eds), *Beyond Employment: Household, Gender and Subsistence*, Oxford: Basil Blackwell.

Pinnaro, G. and Pugliese, E. (1985) 'Informalization and social resistence: the case of Naples'. In N. Redclift and E. Mingione. (eds), *Beyond Employment: Household, Gender and Subsistence*, Oxford: Basil Blackwell.

Polanyi, K. (1944) *The Great Transformation*, Boston: Beacon Press.

—— (1977) *The Livelihood of Man*, New York: Academic Press.

Portes, A. and Walton, J. (1981) *Labor, Class and the International System*, New York and London: Academic Press.

Pugliese, E. (1983) 'Aspetti dell'economia informale a Napoli', in *Inchiesta*, nos 46–7: 89–97.

Ragone, G. (ed.) (1983) *Economia in trasformazione e doppio lavoro*, Bologna: Il Mulino.

Redclift, N. and Mingione, E. (1985) *Beyond Employment: Household, Gender and Subsistence*, Oxford: Basil Blackwell.

Reyneri, E. (ed.) (1984) *Doppio lavoro e città meridionale*, Bologna: Il Mulino.

Roldan, M. (1985) 'Domestic outwork and the struggle for reproduction'. In N. Redclift and E. Mingione, (ed.), *Beyond Employment: Household, Gender and Subsistence*, Oxford: Basil Blackwell.

Rosanvallon, P. (1980) 'Le developpement de l'economie souterraine et l'avenir des societés industrielles', *Le débat*, (June).

—— (1981) *La Crise de l'etat providence*, Paris: Seuil.

Roustang, G. (1982) *Le travail autrement*, Paris: Dunod.

Saraceno, C. (1980) *Il lavoro mal diviso*, Bari: De Donato.

Schumacher, F. (1973) *Small is Beautiful*, New York: Harper and Row.

Szelenyi, I. (1981) 'Structural changes and alternatives to capitalist development in the contemporary urban and regional system', *International Journal of Urban and Regional Research*, vol. 5, no. 1: 1–14.

Thrift, N. J. (1983) 'On the determination of social action in space and time', *Society and Space*, vol. 1, no. 1.

Trigiglia, C. (1978) 'Sviluppo, sottosviluppo e classi sociali in Italia'. In Paci, M. (ed.), *Capitalismo e classi sociali in Italia*, Bologna: Il Mulino.

USA Congress Committee on Ways and Means (1980) *The Underground Economy*, Washington, DC: Government Printing Office, 60–502–0.

Vanek, J. (1974) 'Time spent in housework', *Scientific American*, vol. 231: 116–20.

Wallerstein, I. (1979) *The Capitalist World Economy*, Cambridge: Cambridge University Press.

Wilkinson, F. (ed.) (1982) *The Dynamic of Labour Market Segmentation*, London: Academic Press.

15

Local Mobilization and Economic Discontent

Susan S. Fainstein

The rise, fall and transformation of American cities have always reflected spatially changing patterns of capital investment across the nation and within metropolitan areas. Increasingly, however, cities have also become dependent on international forces. As American capital flows to sites abroad, domestic industry competes with foreign production by driving down labor costs and fleeing expensive inner-city locations; at the same time immigrant workers enter the country from the Third World at a sharply accelerating rate, creating new residential communities and changing the character of local labor markets. Thus, the relatively recent phenomenon of wholesale integration into the world economy has intensified earlier trends towards deindustrialization and increased competition for low-skilled jobs. The new international division of labor, defined as 'a world market for labor and a real world industrial reserve army of workers, together with a world market for production sites' (Fröbel, Heinrichs and Kreye, 1980: 13), has exacerbated the hardships experienced by previously deprived populations, as well as adding to their number.

While people retain roots in their communities, economic enterprises no longer do so. A recent newspaper article on the planned departure of Mack Trucks from Allentown, Pennsylvania, illustrates the point. The company—founded in Allentown, and the source of its motto, 'The Truck Capital of the World' – intended, despite union concessions and increased profitability, to move to the South, thereby laying off 2000 employees. The article noted:

If the plant goes, many residents say, the company's headquarters on Mack Drive, on the city's south side, may be next. Renault, the French car maker, owns 40 percent of Mack's stock and people here note that many members of its board no longer have close ties to the Lehigh Valley. (Gruson, 1986)

The author wishes to thank Norman Fainstein, Michael Smith and Joe Feagin for comments on an earlier draft of this chapter, and Susan Gittelman for her research assistance.

The elusiveness of private economic entities, combined with the susceptibility of local governments to their blandishments and punishments, creates enormous obstacles for community organizations seeking to defend themselves against the equally disrupting forces of investment and disinvestment. In the last two decades local residents have organized to counter the impacts of economic deprivation and competition for scarce urban space on their daily lives. During the 1960s and 1970s urban social movements, focusing on issues of collective consumption (i.e. state-supplied income, goods and services) (see Preteceille, 1981; Saunders, 1981), had at least some success in influencing state programs for social services and spatial reorganization. In the current decade, recognizing the linkage between economic transformation and community deprivation, activists have increasingly sought to combine community-based interests with efforts to transform the local productive economy. These have included designation of a percentage of the proceeds from profitable development to community enterprises and worker and community takeovers of industry.

In the meanwhile the Reagan administration's efforts to restructure the economy through reduction of governmental domestic programs, deregulation and privatization have eroded earlier gains while causing the local, social-service targets of urban movements to evaporate. The legitimation crisis, which O'Connor (1973) and others predicted as a result of a reduction in social services, has apparently not come to pass. The President has defined national urban policy as economic policy; in the words of his national urban policy report: 'the foundation for the Administration's urban policy is the Economic Recovery Program . . . comprising tax cuts, reductions in the rate of government spending, regulatory relief, and monetary restraint' (USDHUD, 1982: 1). Within this context the discontents that urban movements formerly blamed on health, welfare, education and urban renewal agencies now seemed to come from decisions made within the 'private' sector and far removed from the physical boundaries of the metropolis.

This chapter examines the urban impacts of the new international division of labor, their relation to urban political conflicts, and the character of movements formed to combat social inequality. It concludes by discussing the potential for a national progressive movement in the United States that would link geographically-based groups with other transforming elements.

IMPACTS OF THE NEW INTERNATIONAL DIVISION OF LABOR

The term 'new international division of labor' is an inadequate description of the changes occurring in the global economy. They involve not simply a relocation of work sites but the burgeoning of economic sectors which exist precisely because this international division creates new needs for investment mobility, coordination and information. In other words, as control of economic entities becomes centralized at the global level, occupational sectors originate or expand in order to make such control possible. This has led theorists to see not just geographical shifts in production but its qualitative transformation. For example, Castells (1984: i) asserts:

Technological change can only be understood in the framework of two fundamental historical processes that are transforming our societies: the restructuring of the capitalist mode of production and the emergence, within capitalism, of the informational mode of development.

In a similar vein, Touraine (1985: 781), who calls the present epoch 'postindustrial', argues:

Postindustrial society must be defined . . . by the technological production of symbolic goods which shape or transform our representation of human nature and of the external world. For these reasons, research and development, information processing, biomedical science and techniques, and mass media are the four main components of postindustrial society.

In an economy with more upper-level jobs requiring high cognitive skills and more minimum-wage service jobs, but fewer well-paid, blue-collar occupations, income inequality is increasing (see Sassen-Koob, 1984). This situation is clearly indicated by income distribution statistics showing a simultaneous increase, between 1975 and 1983, of families receiving below $10,000 and above $35,000 per year in constant 1983 dollars. The percentage in the below $10,000 category grew from 13.7 to 15.9 per cent in this period, while the number receiving above $35,000 increased from 24.1 to 29.6 per cent (US Bureau of the Census, 1984: 446). Although the geography of this income distribution continues to manifest itself in a large and still growing gap between city and suburb, cities like New York, Boston, and San Francisco, which have become centers of information technology and financial control, encompass growing numbers of both income extremes within their boundaries.

In summary, the restructuring of the American economy has involved the continuing decline in importance of manufacturing industries, the growth of the service sector, characterized by high- and low-wage jobs, persistent high levels of unemployment particularly among minority ethnic groups, and the constant mobility of industry (see Bluestone and Harrison, 1982). Its impacts have varied geographically depending on the economic base of particular regions and cities. For example, old industrial areas have witnessed relatively low housing prices and large-scale mortgage defaults by unemployed workers, while prospering metropolitan areas have suffered extreme pressures on housing markets, pricing housing out of the reach of low-income households. The restructuring process has made localities hostage to the technological and locational decisions of corporate managers.

Until the Carter administration (1976–80) increasing inequality of earnings was compensated by a growing governmental role in the provision of welfare, but after the mid-seventies pubic expenditures ceased to counterbalance labor market trends (Danziger, Haveman and Plotnick, 1981). Thus, while federal social welfare expenditures grew by 450 per cent in constant dollars between 1950 and 1976 (US Bureau of the Census, 1983: 370), they remained virtually stagnant for the next six years (US Bureau of the Census, 1984: 355). Federal aid to state and local governments, after peaking in 1978, declined by 14 per cent in constant dollars between 1978 and 1984 (US Bureau of the Census, 1984: 267).

The poor are apparently not only becoming increasingly deprived as measured by income status, but also more and more isolated socially and politically. Their cause had in the past been pressed through their mobilization into urban social movements. Activism continues in American cities, but the efficacy of community-based organizations is seriously limited by, on the one hand, an unsympathetic federal government and, on the other, the footloose character of industry, which can hold city governments hostage to its demands.

It is possible, however, that the present situation offers new possibilities for overcoming the historic separation between workplace and community demands. Thus, Smith and Judd (1984: 193) argue:

There is a real potential for organized militancy in the sphere of capitalist reproduction that can be directly related to work-place grievances over labor market restructuring. 'Community action' thus need not necessarily contradict, but in particular historical circumstances may even complement, conflicts over control of the production process.

Similarly Sassen-Koob (1984: 164) thinks that unemployment among the formerly well-paid, blue- and white-collar strata will produce the objective conditions for a new alliance between low- and middle-income workers. These writers essentially are asserting that the restructured capitalist economy, having subjected labor to the disciplines of severe recession and depressed wage rates, is providing new structural conditions for movements uniting previously disparate portions of the population. The following sections of this chapter examine the changing focuses of urban activism and inquire as to its potential for overcoming the limitations created by the division between economy and community.

ECONOMIC CHANGE AND URBAN POLITICS

The aphorism, 'the worse, the better' sums up one, facile explanation of the roots of popular mobilization. Much scholarly analysis, ranging from de Tocqueville's (1955) examination of the French Revolution to Davies'

(1969) discussion of the 'J curve', however, denies any simple correlation between declining living standards and rebellion. Rather, the consensus is that mobilization occurs when there is a commonly perceived discrepancy between actuality and expectation (see Fainstein and Fainstein, 1974: Appendix). A further condition, if mobilization is to be effective, is disarray within the ruling elite (see Skocpol, 1979). In the recent history of the United States, sudden and extreme economic decline produced the workplace-based movements of the 1930s (Piven and Cloward, 1977); these were supported by key members of the governing class. The next groundswelling of popular protest – the civil rights and community movements of the 1960s – erupted in a period of general prosperity. While the years of the Great Depression involved significant changes in the structure of the American economy, the 1960s did not encompass any striking deviation from the aggregate economic trends of earlier years. They did involve the culmination of massive migration, resulting from the transformation of southern agriculture that caused blacks to leave the land and head north.

This northward flow, however, had begun long before and only became the basis for mobilization when low-income and minority groups perceived both that they were being excluded from national affluence and that their condition was remediable through political action. As in the 1930s popular movements had allies within political elites who sought to co-opt rebellion and capture new voting constituencies. The 1980s have already spanned postwar extremes of national economic decline and growth. Neither of these conditions, however, has yet inspired a sufficiently high level of militant opposition to cause policy reversals that would mitigate income inequality and enhance collective consumption. Nevertheless, urban grassroots activity remains highly politicized and far more socially inclusive than was the case before the conflicts of the 1960s. Comparison of the situation in the 1960s and 1970s with the present indicates changes in the character of community-based agitation and points to possible future directions.

Movements of the 1960s

There were three social bases for the movements of the 1960s: client status, race/ethnicity and place (Fainstein and Fainstein, 1974). But racial solidarity was a key element in mobilizing even those movements that did not have an explicitly racial program. For the most part, clients of educational, health and welfare programs had more in common than simply their status as recipients of government benefits; they perceived their commonality in a similar, general social status of dependency consequent on racial discrimination. While this was true for both blacks and Hispanics, it was primarily blacks who mobilized against urban bureaucracies. Similarly, the community-based movements that fought urban renewal and demanded neighborhood improvements were predominantly black. They drew their model from the civil rights movement; their potential for threatening urban stability stemmed from the riots; and their passion arose from a shared status that transcended economic interest.

In the North, popular mobilizations were not unified into a national coalition, and few produced leaders of any stature. None the less, they were sufficiently threatening or persuasive to precipitate a national urban policy. Within particular municipalities they succeeded in racially integrating the urban bureaucracies, halting redevelopment programs, and increasing expenditures on social service and neighborhood development programs. Their effectiveness lay partly in the alliances they were able to develop with dominant groups; they obtained financial help from foundations, staffing from middle-class cadres, planning and legal assistance from radical professionals, and supportive policies from sympathetic governmental officials. While the amount of liberal compassion for oppressed groups should not be exaggerated, it was nevertheless sufficient to cause division and insecurities within the ruling elite, thereby greatly enhancing the effectiveness of movements from below.

The neighborhood movement

The 1970s witnessed the decline of the militant groups of the 1960s, but the proliferation of community organizations that have been lumped together under the rubric of the neighborhood movement (Boyte, 1980). Racial militancy receded as the impetus for grassroots activity (Fainstein and Fainstein, 1976; Fainstein and Martin, 1978); the price for a broader social base was a reduction in the emotional commitment that gave earlier movements their forcefulness. The neighborhood movement suffered from all the conditions that circumscribe organizations whose members are united only by common occupation of a non-sovereign territory: (1) narrowness of issues; (2) part-time leadership; (3) cross-cutting cleavages; (4) individual geographic mobility; and (5) limited financial resources.

Overcoming these obstacles requires an overarching ideology as potent as patriotism, but such a meaning system has been extraordinarily difficult to formulate on a neighborhood basis. While racial solidarity had formerly provided a foundation for group coherence, it had also provoked severe counter-reactions, making it a highly risky strategy for people who required powerful allies in order to succeed in their aims. Consequently neighborhood groups sought to formulate an ideology that would affirm the right of ordinary people to control the future of their neighborhoods without emphasizing racial or ethnic exclusion.

According to Castells (1983: 326): 'people tend to consider cities, space, and urban functions and forms as the mainspring for their feelings'. He sees the aim of urban social movements as the imposition of 'a new urban meaning in contradiction to the institutionalized urban meaning and against the interests of the dominant class' (1983: 305). But so ambitious an undertaking only becomes conceivable for neighborhood movements if communal space is in fact a mainspring for emotion, an assertion open to serious challenge. One recent instance of such an intense, spatially-based effort was the gay movement in San Francisco (Castells, 1982; 1983), but the impetus there was shared sexual preference, not territory *per se*. Most neighborhood organizations are drawn together by a limited common interest that does not tap strong emotional involvements. They therefore face great difficulty in overcoming the barriers to organizational coherence. Effective opposition to the interests of the dominant class founders on internal weakness as well as external power.

The achievements of neighborhood organizations have perforce been limited to modifications of development schemes, small-scale neighborhood improvement programs, limited participation in municipal policy-making, and, under the Carter administration, the creation of the now dismantled Office of Neighborhoods within the Federal Department of Housing and Urban Development. To some extent community groups obtained symbolic recognition, evidenced in the report of the National Commission on Neighborhoods (1979) and the rhetoric of local officials. In a few cities like Santa Monica and Cleveland (Shearer, 1982; Clavel, 1985) they captured City Hall, and in a greater number they participated in coalitions that backed successful mayoral candidates. But for the most part neighborhood organizations spent their energy opposing cutbacks in a time of fiscal stringency. Operating in a context of shrinking resources for collective consumption, a reconceptualization of the urban crisis as one of fiscal solvency (Fainstein et al., 1983; Smith and Judd, 1984), and the necessity to compete with other places both here and abroad (Peterson, 1981), not only were they unable to impose a new urban meaning, they had one thrust upon them.

Recent tendencies

Community activists of the 1980s have an increasingly sophisticated view of the relationship between the productive economy and the condition of their localities. They have therefore sought ways of escaping the limits imposed by the vulnerability of cities in relation to the private sector. Because private firms can easily threaten to invest elsewhere, taking with them their employment and tax contributions, city governments are readily persuaded to offer tax concessions, facilitate urban redevelopment, and reduce social services to stabilize the tax rate. Neighborhood and workplace organizations, finding that simple opposition to development, on the one hand, and industry flight, on the other, offered few rewards, have attempted to gain explicit benefits from these tendencies. In addition, they have tried to find other sources of support besides federal funding for neighborhood economic development and low-cost housing, and to achieve worker control of runaway industries. Recognizing the isolation of low-income communities, they have attempted to develop progressive coalitions and to become involved in electoral politics.

Local development corporations (LDCs), which operate both in the commercial and housing areas, are an idea with roots in the poverty programs of the 1960s. Perhaps the best known is the Bedford-Stuyvesant Restoration Foundation in New York City. Enterprises operated by these bodies, while not necessarily offering career opportunities or even very good wages, at least will not flee to the suburbs or Hong Kong. Organizers of development corporations have been attempting to take advantage of the federal thrust toward privatization and have switched from a poverty program orientation to an entrepreneurial one, focusing considerable effort on achieving adequate financing. A discussion of three LDCs in Los Angeles (Haas and Heskin, 1981: 546) describes their strategy as trying 'to turn to their advantage rather than stop the flow of public and private capital in their communities'. In New York State local community development corporations, which concentrate primarily on neighborhood commercial redevelopment, receive state funding to support staff and are eligible for additional grants for specific projects.

A somewhat different, and so far very successful model of the LDC is the Nehemiah Plan, a Brownsville (Brooklyn) housing project led by a coalition of black churches: 'The movement has mobilized the personal incomes and savings of working poor residents to finance their ownership of new, small, single-family homes in the ghetto' (Zukin, 1985: 3). So far the Nehemiah Plan has managed to produce nearly 1000 housing units priced under $50,000, less than half the price of comparable market-rate new housing. While governmental involvement has been required for mortgage interest subsidies, sponsorship has remained private and the homes have passed into individual ownership. Ideally the project promises 'a new mode of integrating Brooklyn's black population into the city's political organization' (Zukin and Zwerman 1985: 18).

While LDCs offer a route to community preservation and autonomy, their search for funding restricts their usefulness as independent neighborhood advocates and produces inherently co-optative tendencies. These problems caused Haas and Heskin (1981: 562), in their analysis of the Los Angeles cases, to conclude that, although the organizations did manage to obtain funding for their projects: 'One of the primary dangers of this approach is that the difficult struggle for economic support and technical competence often undermines the interest, energy or ability of these organizations to establish, maintain and cultivate a mass base.'

Zukin (1985) comments that the thrust for private, albeit community-sponsored, development in Brownsville represents acquiescence to the Reagan administration's emphasis on limiting government's role in social welfare. The danger is that organizations, even non-profit ones, operating in the private market are subject to co-optation both in the narrow sense of the absorption of their leadership into establishment structures and in the broader sense of ideological adherence to a philosophy that supports and reproduces inequality.

Other approaches to the housing issue may be more radicalizing, although they may also prove less successful in providing housing. Heisler and Hoffman (1988) describe an effort in Lorain County, Ohio, to mobilize laid-off workers who were in danger of losing their homes through foreclosure. They note that homeownership is closely tied to labor market status, thus linking the spheres of production and consumption. Because homeownership has so much symbolic as well as economic weight, 'threats to homes' promised a way to mobilize younger blue-collar workers who might normally shun community organizations. But while initial successes in deferring foreclosures by local institutions attracted support for the organization, large out-of-state mortgage companies proved much less vulnerable to pressure. Financial deregulation and the growth of the secondary mortgage market 'contributed to the inaccessibility and invulnerability of mortgage lenders to local level initiative' (1988: 19). Thus, while the 'threat to homes' campaign had the ideological potential of demonstrating connections between work and community and putting pressure on financial institutions, it confronted the same factor that limits the effectiveness of all place-based organizations – the 'enemy' is elusive and cannot be touched within the boundaries of the community.

Unquestionably the accelerating cost of housing offers a basis for mobilizing city residents who, even with middle-class incomes, cannot afford a home. Rent control has attracted passionate adherents in California, New York and New Jersey. Low-income housing groups, using court cases and lobbying, have succeeded in a number of places in obtaining housing trust funds derived from mandatory contributions by private developers. ACORN, which has had a history of organizing around economic as well as neighborhood issues, has been sponsoring squatter movements that have gained the support of local politicians (Lamiell, 1985). Threats of displacement quickly stimulate the development of oppositional neighborhood groups. But unless housing issues can be linked organizationally and ideologically to other programs, groups concerned with them inevitably suffer the limitations associated with locally-based, single-issue politics.

The most explicit linking of economic and community issues has been in the efforts to combat runaway industry and to achieve worker ownership of firms. These endeavors have achieved union–community coalitions and in some instances have managed to attain economically viable industries rooted in their communities. The failure of the most significant effort of this sort, however, a worker takeover of Youngstown Sheet and Tube, points to the contradictions of this approach when the capital needs are very large:

Despite minor and short-terms successes [in gaining funding for studies, some start-up financing, and considerable political support] ... the Youngstown experience demonstrates the basic contradiction of the entrepreneurialist game. On the one hand, [private financial institutions] ... will not invest in new enterprises which are not massively backed by government-provided collateral, while, on the other hand, public budget officials will not supply the large sums necessary for successful enterprise formation because of the state's own fiscal constraints, and the rhetoric which it has been increasingly stressing to the effect that 'new business enterprise is the business of private enterprise'. (Cooke, 1984: 425; see also Buss and Redburn, 1983: appendix B)

One solution that has been proposed to the problem of financing worker-owned industry is 'pension fund socialism' – the seizure of control by workers of their pension fund assets to be invested in enterprises that would benefit themselves and their localities (see Rifkin and Barber, 1978). Theoretically this approach offers by far the most effective means of overcoming the contradiction between the economic development and community-based interests of workers. But, except in the instance of divestiture from firms doing business in South Africa, there has been no powerful movement to support aggressive use of pension funds and considerable fear that such use might jeopardize security.

If focus on a single issue in a single place severely hampers the ability of organizations to attain their goals, then one obvious response is to form broad coalitions. In the words of Miller and Tomaskovic-Devey (1983: 8):

The abundance of single-interest organizations testifies to the variety of concerns, many noneconomic, that are important to people, propelling them to fight for this goal or prevent that action, such as those relating to nuclear waste, the threat of nuclear war, energy costs, environmental protection, battered women, occupational health, et cetera. It is good that people are being drawn into activity on those issues close to them. On the other hand, only pockets of limited influence develop among these and the community groups that dot the political landscape. Most are politically weak or can win only minor concessions. Many have not thought of themselves as groups fighting off encroachments and dangers rather than 'for' groups moving on to their deeper goals. Their political weakness could be overcome if their interests blended together in an effective political way. Many are beginning to envision that possibility.

Indeed, coalition seems the necessary precursor to any effective method of dealing with the growing disjunction between the internationally controlled economy and locally-rooted communities. Various efforts in this direction already exist (see Kelsey and Wiener, 1983; Cantor, 1983; Creamer, 1983; Miller, 1983; Handman and Adler, 1983); the voting registration drive of 1984, in which unions and community groups mounted a joint nationwide effort to enroll the unregistered, demonstrated that unified action is possible (see Cloward and Piven, 1983). Whether coalitions will actually form the underpinnings of a national social movement, however, remains to be seen.

Much depends, as will be discussed below, on the ability of the left to formulate an ideological program capable of attracting a mass following.

THE POTENTIAL OF URBAN MOVEMENTS

The attention given to urban movements in the United States and Europe since 1968 had both theoretical and practical roots. Theoretically, the Marxist interpretation of class struggle as the primary force for change within capitalist societies lost its persuasiveness. Even if the proletariat had displayed far more militant class consciousness than was the case, the diminishing proportion of workers engaged in industrial production meant that the working class, as traditionally defined, could no longer claim to be even nearly a majority. Growing numbers of people occupied contradictory class positions; only the most tendentious of theoretical analyses could pretend that the interests of the 'new middle class' were identical with those of labor. Practically, the persistence and fundamental importance of conflicts based on race, ethnicity, territoriality and gender indicated alternative bases for social change (Giddens, 1981). From both an objective standpoint (What are the structural cleavages that give rise to social action?) and a subjective one (What are the conflicts that stir people's passions?) the categorization of people's social bases and communal allegiances wholly in terms of class, under the direction of the class-based party, clashed with observed reality.

Examination of Castells' *The City and the Grassroots* (1985) indicates both the source of current emphases on urban consumption-based movements as agents of change and an interpretation of the transforming potential of grassroots actions. The stress that Castells and other contemporary Marxists place on urban social movements did not emanate from an initial theoretical formulation that predicted the displacement of class struggle into the urban arena. Rather, observation of contemporary struggles indicated that conflict had become manifest within housing projects and urban bureaucracies as well as factories and that insurgent leadership did not come from traditional working-class parties:

So why still worry about social movements? And why urban? First of all, because of experience, both contemporary and historical: May 1968 in France; the Autunno Caldo in the Italian factories in 1969: the 1960s in America: the worldwide mobilization against the Vietnam War; the Spanish Resistance against Franquism; the German Student Movement; the national liberation movements in the Third World; the Unidad Popular in Chile; the uprising of the feminist movement; all over the world conscious people have continued to mobilize collectively to change their lives and propose new ones against those who want to preserve the old order. (Castells, 1983: 299)

Although he traces urban conflict to the capitalist mode of production, Castells (1983: 319–20) does not describe the objectives of urban social movements as the attainment of economic equality but instead lists three, essentially humanistic goals: (1) a city organized around use rather than exchange values; (2) cultural identity; and (3) political decentralization and urban self-management. Objectives phrased in these terms, of course, allow for a broader social base than an end defined specifically as control of the means of production:

> Movements are urban actors, defined by their goals and their urban condition. They are not, then, another form of class struggle, gender struggle, or ethnic struggle. The components of the urban movements come from a variety of social, gender, and ethnic situations . . . They are neither working class movements nor a middle-class movement. (1983: 320)

But this vagueness dodges the question of the potentially conflicting economic interests of constituent groups, as well as, more fundamentally, the mode by which the economic base can be reorganized sufficiently that use values become the determinant of city life. Castells argues that demands for adequate housing, parks or historic preservation constitute such a reorganization and calls this form of mobilization 'collective consumption trade unionism' (1983: 319). These kinds of popular activity were central concerns of his earlier works (Castells, 1975; 1977; 1978), and they have indeed been the dominant forms of recent mobilization. But the development of a public housing project or the saving of an historic site is a far cry from 'a city organized around its use value' (1983: 319).

In his emphasis on cultural identity and community empowerment, on the uniqueness of urban movements in their capacity to change urban meaning, Castells goes beyond the heterodox Marxism of his earlier stress on collective consumption and the realm of production. He attributes far greater importance to aspects of social life normally dimissed as superstructural, or at any rate dependent, than do most Marxists. But he undercuts his enthusiasm for the potential of urban social movements by terming them 'reactive Utopias' (1983: 327), indicating that their continued usefulness depends on the successes of 'new central social movements (feminism, new labor, self-management, alternative communication) . . .' (1983: 327). Overall he is moderate in his concusions:

> Urban movements are [not] the new historical actors creating social change, nor the pivotal source of alternative social forms. (1983: 319)

> They are not agents of structural social change, but symptoms of resistance to the social domination even if, in their effort to resist, they do have major effects on cities and societies. (1983: 329)

> [Yet] urban movements do address the real issues of our time, although neither on the scale nor terms that are adequate to the task. (1983: 331)

Ultimately, for Castells, the role of urban social movements is that of midwife, 'nurturing the embryos of tomorrow's social movements within the local Utopias that urban movements have constructed in order never to surrender to barbarism' (1983: 331).

In a brief phrase Castells sums up the overwhelming difficulty faced by popular movements: 'Relationships of production are integrated at the worldwide level, while experience is culturally specific . . . our world exists in a three-dimensional space whose dynamics tend to be disjointed' (1983: 310). It is the fact of this disjunction that causes him to call on 'new central movements'. But besides his passing reference to the nurturing role, he offers little specific analysis of the connections between community-based and central movements, and none concerning the conjunction of cultural and production-based movements.

Ideology and organization

The increasingly integrated international economy and the highly decentralized character of production within the new international division of labor require a reinterpretation of the political importance of place. They imply that place-based movements, whether rooted in work or residence, were historically-specific phenomena. The growth of national unions long ago implied recognition of the loss of autonomy of the single production site; the current weakness of these unions reflects the end of national autarky. In residential neighborhoods the movement for community control was an attempt to reverse centralizing tendencies and reimbue the locality with political meaning. While urban social movements did achieve an institutional framework for participation and some devolution of social services, their gains were necessarily restricted by their parochialism. Because places still matter profoundly to the people who occupy them, they cannot be disregarded by any progressive movement. Nevertheless, place must be subsumed into a more encompassing commonality if an effective force is to confront power organized at the national and international levels.

Developing a popular force with a broad enough social base to redefine relationships that are 'integrated at the worldwide level' requires the formulation of an overarching ideology to link potential constituent groups. Gottdiener (1984: 215–16) contends that it is not the objective character of territorial fragmentation that prevents spatially-based groups from coalescing into a national movement but rather 'ideological mind-sets' which presumably can be overcome through theoretical demystification and practical activity. At this moment, however, despite a 38 per cent increase in the number of people at or below the official poverty line from 1978 to 1984 (US Bureau of the Census, 1985), there is not a sufficiently widespread sense of grievance and concept of reform to give rise to ideological solidarity.

There are several reasons why economic restructuring has not produced an aroused radical consciousness in the present period:

1 The massive entry of women into the labor force masked male unemployment and wage cuts by maintaining a family income. Moreover, the reduction of male blue-color employment and increase in female white-collar work meant that an increasing proportion of the workforce was in occupational categories that were traditionally hard to mobilize.

2 As has been the case throughout the century, ethnic and racial divisions have restricted working-class solidarity. New immigration, and particularly the recruitment of illegal immigrants into manual jobs, has exacerbated the difficulty of mobilizing low-income workers.

3 Conservatives have succeeded in developing a coherent ideology in which individuals are seen as the victims of clumsy and misguided government programs, to be saved by private sector initiatives. The left has not been able to generate a counter-ideology that specifies a villain and offers a path of redemption.

A left coalition which hopes to attain majority support must reach out to the new social movements (anti-nuclear, feminist, environmental) that have formed in the last twenty years as well as to the work- and community-based groups which have more specifically economic grievances. These new social movements have tended not to be tied to the working class and have had objectives that transcend material gains and state programs: 'New social movements are less sociopolitical and more sociocultural. The distance between civil society and State is increasing while the separation between private and public life is fading away' (Touraine, 1985: 780). Their subjectivism and varied ambitions militate against the generation of a unifying organizational framework. Yet without such a framework political effectiveness and the capacity to deal with the forces causing economic deprivation are seriously jeopardized:

At the beginning of the eighties almost nothing seems to survive of these epic representations [of social movements as major historical actors]. Movements are lost, and there is no character occupying the scene. But there are a lot of submerged networks, of groups and experiences that insist on considering themselves 'against.' But who cares about them? They seem more interested in themselves than in the outer world, they apparently ignore politics, they don't fight against power. They don't have big leaders, organizations seem quite inefficient, disenchantment has superseded great ideals. Many observers consider these realities, which don't challenge the political system and are not interested in the institutional effects of their action, as residual, folkloristic phenomena in the big scenario of politics. (Melucci, 1985: 809–10; see also Offe, 1985: 819–20)

Melucci (1985: 810) contends that even though the new social movements are disorganized and 'submerged', they are 'the seeds of a qualitative change in contemporary collective action'. But even he concedes that 'social movements can't survive in complex societies without some forms of political representation' (1985: 815).

André Gorz, who once sought a strategy for labor (Gorz, 1967), has more recently attempted to delineate the relationship between new elements arising from postindustrial capitalism and the political arena. He identifies a broad-based movement comprising environmentalists, feminists and marginally employed workers as an agency for the rejection of the accumulation ethic. Contending that the changing character of capitalist production has obviated the need for labor in the traditional sense, he claims (1982: 74) that it is now possible to envisage a world largely freed from soul-destroying toil: 'the logic of capital has brought us to the threshold of liberation.'

It is through politics that Gorz discerns the possibility of social action to this end. Political organizations are both parties *and* other groupings; because of the rigidities of political parties, 'fundamental debates over the production and the transformation of society have shifted to clubs, churches, universities, associations and movements . . .' (1982: 118). But Gorz recognizes that politics will always involve contradictions resulting in permanent tension, and, while critical of contemporary political parties of the Left, he nevertheless sees the need for dealing with them. Social movements cannot achieve their aims autonomously, even while they cannot succeed if they submerge themselves in normal politics: 'The process of transforming society in accordance with the aims of the movement will certainly never be an automatic effect of the expansion of the movement itself' (1982: 12). Thus, while movements must remain distinct from political parties, the tension between them can be fruitful.

The political party today which seems best to reflect the kind of creative tension to which Gorz refers is the West German Green Party (see Aronowitz, 1984). While favoring worker control of industry, the Green Party opposes centralism, whether of state or party. It incorporates a variety of left political tendencies, including environmentalism, socialism, pacifism, cultural radicalism, and feminism. Because the Greens have attained parliamentary representation, they are subject to the same forces of co-optation and routinization which have plagued all left-wing parties that hold electoral office. But the institutionalized vehicle of the party continues to coexist with the more anarchic social movement that underlies it.

Could a similarly constituted mass party develop within the United States? The American Left has time and again foundered on its inability to build an influential political party. Europeans, disillusioned with the narrow rigidity of communist parties and the co-optation of socialist ones, tend to scoff at American leftists who dream of working-class parties in the US. Yet the absence of such institutions has been critical in keeping the United States as conservative as it is – in narrowing both the range of ideology and the extent of welfare state programs. Now, in the face of a drastically weakened labor movement, a traditional leftist party seems a particularly unpromising vehicle for effecting social change. But a party engaging the energies of the new social movements offers one possibility for exceeding the present limits on popular radicalism (see Capra and Spretnak, 1984: chapter 9).

NEW MOVEMENTS AND THE AMERICAN POLITICAL TRADITION

Efforts at social reform in the United States, with the partial exception of the Socialist Party, have typically been rooted in the populist or progressive traditions. Populism has reflected a nebulous unity of the masses against the classes – an anti-business stance often combined with nativism. Progressivism has usually been directed at reordering the political structure, with the intention of removing venal politicians and enhancing either democracy or professionalism in government. These two political traditions have involved both electoral politics, either through a third party or reform of an existing one, and an underlying broader social movement. Neither tradition called for drastic transformation of the economy: populism stressed regulation of big business, localism, participation and protection of small property-holders; progressivism emphasized economic efficiency and, in its different variants, more businesslike government and social programs to improve living conditions and economic opportunity for the poor.

A movement made up of peace activists, environmentalists, feminists and community groups builds on elements of traditional populist/progressive sentiment. Like its predecessors, it would not be fundamentally oriented towards transformation of the mode of production; but similarly, if its reform agenda were enacted, it would have profound implications for economic organization. Its programmatic thrust would be for more progressive taxes, regulation of business, governmental decentralization, and collective con-sumption programs. Unlike a purely labor-based movement, such an amalgam could appeal to middle-class suburbanites as well as blue-collar workers. While cross-class alliances are clearly subject to underlying cleavages, they also possess advantages not available to homogeneous working- or lower-class organizations. Besides the obviously greater political access and potency associated with middle-class status, groups drawn from the occupational elite possess important leadership capabilities. Thus, Offe (1985: 805–1) argues:

A high level of formal schooling leads to some (perceived) competence to make judgments about complicated and abstract 'systemic' matters in the fields of economic, military, legal, technical, and environmental affairs . . . Higher education increases the capacity to think (and conceivably even to act) independently, and the preparedness to critically question received interpretations and theories about the world.

Attempts to institutionalize a broad alliance spanning economic and cultural issues exist today in various guises: Democratic Socialists of

America; Jesse Jackson's rainbow coalition: widespread voter registration drives being operated by coalitions of community organizations, social service professionals, church groups, and statewide advocacy groups like Citizen Action. The failure so far of an organization to jell sufficiently to attain the prominence of the Green Party does not preclude such a future event, particularly if a charismatic leader appeared. Social theory is extremely weak in its ability to predict sudden shifts in popular consciousness; while structural preconditions can be identified, none can be adequate in itself to guarantee the development of a social force.

Of course, the existence of a large-scale, electorally potent movement would not necessarily mean that it would be programmatically effective. As soon as its efforts began to threaten corporate profitability, it would be subject to severe counterattack (see Molotch and Logan, 1984) – the battles over rent control in California, where real-estate interests have contributed enormous resources to overturn ordinances and defeat referenda, illustrate how potent opposition to regulation can be (Fainstein et al., 1983: 237–8). Racial divisions will continue to plague any alliance that tries to bring together inner-city blacks with suburban whites. Nevertheless, changes in the Democratic Party over the last two decades imply that progress in this respect is not impossible.

If the current expansion of the economy continues, challenges to Reaganism will constantly confront the proposition that you cannot argue with success. But rapid growth will also reinforce all the conditions that brought environmentalism and anti-consumerism to the fore during the 1960s. Environmental deterioration, gross materialism and increasing inequality will displace rising unemployment as major sources of dissatisfaction. The foolhardiness of an accelerating military budget will continue to gain adherents for the peace movement and supporters for alternative ways of spending public money. Prosperity, as discussed earlier, does not necessarily obviate discontent, and it provides resources that can be used for public programs. The anti-growth mentality of the Green Party is one element of its ideology that probably would not gain popularity in the US, but an emphasis on better use of the growth dividend might.

This paper began by noting the dependency of urban communities on higher levels of decision-making. Just as local governments are tied into national economic and political structures, so the fate of urban social movements depends on social action at these higher levels. But the basis of American electoral politics in relatively small territorial jurisdictions means that political organizing at the grassroots level, even when inspired by primarily local issues, can feed into broader movements. Urban social movements in themselves can do little to affect economic discontent, but they can be significant contributors to a national political coalition aimed at redirecting the course of the American economy and the distribution of its benefits.

REFERENCES

Aronowitz, Stanley (1984) 'Seeing green', *Voice Literary Supplement*, no. 27 (June): 19–21.

Bluestone, Barry and Bennett Harrison (1982) *The Reindustrialization of America*, New York: Basic Books.

Boyte, Harry C. (1980) *The Backyard Revolution*, Philadelphia: Temple University Press.

Buss, Terry F. and F. Stevens Redburn (1983) *Shutdown at Youngstown*, Albany: SUNY Press.

Cantor, Daniel (1983) 'ACORN, the UAW, and the Teamsters', *Social Policy*, 13 (Spring): 19–22.

Capra, Fritjof and Charlene Spretnak (1984) *Green Politics*, New York: E. P. Dutton.

Castells, Manuel (1984) 'Towards the informational city?'. Working Paper no. 430, Institute of Urban and Regional Development, University of California, Berkeley (August).

—— (1983) *The City and the Grassroots*, Berkeley: University of California Press.

—— (1982) 'Cultural identity and urban structure: the spatial organization of San Francisco's gay community'. In Norman I. Fainstein and Susan S. Fainstein (eds), *Urban Policy under Capitalism*, Beverly Hills: Sage.

—— (1978) *City, Class, and Power*, New York: St Martin's Press.

—— (1977) *The Urban Question*, Cambridge, Mass.: MIT Press.

—— (1975) 'Advanced capitalism, collective consumption, and urban contradictions'. In Leon Lindberg et al. (eds) *Stress and Contradictions in Modern Capitalism*. Lexington, Mass.: D. C. Heath.

Clavel, Pierre (1985) *The Progressive City: Planning and Participation*, New Brunswick, N.J.: Rutgers University Press.

Cloward, Richard and Frances Fox Piven (1983) 'Toward a class-based realignment of American politics: a movement strategy', *Social Policy*, 13 (Winter): 3–14.

Cooke, Philip (1984) 'Workers' plans: an alternative to entrepreneuralism?', *International Journal of Urban and Regional Research*, 8 (September): 421–37.

Creamer, Bob (1983) 'Illinois Public Action Council', *Social Policy*, 13 (Spring): 23–5.

Danziger, Sheldon, Robert Haveman and Robert Plotnick (1981) 'How income transfer programs affect work, savings, and the income distribution: a critical review', *Journal of Economic Literature*, 19 (September): 975–1028.

Davies, James C. (1969) 'The J-curve of rising and declining satisfactions as a cause of some great revolutions and a contained rebellion'. In Hugh Davis Graham and Ted Robert Gurr (eds) *Violence in America*. New York: New American Library, pp. 671–709.

Fainstein, Norman I. and Mark Martin (1978) 'Support for community control among local urban elites', *Urban Affairs Quarterly*, 13 (June): 443–68.

Fainstein, Susan S., Norman I. Fainstein, Richard Child Hill, Dennis Judd and Michael Peter Smith (1983) *Restructuring the City*, New York: Longman.

Fainstein, Susan S. and Norman I. Fainstein (1976) 'Local control as social reform: planning for big cities in the seventies', *Journal of the American Institute of Planners*, 42 (July): 275–85.

—— (1974) *Urban Political Movements*, Englewood Cliffs, N.J.: Prentice-Hall.

Fröbel, Folker, Jürgen Heinrichs and Otto Kreye (1980) *The New International Division of Labour*, Cambridge: Cambridge University Press.

Giddens, Anthony (1981) *A Contemporary Critique of Historical Materialism*. Berkeley: University of California Press.

Gorz, André (1982) *Farewell to the Working Class*, Boston: South End Press.

—— (1967) *Strategy for Labor*, Boston: Beacon Press.

Gottdiener, Mark (1984) 'Debate on the theory of space: toward an urban praxis'. In Michael Peter Smith (ed.), *Cities in Transformation*, Beverly Hills: Sage, pp. 199–218.

Gruson, Lindsey (1986) 'Tremors at Mack Truck jolt Pennsylvania town', *New York Times*, 17 January.

Haas, Gilda and Allan David Heskin (1981) 'Community struggles in Los Angeles', *International Journal of Urban and Regional Research*, 5 (December): 546–63.

Handman, Edward and Norman Adler (1983) 'District Council 37 (AFSCME) and the community', *Social Policy*, 13 (Spring): 42–4.

Heisler, Barbara Schmitter and Lily M. Hoffman (1988) ' "Threats to Homes" as a mobilization grievance: targets and constituencies', forthcoming.

Kelsey, Janet and Don Wiener (1983) 'The citizen/labor energy coalition', *Social Policy*, 13 (Spring): 15–18.

Lamiell, Pat (1985) 'Squatting in New York', *City Limits*, 10 (October): 12–16.

Melucci, Alberto (1985) 'The symbolic challenge of contemporary movements', *Social Research*, 52 (Winter): 789–816.

Miller, Mike (1983) 'San Francisco models', *Social Policy*, 13 (Spring): 30–2.

Miller, S. M. and Donald Tomaskovic-Devey (1983) 'A framework for new progressive coalitions', *Social Policy*, (Spring): 8–14.

Molotch, Harvey and John Logan (1984) 'Tensions in the growth machine: overcoming resistance to value-free development', *Social Problems*, 31 (June): 489–99.

National Commission on Neighborhoods (1979) *People, Building Neighborhoods*, Washington: USGPO.

O'Connor, James (1973) *The Fiscal Crisis of the State*. New York: St Martin's Press.

Offe, Clause (1985) 'New social movements: challenging the boundaries of institutional politics', *Social Research*, 52 (Winter): 817–68.

Peterson, Paul (1981) *City Limits*, Chicago: University of Chicago Press.

Piven, Frances Fox and Richard A. Cloward (1977) *Poor People's Movements*, New York: Pantheon.

Preteceille, Edmond (1981) 'Collective consumption, the state and the crisis of capitalist society'. In Michael Harloe and Elizabeth Lebas (eds), *City, Class and Capital*, London: Edward Arnold, pp. 1–16.

Rifkin, Jeremy and Randy Barber (1978) *The North Will Rise Again*, Boston: Beacon Press.

Sassen-Koob, Saskia (1984) 'The new labor demand in global cities'. In Michael Peter Smith (ed.), *Cities in Transformation*, Beverly Hills: Sage, pp. 139–71.

Saunders, Peter (1981) *Social Theory and the Urban Question*, New York: Holmes and Meier.

Shearer, Derek (1982) 'Planning and the new urban populism', *Journal of Planning Education and Research*, 2 (Summer).

Skocpol, Theda (1979) *States and Social Revolutions*, New York: Cambridge University Press.

Smith, Michael Peter and Dennis R. Judd (1984) 'American cities: the production of ideology'. In Michael Peter Smith (ed.), *Cities in Transformation*, Beverly Hills: Sage, pp. 173–96.

Tocqueville, Alexis de (1955) *The Old Regime and the French Revolution*, New York: Doubleday-Anchor.

Touraine, Alain (1985) 'An introduction to the study of social movements', *Social Research*, 52 (Winter): 749–87.

US Bureau of the Census (1985) 'Money income and poverty status of families and persons in the United States: 1984 (advance data from the March 1985 Current Population Survey)', *Current Population Reports*, Series P–60, no. 147 (August).

—— (1984) *Statistical Abstract of the United States: 1985*. Washington, D.C.

—— (1983) *Statistical Abstract of the United States: 1984*, Washington, D.C.

US Department of Housing and Urban Development (USDHUD) (1982), *The President's National Urban Policy Report, 1982*, Washington, D.C.

Zukin, Sharon (1985) ' "Reprivatizing" a New York City ghetto: Housing the working poor in the 1980s', unpublished manuscript.

Zukin, Sharon, and Zworman, Gilda (1985) 'Housing for the working poor: A historical view of Jews and Blacks in Brownsville', *New York Affairs*, 9(2): 3–18.

16

Restructuring and Popular Opposition in West German Cities

Margit Mayer

The particular nature and intensity of urban conflict and social movements in West Germany during the 1970s and early 1980s can be understood if analyzed in the context of the far-reaching and all-embracing restructuring and modernization process of German society, which the Social-Democrat government (1969–82) implemented in an attempt to maintain the nation's leading position within a changing world economy. The adaption to changing world market conditions was successfully managed by a policy of modernization, which resulted, however, in creating new divisions, and intensifying the dichotomy in German society between the 'core' and the 'margins'. It thereby created not only a need for more state intervention and social regulation, it also created its own opposition.

The marginal sector, or internal periphery, comprises not only the fractions of capital threatened by structural change and those without economic privileges (the unskilled, redundant, and surplus workers), but also all non-productive interests, e.g. environmental interests. Thus, people who opposed the destruction of cities or the natural environment were marginalized and presented as a threat to 'stable employment'. But even though every attempt has been made to exclude and marginalize this opposition – the so-called new social movements – it has succeeded, possibly because of its disrespect for parliamentary procedure, in exerting a stronger influence on the *substantive definition* of political conflicts of interest and on the definition of social problems than the traditional parties.

In this process, German cities have not only felt the concrete effects of restructuring, such as decay, renewal and gentrification; they have also experienced the narrowing of social and cultural life-styles, which reinforces the marginalization and discrimination of those social groups who cannot or do not want to adapt to this form of modernization. The process of 'colonization of living spaces' (Kolonisierung von Lebenswelten, Habermas, 1981) is most acutely felt in the inner cities, where restructuring threatens to expropriate the complex substructures of long-established social relations;

and where those social groups who are most vulnerable to the negative impacts of the modernization process (the so-called 'social problem groups' *and* those groups who play a pioneering role in the cultural reorientation and social innovation of life and work-styles are concentrated (like the young urban professionals of the new middle classes, students and young trainees).

Thus, cities constitute strategic arenas where the impacts of the economic and social restructuring and opposition to it take shape (Grottian and Nelles, 1983). As the role of most cities within the new international division of labor has changed, the necessary adaptation processes (the development of certain inner city areas for the new middle classes, intensified socio-spatial segregation, liberalization of housing policies and redevelopment), which the government sought to implement, effected not only large-scale changes of inner cities (Schwartz, 1982), but impacted also on the problem-solving capacity of the municipal governments. Both factors provided a basis for the emergence of a broad-based urban opposition.

The effects of these diverse factors coming together in the field of local politics are presented in this essay. It will be argued in effect, that a new political actor – constituency-based, (dis-)affected local interest groups which emerged from the social movement groups – has been created and absorbed into the local political machinery. Given state intervention (under a Christian-Democratic federal government) both to create conditions for technological restructuring and to dismantle welfare state functions, the future of these new political actors and of the innovative 'alternative' movement collectives remains uncertain.

In order to show what their potential and their limitations might be, we shall use a concept of the state as an historically specific (and dynamic) social relation. The theoretical framework underlying this analysis assumes that the position of the state within the reproduction context of capitalist societies, like the relationships between social classes and the state, does not remain static. Thus, the 'Fordist' form of capitalism, which is now entering a fundamental and secular crisis, implies not only a particular mode of surplus value production (Taylorism, mass production of consumer durable goods, division of labor at the level of the world market), but also a distinct form of the state: the Keynesian, social-democratic and corporatist welfare state.[1] Depending on the position of each country within the 'imperialist chain' and on its national, cultural and political traditions, Fordist societalization took on a specific form in each advanced industrialized country, but everywhere the modern welfare state emerged as a necessary corollary to the Fordist form of intensive accumulation (Aglietta, 1979). In this process, political parties and trade unions developed more bureaucratic and state-like apparatuses ('mass integrative apparatuses': Hirsch, 1980). Intensified competition on the world market forced national governments to orchestrate rapid and far-reaching changes in their economic and social structures. The resulting contradiction between world market-determined conditions and political legitimation produced conflicts which can no longer be described in simple class terms. As an essential means of mitigating these conflicts, bargaining between centralized and bureaucratized interest groups and the state administration emerged.

The crisis of the Fordist formation began worldwide in the mid-1970s: low growth rates, increasing mass unemployment, severe monetary crises, etc. began to show that capital can no longer profitably valorize under conditions of the Tayloristic labor process, egalitarian mass consumption and the welfare state. The whole institutional setting of the Keynesian state with its corporatist mode of institutionalizing class conflicts is becoming an impediment to the accumulation of capital.

The restructuring of cities can be interpreted both as a consequence of this crisis and as one of the ways to resolve it. Understanding the social and political conflicts which emerged in the 1960s and 1970s as a reaction to the Fordist form of societalization and to the political structure of the Fordist state *and* as part of its current hegemonic crisis is essential to this analysis, as it highlights the dynamic and direction of the political-economic processes which shape the local terrain and the role it will play in a new hegemonic strategy.

ECONOMIC RESTRUCTURING

Until the mid-1960s, the economic and social development of the Federal Republic of Germany was characterized by extremely rapid capital growth, leading to the rise of West Germany as a hegemonic center (Modell Deutschland). Annual GNP growth rates between 1950 and 1960 averaged 8 per cent, between 1960 and 1965 5.1 per cent, 1965 and 1970 4.7 per cent, but decreased to an average of 1.7 per cent during 1970–5 (cf. Kommission, 1977). During this period (1970–5), the manufacturing sector increased from 31 per cent of the GNP to 43.2 per cent, whereas the US manufacturing sector declined from 28.2 to 26 per cent of GNP (Semmler, 1982: 22). While the 1950s and the early 1960s were marked by unprecedented rates of growth in domestic production, in wage increases and declining rates of unemployment, this was also the result of an exceptional confluence of factors: relatively modern industrial plants, the weakened position of the working class and its organizations which had been destroyed by Fascism (cf. E. Schmidt, 1970; Rupp, 1978), the expansion of the world market, into which the specific structure of West German exports fit so well, and, lastly, a conservative and efficient bureaucratic state, which intervened massively in favor of the formation of capital. By international comparison, the wage rates were exceptionally low, thereby guaranteeing West German capital important competitive advantages in the world market.

The political-economic weakness of the working-class also facilitated this process of Fordist modernization: the thorough restructuring of industry, and major changes in regional development.

Hence, the proportion of investment goods within industrial production rose, in 1950–79, from 53 to 68 per cent, while that of consumption goods decreased from 33 to 28 per cent. During the same period, the (value) share of technologically advanced industries (chemicals, electronics, oil refining, plastics, cars) within industrial production rose from 17 to 38 per cent (Hirsch, 1974: 119 ff.). Export-led industries within the manufacturing sector have been leaders of this tremendous growth. They were well-placed for the world market boom of the 1950s as they were based in heavy industrial goods, durable manufactured goods, and oil-based chemicals and pharmaceuticals. The West German share of total world trade increased from 19.3 to 20.8 per cent in 1977 (Semmler, 1983: 23–8). The Federal Republic then established itself on the international market as leading supplier of producer and investment goods and thereby profited from the expanding world economy. Internal consequences were a predominance of technologically advanced and export-led capital, a shrinking of the agricultural sector, and the expansion of the service sector, all of which effected changes in the class structure of West German society, increasingly uneven regional strains, and, over time, grave ecological and infrastructural problems. These were exacerbated, as we shall see in the next section, by the political-administrative manipulation which aided in advancing the destruction of nature and environment in order to bring about profitable changes in the technology of production.

The intense world market penetration of West German industry, which was possible on the basis of specific power relations between the classes and of the conditions of accumulation during the so-called 'reconstruction period' implied that the *process of economic reproduction had become absolutely dependent upon the competitive position of West German capital on the world market*. This competitive position began to *fade* by the late 1960s with rising wage rates and with the end of the era of the undervalued Deutsch mark. The result was a sharp fall in the rate of profit culminating in the crisis of 1966/7 (Altvater et al., 1979: 84–7). Mediated through this first recession, capital began to accelerate the modernization of production technologies and to develop new forms of regulating the working class.

With increased international instability in the 1970s and the slower growth of world trade, exports could no longer function as a prevention against recessions. Instead, Germany increased its direct investments abroad and allowed the unemployment rate to rise (from 0.7 per cent in 1970 to 2.6 per cent in 1974: Hirsch, 1980: 16). The world economic crisis of 1974/5 marked a further change in the power relations between the classes: unemployment rose to 4.8 per cent in 1975, real wages began to fall and capital profits rose (and Helmut Schmidt took over from Willy Brand as Chancellor).

Both continued technological restructuring (increasing the capital-intensity of production) and changed market structures (monopolization, international capital penetration) set limits to the traditional Keynesian (demand-oriented) form of crisis regulation. Instead, since the mid-1970s, the government has followed a policy of selective measures to restructure industrial production in favour of industries which are more competitive on the world market. Guaranteeing capital's realization in Germany has meant and still means securing and expanding the relative hegemonic position of the FRG within the context of inter-imperialistic competition. West Germany's capacity for economic penetration of other areas, which had been the basis of exceptional economic stability and prosperity, also generated an intensifying pressure to adjust to changed competitive conditions on the world market. This adjustment has presupposed a *smooth* implementation of the restructuring processes of economic and social conditions – including their adverse impacts on the working and living conditions of the population. Participation in the new international division of labor implied the export of labor-intensive production and the tendency to (job-shedding) technological rationalization of the remaining production. Hence it implied that structural unemployment would rise, and that certain population groups would become marginalized (which presented a new potential for social conflict and a new need for state regulation). The ensuing shift towards the expanding service sector and also to the greater spatial separation of headquarters and production functions changed the regional distribution of unemployment: it is now concentrating in the urban agglomerations, with rates varying between 7 and 9 per cent.

The *political* organization of the export-accumulation strategy (Lankowsky, 1983: 111) has tended to take the form of *overall* regulation of the conditions of socialization and reproduction; assuming a stance of neo-realism, policies to balance the uneven regional development are given up.

POLITICAL DEVELOPMENT

Based on the 'economic miracle' of the 1950s and early 1960s, a consensus was shared by the political parties, which articulated the common belief in the social market economy, in an authoritarian form of democracy, and in joint West foreign politics. The Christian-Democratic Party, beginning with the first national election in 1949 and lasting until the 'Grand Coalition' of 1966, proved itself as the 'umbrella organization' of German industry and agriculture. While the economic policy pursued by the Adenauer regime refrained from direct national planning or a formal incomes policy, it played a crucial role in organizing postwar German capital through sectoral and regional economic policies. Among them were national agricultural policy, railway and highway development policy, massive housing and urban development projects, and state subsidies for the coal industry (later extended to other key industries such as shipbuilding and steel).

The changing capital realization conditions in the world market context in the mid-1960s required, however, intensified intervention of the state into the process of social reproduction. Administration was centralized, planning and decision-making agencies with regard to 'structural politics' were made autonomous, the repressive apparatus expanded. These changes did not so much mean an augmentation of the 'steering capacities' of the state; rather, the technologically dominant capital fractions/monopolies used the financial and organizational capacities of the state for their development and investment strategies. The necessary processes of social and economic restructuring could only be accomplished by administrative means.

State policies comprising crisis management since the 1966/7 recession (first under the 'Grand Coalition' from 1966 to 1969; and since 1969 under the Social-Democratic government) accompanied and accelerated drastic societal restructuring, which implied not only deleterious consequences (especially of ecological nature), but which also produced specific new (dis-)affected groups. The intensification of state intervention, and the expanding reach of the state into all spheres of society; the shift of political decision-making to the executive; the growth of service functions of the public administration; and the transition to political planning which occurred as part of the crisis-management policies which the SPD initiated (cf. M. Schmidt, 1978), all caused on the one hand an 'overall responsibility' of the administration, and, on the other hand, a fragmental field of social conflicts.

The world market-oriented economic strategies thus presented new sources for structural crisis and produced a division of society into a core, which is economically and socially secure, and insecure margins of permanently unemployed, of welfare recipients, and of high concentrations of women and youths. The economic adjustment process to new world market conditions, which underlies the crisis management attempts since 1966/7, thus required a concomitant *societal* restructuring: domestic policies from the Urban Development Act 1971 (*Städtebauförderungsgesetz*) to the Federal Spatial Zoning Program (*Bundesraumordnungsprogramm*) have been geared to make production structures more flexible. The Urban Development Act expanded government powers to engage in urban renewal and redevelopment to rationalize inner-city land uses. The mid-seventies also saw the demise of the traditional policies of urban expansion and renewal which had accompanied the growth of the working class.

In short, the intensification of world market competition led to pressures to rationalize and to innovate in the dominant industries. In order to protect and maintain the profitability of the national location for increasingly internationally operating capital, the national 'intervention state' chose to pursue a ruthless modernizing strategy, which, over time, produced severe social, cultural and ecological destruction.

Legitimate political action was, however, restricted to party-based action, and limited to those parties which were seen as safeguarding the 'free, democratic basic order'.

These parties had undergone quite a transformation from their traditional function of articulating and mediating different and opposing interests to the political decision-making process. They had become 'mass integrative parties' operating as regulative transmission agents between the state bureaucracy and the people subject to their measures. In other words, their role has become one of mediating the constraints *to* the affected social groups, as they seek to destabilize them, to filter and process their interests in such a way as to make them congruent with the requirements of world market integration.

The Social-Democratic Party played a crucial role in implementing the state interventionist modernization strategy, which made continued economic growth and relatively low unemployment rates possible. It also played a significant role for the political integration of the working class and for the corporatist inclusion of the unions. What this also meant, however, was that the SPD no longer functioned as a potential focus for extra-parliamentary opposition movements. The ensemble of political institutions in Germany during the 1970s was thus characterized by a high degree of selectivity with regard to which interests it would respond to. It limited access to the process of political decision-making to the major interest groups (who were quite capable of articulating and achieving their demands both within the party apparatuses and within the sectoral political arenas); it was further characterized by a sectoral interpenetration of the peaks of the major associations, bureaucracies and party apparatuses, who effectively undermined the formal decision-making powers of parliaments. The participation and decision-making procedures thus systematically excluded all interests which were adversely affected by the consequences of the modernization strategy. Hence, these interests mobilized outside of and against the institutions of the established system. The heterogeneous and scattered opposition forces of the 1960s clustered into grassroots structures of their own and developed new organizational forms, which were intensely geared towards autonomy and independence from the state.

So, while the coalition parties' implementation of modernizing strategies, in which the state apparatus and the central interest organizations of the 'social partners' cooperated, was a splendid success in terms of institutionalizing the traditional forms of class struggle, these very strategies produced at the same time new conflicts and opposition, which the parties were ill-equipped to handle. In fact, what developed was a frontal opposition between parliamentary parties and the new social movements, whose demands the parties could not satisfy. On the one hand, the statist form of modernization was experienced as administrative intrusion into people's living space; urban renewal and zoning reforms (i.e. adapting land use patterns to the modernization process) were experienced as paternalistic intervention. On the other hand, new and autonomous interest groups emerged in opposition to this hegemonic political culture, which were shaped by their anti-statist conception of politics. The emergence of citizens' initiatives in the 1970s, then, is not only due to the proliferation of adverse consequences of capital restructuring at the local level, but also to the *statist* and technocratic form reform politics took on in West Germany.

The stronger the protest movements grew in the course of the early 1970s, the more the defensive reactions of the established parties against the *form* of politics as well as against the demands (especially ecological and democratic demands) they formulated, intensified. (The pressure to conform to the party form of politics eventually led to the formation of the Green Party nationally.)

Notably since the economic crisis of 1974/5, when the margin for reform-oriented political incorporation and for material concessions diminished, and the SPD dropped all reform projects in favor of direct subsidization of modernization, mobilization against the negative effects of urban restructuring as well as against the monopoly of established parties to articulate political interests intensified. At the same time, the 'representative absolutism' (Roth, 1985), combined with the repressive and marginalizing strategies applied by the administration, exacerbated the tendency of extra-parliamentarian movements to politicize into the autonomous, anti-statist stance, which opposes the restriction of legitimate political action to parliamentarism and the monopoly of that arena by the established parties.

In short, a 'corporatist regulation cartel' (Hirsch, 1983: 83), consisting of the mass parties, the bureaucratic unions, employers' associations, and a state administration with broad social and economic regulating functions, succeeded in containing 'old' class conflict. It succeeded through welfare-statist class compromise and through industrial growth. Its very modernizing strategies however, created new conflicts and new victims. Uneven regional development, environmental destruction, rising unemployment rates and growing marginalization all challenged the acceptance and legitimacy of the politics of the regulation cartel. As the contradictions between the imperatives of the world market-centered growth politics and a mass integrative system based on the availability of material concessions have increased, a new opposition emerged in the form of a socially heterogeneous alliance of social movements and organizations. Against the values of affluence, economic stability and security, they posit participation, solidarity, self-realization and the recovery (or conservation) of cultural and natural resources.

The Berlin squatters directly challenged local 'regulative cartel' control but also offered an innovative housing reform strategy. Citizens' initiatives in all major cities have formed since the early 1970s to protest against large-scale redevelopment in inner cities, as well as airport expansions, environmental depredation, or the lack of access to decision-making processes. The so-called alternative movement has organized democratic self-managed cooperatives both in the production as well as in the service sector, thereby challenging the social-levelling and uniform life- and work-styles imposed by social-democratic welfare politics. The women's movement in particular raises issues of identity and gender in a way that challenges their increasing commodification and subjection to the capitalist norm. And the cultural experiments of collectives, who have attempted to live in nascent utopian communities, offer experiences which challenge the imposition of the Fordist discipline (cf. generally Brand et al., 1984).

THE MOVEMENTS

Urban movements represent the politically active side of a (far larger) social sector which has become marginalized in the process of economic structural change. They took a different form from movements in the United States because restructuring policies there produced an increase in poverty combined with a decline in access to affordable housing and social services (Fainstein and Fainstein, 1985). Rather, they coalesced and acquired their ideological slant during the era of growth, and hence on a relatively higher economic level, so that marginalization tendencies have not been as pronounced, and social homogeneity and stability have been maintained to a greater degree than in the United States. The marginalization tendencies which do take place, transcend communities rather than manifest themselves spatially in segregated neighborhoods. This stability served as a precondition for their specific self-expression and for the political thought which expressed itself in the new social movements, just as later developments indicate intensifying marginalization and increasing spatial segregation in German cities – a recent trend which has been called the 'Americanization of the German cities'.

At their height, the housing struggles were not just about a need for more houses. Rather, they constituted a defense of urban living space against the grasp of expanding welfare state bureaucracies and capitalist corporations; they were about the self-determined structure of living conditions. The squatter movement in particular explored alternative, self-defined life- and work-styles in direct action by squatting in vacant houses (Brandes and Schoen, 1981; Laurisch, 1981; Roth, 1981; Aust and Rosenblad, 1981). The corresponding political form of collective disobedience fundamentally questioned the prevailing system. The interests and needs which were articulated in this struggle, and the real problems of the housing market, took on a symbolic significance for a host of other protest reasons. They crystallized the desire for alternative, non-Taylorized uniform/bureaucratized life-styles; a critique of mass consumption models; and the demand for participation in politics and personal self-fulfilment against bureaucratic alienation and oppression. Not surprisingly then, the motives of the squatters frequently overlapped with the interests of more moderate citizens' initiatives in self-help housing rehabilitation, or with the interests of alternative collectives in suitable conditions for expanding their projects. But just as often the motives diverged.

The diversity and specificity of issues dissolved in each city into a local movement culture. This process was accelerated by the strong anti-authoritarian protest movements of the 1960s and early 1970s. Thus, the emergence of a complex network of self-organized living and work collectives – albeit dependent on the benefits of the German welfare state – has been a characteristic of the West German movement culture. The substantial infrastructure created also provided the material basis for the movement's political image of autonomy. This sense of autonomy, the concept of politics as anti-statist, and the slower (compared to the United States) process of separation between political protest and an alternative culture, which characterize the urban social movements in West Germany, are a result of the global context and Germany's role within it, as described above.

Rather than the insular issue definition characterizing American movements, there has been a more complex challenge to hegemonic values. Given the relatively centralized German federal system, and the integrated party structure, but especially given the highly statist and corporate system of interest regulation, most German citizens' initiatives, while locally based, frequently became nationally focused. Whenever opposition to a local issue emerges – be it a large-scale industrial or nuclear plant, a highway, toxic wastes, plant closure or even urban renewal – the protest immediately confronts the whole state and the whole party apparatus. This kind of politicization through and against the 'nuclear state' takes place almost automatically.

While materially these movements quite obviously never could maintain themselves independently of the state, and were in fact built upon the material conditions provided by the German welfare state, their image as anti-institutional and anti-statist has been a strong unifying thread of the so-called 'second culture'. This unity was reinforced by the fact that the needs they expressed confronted a political system which initially was incapable of responding to or mediating their interests.

By the end of the 1970s, the beginning of a shift in the relationship between movements and the state could be observed. Due to the rise in unemployment and the dismantling of the 'social net', more pragmatic and need-oriented claims began to edge out the oppositional utopian demands of the earlier years. Pressures for programs, policies and funding for alternative projects began to be directed at the state, and particularly at the various local states. A long conflictual process took place inside the movements concerning this shift away from autonomy and pure opposition. In all the different kinds of alternative project (in squats, in production collectives, in alternative social service projects) one could find very difficult, often mutually exclusive definitions of the situation and of the social practice they were engaged in.

The 370 squats in the Federal Republic were not only symbols of resistance; the appropriation of 'free spaces' was also a means for divergent, frequently contradictory purposes: while to some they were means of militant struggle against the state or of a radical political critique, others used them as means for self-realization or for exemplary alternative, constructive projects (Hilgenberg and Schlicht, 1981; Brandes and Schoen, 1981). While all movement participants had in common the critique of the prevailing norms of production and consumption, only a small fraction of the movement was able to project alternative models. Even during the peak of the squatters' movement in West Berlin, the attempt to create a common organizational infrastructure for a squatters' movement that involved thousands of people (the Squatters' Council) failed because of the inherent diversity of the movement. The different interests – alienated youths in niches in a protected milieu; citizens' and tenants' initiatives in 'careful' urban renewal and in self-help; the left trying to impose their critical positions on the ongoing struggle; and the various political, alternative and women's groups in favorable environments for expanding their own projects – facilitated joint action in certain mass protests, but did not allow the common development of feasible politics.

Targeted, harsh repression by the state, especially with regard to the squatters' movement in West Berlin (where 54 police evictions, 410 police raids, 4687 criminal investigations and 2287 arrests took place: Der Senator für Inneres, 1984: 6) played a complementary role in exacerbating and isolating the different interests.

At the same time, the physical state of the houses, which had more often than not been systematically run down by the development agencies, made the demand for subsidization of rehabilitation measures a necessity for those groups remaining in the houses after the eviction/legalization phase. For that purpose, they would have to organize within the appropriate legal framework and gradually take on the behavior that is typical of interest representation organizations.

A similar development could be observed with the approximately 160 different citizens' initiatives, women's projects and alternative collectives, which in 1981 in Berlin formed an umbrella organization in order to get public funding for their projects on the grounds that they were doing 'socially useful work'. While the activists among them understood this demand as a political offensive on the voluntarism propagated by the Christian Democratic Party, more and more projects joined the umbrella

(*Arbeitskreis Staatsknete*), which were new, with little political experience, and with high hopes for *individual* funding. Still, it should be emphasized that such different groups, ranging from explicitly political citizens' initiatives to protest and women's groups, and projects experimenting with self-help in social services as well as in production, did organize in a *common* interest for the purpose of supporting their different projects.

Berlin's *Arbeitskreis Staatsknete* spearheaded a development which began to take place soon after in other cities, as economic conditions and marginalization (especially youth unemployment) undermined the position of alternative projects everywhere. Their financial situation throughout West Germany began to deteriorate by 1982 (Grottian, 1983: 28; Beywl, 1983: 97; Kohlenberger and Schwartz, 1983). Professionalization and a readiness to participate in the political bargaining process wherever it opened up were the consequences.

The originally polarized relationship between the urban social movements and the state has thus subtly changed into one between interest groups and a welfare bureaucracy increasingly confronted with its own limitations. The projects – either in order to survive or, less egotistically, in order to revitalize a neighborhood, or deliver a social service which otherwise would be inadequate or not exist – decided to cooperate.

FORMS OF INCORPORATION

The incorporation of the oppositional and marginalized sectors of the 'second society' via parliamentary representation by the Green and Alternative Lists is one of the most important changes in the West German political landscape in the past twenty years. The effects of parliamentary compromise, of time constraints, of concentration on elections and budgets, of pressure to jettison symbolic counter-politics and pay due respect to established parliamentary ritual – in other words, of the parliamentary form itself – on movement goals are becoming evident with the development of the Green Party since it gained its first seats in Parliament (cf. Zeuner, 1985). Less obvious are the forms of incorporation through 'decentralized corporatism', which are emerging in certain policy sectors.

This form of incorporation (as opposed to the experience of the United States) has been quite difficult to achieve. First, the American neighborhood movement of the 1970s was much more goal-oriented and far less dominated by political-ideological themes. Second, political access at the local level is much easier in the United States than has been the case in Germany. These and other factors facilitated a development 'from protest to program' and from 'movement to interest group activity' (Warren, 1982; cf. Clarke and Mayer, 1986). In spite of the lack of these factors, in West Germany too, channels of communication have been established at the local and regional levels, often between alternative projects and conservative Christian Democratic administrations.

In West Berlin, a modern social services program organized by CDU officials funds social projects based on client self-help and voluntary co-production of health services. This program was established in response to the demands for state funding of alternative social, cultural and political projects. While the umbrella organization *Arbeitskreis Staatsknete* had demanded funding for a self-administered fund from various departments (Health, Social Services, Culture, Science, Urban Development, Economics, Education), the CDU offer was limited to social services and health-related activities. This program, to which 266 self-help groups applied (for a total of DM 36 million) during its first year (1983), funded 144 self-help groups (with DM 4 million) active in health and social projects working with women, immigrants and handicapped people. The funding conditions encourage voluntary staff rather than the recruitment of salaried staff: and they require that a large share of their work be channelled into form-filling and writing reports so that a number of the projects decided not to renew their applications after the first year. They found the control over their work and the redefinition of their goals too intrusive. Instead they seek support from Netzwerk, the largest alternative self-help organization, which distributes donations from approximately 6000 members in support of democratically-organized, self-administered economic, political and social projects, from the Oeko-funds (see below, p. 358), or private donors.

In West Berlin too, in part as a response to the housing problems which the squatter movement has made so public, a self-help rehabilitation program was institutionalized by the Housing Senate. Various intermediary organizations, both technical assistance and socially-oriented renewal agents, have been included in the planning, formulation and implementation of housing and social policies (cf. Mayer, 1984: 20–31).

The Christian-Democratic government in West Berlin has exhibited the two faces of the state: liberal (by its Departments for Social Affairs and Housing) and authoritarian (by its Department of Interior). The case is so clear-cut that it may lead the way to the 'post-fordist' authoritarian state, which is paralleled by a decentralized and fragmented corporatism. Meanwhile, other local governments have responded with different emphases to the urban social movements of the 1970s and early 1980s.

Because of its unique political and economic situation, and because it attracts such large numbers of marginalized groups, Berlin has often been used as a testing ground for experimenting with innovative social policies; but conservative governments in Germany's southern growth belt (Baden-Württemberg, Bavaria) has displayed a similar readiness to absorb solutions developed by the alternative scene. While these cities, characterized by new, hi-tech growth industries and tertiary expansion do not (yet) have to deal with marginalized groups, their Christian-Democrat governments have also begun to encourage self-reliance and self-help as 'limited social experiments' (Landesregierung von Baden-Württemberg, 1983: 137). Leading CDU politicians, who are promoting the role southern cities will have within the new national division of labor, anticipate that this growth will also produce social disintegration and divisions. Precisely for that reason, the local state is called upon to mobilize small groups and associations and private households, so that not only cheaper, but also more effective versions of a social welfare society can be explored.

On the other hand, those traditional industrial regions of Germany (the Ruhr valley, Nordrhine-Westphalia) which experience massive deindustrialization and high unemployment rates (due to huge job losses in steel, etc.), and where locally the Social-Democrats are in power, have experienced a more hesitant response by the local state to the social movements. Because job creation has been the primary goal of the Social-Democrats, they have responded to those sectors of the movement which promise to give employment to the structurally unemployed in the German Model. SPD-run states (*Länder*) have initiated funding programs for worker cooperatives; they are also responsive to pressures to correct economic promotion policies and enterprise laws, so that small and unconventional businesses can more easily receive public funding.

In the state of Hesse, alternative collectives from various spheres have formed an association to represent their financial needs to the Green and Social-Democratic Parties, which have formed a majority government. In return for supporting the SPD, the Green Party has secured state funding for cooperative models of self-management (cf. Voigt, 1985).

The city state governments of both Bremen and Hamburg have also started (and the state of Nordrhine-Westphalia is preparing to start) funding programs aimed at generating jobs in the alternative 'industry'. These SPD-initiated programs, while pursuing labor market goals which are specific to Social-Democratic politics, are also responses to alternative production collectives, which had come together to demand legal changes and start-up help to facilitate their productive enterprises. Unconventional employment initiatives are explored particularly in the new technologies sector (cf. Sund, 1984).

THE PARTIES

It is easy to see that the Social-Democratic concept of restructuring the cities is still strongly influenced by a Keynesian growth agenda and oriented towards the sectors of the social core. 'Etatist corporatism', based on the cooperation between the state and centralized interest organizations on the one hand and an institutionalized compromise formation between social partners on the other, characterizes the Social-Democratic mode of regulation; in their struggle to recapture power both locally and nationally, the SPD hesitates to replace 'egalitarian' welfare state services with self-help forms of provision. Only in the sphere of employment policies and job-training can the SPD promote innovative strategies, but mostly as strategies for the margins, for the so-called 'second labor market'.

While the Social-Democratic Party leadership insists on a marginalizing and only tactically instrumental cooperation with Alternatives and Greens (cf. Glotz, 1984: the SPD has to become the 'organizing center of a German Left capable of coming a majority'), in various SPD-run cities (e.g. Munich) programs have been initiated outside the official job market-related policies: experiments in new and old (cooperative) forms of non-state organized social security and politics are being tested in social and housing areas, even if in the attempt to recapture the Green vote.

Generally, the instrumentalizing SPD strategy still aims to defend 'the welfare state' at a time when the state-organized and the traditional professional social service system clearly can no longer adequately deliver to the specific social welfare needs that are the result of the adverse effects of the modernizing strategies.

The Christian-Democratic Party faced fewer barriers to including collective self-organization and self-help in their program. In fact, it is argued that new, co-production involving forms of problem management, represent a qualitative improvement of the welfare state. The frequently invoked concept of *Subsidiarität* (loosely translated as 'help for self-help') implies a transformation rather than a dismantling of the welfare state. The goal of the various local CDU-sponsored programs for self-help groups is to deal with the current problems of the welfare state: mobilizing social self-organization is to counter the dependency of citizens on the state, the anonymity of social welfare systems, and the bureaucratization and centralization of all spheres of life (Dettling, 1984). The cut-back measures of the conservative coalition were portrayed as a means to strengthen the solidaric structures of the social security system through more individual responsibility.

Thus, the CDU version which provides a key role to small-scale networks and self-organized citizens' activity, opens up both more (than the SPD strategy) and less (because of its individualizing and privatizing form) space for the activity of counter-cultural groups.

The Green Party, which has become the parliamentary representative of oppositional and marginalized sectors of the so-called 'Second Society', is only just beginning to formulate concepts of how a direct communication between alternative groups and the state could be shaped. At this point, positions within the party are both varied and ill-defined.

While a platform submitted by the Baden-Württemberg Greens prior to the 1983 national elections contained a rather naive proposal for an 'ecological social politics' as the alternative both to conservative dismantling and Social-Democratic defense of the welfare state, by 1984 most Green thinkers had recognized that the CDU also envisaged a restructuring of the state that goes beyond 'dismantling'. Efforts to define more precisely a counter-concept to the prevailing social politics are, however, still under way. Meanwhile, the Green Fraction in Bonn has published party proposals for legal changes regarding funding for alternative enterprises and technical assistance agencies (*Arbeitsföerderungsgesetz*) and regarding cooperatives (*Genossenschafisgesetz*). These proposals are incorporated in a draft (Gesetz-entwurf zur Förderung von örtlichen Beschäftigungsinitiativen, 1984) submitted to Parliament during the recent round of budget negotiations. Their focus is job-creation in and through non-profit, democratic enterprises engaged in ecological and socially useful production. While this effort can not really be more than an impulse to advancing at the national level the debate on state-funding for alternative projects, the result of the coalition between the Greens and the SPD in Hesse is a practical example of shaping a link between (an association of) alternative projects and the state. Since such state funding has been quite meager to date, the Green Party has also established a so-called 'Eco-fund' (Oeko-Fonds) to support alternative projects (including, importantly, political projects) with campaign income received by the party under West German laws governing public financing of elections. So far, these Eco-funds are in operation in eight German states, and are governed by an advisory board made up of representatives of alternative projects and of 'public figures'.

EFFECTS OF THE NEW FORMS OF INCORPORATION

Our first hypothesis was that the patterning of new state policies oriented towards alternative projects would advance the process of differentiation and fragmentation within the urban movements. It appears that this has been the case: the West German 'movement sector' now appears fragmented into parts which fit in to the respective administrative bureaucracies. The self-organized forms of movement decision-making which have developed over the years or in conflict situations have either been pushed aside by the state bureaucracy itself, or have been restructured into constrained stable 'addressees' for the state as a result of meeting the legal and organizational conditions for funding. Moreover, since these representative organizations must continue to be connected to and be seen as minimally legitimate by their constituency, many such intermediary organizations experience internal conflict, competition for recognition as representatives, and goal dissonance. In all cases under study, conflicts appeared between the self image of the groups and the criteria of the funding agencies. Grassroots groups continued to see themselves in opposition to the state, even as intermediary representatives already marketed their labor as workable solutions to social conflict and policy innovation. Many such 'basis groups' did not see themselves as 'marginal groups who are into interesting social projects', despite the fact, for example, that a marked shift was observable from self-organization as a component of political struggle to self-help as an aspect of social welfare policy.

A second hypothesis was that the beginnings of a form of incorporation through 'decentralized corporatism' on the local level, similar to that in the United States (cf. Clarke, 1984), would be observable. Indicators of such a phenomenon would be changes in the patterns of participation and decision-making, in which smaller agencies, self-help groups and alternative projects formally and administratively shared in policy formation and implementation with established agencies. In so far as interest organizations of alternative projects, self-help groups and community-based organizations are in fact included in state agency procedures from which they had previously been excluded, then it can be said that this hypothesis has been confirmed. Groups such as these participate in legislative negotiations and influence the manner in which policies directly affecting their interests are implemented. Also, these new institutions tend to stabilize a tripartite relationship among (1) alternative groups active in social and community politics, (2) the large, established (private) non-profit social welfare or urban development organizations, and (3) state agencies. This reinforces the argument in favor of the emergence of decentralized corporatism, and suggests that a new political terrain – and not simply a symbolic playground – is being formed.

Finally, a third hypothesis was that these new forms of incorporation would serve as models in debates and practices leading to a restructuring of the welfare state; that is, it would be possible to observe the emergence of a new structure of politics. What has so far appeared, however, leaves this hypothesis unanswered. It can be argued that the pattern according to which social policy is being carried out in West Germany has quantitatively expanded by the incorporation of newly recognized intermediaries and constituencies into the process. This, however, has not brought about a qualitative transformation of social welfare or urban development policy formation and program implementation structures. Hence the inclusion of constituency-based intermediaries into the established framework appears to improve the regulatory capacities of the local administrative apparatus, and does not imply a growth of local democracy as is often suggested.

As we have seen in the first sections, the world market-oriented socio-economic and infrastructural processes have brought about various changes with which the traditional forms and procedures of formally democratic political decision-making could not adequately deal. For example, the increasingly uneven regional strains required a new way to deal with the role of regional minorities in the implementation of large-scale industrial projects. Or the increases in social and cultural marginalization are calling for a harmonious way of processing potential conflict.

So, the question of the possible restructuring of the welfare state through corporatist forms of self-help, voluntarism and co-production may have less to do with expanding democracy than with streamlining conservative strategies of privatization. The Christian-Democrats may be more capable than the Social-Democrats of establishing a new balance between the private and the public sector (between 'individual responsibility and solidarity' as they call it: Landesregierung von Baden-Württemberg, 1983: 193), with a greater emphasis on authoritarian and self-policing forms of social control than on integrative and monetary forms. As Michael Davis has oberved with respect to 'post-Fordist America', the new conservatives share a 'vigorously anti-statist' rhetoric with the alternative culture. However, the 'real programmatic intention' of the conservatives is the 'restructuring, rather than diminution, of state spending and intervention in order to expand the frontiers of entrepreneurial and rentier opportunity' (Davis, 1984, 35). The new corporatism may prove to be the vehicle by which such a strategy could be implemented. Then, the hidden function of the alternative scene could turn out to be advancing the adjustment to new technological requirements; the squatters would have spearheaded the type of urban renewal/revitalization which paves the way for the necessary restructuring of the cities (Siebel, 1983); alternative production collectives would have functioned as fore-runners of those new jobs which are likely to emerge in small-scale rather than large, but high-tech outfits, in service rather than industrial sectors (Personick, 1981, 28–41; Henckel et al., 1984).

Whether such scenarios will actually become reality, will depend not only on the way the international competition develops and the way German society is restructured in order to meet its pressures. It will also depend on the contradictory possibilities that are now emerging for the new social needs and interests to express themselves. The innovations in the patterns of interest intermediation which have been observed consist of incorporating new social needs and desires for collective, democratic forms of work and living arrangements into existing program structures. The social content of self-organization and direct labor of 'affected' local/urban constituencies, which are brought into the regulation mechanism by interest groups that were not formerly organized as such or used to be marginalized, does resonate with some conservative austerity strategies. The outcome will remain a question of unfolding power relationships within the new political arrangements in a society fissured by more divisions and more cross-cutting cleavages than ever before.

NOTE

1 The 'Fordist' form of capitalism emerged first in the U.S. between the 1930s and 1950s. According to Aglietta (1979: 116–17): 'It marks a new stage in the regulation of capitalism, the regime of intensive accumulation in which the

capitalist class seeks overall management of the production of wage-labour by the close articulation of relations of production with the commodity relations in which the wage earners purchase their means of consumption. Taylorism is the mode of organization of the production process, when increased division of labor allows for its automation, for example, on the assembly line.'

REFERENCES

Aglietta, Michel (1979) *A Theory of Capitalist Expansion. The US Experience*, London: NLB.

Altvater, Elmar, Jürgen Hoffmann and Willi Semmier (1975) *Vom Wirtschaftswunder zur Wirtschaftskrise*, Berlin West

Aust, Stefan and Sabine Rosenblad, (eds) (1981) *Hausbesetzer: Wofür sie kaempfen, wie sie leben, und wie sie leben wollen*, Hamburg: Hoffman and Campe.

Beywl, Wolfgang (1983) 'Alternative Ökonomie – Modell zur Finanzierung von Selbsthilfeprojekten'. In Lother Bertels and Hans-Gerd Nottenbohm (eds), *Ausser man tut es. Beitraege zu wirtschaftlichen und sozialen Alternativen*, Bochum: Germinal.

Brand, Karl-Werner, Detlef Büsser and Dieter Rucht (1984) *Aufbruch in eine andere Gesellschaft. Neue soziale Bewegungen in der Bundesrepublik*. Frankfurt: Campus.

Brandes, Volker and B. Schön, (eds) (1981) *Wer sind die Instandbesetzer?* Bensheim: Paedextra Verlag.

Clarke, Susan (1984) 'Urban America, Inc.: A corporatist convergence of power in American cities?'. Discussion Paper no. 18, Center for Public Policy Research, University of Colorado.

Clarke, Susan and Margit Mayer (1986) 'Responding to grassroots discontent: Germany and the United States', *International Journal of Urban and Regional Research* vol. 10, no. 3, (September).

Davis, Michael (1984) 'The political economy of late-imperial America', *New Left Review* 143 (Jan./Feb.).

Dettling, Warnfried (1983) 'Krise des Wohlfahrtsstaats'. In *Krise der Arbeitsgesellschaft. Verhandlungen des 21. Deutschen Soziologentags in Bamberg 1982*, Frankfurt: Campus.

—— (1984) 'Neues Verständnis von staatlicher Politik', *Neue Gesellschaft*, Heft 4.

Deubner, Christian et al. (1979) *Die Internationalisierung des Kapitals*, Frankfurt: Campus.

Fainstein, Susan and Norman Fainstein, 1985. 'Economic restructuring and the rise of urban social movements', *Urban Affairs Quarterly*, 21/2 (December 1985).

Froebel, Folker, Jürgen Heinrichs and Otte Kreye (1980) *The New International Division of Labor: Structural Unemployment in Industrialized Countries and Industrialization in Developing Countries*, Cambridge, Mass.: Cambridge University Press.

Gesetzentwurf der Fraktion DIE GRUENEN (1984) 'Entwurf eines Gesetzes zur Förderung örtlicher Beschäftigugsinitiativen', 16 December. Deutscher Bundestag, Drucksache 10/2576, 16 December.

Glotz, Peter (1984) *Die Arbeit der Zuspitzung. Über die Organisation einer regierungsfähigen Linken*, Berlin West.

Grottian, Peter (1983) 'Steuergelder für Alternativprojekte?'. In Peter Grottian and Wilfried Nelles (eds), *Großtadt und soziale Bewegungen*. Basel: Birkhäuser Verlag.

Habermas, Jürgen (1981) *Theorie des kommunikativen Handelns*, Frankfurt: Suhrkamp.

Henckel, D., E. Nopper and N. Rauch (1984) *Informationstechnologie und Stadtentwicklung*, Stuttgart: Kohlhammer.

Hilgenberg, D. and U. Schlicht (1981) 'Was Hausbesetzer denken. Auswertung von 57 Interviews, *Der Tagesspeigel*. 10 October.

Hirsch, Joachim (1974) *Staatsapparat und Reproduktin des Kapitals*, Frankfurt: Suhrkamp.

—— (1980) *Der Sicherheitsstaat. Das 'Modell Deutschland', seine Krise, und die neuen sozialen Bewegungen*, Frankfurt: Europäische Verlagsanstalt.

—— (1983) 'Fordist security state and new social movements', *Kapitalistate*, 11.

Kohlenberger, Lothar and Hans-Albrecht Schwartz (1983) 'Mit den Alternativen in eine neue Zukunft? Überlegungen zu einigen Aspekten der Alternativbewegung'. In Grottian and Nelles, *op. cit.*

Kommission für wirtschaftlichen und sozialen Wandel (1977) *Wirtschaftlicher und sozialer Wandel in der Bundesrepublik Deutschland*, Göttingen.

Landesregierung von Baden-Württemberg (ed.) (1983) *Zukunftsperspektiven gesellschaftlicher Entwicklungen*, Stuttgart.

Lankowski, Carl F. (1982) 'Modell Deutschland and the international regionalization of the West German state in the 1970s', in A. Markovits (ed.), *The Political Economy of West Germany*, New York: Praeger.

Laurisch, Bernd (1981) *Kein Abriss unter dieser Nummer*, Göttingen: Anabas.

Markovits, Andrei (ed.) (1982) *The Political Economy of West Germany. 'Modell Deutschland'*, New York: Praeger.

Mayer, Margit (1984) 'Stadtteilbezogene Interessen und soziale Bewegungen. Eine vergleichende Untersuchung von Entwicklungstendenzen im Verhaeltnis zwischen staedtischen Bewegungen und Staat in den USA und der BRD'. DFG-Projektbericht, May.

Personick V. (1981) 'The outlook for industry output and employment through 1990', *Monthly Labor Review*, August.

Roth, Roland (1981) 'Die Magie des fliegenden Pflastersteins. Zu einigen Neuerscheinungen ueber die Hausbesetzungen und Jugendrevolten 1980/81', *Kriminalsoziologische Bibliographie*, 31/32.

Roth, Roland (1985) 'Neue soziale Bewegungen in der politischen Kultur der Bundesrepublik Deutschland'. In K.-W. Brand (ed.), *Neue soziale Bewegungen in Westeuropa und den USA*, Frankfurt: Campus.

Rupp, Hans-Carl (1978) *Politische Geschichte der Bundesrepublik Deutschland*, Stuttgart.

Schlupp, Frieder (1980) 'Modell Deutschland and the international division of labor: The FRG in the world political economy'. In Ekkehard Krippendorf and Volker Rittberger (eds), *The Foreign Policy of West Germany: Formation and Contents*, Beverly Hills: Sage.

Schlupp, Frieder (1979) 'Internationalisierung und Krise. Das "Modell Deutschland" im metropolitanen Kapitalismus', *Leviathan* I: 12–35.

Schmidt, Eberhard (1970) *Die verhinderte Neuordnung 1945–1952*, Frankfurt.

Schmidt, Manfred G. (1978) 'The politics of domestic reform in the Federal Repubic of Germany'. *Politics and Society*, 8: 165–200.

Schwartz, Gail Garfield (ed.), *Advanced Industrialization and the Inner Cities,* Lexington, Mass.: Lexington Books.

Semmler, Willi, (1982) 'Economic aspects of Model Germany: A comparison with the United States'. In Markovits (ed.) *op. cit.*

Der Senator für Inneres (1984) *Hausbesetzungen und Hausbesetzer in Berlin: Eine Statistik über die Entwicklung seit 1979,* Pressemitteilung 16/84 (29 February).

Siebel, Werner (1983) 'Frankfurt 2000', *Frankfurter Rundschau,* (31 December).

Sund, Olaf (1984) 'Neues Feld entwickeln', *Neue Gesellschaft* 31/4 (April).

Voigt, Stefan (1985) 'Cooperatives flourish despite pitfalls, cynics, low wages and long hours', *The German Tribune* (September).

Warren, D. I. (1982) *The Health of American Neighborhoods: A National Report,* A Report to the Charles F. Kettering Foundation.

Zeuner, Bodo (1985) 'Parlamentarisierung der Grünen', *Prokla,* 61 (December).

17

Urban Protest and the Global Political Economy: The IMF Riots

John Walton

Bread riots have returned to recent history. With distressing familiarity newspaper headlines chronicle a new international wave of urban insurrections: 'Dominican Toll in Price Rioting is 29 in 2 days'; 'Food Price Rioting Persists in Sudan' (*New York Times*, 25 April 1984 and 29 March 1985). Attentive readers will recall nearly a decade of similar violent episodes that flashed like cutting torches at the joints of a listing structure of international fiscal crisis. Mayhem in Santo Domingo re-enacted scenes from São Paulo, Ankara, Lima, Kinshasa and Cairo. Beginning in the mid-1970s a series of bread riots and political risings swept across continents with little regard for geopolitical divisions or domestic conventions of political expression. In one country after another workers, civil servants, students, shopkeepers and the urban poor took to the streets, fundamentally because their governments were in trouble; in debt to international agencies and syndicates of western banks, looking for solutions that would mollify creditors, and compelled to adopt a desperate orthodoxy of economic austerity.

So far, no explanation has been offered for these contemporary events. Food riots are usually understood as key moments in the history of modern Europe; the Great Fear of urban food shortages in revolutionary France that drew *sans-culottes* into the current of national protest (Rudé, 1952) or the English crowd in the eighteenth century that reformulated traditional rights in a new moral economy of the poor. Social history has taught us the meaning of such events. 'The food riot in eighteenth-century England was a highly complex form of direct popular action, disciplined and with clear objectives' (Thompson, 1971: 78). These disturbances reflected domestic conflicts; class struggles of early industrialization between the aristocracy and landlords on one hand, and the rising merchant and urban working classes on the other. Indirectly, they also involved the international economy with the protracted opposition to protective Corn Laws in nineteenth-century England. We know, too, that the state was involved from the early modern period, ensuring the urban food supply or promoting exports in lieu of meeting local demand, depending on the exigencies of political rule (Tilly, 1975).

Such broad historical parallels notwithstanding, little theoretical interpretation has been generated for the austerity protests of the last decade. This essay is a beginning. It sketches briefly the origins and responses to the international debt crisis, notably the austerity policies urged by creditor nations and multilateral agencies, such as the International Monetary Fund, which created the conditions of social protest. Next, it attempts an exhaustive inventory of the protests themselves, describing patterns, inferring causes, and assessing short-run effects. Finally, some concluding observations are offered about the changing international political economy.

Several prefatory observations set the stage for this analysis and relate it to themes of the city in the new international division of labor. First, the debt crisis and austerity protests are global concerns. Some 80 countries around the world are overburdened with debts to international banks and agencies and find themselves forced to adopt unpopular 'stabilization' programs. Western banks, including most of the major United States banks and their syndicated regional partners, are seriously 'exposed' in Third World loans – compromised to the extent that their stability and profits depend on continuing debt service. Second, this financial crisis is closely linked to the new international division of labor, to the competitive and uneven development in the advanced countries and their quest for investment opportunity in the Third World. Third, by contrast to previous decades when policies of economic growth favored cities and led to rural discontent (e.g. de Janvry, 1981), the new austerity has stifled growth and transferred the social costs of indebtedness mainly to the cities. In the late 1970s and 1980s political unrest in the Third World is principally an urban phenomenon owing to the manner in which the crisis developed and specific policies for addressing it. Finally, the social protest analyzed in this paper must be understood as the product of an interaction between global, national and urban community forces, rather than any externally imposed conflict or achievement of urban social movements. The nation–state in the Third World is the critical pivot around which pressures from above and below work their effects. This is not to discount the potency of global capitalism or the vitality of people's movements, but to locate the arena in which contending forces are resolved.

THE PROVENANCE OF ECONOMIC CRISIS

The international monetary crisis of the 1970s, and its extension to the world debt crisis in the 1980s, has been the subject of several scholarly monographs (e.g. Block, 1977; Brett, 1983; Moffitt, 1983) and countless tretaments in the financial press (e.g. *The Wall Street Journal*, 22 June 1984).

For the purpose of locating contemporary political protests in their economic context, only a portion of the etiology of the crisis needs development.

The most salient and ironic feature of the current debt crisis is that its roots sprouted as early as 1960 and grew in the compost of trade deficits accumulated *by the United States*. The US deficit resulted from the very success of its postwar recovery programs. The rejuvenated European and Japanese economies performed so well, and US industrial supremacy waned so much by comparison, that US deficits began to mount dangerously. Dollars 'overhung' in the current accounts of successful exporting countries or worse, for the US, were redeemed in gold:

By the early 1960s the deficit had reduced gold reserves below the value of external dollar holdings . . . they fell from $17.8 billion in 1960 to $11 billion in 1970 despite the very powerful pressures exerted on countries which, like France, attempted to transform their dollar assets into gold in order to forestall the possibility of an American devaluation. (Brett, 1983: 164)

The root of the problem was the large and growing U.S. deficits. In the first half of the 1960s, U.S. balance of payments deficits averaged $742 million per year. From 1965 to 1969, they ballooned to $3 billion annually. The U.S. balance of payments veered out of control for two main reasons, both related to the decline of U.S. power. First, by the mid-1960s, Europe and Japan had reemerged as formidable economic competitors. . . . The second major cause was Vietnam [which] added billions to the U.S. deficit. (Moffitt, 1983: 30)

The looming US debt crisis was averted in 1971 when the Nixon administration unilaterally abrogated the Bretton Woods system by twice devaluing the dollar, abandoning the gold standard, and converting to a floating exchange rate. As France feared, international dollar holdings abruptly lost value. The United States used its decided political advantage in the world economy to export its debt and the inflationary cost of the war in Vietnam. Those adjustments inaugurated the 'international economic disorder' of the 1970s and the current world debt crisis.

Equally important, however, was the parallel and related development of international banking. Beginning in the early 1960s when the US government attempted a series of capital control programs, themselves aimed at the domestic side of the dollar overhang, banks responded by moving abroad. A legion of US regional banks joined the pioneering Chase Manhatten, Bank of America and Citibank, establishing foreign offices unfettered by national regulations. In 1964 just eleven US banks operated overseas from 181 locations; a decade later 129 banks were doing business out of 737 branches. International banking was stimulated by positive lures that went far beyond the self-defeating capital controls. It followed transnational corporate clients abroad, learned painfully how to profit in foreign currency speculation (often against the US dollar, which the government was meanwhile trying to bolster after 1971), and attracted major Eurodollar accounts swollen by the surpluses of oil-exporting countries.

The world debt crisis was born in a union of these trends. The United States strove to regain favorable trade balances partly through exports to newly industrializing countries and tied aid for costly development projects in countries such as Brazil. Political alliances were cemented with loans to strategic countries such as Poland, Yugoslavia, Turkey, Egypt, South Korea, the Philippines and Indonesia. The increasingly competitive international banking system fell over itself making loans to developing countries since, the lore held, sovereign nations never went bankrupt. The new mood of intrepid banking was propelled by windfall fees for large loan syndications and by the unquestioned credit-worthiness of petroleum exporters such as Mexico or prosperous countries relatively self-sufficient in oil such a Argentina. Most developing countries glady accepted the loans, projects and halcyon promises of the 'development decade'. And, at the outset, the banks profited enormously (Honeywell, 1983). Like a good party and an expensive restaurant, the mounting bill was out of sight and mind. Economic theory, after all, promised the imminent appearance of benefactor growth to pick up everyone's bill.

Two statistics summarize the growth and composition of the debt crisis. First, the total debt of developing countries grew from $64 billion in 1970 to $686 billion at the end of 1984 (*World Development Report*). Other estimates including selected 'developed' countries put the present sum at over $900 billion. Second, in 1973, according to the IMF, private banks accounted for about one-third of the total debt of Third World countries. By 1982, it stood at considerably more than half (Moffitt, 1983: 102).

IMF AUSTERITY

The public appearance of a world debt crisis is usually dated in August 1982 when Mexico came close to panic and national bankruptcy. The arbitrariness of this onset date is matched only by present (early 1986) opinion that the debt crisis has passed as a result of major rescheduling in Brazil, Mexico and Argentina. It was clear from the mid-1970s onwards that many developing countries were moving dangerously upwards in the ratio of external debt to GNP or export earnings. A rule of thumb, that debt *service* should not exceed 20 per cent of export earnings, was increasingly violated (and later applied to 40 of the 81 debtor countries surveyed in 1984). The US government and international agencies began placing stricter conditions on new loans and aid programs; conditions designed to reform alleged misuses of foreign assistance, to promote free market mechanisms with all their purported efficiencies, and, in the end, to ensure the regular repayment of the debt service on which the banks computed their profits, if not on the principal.

The notion of 'conditionality' soon became associated with the IMF since that institution not only applies conditions to its own ('last resort') loans and drawing rights, but also has assumed the dual role of a credit-rating service and negotiator in loan agreements between the international banks and borrowing countries. As an increasingly enforced basis on which debt-ridden countries are able to obtain new or renegotiated loans from *any* source, IMF conditionality involves several elements. In the general case of financially troubled countries:

if the difficulty is caused by deep-seated factors such as a deterioration in the terms of trade that is unlikely to be reversed, *excessive domestic demand*, cost-price distortions including overevaluation of the domestic currency, or a permanent decline in net capital inflows, *a change in the member's policies will be needed.* (Hooke, 1982: 34; emphasis added)

This theoretical axiom and IMF policy mandate translates into a set of particular measures imposed on borrower countries with striking regularity. These include: devaluation, reduced public spending, elimination of public subsidies for food and other essentials such as cooking oil and gasoline, wage restraint despite inflation, increased ('positive') interest rates, taxes related to demand curbs, elimination of state-owned or supported enterprises, greater access for foreign investment, reform of protection for local industries, export promotion, and application of new foreign exchange to debt services. 'The general thrust of IMF programs is to promote market-oriented, open economies geared to export production' (Loxley, 1984: 29).

The purely economic effects of austerity defy precise identification in the aggregate. From varied starting points on a scale of world poverty, debtor countries have experienced different combinations of reform measures imposed at different times with mixed enthusiasm. The rigor of IMF conditions and enforcement varies, too, with political considerations – gentle persuasion for Israel, exceptions for the Philippines, and cold theory for the Dominican Republic. From the standpoint of social equality, however, austerity produces a clear pattern of regressive consequences independent of how far particular countries move in that direction.

Wage restraint below levels of inflation obviously penalizes the working and salaried middle classes. Attacks on 'excessive domestic demand' in poor countries, particularly cuts in subsidized staple foods, deprives the underemployed slum-dwelling population of the means of survival and pushes the working-class poor into desperation. Public spending cuts eliminate services for the same populations and jobs for middle-class civil servants. Businesspeople from the shopkeeper to the national industrialist are hurt by import restrictions, rising interest rates, and reduction of the troublesome excessive domestic demand. Everyone faces higher, 'undistorted' prices that tend to follow devaluation. Domestically, only the upper classes benefit and, of this strata, only a special fraction, namely, the exporting interests with the least reliance on imports and the domestic market. When the austerity measures 'work', and export-earned foreign exchange is applied to the debt, of course the international bankers benefit.

These are more than speculative effects or trial scenarios. In Mexico, where IMF austerity has been applied with some alacrity, annual inflation continues at 80 per cent, 1983 purchasing power dropped by 40 per cent (*Latin America Weekly Report*, 1 June 1984), reduced public spending has produced 'massive lay-offs' in industries such as construction. Yet for a time, Mexico was considered a shining success story at the IMF because reduced public spending enabled repayment of emergency loans. As Brazil conceded to IMF demands limiting the indexing of wages in July 1983, despite continuing inflation above the index correction, Albert Fishlow observed: 'This is the third year in a row in which per capita income has declined, surpassing even the worst years of the Great Depression' (*Los Angeles Times*, 21 July 1983). Declining wages were the lot of those who kept their jobs. 'Many did not, particularly those working for small and medium-sized businesses. . . . Unemployment has risen sharply in Brazil's towns and cities since 1980' (*The Economist*, 12 March 1983). In Peru, the sociologist Julio Cotler explained that striking workers 'are desperate. The debt has blocked any progress. Average income is as low as it was twenty years ago. All this has produced a high degree of social unrest' (*The Wall Street Journal*, 13 July 1984). This pattern is repeated in country after country beyond the confines of Latin America or the Third World as it is usually understood:

Usually the urban working class is worst affected, by lay-offs induced by restraint and by deteriorating real incomes in the face of inflationary pressures resulting from devaluation, subsidy cuts, and the imposition or raising of fees and prices for public services. In extreme cases this has given rise to what are now called 'IMF riots' which are, essentially, urban phenomena. (Loxley, 1984: 30)

POPULAR PROTEST

Austerity protests began in Peru in 1976, although Egypt witnessed the first bread riot directly linked to austerity measures in January 1977. Similar outbreaks continue at the time of writing, with national srikes and massive political demonstrations during late 1985 and early 1986 in Guatemala and El Salvador. The cases of 'mass action protesting economic austerity' in table 17.1 are intended to include a universe of events, defined by large public protests over state economic policies that stem from international agencies and national governments and aim at resolving the debt crisis.

Naturally, the claim that the set of 22 cases constitutes the universe so defined is vulnerable to every reasonable criticism about its coverage, unlike a sample. Additional cases were considered and dismissed for various reasons. Illustratively, food riots in Poland in 1970 were tenuously connected to international authority. In June 1984 when 200,000 Honduran workers threatened to strike over new taxes (on alcohol, cigarettes, telephone service, and cinema tickets) requested by the IMF, the president suspended

TABLE 17.1 *Summary by country of mass action protesting economic austerity*

Country/cities	Date	Action/duration	Severity	Precipitating events	General policies and their source	Consequences
Peru Lima Sicuani Ayacucho Trujillo Urubamba Cuzco Arequipa Huancayo Puno Chiclayo Piura Chimbote	July 1976, June–July 1977, May 1978, Jan. 1981, Mar. 1983, Sept. 1983, Feb. 1984, June 1984, Nov. 1984, May 1985.	Initially, street demonstrations and riots in Lima. Protest spreads to other cities and to strikes. General strikes by labor unions, students, teachers, civil servants. Persistent 1–3-day strikes. Demonstrations by students and in shanty towns; 10,000 march on government palace. General strike of public employees and industrial unions.	Initially, 5 killed, then 6. 200 union officials arrested. Approximately 10 killed. 'Dozens' injured. 300–800 arrests.	Price increases in basic foods and gasoline, elimination of government subsidies, inflation, unemployment, cuts in university funding.	Reductions in public spending and devaluation ordered by IMF and World Bank as conditions for new loans and debt rescheduling.	Martial law, price increases reduced, price freeze on basic foods, devaluation halted. Return to civilian government. Government resistance to IMF, especially wheat and gas price increases. Protracted negotiations on rescheduling. Alternately austerity measures imposed and ameliorated. State of siege finally called to end strikes.
Egypt Alexandria Cairo Suez Aswan Helwan	Jan. 1977	Food riots. Attacks on public transportation, buildings, and police stations. Two days.	47–49 killed. Hundreds wounded. 600–1200 arrests.	Price increases due to cutbacks in government subsidies of food (rice, sugar, bread, tea) and cooking gas.	Devaluation, import reduction, and cuts in government spending recommended by IMF as a condition of new credits.	Food subsidies restored. Wage and pension increases for public sector workers. New US, IMF and Saudi loans. Growing instability of Sadat government.

Ghana Accra	Sept.–Nov. 1978	More than 80 strikes over several months in aviation, breweries, civil service, state information media, oil refinery, etc.	Extensive strikes, no reported casualties.	Devaluation, 80 per cent increase in petroleum prices, food price rises.	Government austerity programs to reduce budget deficits and attract IMF and bank assistance.	Workers given ultimatum to return to work or be dismissed. Police and military politicized.
Jamaica Kingston Montego Bay Ochos Rios Negril May Pen	Jan. 1979, Jan. 1985	Three days each of street demonstrations, barricades, looting of stores, protest marches on government house.	5 killed (1979). 10 killed and 20 arrested (1985).	Price increases in gasoline, food.	Government elimination of subsidies and devaluation in response to IMF recommendations.	Government held fire on austerity measures, contained disorder.
Liberia Monrovia	April 1979	Political demonstration to food riots. Looting of stores and markets. Two days.	29–74 killed. 400 injured. 200–400 arrests. University closed.	Government increases in price of rice.	Government policy to increase farm income and production, lower imports and out-migration.	Price increase moderated. Military and police pay increases. Amnesty for protestors. Weakened government overthrown by army coup within a year. US and World Bank loans follow.
Zaire Kinshasa	May 1980	Political demonstration, burning of cars and buses. Other protests for months.	Hundreds arrested, university closed.	Price increases in food and consumer goods; and transportation corruption.	Devaluation, exchange controls, and anti-corruption credit restrictions demanded by IMF for new credits.	Wage increases, new US and IMF loans.
Turkey Ankara Izmir Istanbul Fatsa	Feb.–Sept. 1980	Food riots, looting, strikes, factory occupations.	2000 killed. Thousands arrested.	Government austerity measures lifting price controls on food transportation, and basic services; elimination of subsidies and mass dismissals from state-run	Devaluation, move from state-controlled to free market economy, elimination of state price and industrial subsidies, all urged by IMF for $1.6 billion	Civil violence. Political unrest. Military coup. New US loans and debt rescheduling.

TABLE 17.1 (Continued)

Country/ cities	Date	Action/ duration	Severity	Precipitating events	General policies and their source	Consequences
Poland Lublin Warsaw Gdansk Gdynia Sopot Lodz Wroclaw Szczerin Elblag	July 1980– Dec. 1981	Strikes, blockades of transportation and services, industrial occupations, work stoppages, political demonstrations.	Hundreds of thousands striking. Hundreds jailed.	Elimination of meat price subsidies, price increases, shortages, consumer goods shifted to more expensive 'luxury shops' dealing in foreign currency.	Government economic program to increase production and reduce heavy public subsidies as urged by western banks.	Wage increases granted to strikers. Independent trade unions recognized and later banned. Top government and party leaders replaced by hard-liners. Debt rescheduling.
Sudan Khartom	Jan. 1982, Mar.– April, 1985	Riots, students demonstrations, shops and gas stations burned. One day. Riots of 1985 lead to street demonstrations, looting, attacks on embassy. Doctors call for general strike with other professionals (lawyers, engineers, professors, pilots) and strikes shut down business, transport & all basic services, events cover 2 weeks.	Universities closed. 20+ killed, 2000 arrested.	Cutbacks in government subsidies of sugar, gasoline, wheat and cooking oil. Price increases for bread, staples, gasoline.	Devaluation, end to government subsidies of food and petroleum prices, tax increases on imports, all demanded by IMF and western banks as conditions for emergency loans. Pressure from US which froze aid in February, and from IMF and foreign creditors led to austerity measures, especially elimination of food subsidies.	IMF grant of $225 million in credits. US restores aid, president ousted by military coup, economic measures cancelled.

	Dates	Protest	Arrests/Closures	Price/Policy Issues	IMF/Austerity Action	Outcome
Argentina Buenos Aires Mendoza	Mar. 1982, Oct. 1983, June 1984, Sept. 1984, May 1985, Aug. 1985.	Demonstrations by labor unions, series of 24-hour strikes, general strike, some looting.	Hundreds arrested.	Price increases, inflation, policies on foreign debt.	Austerity measures by military and, later, Alfonsin government in negotiation with IMF.	Economic problems contribute to military withdrawal from government. Alfonsin administration first resists IMF granting wage increases then implements its own comprehensive austerity program with broad acceptance.
Ecuador Quito Guayaquil	Oct. 1982, Mar. 1983, Jan. 1985.	General strikes, one and two days. Demonstrations, street violence.	Schools and universities closed. 7 killed, 50 wounded, 500 arrested.	Price increases and elimination of government subsidies on flour, gasoline. Price increases of milk and fuel oil.	Devaluation and subsidy cuts required by IMF as condition for refinancing debt.	Approval for rescheduling and new IMF special drawing rights. Agreement to delay debt repayments. Compensatory wage increases.
Bolivia La Paz Cochabamba	Mar. 1983, Nov. 1983, Dec. 1983, Apr.-May 1984, Nov. 1984, Feb.-Mar. 1985, Sept. 1985.	General strikes, one to four days. Strike of bank employees responsible to implementing austerity measures. Demonstrations, street violence, looting, protest marches.	Approximately 10 killed, 1500 arrested. Industry, mines, banks, shops and universities shut.	Proposed austerity measures that would have increased basic food prices and gasoline and a proposed devaluation. Unemployment, inflation, devaluation.	Devaluation and subsidies elimination urged by IMF as a condition for new loan.	Replacement of Cabinet and key Ministers. Government-labor agreement not to implement austerity measures, wage increases to partly offset inflation, postponement of debt payments. Renewed austerity with elected government and state of seige to end general strike.

TABLE 17.1 (Continued)

Country/cities	Date	Action/duration	Severity	Precipitating events	General policies and their source	Consequences
Chile Santiago Valparaiso	Mar. 1983–May 1983, June 1983, Aug. 1983, Sept. 1983, Oct. 1983, Nov. 1983, Sept. 1985.	Near-monthly political protests over unemployment, inflation, and Pinochet government. Many one-day protests. Demonstrations, 'National Social Protest', general strikes, looting.	30–60 killed. 1000+ arrests. Several thousands detained.	Pinochet dictatorship and unemployment, devaluation, price increases.	Devaluation, end to state subsidies and enterprises, and free market system urged by monetarist advisors and IMF.	Emergency public works projects and jobs. Mass detentions of protestors and poor neighbourhood residents. Debt rescheduling.
Brazil Saõ Paulo Rio de Janeiro Santos Campinas Fortaleza Ribeirao Pretto	Apr. 1983, Oct. 1983.	Political demonstrations, riots over food prices and unemployment, looting of supermarkets. Three days + persistent looting.	2 killed. 130 injured. 566 arrests.	Price increases, devaluation, elimination of subsidies, inflation and unemployment.	Devaluation and austerity measures adopted in order to meet IMF conditions for new loans.	Emergency job program promised for 170,000. New loans and debt rescheduling agreed with IMF. Food stamps, incentives to small and medium firms.

Country/City	Date	Protest	Casualties	Government action	Cause/IMF	Outcome
Philippines Manila	Sept.–Oct. 1983, Aug.–Sept. 1984.	Political demonstrations, strikes. 2–3 days each and continuous one-day protests by unions, students, churches and office workers.	Approximately 50 killed, 500 injured, 1000+ arrests. Demonstrations of 500,000.	Devaluations, price increases, Marcos regime, Aquino assassination.	Dictatorial rule. Several devaluations, delayed wage increases, austerity measures demanded by IMF and banks.	Tax and price freezes. New IMF loans, debt payment delays, debt rescheduling. US, Japan, and South Korea loans. Government repression. New price increases.
Panama Panama City Colon	Oct. 1983, Sept. 1985.	General strike. Demonstrations, national legislature occupied, strikes, protest marches.		Proposed freeze on wages of public employees, reduced subsidies to business and industry.	Recommended by IMF and world bank.	President resigns under pressure from labor, business and military (and other mysterious military intrigue). No austerity measures implemented.
Tunisia Tunis Sfax Gafsa Kabili Hamma Kasserine Gabes Mareth LeKef	Jan. 1984	Food riot, looting, attacks on shops, public buildings, airline offices, appliance stores, and foreign cars. One week.	57–110 killed. 'Many' arrests. Schools and universities closed.	Government price increases for bread, pasta, flour, and grains.	Government policies to reduce expenditures and imports, raise taxes and apply savings to debt as recommended by the IMF and World Bank.	Price increases reversed or moderated. Rent freeze. Promised cash allotments to poor. New policies to reduce subsidies and raise taxes more slowly. New aid from France.
Morocco Casablanca Mohammedia	June 1981	General strike to protest price rises. 5 days. Called by labor unions and confederation.	200 killed. 5,000 injured. 750 arrested. Many thousands of participants. Newspapers closed.	Government reduced food subsidies and rapid rise of basic food prices.	IMF pressure to improve balance of payments following a $1.2 billion loan.	Price increases cut by half, government retreated temporarily.

TABLE 17.1 (Continued)

Country/ cities	Date	Action/ duration	Severity	Precipitating events	General policies and their source	Consequences
Oujda Marrakesh AlHoceima Rabat Tetuan Nador Ksar el-Kebir	Jan. 1984	Student protest demonstrations, worker protests, riots. Two weeks.	60–200 killed. 800–900 arrests.	Increases in student fees and announced price increases for bread, sugar, and cooking oil.	Government cuts in food subsidies and other austerity measures demanded by the IMF.	No food price increases implemented.
Dominican Republic Santo Domingo Santiago San Francisco de Macoris San Cristobal	April. 1984, Feb. 1985	Food price riots. Organized protest by church, business, and labor. Strikes. Three days. Protests and strikes by shop-keepers, transit workers, and middle-class neighbourhoods. Three days.	60 killed. 150–300 injured. 1000 arrests. Schools, uni-versity, and ratio station closed. Two killed (1985).	Government announc-ed price increases on food staples, all imports including medicine, and gasoline. New price increases, devalu-ation.	Elimination of govern-ment subsidized prices part of an agreement with the IMF for a $600 million loan. Measures urged by IMF and creditors in 1984, but rescinded, imposed again.	Some basic food and medicine prices moderated, but not gas and most imports. Labor leaders jailed to pre-vent further protest. New IMF agreement. Some re-newed price increases moderated and wage in-creases proposed.
Haiti Cap Haitien Conaives Bombardopolis	May 1985	Riot, attack on local barracks, looting of food stores and ware-house.	Three killed. Several hundred riot.	Food shortages, cor-ruption in government distribution of food aid, restriction of emigra-tion, police brutality.	Government crack-downs. IMF austerity measures and suspend-ed public works employment.	Replacement of Cabinet and local government officials. Government distribution of food and money.

Guatemala Guatemala City	Sept. 1985	Protest, riot, looting, demonstrations, job actions, strikes. One week. Strikes by teachers and public employee job actions in support.	2–10 killed, 1000 arrested. Troops invade university.	Government announced increases in bus fares, bread and milk.	IMF urging to reduce government deficit, increase taxes, and cut public spending.	Government agreed to freeze prices of basic goods and rescind bus fare increase. Agreed to raise salaries of public employees and to urge same from private employers.
El Salvador San Salvador	May–July, 1985. Feb. 1986.	Demonstrations by 30,000 workers for salary increases (May), by 50,000 students and teachers for university budget (July), by 15–50,000 workers and public employees protesting economic policies (Feb.)	Work stoppages, hospital take-over. Armed forces occupied hospital. 15 union, teacher and student leaders arrested.	Initially, price rises and inadequate university budget. Later, January 1986 austerity program and devaluation.	Devaluation and sharp increases in gasoline prices with moderate wage increases and price freeze. Economic policy influenced by US advisors.	Growing opposition to Duarte administration from once-supportive moderate unions and from business groups and coffee exporters.

Sources: New York Times; Wall Street Journal; Economist; Latin American Weekly Report; Time; Newsweek; Business Week; Veja.

the taxes. In August 1981 a general strike in Sierra Leone over the cost of living and demands for government subsidies was barely reported, made no mention of international actors, and apparently met with amicable settlement. Recent demonstrations in Mexico demanding debt repudiation have been peaceful – at least according to available accounts. Excluding doubtful cases for one or another of these reasons, table 17.1 attempts to summarize all of the protests in their essential aspects.

The first valuable lesson is the generality of austerity protest. Unrest is most common in the more heavily indebted Latin American and Caribbean countries (12 cases), but North and sub-Sahara Africa are well represented (7 cases), with the small remainder coming from Europe (2) and Asia (1). The nations themselves range from the heavily industrialized, and indebted, Brazil and Poland to diminutive Liberia and rustic Sudan.

The protests are mounted in cities and, impressively, in networks of cities. This is not to say that rural areas are unaffected or quiescent. It appears, however, that instances of rural protest (e.g. sympathy strikes in Peruvian mines) are orchestrated from national centers. Typically, the capital city is the focus, but the demonstrations do not regularly begin or end there. In Egypt, Turkey, Poland, Brazil, Tunisia and Morocco the protests began in regional cities experiencing stagnant industry, unemployment and the inequities of uneven regional development. In more than two-thirds of the cases, protest spread in a wave of urban unrest. Mass dismissals to reduce costs at a state-run factory in Izmir, Turkey spawned a workers revolt that was promptly taken up by disgruntled residents of Istanbul and Ankara recently hit by soaring prices for food and essential services (both policies stemming from IMF recommendations to transform the state-controlled economy to a liberal free-market system). Strikes in Lublin, Poland over meat price increases resonated in Gdansk before Solidarity was heard of. In all instances the wave of protests decried a homogeneous set of conditions which took on national colors and urban salience, but the basic grievances were societal and international.

The protests themselves vary in the form of political expression and encompass three equally common types of mass action: food riots, general strikes and political demonstrations. The classical bread riot precipitated about a third of the actions; shops and supermarkets were looted from Monrovia to Rio. In countries with a strong tradition of trade unionism, such as those of Latin America, general strikes were called which rallied a phalanx of social classes. In the celebrated Polish case, strikes grew into a social movement. Political demonstrations typified the remaining instances; usually huge marches sponsored by students, unions and political groups carrying plaintiff banners to official or symbolic staging areas.

Less significance attaches to these types than to their interaction and constraining political environment. In the first place, protest actions are mixed: food riots and looting spilled over to attacks on public buildings and buses (Egypt, Tunisia, Dominican Republic, Peru, Panama); political demonstrations degenerated into riots with and without police incitement (Liberia, Zaire, Brazil); general strikes usually included demonstrations. Moreover, as protest spread across cities its form changed; a riot or violent confrontation here engendered a strike there. Second, protests follow the contous of national politics. In the dictatorial settings of Chile and the Philippines the pains of austerity are constricted in risky demonstrations expressing dissent from regime policies. Polish Solidarity calibrated its protests to elicit something between indifference and Soviet intervention. From another angle, the protests were often violent and sometimes extraordinarily fatal. The highest death tolls, however, correlate more with repressive regimes and domestic factional strife than with the size or stimulus to mass action. (Compare the reduced casualities in Brazil or even Poland with the carnage in Egypt, Liberia, Turkey, Morocco and Chile.) Once again, the impression is of a singular phenomenon – organized and allied social class opposition to regressive measures that threaten the livelihood of people who respond where and how they can.

THE TEXTURE AND BASES OF URBAN POLITICAL ACTION

When coherent accounts of the protests are available, the manner in which global austerity affects the texture of urban political organization comes to life. In the Dominican Republic, for example, a great deal more than a food riot took place:

The demonstrations which deteriorated into rioting in the week after Easter were very largely spontaneous, though the action which sparked them was carefully, if rapidly, prepared. This was a planned 12-hour strike called for 23 April by residents of the working class suburb of Capotillo, which three other neighborhoods also decided to observe, in protest at the dramatic price rises and the government's agreement with the IMF. The main influence in the strike committee (the *Comité de Lucha Popular del Barrio Capotillo y Zonas Aledanas*) came, our sources say, from local *comunidades de base* of the Catholic Church. . . . The organisers of the original protest in Capotillo were thus well-prepared. The mass meeting which decided to declare the strike appointed groups to contact the media, collect money and carry out door-to-door canvassing for support. The strike in Capotillo was totally successful, but it rapidly ran out of the control of the organizers. (*Latin America Weekly Report*, 11 May 1984)

The riot surprised community organizations and the cooperating Front of the Dominican Left. The whole affair surprised the ruling and opposition political parties, which then began struggling for advantage by publicly rehearsing the speech each would have delivered to the IMF. The Dominican National Workers' Union vied for popular support by calling for a general strike, which resulted only in their own arrest. President Blanco's representatives carried all of these concerns to a new round of talks with the IMF. The base community initiative, in short, transformed the national political agenda.

Perhaps the most chronicled austerity protests and rioting took place in Brazil during April 1983. Previously, and on a broader scale, Brazilians enacted a drama repeated in the Dominican Republic and, indeed, many of the cases. Once again, the locus of protest was a working-class community; the São Paulo *barrio* of Santo Amaro which houses one million people, including 100,000 slum-dwellers and 80,000 unemployed. Santo Amaro had experienced unrest prior to the fateful 4 April 1983. In 1981 squatters invaded a state farm and just one month before the riots protestors destroyed 27 buses of the private transport company which locked out passengers to force the government to agree to a fare increase. A 30 per cent devaluation in February threatened to drive meager incomes below the subsistence level. Recently the number of employed steelworkers in Santo Amaro dropped from 100,000 to 80,000 and the local Telefunken factory moved to a tax-free zone in Manaos, taking 6000 jobs with it. The *barrio* supports 93 neighborhood improvement organizations, an active union movement, and political groups ranging from the Brazilian Communist Party and the Workers Party to the center-left Brazilian Democratic Movement.

On 4 April a demonstration was called by an *ad hoc* 'Committee Fighting Against Unemployment', backed by the left political parties and unified under the slogan 'We won't die of hunger and be quiet about it'. Two hundred demonstrators gathered in front of an ice-lolly factory which recently had attracted throngs of applicants for just five jobs. As the demonstrators moved to a nearby square to hear speeches, their numbers swelled to 2000, many of whom picked up oranges from a delivery truck parked along their route. Somewhere in the perorations, the oranges were hurled, bombarding the surrounding commercial zone. A 30-hour riot was underway, drawing 3500 protestors and opportunistic 'marginals' who looted 200 stores, invaded 48 homes, and destroyed 125 cars and buses.

On the third day organizers of the initial demonstration sought to refocus action on their complaints about unemployment and rallied a new march of 3000 on the State Governor's palace. When the Governor sent the Labor Secretary out to meet the assembly, and palace guards tried to lure the demonstrators within range of water cannon, more mayhem followed. Symbolically, perhaps, the iron fence around the palace was torn down. Eventually the Governor did meet representatives of the crowd, but apparently to no one's satisfaction; the protestors smashed buses which the Governor had provided for their peaceful return home and police were finally unleashed on the crowd. Prophetically, the Governor of Rio de Janeiro, who was lunching at the palace as the demonstrators grew militant, observed that São Paulo was only the first Brazilian city to face austerity riots.

Protests around the world emanated from depressed, yet organized urban communities; Kinshasa's vast La Cité and the Santiago *barrios* once mobilized around the Unidad Popular. Among the many Polish towns that joined the 1980 summer of strikes, food-price demonstrations and lockouts, it was the more politically experienced Gdansk workers who locked themselves *into* the shipyards demanding independent unions. As austerity rained down from international agencies and state reform, the seeds of protest grew in soils that mixed urban poverty, community organization, and mobilized political groups.

In all cases, the protests were patently political actions as opposed to crowd convulsions, subversive conspiracies, or criminal mischief. Dominant interests, of course, engaged in the usual scapegoating. Brazil's popular magazine *Veja* blamed the communists and, more creatively, Morocco's King Hassan II indicted an unlikely trio of 'professional Marxist, Zionist, and Khomeinist agitators'. But the evidence spoke otherwise. Class politics were clearly expressed in Brazilian protest banners and grafitti that blamed not only the IMF, but Yankees, the nation's leaders, political parties and labor unions. Urban communities demonstrated, for jobs, wage increases and affordable food within the established political process.

When riots ensued, selected targets included government buildings, police stations, public transport companies guilty of fare increases, well-stocked supermarkets and warehouses, appliance stores, gas stations and private automobiles – in short, most of the available symbols of government policy, basic necessities and upper-class affluence. Egyptian and Tunisian crowds attacked sports cars, airline and travel offices, and public offices. Haitians looted food warehouses maintained by CARE, protesting against corruption in relief aid. Peruvians marched on the national palace, and Panamanians occupied the national legislature chanting: 'I won't pay the debt, let the ones who stole the money pay.'

The protestors themselves came from social strata within a limited range. Typically, as in Brazil and the Dominican Republic, participants represent the employed working class and the underemployed urban poor. Sometimes these include or attract students. In a smaller but significant number of cases, those groups were joined by national business interests, churches, office workers and civil servants (e.g. Peru, the Dominican Republic). In the Philippines economic protest marches regularly began at Manila's financial district and were led by prominent business persons. A general strike in Bolivia owed its success to sympathetic bank employees who walked out rather than comply with new austerity measures. Teachers and university students played a critical role in Guatemala and Haiti. In summary, the protests are multi-class affairs. In the aggregate, workers and the urban poor contribute the largest number of participants, but public employees, students, churches, unions and small businesses are frequently represented and are sometimes in the vanguard.

The actions were short-lived, if often episodic. Protestors organized for a specific and typically reformist purpose; a forty-eight hour general strike, for example, called to demonstrate the depth of public concern to officialdom. If riots flared, efforts were made by politicians and dissenters to incorporate their grievances into the political dialogue. Sometimes this was nothing more than a tactical maneuver, an effort to defuse the situation until the same measures could be introduced more gradually. But the tactic did not regularly succeed. Renewed demonstrations occurred in two-thirds of the cases; and in several countries that experienced one protest no new austerity measures were attempted.

One generalization that should not be overlooked is the precipitate occasion of the protests. Their origins lie not only in the perceived crisis that engulfed the international economy in the space of a few years, but typically in the abrupt introduction of exactions on the poor. Devaluations set off rapid domestic price rises. Wage restraints eroded real income. Public subsidies were suddenly removed from such necessities as staple foods, cooking oil, gasoline, transportation and even medicine. These, accompanied by escalating unemployment, aggravated the deteriorating condition of the poor. Intentional IMF 'shock treatments' produced unprescribed fits as electrified patients turned on their tormentors.

In some cases the prescription came straight from the IMF, World Bank, or US Treasury tied to new or renegotiated loans and aid. This was not always the case, nor need it have been to conclude that the source of austerity was the international economy and its power brokers. Sometimes recipient governments anticipated or concurred with the standard austerity package. In other cases – notably Argentina, Ecuador, Brazil and Peru – they demurred and won some concessions in the tough negotiations that followed. Sometimes their economies were suffering under policy mistakes largely of their own making and some sorts of reform were needed. Under such conditions the IMF provided a convenient villain to be blamed for unpopular measures that governments were required to take themselves. In that sense, national states were caught between popular and international pressures. The extent to which the state aligned with one side or another varied, for example, from the Chilean government's embrace or foreign interests to the economic nationalism of Manley's Jamaica, or of the Peruvian government elected in 1985.

THE CONSEQUENCES OF PROTEST

Inevitably, the question arises: 'What have the protests accomplished?' It is a fair question with an inconclusive answer, at least for the moment. Mass actions have had varied and significant effects around the world. Some of their consequences are still unfolding. Nevertheless, a first approximation of effects can treat the consequences that followed directly on the precipitating events and their underlying policies.

The protests generated a variety of consequences ranging from clear victories to renewed repression. The effects are best summarized under two general categories, each with its own species: immediate economic reform and sustained political transformation. In the first case, mass action typically brought swift official response. All of the protests succeeded, in the sense of shaking their societies into alert appreciation of the regressive policy effects and deepening urban poverty.

In the short run these economic effects take four specific forms. First, sometimes the austerity measures were defended and applied more rigorously with a combination of new ameliorative concessions and police repression. In Chile, the example, the free market was praised at the same time that the Pinochet regime created jobs in highway repair, on one hand, and conducted raids and mass arrests on organized working-class *barrios*, on the other. Second, and more common, the riots caused stunned governments to moderate or abandon the new austerity programs. In countries such as Liberia, Bolivia, Tunisia and Peru, the protestors gained immediate satisfaction. Third, beyond rescinding the austerity measures, governments in about half the cases introduced new wage and welfare benefits. Food subsidiaries were restored along with inflation-correcting wage increases and jobs programs (e.g. Egypt, Zaire, Poland, Brazil). Fourth, concessions granted in the majority of cases were underwritten by new and renegotiated loans in almost all countries. Residents of Third World slums spoke directly to Washington policy-makers and London bankers.

Popular uprisings alone did not produce all these changes. The protests took place in the midst of other crisis-induced action, including loan renegotiations, and revised aid arrangements were also provided in countries that did not protest. Conversely, however, protests within a given country were usually followed by relief: 'Perhaps the strongest force motivating the call for reform [has been] the unrest that economic stagnation and austerity programs have brought even to long tranquil countries' (*Washington Post*, 24 June 1984).

In the longer run, mass action has initiated a political transformation that continues to the present and suggests a realignment of the global political economy. Three features are discernible. First, in several instances the protests were the push that toppled unsteady governments, for better or worse, in Turkey, Poland, Liberia, Bolivia and the Sudan. Austerity protests in Haiti and the Philippines began the popular movements that grew and expanded their aims to the successful overthrow of the Duvalier and Marcos regimes.

Second, the mobilized and spontaneous participation in mass actions, official concessions and the leverage which insurgent groups perceived in crisis conditions all combined to activate established popular movements.

The irrepressible social movement of Polish Solidarity is a choice, but not isolated, example. In a number of cases partially successful protests have led to repeated demonstrations, joined now, if not before, by political parties, labour unions and business associations. In countries such as Brazil, where the protest coincided with a restoration of democratic government, the political interests of the urban poor have at least a better chance of influencing the emergent state. Ironically, the debt crisis has played an important causal role in bringing about new democratic regimes around the world, while at the same time burdening them with enormous economic liabilities.

Third, the new uprisings of the world's poor have altered the international political economy. On one hand they have, at least temporarily, shifted the distributive burden for crisis solutions. The banks are not regularly collecting debt service, except where emergency loans have been provided for that purpose. Repayment of principal has become a fantasy. Some developing nations (Peru, Nigeria) have limited the amount of debt service to a percentage of exports, and others have taken a tougher nationalistic line with international authorities – in both cases for reasons of domestic political support. On the other hand, international agencies and banks have been chastened by the unrest and what it implies for their authority or liquidity. Lenders and the IMF, quick to perceive their vulnerability to a debtors' alliance, or simply to the non-compliance of governments against the political wall of further exactions from the domestic economy, have temporized and moved to renegotiate. This response is less than charitable. Indeed, it involves an attempted divide-and-rule strategy in which favorable renegotiations for one country (e.g. Mexico) are speciously held up as a model of good faith and compliance to other countries which do not receive the same concessions in renegotiation. In any case, the system of control is weaker; 'now the bankers are beginning to face that reality – and they are scared. It's one thing, they say, to deal with inflation, balance of payments and capital flows. but politics are a wild card that most bankers don't understand' (*Wall Street Journal*, 7 October 1983).

CONCLUSION

A number of critical economists have concluded that the IMF approach to economic crisis will not successfully resolve the problem by punishing the poor and destroying domestic production (e.g. *Development Dialogue*, no. 2, 1980). Not only is the medicine wrong for the ailment in closely examined and key cases such as Brazil (Fishlow, 1982; Dornbusch, 1984), but the theoretical epidemiology appears mistaken (Brett, 1983). The continuing crisis is not one of a self-regulating system temporarily out of kilter, but a self-consuming addiction in which today's euphoric 'fix' exacerbates tomorrow's withdrawal pain.

To these judgements gleaned from political economy we may add that austerity for the poor has foundered on the moral economy. In developing nations around the world, someone else's debt crisis is an experienced social crisis. Militant crowds and urban communities have said no to politics of hunger and unemployment that would ensure servicing bank loans. At least they have said they won't be quiet about it in tones that convince the crisis managers.

The role of urban political action in this transformation has been crucial. Austerity policies have altered the schedule of winners and losers that prevailed during earlier 'decades of development'. Rural producers who suffered previously under price controls and artificially low exchange rates (de Janvry, 1981) may now get more sympathetic treatment. The urban working classes, public employees and national business, many of whom did enjoy the trickle-down benefits of rapid growth in the 1960s and early 1970s, are now paying the price of stabilization. The contours of political unrest in the Third World have shifted accordingly. From this we may conclude that urban and rural are not intrinsically meaningful analytic categories, but gross descriptive terms the features of which shift with circumstance. In this instance, urban class struggles have superseded the peasant rebellions of previous decades as a result of changes in the global political economy as these are mediated by states.

The confrontation of debt crisis and austerity protest brings into sharp relief the position of states mediating the cross-pressures of an international class struggle. The review of protest actions shows that states vary from opportune implementation of austerity programs to grudging compromises and nationalistic opposition. But the balance is delicate and the conditions volatile. Ironically, the crisis which has brought the most systematically regressive standard of living to the world's urban poor and national enterprise since the Depression may also introduce the space and the occasion for a new pattern of democratic development. Much depends on which way those states will turn in the face of demands from their workers and their bankers.

REFERENCES

Block, Fred L. (1977) *The Origins of International Economic Disorder: A Study of United States International Monetary Policy from World War II to the Present*, Berkeley: University of California Press.

Brett, E. A. (1983) *International Money and Capitalist Crisis: The Anatomy of Global Disintegration*, London: Heinemann.

Cardoso, Fernando H. and Enzo Faletto (1977) *Dependency and Development in Latin America*, Berkeley: University of California Press. (Original Spanish edition, 1969).

de Janvry, Alain (1981) *The Agrarian Question and Reformism in Latin America*, Baltimore, MD. Johns Hopkins University Press.

Fishlow, Albert (1983) 'Brazil gets bad medicine for its ailment', *Los Angeles Times*, 11 December.
—— (1985) 'State and economy in Latin America: New models for the 1980s'. Paper presented at the conference on The Impact of the Current Economic Crisis on the Social and Political Structure of the Newly Industrializing Countries, Sao Paulo, Brazil, February.
Girvan, Norman, Richard Bernal and Wesley Hughes (1980) 'The IMF and the Third World: The Case of Jamaica, 1974–80', *Development Dialogue*, no. 2: 113–55.
Honeywell, Martin (1983) *The Poverty Brokers: The IMF and Latin America*, London: Latin American Bureau.
Lever, Harold (1984) 'The debt won't be paid', *New York Review of Books* (28 June): 3–5.
Loxley, John (1984) 'Saving the world economy', *Monthy Review* (September): 22–34.
Moffitt, Michael (1983) *The World's Money: International Banking from Bretton Woods to the Brink of Insolvency*, New York: Simon and Schuster.
Stallings, Barbara (1985) 'The debt crisis: Back to the dependency syndrome?'. Paper presented at the conference on The Impact of the Current Economic Crisis on the Social and Political Structure of the Newly Industrializing Countries, Sao Paulo, Brazil, February.
Thompson, E. P. (1971) 'The moral economy of the English crowd in the eighteenth century', *Past and Present*, 50 (February): 76–136.
Tilly, Charles (1975) 'Food supply and public order in modern Europe'. In Charles Tilly (ed.), *The Formation of National States in Western Europe*, Princeton N.J.: Princeton University.
The Wall Street Journal (1984) 'World debt in crisis' (27 June.)
World Development Report 1985 (1985) Washington: World Bank and Oxford University Press.

Contributors

Sophie Body-Gendrot is Lecturer in Political Science, Institut d'Etudes Politiques, Paris.

Susan S. Fainstein is Professor of Urban Planning and Policy Development, Rutgers University.

Joe R. Feagin is Professor of Sociology, University of Texas, Austin.

Norman J. Glickman is Hogg Professor of Urban Policy, Lyndon Baines Johnson School of Public Affairs, University of Texas, Austin.

Richard Child Hill is Professor of Sociology, Michigan State University.

Desmond S. King is Lecturer in Politics, University of Edinburgh.

Margit Mayer is Lecturer in Political Science, JWG Universität, Frankfurt, West Germany.

Enzo Mingione is Professor of Economic Sociology, University of Messina, Italy.

June Nash is Professor of Anthropology, Graduate Center, City University of New York.

David C. Perry is Professor of Environmental Design and Planning, State University of New York at Buffalo.

Helen I. Safa is Director, Center for Latin American Studies, University of Florida.

Saskia Sassen-Koob is Associate Professor of Planning, Columbia University, New York.

Michael Peter Smith is Professor of Community Studies and Development and Chairperson, Department of Applied Behavioral Sciences, University of California, Davis, California.

Edward W. Soja is Professor of Urban and Regional Development, Graduate School of Architecture and Urban Planning, University of California, Los Angeles.

Richard Tardanico is Fulbright Professor, Escuala de Historia y Geografía, Universidad de Costa Rica and Visiting Professor, Facultad Latinamericana de Ciencias Sociales, San José.

Michael Timberlake is Assistant Professor of Sociology, Memphis State University, Tennessee.

John Walton is Professor of Sociology, University of California, Davis, California.

Patricia Ann Wilson is Associate Professor, School of Architecture and Planning, University of Texas, Austin.

Index